NOTABLE
AFRICAN AMERICAN
WRITERS

NOTABLE
AFRICAN AMERICAN
WRITERS

Volume 3

Sonia Sanchez — Al Young
Essays
Appendixes
Indexes
901 – 1350

from

THE EDITORS OF SALEM PRESS

SALEM PRESS, INC.
Pasadena, California   Hackensack, New Jersey

∞ The paper used in these volumes conforms to the American National
Standard for Permanence of Paper for Printed Library Materials, Z39.48-1992
(R1997)

Essays originally appeared, in whole or in part, in *Critical Survey of Drama*
(2003), *Critical Survey of Poetry* (2003), *Critical Survey of Short Fiction* (2001), and
Critical Survey of Long Fiction (2000), and *Magill's Choice: 100 Masters of Mystery
and Detective Fiction* (2001). New material has been added.

Library of Congress Cataloging-in-Publication Data
Notable African American writers.
    p. cm. — (Magill's choice)
    Includes bibliographical references and indexes.
    ISBN-13: 978-1-58765-272-1 (set : alk. paper)
    ISBN-10: 1-58765-272-2 (set : alk. paper)
    ISBN-13: 978-1-58765-275-2 (v. 3 : alk. paper)
    ISBN-10: 1-58765-275-7 (v. 3 : alk. paper)
    [etc.]
    1. American literature—African American authors—Dictionaries.
2. African American authors—Biography—Dictionaries.   3. African
Americans in literature—Dictionaries.   4. African Americans—Intellectual
life—Dictionaries.   I. Title.   II. Series.
    PS153.N5N68 2006
    810.9'89607303—dc22
                                                        2006002916

First Printing

PRINTED IN CANADA

Contents

Indexes

Complete List of Contents

Volume 1

Volume 2

Volume 3

NOTABLE
AFRICAN AMERICAN
WRITERS

Sonia Sanchez

(Wilsonia Benita Driver)

Poet and playwright

Born: Birmingham, Alabama; September 9, 1934

DRAMA: *The Bronx Is Next*, pb. 1968, pr. 1971; *Sister Son/ji*, pb. 1969, pr. 1972; *Uh, Huh; But How Do It Free Us?*, pb. 1974, pr. 1975; *Malcolm Man/Don't Live Here No Mo,'* pr. 1979; *I'm Black When I'm Singing, I'm Blue When I Ain't*, pr. 1982; *Black Cats Back and Uneasy Landings*, pr. 1995.

POETRY: *Homecoming*, 1969; *We a BaddDDD People*, 1970; *A Blues Book for Blue Black Magical Women*, 1973; *Love Poems*, 1973; *I've Been a Woman: New and Selected Poems*, 1978; *Homegirls and Handgrenades*, 1984; *Under a Soprano Sky*, 1987; *Wounded in the House of a Friend*, 1995; *Does Your House Have Lions?*, 1997; *Like the Singing Coming Off the Drums: Love Poems*, 1998; *Shake Loose My Skin: New and Selected Poems*, 1999.

NONFICTION: *Crisis in Culture: Two Speeches by Sonia Sanchez*, 1983.

CHILDREN'S/YOUNG ADULT LITERATURE: *It's a New Day: Poems for Young Brothas and Sistuhs*, 1971; *The Adventures of Fat Head, Small Head, and Square Head*, 1973; *A Sound Investment, and Other Stories*, 1979.

EDITED TEXTS: *We Be Word Sorcerers: Twenty-five Stories by Black Americans*, 1973.

Achievements

A political activist of the 1960's Civil Rights movement, Sonia Sanchez has been recognized for her considerable poetic talents. Called "a lion in literature's forest" by poet Maya Angelou, Sanchez has authored many books. From her critically acclaimed *Homegirls and Handgrenades*, winner of the American Book Award, to her academic recognition as director of the women's studies program at Temple University, Sanchez has earned worldwide accolades for her art, which was born out of her political activism. As part of her major role in the Black Arts movement of the 1960's, she began teaching the first black studies curriculum in the United States at San Francisco State College in 1969 with fellow Black Arts movement members Askia Toure and Amiri Baraka.

Her early poetry earned a PEN Writing Award (1969), a grant from the National Institute of Arts and Letters (1970), and a National Endowment for the Arts award (1978-1979). She has received recognition for her commitment to teaching and to social activism from community organizations including the Black Students of Smith College (1982), the Mayor's Commission for Women in Philadelphia (1987), the Peace and Freedom Award from the Women's International League for Peace and Freedom (1988-1989), and the Young Men's Christian Association (YMCA) Women Pioneers Hall of Fame (1992). She won a PEN Fellowship in the Arts (1993-1994) and was given the Legacy Award from Jomandi Productions (1995). She has been a distinguished poet-in-residence at Spelman College and was awarded an honorary doctorate by Wilberforce University.

Sanchez represents the best in American literature. In her works, she has described the struggles of people of color and other global themes, earning recognition for both her work and those humanistic ideals. Her 1997 work *Does Your House Have Lions?* was nominated for both the National Book Critics' Circle Award and the National Association for the Advancement of Colored People (NAACP) Image Award. In 2001, she was awarded the Frost Medal for distinguished lifetime service to American poetry. Sharing her poetry in Africa, Cuba, China, Norway, and Nicaragua, she has also traveled to more than five hundred U.S. universities and colleges, lecturing and providing poetry readings.

Biography

On September 9, 1934, Wilsonia Benita Driver—who later took the name Sonia Sanchez—was born to Wilson and Lena Driver in Birmingham, Alabama. A drummer in a jazz band, her father lost his wife when she and the twins she was carrying all died in childbirth. This family tragedy, occurring only a year after Sanchez's birth, resulted in tremendous upheaval for her and her older sister. Often cared for by her paternal grandmother, Sanchez grew attached to "Mama," the woman whom she credits with teaching her to read at age four and encouraging her great love of language. Describing how she used to fall to the floor laughing at her grandmother's words, Sanchez states: "I used to take the words and mull them over my tongue and give them back to her." When her grandmother died, the six-year-old Sanchez started to stutter. Her stuttering left her shy and somewhat isolated, but it also left her alone to write poetry, sometimes hiding it under the family's old, standing bathtub, which she was responsible for cleaning once a week.

When Sanchez was nine, her father moved the family to New York City. Living with her father and stepmother, she struggled with her shyness and stuttering. She was conscious of the rhythm of the black dialect spoken in the city streets, but it was not permitted in her parents' home. Still, she absorbed a vernacular that became an important influence on her poetry. Her poetry also gave her an outlet for her dismay at family changes—including three different stepmothers—and an often-distant father.

She graduated from Hunter College in 1955 with a degree in political science. Although she had read the work of African American poets in school in the South, the encouragement of librarians and a visit to the Schomburg Library, a black culture museum, opened her eyes to the history of slavery and to the works of other African American writers. Sanchez did graduate work in poetry with Louise Bogan at New York University, who she says taught her the craft of poetry.

Sanchez has supported herself through a series of academic appointments, beginning at San Francisco State College in 1966 and including the University of Pittsburgh, Rutgers University, City College of New York, Amherst College, University of Pennsylvania, and Temple University. She initiated the black studies movement, a drive to include African American literature in the college curriculum, in 1966 at San Francisco State College. At the University of Pittsburgh, she taught the first seminar on literature written by black women. A popular professor, she has won acclaim for teaching, including the Lindback Award for distinguished teaching and four honorary degrees, including a 1998 honorary doctorate from Temple University and the Robert Frost Medal in poetry in 2001.

She believes that teachers are responsible for transmitting the legacy of the past and for creating social change, and she is widely acclaimed as a teacher. In both her teaching and writing, Sanchez emphasizes that African Americans must refuse to see themselves as victims and must develop the self-confidence to survive in a white world that oppresses them. Her books for children promote positive self-images. She has militantly opposed drugs in the black community and sees literacy and education as the hope for the future. She believes that African Americans have a personal responsibility for self-development but must move beyond this to a larger commitment as members of the black community.

Sanchez is a prodigious worker. While raising her three children—Anita, Morani Neusi, and Mungu Neusi—and fulfilling her duties as a college professor, she continued to write in longhand from midnight to three o'clock in the morning. When asked why she writes, she responded, "I write because I must. I write because it keeps me going. I have not killed anyone in America because I write." Literary critics have said that her poetry is based on the African oral tradition, in which the poet is a source of history, instruction, and inspiration. She is gratified that white audiences have come to appreciate her work but says that she writes for herself and for an African American audience.

Analysis: Poetry

Innovative in her use of language to convey provocative themes, Sonia Sanchez explores the various forms language takes. Using street language to lyrical haiku, she confronts and takes the reader on a metaphoric journey through both black and white

America. Her political activism, born in the 1960's, is fused into her poetic voice and vision, as she stated in a 1999 interview: "All poets, all writers, are political." She further contends that her work has been built on her desire to change the world "for the better." Influenced by Malcolm X, a political activist along with Sanchez in Harlem, she asserts that she learned a great deal from this African American leader about language, presentation, and keeping the audience's attention. Moreover, she uses her poetry to share her vision of the world, both past and present. Integrating important figures in African American history such as Malcolm X and Martin Luther King, Jr., into her poetry, she dramatizes significant periods for her readers, both young and old, black and white.

Sanchez's poetic voice is always revealing and instructive. Elemental to her work is the articulate, engaging voice of the teacher, who with humor and technique labors to guide her students toward understanding and even revelation.

Homegirls and Handgrenades

Critically acclaimed, this significant Sanchez collection is divided into four sections: "The Power of Love," "Blues Is Bullets," "Beyond the Fallout," and "Grenades Are Not Free." The thematic opposites of rage and love, cynicism and compassion, and pain and joy coalesce in this volume.

The varying rhythmic style of the poems reflects the forms language takes in articulating diverse, sometimes conflicting, views. For example, the language of the street often labeled by Sanchez as "black English," spoken by her stepmother and her beloved grandmother, is used to describe "Poems Written After Reading Wright's 'American Hunger'": "such a simple need/ amid yo/easy desire."

In four of the poems she uses haiku, a Japanese lyric form that represents a single, concentrated image in seventeen syllables and arranged in three unrhymed lines of, traditionally, five, seven, and five syllables. Aptly named "Haiku," each poem conveys a single impression of a scene in motion: "your love was a port/ of call where many ships docked/ until morning came." In the section "Beyond the Fallout," the haiku exhibits raw anger: "I see you blackboy/ bent toward destruction watching/ for death with tight eyes."

The visionary quality of Sanchez's poem is articulated in poetic language that projects versatility because American life cannot be reflected in one homogenous voice. Sanchez uses the English vernacular to apprehend the complexity of human existence, as she states in a 1985 interview with Herbert Leibowitz: "Playing with words, as I used to, was like going outside and running and jumping over walls." As she explains further in the same interview, "A lot of my poetry expresses what it means to let people taste and feel sweetness and power running together, hate and love running together, beauty and ugliness also running together."

We a BaddDDD People

In the 1970 collection *We a BaddDDD People,* her political voice resonates in her poems as a way of protesting about how she could grow up in a country that did not "tell me about black history" and yet "ma[d]e me feel so inferior." In many ways her poetry becomes a way of answering those questions for herself. The discovery is certainly thematically addressed in the poem "Questions" and in the section titled "Survival." Depicting the political unrest of the period of the late 1960's, the collection has been criticized for being unoriginal in its political diatribe. However, the importance of the work in posing the political and personal questions of black existence for the poet and her readers is articulated in the following lines from "QUESTIONS": "we suicidal/ or something/ or are we all bugalooers/ of death:/ our own???" and "why they closing down/ prisons as they close off/ our blk/ minds."

The structure of the poems often represents the urgency of the poetic voice. For example, lines are fractured and split off by slashes and spaces. In "right on: wite america," the first stanza uses virgules and abbreviations:

> starting july 4th is
> bring in yr/guns/down/to
> yr/nearest/po/lice/station/

The troubled tone of the collection, reinforcing the structure, is loud and vociferous, as in "words for our children (from their many parents)":

> we are the
> > screeeeeamers/
> > > seaaaarcherrrs/
> > > > weepeeers

Although the tone is often soul searching, the thrust of the poetry strives metaphorically to force change.

More than featuring poems of political dissent, the collection reaffirms the need for poetry, the desire to chant or even shout out one's thoughts, as exhibited in "a/coltrane/poem":

> stretchen the mind
> > till it bursts past the con/fines of
> solo/en melodies

and concluding with the need to listen:

> > > > showen us life/
> > > > > liven.
> a love supreme.
> > > for each
> > other
> if we just
> lisssssssSSSTEN.

Does Your House Have Lions?

A deeply personal collection of poems that describe her brother's battle with AIDS, *Does Your House Have Lions?* captures the conflict and ultimate reconciliation among the voices identified in the sections as "sister's voice," "brother's voice," "father's voice," and "family voices/ancestors' voices." The journey unfolds in a rime royal pattern, a stanza form consisting of seven five-stress lines in iambic pentameter with a specific rhyme pattern (*ababbcc*). This unique form of English verse, first used by Geoffrey Chaucer, initiates and ties the metaphoric thread of the poems between each of the sections, linking the voices together through time—the present (the sister's, the brother's, and then the father's) with the past, as represented by the ancestral voices.

Sanchez described the process of creating the work: "I envisioned the last section as father, sister, and brother in counterpoint, but the ancestors insisted on being included." Invoking African words and phrases, the poetry embraces a timeless quality and an ancestral continuity. In "brother's voice," history provides the landscape for a personal, painful journey: "came the summer of nineteen sixty/ harlem luxuriating in Malcolm's voice/ became Big Red beautiful became a city/ of magnificent Black Birds steel eyes moist/ as he insinuated his words of sweet choice." With this, the protagonist's voice describes his connection: "then I began to think me alive with form and history/ then I made my former life an accessory." The question of how to create such a life in "a country of men/ where dollars pump their veins" appears unanswerable.

In "father's voice," the persona attaches significance to his background as a "southern Negro man playing music," not prepared for the struggles of a young widower attracted to "this ruby-colored girl." Leaving son, daughter, and mother, he becomes an "absentee father" and carefree nightclub owner. Now, at seventy-eight, the voice radiates regret: "i sing a dirge of lost black southern manhood/ this harlem man begging pardon." In reference to this particular section, Sanchez asserts that in assuming the father's voice, she was trying "to reexamine him [her father] and his movement with women" and his relationship with his own children. Also, she learned through doing this how he felt about the loss of his first wife—the only woman he ever loved—and included the following in one of the poems: "this love . . . died in childbirth" and he "never called her name again, wrapped my heart in gauze."

In "family voices/ancestors' voices," the final section, the merging of diverse points of view is reflected in the dialogues between the personas. Challenging the reader, this final section unifies the personal theme with the universal one: the struggles and accomplishments of family. It becomes one family's history crystallized with past familial histories. Integrating the African word *nyata,* meaning how much, in the following, the ancestors' male voice asks, "*nyata?* how much for the walking air?"

Ultimately, the brother's voice finds comfort in the language of the ancestors: "I come ancestor" is his reply to their voices. Moreover, Sanchez declares that "we must at some point understand our history . . . . We must open our eyes to our ancestors to help us live and stay alive."

Analysis: Drama

Sonia Sanchez's strong political views have created controversy surrounding her work among both black and white audiences. Her plays are revolutionary in their content and in their blunt language describing the evils of racism. Her characters often speak in the profane language of urban black English, shocking readers and playgoers. Her exploration of the oppression of black women by black men is a constant theme in her drama, often drawing the criticism of the black community. Her views, however, are not traditionally feminist, as her central theme is the evil of racism. As in all of her writing, her plays stress the responsibility of the members of the African American community to love themselves and one another as a way of transcending racism. She has attempted to bridge the gap between the elite world of academia and the reality of the black experience in the United States. Sanchez's plays are an outgrowth and extension of her poetic craft. She calls on her heritage from black music: blues, jazz, and gospel. Her dialogue is innovative in its typography and rhythm and rejects traditional spelling and capitalization (for example, "blk" and "u" for "black" and "you"). The language of white people, she believes, is a form of oppression. While Sanchez is skilled in playing with words and can express herself in a variety of forms, including traditional English prose and poetry and Japanese haiku, in both her poetry and drama she rejects "Eurocentric" language and traditions. She has moved away from her use of vulgarity in her earlier plays toward a more loving, spiritual expression, and her later work in poetry seems less angry, although it still has strong political content.

The Bronx Is Next

Sanchez's first brief play was, she says, a condemnation of what Harlem was becoming in the 1960's. Once the site of the great outpouring of creativity called the Harlem Renaissance, the area was being destroyed by drugs and violence. The play's two major characters are Old Sister, representing the past oppression of African Americans in the Old South, and Black Bitch, a sexually promiscuous woman accused by the black male characters of sleeping with a white police officer and failing to support the revolution. When Black Bitch accuses the black male leader of abusing women, he brutally rapes her. The black male revolutionaries force both women back into the burning buildings to die. Sanchez's language is explicitly sexual and violent in this play. Although some critics believe the work contains one of the first examples of strong black women characters in drama, others find the message disturbing, with the playwright seeming to blame the women characters for not supporting the revolution.

Sister Son/ji

The narrator in this one-act play is an African American woman in her fifties recalling important episodes of her history as a revolutionary. By changing her makeup and costumes, she recalls her early college days, her first sexual experience, her black consciousness awakening through the speeches of Malcolm X, an episode of near insanity when she loses control of her life, and the death of her teenage son in the revolution. Sanchez portrays the conflicted relationship between black men and women, with the men exploiting their power and expecting the women to take a subservient role in the movement. Sister Son/ji pleads with black men to admit women as equals and respect love and family life rather than a false idea of manhood.

By tracing Sister Son/ji's experiences, Sanchez explores themes that dominate all her work: the exploitation of black women by black men, the destructive power of drugs and violence, the urgent need for African American men and women to work together to combat racism. The play concludes with a statement of Sister Son/ji's strength and survival skills:

Death is a five o-clock door forever changing time. And wars end. Sometimes too late. i am here. still in mississippi. Near the graves of my past. We are at peace . . . but I have my memories. . . . i have my sweet/astringent memories becuz we dared to pick up the day and shake its tail until it became evening. A time for us. blk/ness. blk/people.

Uh, Huh; But How Do It Free Us?
This play, the longest of the three, is experimental in form, with three unrelated scenes connected by dance sequences. In the first scene, three characters (Malik, Waleesha, and Nefertia) represent the black male's need to dominate women to assure his manhood. Both women are pregnant and enemies of each other, rather than sisters, as they try to hold on to Malik's love.

The next scene is a surreal dramatization of male cocaine addicts, four black and one white, riding horses that represent their drug-induced fantasies. Two prostitutes, one white and one black, are whipping them and providing drugs. At the end of this scene, the white man dresses in drag, proclaiming himself the "real queen." Sanchez represents black men as superior to white men, but sees women, both black and white, as subordinate to the degenerate needs of men of both races.

The final scene portrays a black male revolutionary called Brother in relationships with both a black woman and a white woman. The white woman functions as a symbol of the white man's property. She supports him financially and makes him feel powerful. Sister, the black woman, is conflicted in her role as angry lover demeaned by Brother's betrayal with the "devil/woman" and her hopes that he will reform himself and return to his true responsibility as a man committed to his role in the black communiy. Sanchez stops short of supporting the sisterhood of black women, emphasizing Sister's individual strength and ability to survive both racism and her oppression by the black male.

Other Literary Forms
Sonia Sanchez's literary reputation rests primarily on her poetry. She sees her plays as an extension of her poetic art, saying

that their longer form gives her more room to express her ideas. She has written short stories, children's books, essays, literary criticism, and social commentary. She has an impressive record as a university teacher and political activist and has been a driving force behind the movement to include writings by African American authors in the college curriculum. She frequently gives public readings, performances that are noted for their dramatic power and include music, drum beats, and chanting. Some of her best-known works were inspired by the Black Arts movement of the 1960's, and her later writings have continued to focus on African American themes.

Sanchez has also included prose in her collections of poetry, most notably in *Homegirls and Handgrenades.* Interspersed through the four sections of poems, she includes autobiographical narratives. In addition, she has published speeches in *Crisis in Culture: Two Speeches by Sonia Sanchez* and stories and poems for children.

Bibliography

Brown-Guillory, Elizabeth. Introduction to *Sister Son/ji*, by Sonia Sanchez. In *Wines in the Wilderness: Plays by African American Women from the Harlem Renaissance to the Present*, edited by Brown-Guillory. New York: Praeger, 1990. Brown-Guillory provides a synopsis of the play and analysis of Sanchez's work as a whole.

Davis, Eisa. "Lucille Clifton and Sonia Sanchez: A Conversation." *Callaloo* 25, no. 4 (Fall, 2002): 1038-1075. An interesting interview with two of the most important figures in contemporary literature.

De Lancey, Frenzella Elaine. "Refusing to Be Boxed In: Sonia Sanchez's Transformation of the Haiku Form." In *Language and Literature in the African American Imagination*, edited by Carol Aisha Blackshire-Belay. Westport, Conn.: Greenwood Press, 1992. Focuses on Sanchez's use and adaptations of the haiku form.

Evans, Mari, ed. *Black Women Writers, 1950-1980: A Critical Evaluation.* Garden City, N.Y.: Anchor Books, 1984. Contains an essay on Sanchez, analyzing her inventive use of urban black

English in her work, and one by Sanchez, in which she explains her belief that the poet has a responsibility to change social values and discusses her personal life and working methods.

Jennings, Regina B. "The Blue/Black Poetics of Sonia Sanchez." In *Language and Literature in the African American Imagination,* edited by Carol Aisha Blackshire-Belay. Westport, Conn.: Greenwood Press, 1992. Offers insight into critical views of Sanchez's use of language and culture.

Joyce, Joyce A. *Ijala: Sonia Sanchez and the African Poetic Tradition.* Chicago: Third World Press, 1996. A comprehensive look at Sanchez's body of work, covering almost thirty years, and its primary influences. In the introduction, Joyce argues that Sanchez's original contribution to African American literature is inspired by her deep knowledge and understanding of the African oral tradition in poetry.

Lee, Felicia R. "A 'Spiritual Mother' of Spoken Word for a Hip-Hop Generation." *The New York Times,* January 29, 2005, p. B11. A profile of Sanchez's upbringing, career, and recent participation in the HBO series *Def Poetry.*

Reich, David. "As Poets, as Activists." *World,* May/June, 1999, 1-11. In a revealing interview, Sanchez describes the process of writing *Does Your House Have Lions?* as well as other significant familial experiences. Details personal and historical events that influenced her poetry. Provides both personal and literary philosophy.

Sanchez, Sonia. "Disciple and Craft: An Interview with Sonia Sanchez." Interview by Susan Kelly. *African American Review* 34, no. 4 (Winter, 2000): 679-687. Sanchez discusses the body of her work, her literary influences and personal history, and the importance of discipline and craft.

_____. "Exploding Myths: An Interview with Sonia Sanchez." Interview by Herbert Leibowitz. *Parnassus,* Spring/Summer/Fall/Winter, 1985, 357-368. Points to important themes chronicled in *Homegirls and Handgrenades.* Links poetic analysis to poetic intent and purpose. Furnishes an examination of the award-winning collection.

_____. "Sonia Sanchez." In *Black Women Writers at Work,* edited by Claudia Tate. New York: Continuum, 1983. In this interview, Sanchez discusses racism and the need for black women to refuse to see themselves as victims.

Wood, Jacqueline. "'To Wash My Ego in the Needs of My People': Militant Womanist Rhetoric in the Drama of Sonia Sanchez." *CLA Journal* 48, no. 1 (September, 2004): 1-33. Examines the ways in which Sanchez has impacted African American speech, placing it in contrast to the protest work of other prominent writers.

Ya Salaam, Kalamu. "Sonia Sanchez." In *Afro-American Poets Since 1955*, edited by Trudier Harris and Thadious M. Davis. Vol. 41 in *Dictionary of Literary Biography*. Detroit: Gale, 1985. A brief but comprehensive coverage of Sanchez's life and work.

— *Cynthia S. Becerra; Marjorie Podolsky*

Ntozake Shange

(Paulette Williams)

Playwright, novelist, and poet

Born: Trenton, New Jersey; October 18, 1948

LONG FICTION: *Sassafras: A Novella*, 1976; *Sassafras, Cypress, and Indigo*, 1982; *Betsey Brown*, 1985; *Liliane: Resurrection of the Daughter*, 1994.

DRAMA: *for colored girls who have considered suicide/ when the rainbow is enuf*, pr., pb. 1975; *A Photograph: Still Life with Shadows/A Photograph: A Study in Cruelty*, pr. 1977, revised pr. 1979, pb. 1981 (as *A Photograph: Lovers in Motion*); *Where the Mississippi Meets the Amazon*, pr. 1977 (with Thulani Nkabinde and Jessica Hagedorn); *From Okra to Greens: A Different Kinda Love Story*, pr. 1978, pb. 1985; *Spell # 7: Geechee Jibara Quik Magic Trance Manual for Technologically Stressed Third World People*, pr. 1979, pb. 1981; *Boogie Woogie Landscapes*, pr. 1979, pb. 1981; *Mother Courage and Her Children*, pr. 1980 (adaptation of Bertolt Brecht's play); *Three Pieces*, pb. 1981; *Betsey Brown*, pr. 1991 (adaptation of her novel); *The Love Space Demands: A Continuing Saga*, pb. 1991, pr. 1992; *Plays: One*, pb. 1992; *Three Pieces*, pb. 1992.

POETRY: *Nappy Edges*, 1978; *Natural Disasters and Other Festive Occasions*, 1979; *A Daughter's Geography*, 1983, 1991; *From Okra to Greens: Poems*, 1984; *Ridin' the Moon in Texas: Word Paintings*, 1987; *I Live in Music*, 1994; *The Sweet Breath of Life: A Poetic Narrative of the African American Family*, 2004 (photos by the Kamoinge Workshop; photos edited by Frank Stewart).

NONFICTION: *See No Evil: Prefaces, Essays, and Accounts, 1976-1983*, 1984; *If I Can Cook, You Know God Can*, 1998.

CHILDREN'S/YOUNG ADULT LITERATURE: *Whitewash*, 1997; *Muhammad Ali: The Man Who Could Float Like a Butterfly and Sting Like a Bee*, 2002; *Daddy Says*, 2003; *Ellington Was Not a Street*, 2004.

EDITED TEXTS: *The Beacon Best of 1999: Creative Writing by Women and Men of All Colors,* 2000.

Achievements

Ntozake Shange's work embodies a rich confusion of genres and all the contradictions inherent in a world in which violence and oppression polarize life and art. These polarizations in Shange's work both contribute to her artistry and complicate it. She has been criticized and praised for her unconventional language and structure, for her almost religious feminism, and for her stand on black/white and male/female issues. Her first play, *for colored girls who have considered suicide/ when the rainbow is enuf,* produced in 1976 by Joseph Papp's New York Shakespeare Festival, was honored in that year by the Outer Critics Circle, which consists of those who write about the New York theater for out-of-town newspapers. That play also received Obie and Audelco Awards as well as Tony and Grammy Award nominations in 1977. Shange's 1980 adaptation of Bertolt Brecht's *Mother Courage and Her Children* won an Obie Award from *The Village Voice.* Among her many other awards are a *Los Angeles Times* Book Prize for Poetry and a Pushcart Prize.

Biography

Ntozake Shange (pronounced "En-to-zaki Shong-gay") was born Paulette Williams in Trenton, New Jersey, on October 18, 1948, daughter of a surgeon and a psychiatric social worker and educator. She grew up surrounded by music, literature, art, and her parents' prominent friends, among them Dizzy Gillespie, Chuck Berry, and W. E. B. Du Bois, as well as writers and musicians from developing countries. Her ties with her family were strong; she also was close to her family's live-in black maids. She was graduated from Barnard College with honors in 1970, then received a graduate degree at the University of Southern California in Los Angeles. While in California, she began studying dance, writing poetry, and participating in improvisational works (consisting of poems, music, dance, and mime) at bars,

(Jules Allen)

cabarets, and schools. These gradually grew into *for colored girls who have considered suicide/ when the rainbow is enuf,* which she carried across the country to perform in workshops in New York, then at the Public Theatre, and eventually on Broadway. The contrasts between her privileged home and education and the realities of the lives of black women led her, in 1971, to change her name legally from what she called the "slave name" of Paulette Williams to Ntozake Shange, meaning "she who comes with her own things" and "she who walks like a lion" in Xhosa (Zulu). Her two failed marriages, her suicide attempts, and her contact with city violence resulted in an anger that found its outlet in her poems. During the late 1970's, she lived in New York City, but she later moved to Houston, Texas, with her daughter, Savannah. She has taught and lectured at many colleges and universities, including Mills College in Oakland, California; the State University in Rutgers, New Jersey; the University of California, Berkeley; the University of Houston; Rice University; Yale University; Howard University; and New York University.

Her work with Emily Mann on the script version of *Betsey Brown* brought her into prominence among feminists and experimental theaters. Working under the auspices of the New York Shakespeare Festival, the two women brought the play into its production form through a series of staged readings, workshops, and tryouts, and their collaboration techniques were the subject of forums among dramaturges in 1990.

Shange's poetic "reading/performance" piece *The Love Space Demands,* in which she reads her own work (accompanied by guitarist Billie Patterson), was performed in New Jersey at the Crossroads Theatre and in San Francisco at the Hansberry Theatre in 1992.

Analysis: Drama

In Ntozake Shange's introduction to the volume *Three Pieces,* she makes this statement about drama:

> as a poet in american theater/ i find most activity that takes place on our stages overwhelmingly shallow/ stilted & imitative. that is probably one of the reasons i insist on calling myself a poet or writer/ rather than a playwright/ i am interested solely in the poetry of a moment/ the emotional & aesthetic impact of a character or a line.

Her plays have evoked a range of critical responses commensurate with their unconventional nature. Should her work be characterized as poetry or drama, prose or poetry, essay or autobiography? Her choreopoems, made up of poetry, drama, prose, and autobiography, are unified by a militant feminism in which some critics have seen a one-sided attack on black men. Others, however, point out the youthful spirit, flair with language, and lyricism that carry her plays to startling and radical conclusions. Her style and its seeming contradictions, such as the use of both black English and the erudite vocabulary of the educated, are at the heart of her drama. Influenced by their method of development—public poetry reading in bars, cafés, schools, Off-Off-Broadway theaters—the plays are generally somewhere between a poetry reading and a staged play.

First among the contradictions or contrasts is her blending of genres: Her poems shade into drama, her dramas are essentially verse monologues, and her novels incorporate poetic passages. Second, her language varies radically—on a single page and even in a single phrase—from black dialect ("cuz," "wanna," "awready," "chirren") to the language of her middle-class upbringing and education ("i cant count the number of times i have viscerally wanted to attack deform n maim the language that i waz taught to hate myself in/"). In the published texts of her poetry, plays, and essays, in addition to simplified phonetic spellings, she employs the slash instead of the period and omits capitalization. Many recordings of her work are available, and these provide the listener with a much fuller sense of the dynamic quality of her language in performance.

Shange's bold and daring use of language, her respect for people formerly given little value, and her exploration of the roles of black men and women have opened a new dimension in theater. Her blendings of poetry, music, and dance bring theater back to its origins and simultaneously blaze a trail toward the drama of the future.

for colored girls who have considered suicide/ when the rainbow is enuf

Shange's first dramatic success, *for colored girls who have considered suicide/ when the rainbow is enuf,* is the recital, individually and in chorus, of the lives and growth of seven different black women, named according to their dress colors: "lady in red," "lady in blue," "lady in orange," "lady in brown," "lady in yellow," "lady in purple," and "lady in green." The term "colored girls" in the title evokes a stereotype of black women yet also contains a germ of hope for the future (the "rainbow," both of color and of eventual salvation).

These seven stylized figures are representative voices of black women, and they express their fury at their oppression both as women and as blacks. The first segment shows high school graduation and the social and sexual rite of passage for "colored girls" in the working-class suburbs. Some of the women who have been cruelly disappointed in relationships with men discuss their spiritual quests. A black woman pretends to be Puerto Rican so that she can dance the merengue in Spanish Harlem. A woman breaks up with her lover by returning to him his plant to water. The scenes become more somber, portraying rape, abuse, city dangers, and abortion. Ties with a more heroic black past appear in "Toussaint," while the glamorized prostitute evicts her lover from her bed. The women begin to analyze their predicaments and to assert their independence in segments entitled "somebody almost walked off wid alla my stuff" and "pyramid," in which three women console one another for the actions of the faithless lover whom they share. In the brutal culminating scene, a crazed Vietnam veteran, Beau Willie Brown, abuses his woman, Crystal, and kills their infant children, dropping them from a window.

The recurrent motif of the recitation is the thwarting of dreams and aspirations for a decent life by forces beyond one's control: war, poverty, and ignorance. There is, however, a saving grace. Toward the end of the play, the seven women fall into a tighter circle of mutual support, much like a religious "laying on of hands" ceremony, in which they say, "i found god in myself/ & i loved her/ i loved her fiercely." Their bitter pain, shown throughout the dramatic episodes, turns into a possibility of regeneration. Thus, the play is a drama of salvation for women who do not receive their full value in society.

Though it was a landmark in the emergence of new black women playwrights, *for colored girls who have considered suicide/ when the rainbow is enuf* has been criticized for its lack of discussion of black traditions in religion, family, and ordinary work, and for its omissions of both black literary and political history and the influence of whites. Its style, considered as an attack on language, part of blacks' "enslavement," has also been criticized. Later plays, however, include these elements in a constantly enriching network of allusions.

A Photograph

In *A Photograph*, a set of meditations and sketches involving an ideal black woman named Michael and her lover Sean, a failed photographer, Shange explores her idea of art—"the poetry of a moment"—as well as representative stages of the African American experience. Photography, dance, and drama are shown to be art forms that capture meaningful moments and present them to viewers and readers so that they might behold and understand the essence and the value of art and life. The young professionals that reside in or pass through Sean's San Francisco apartment-studio are shown to examine the psychological factors that impede and that motivate them and other African Americans.

The five figures of this piece are representative of other aspects of black life than those put forward in her first play. Nevada, a lawyer and lover-supporter of Sean, the struggling artist, sets herself above other "common" African Americans: Her family, she boasts, "was manumitted in 1843/ [when] yall were still slaves/ carrying things for white folks . . . /" The upwardly mobile Earl, also a lawyer, former lover of Claire and long-time friend of Sean, pleads Nevada's case to Sean when the latter rejects her. Claire is a dancer who dances seductively for Sean as he photographs and then ravishes her. Michael is a dancer and the woman Sean comes truly to love as she shares herself and her ideas of art and of the African experience with him.

Early in the drama Sean tells Michael, "i'm a genius for unravelling the mysteries of the darker races/ . . . i know who we are." After he rejects Nevada and is rejected by her, Sean reveals his insecurities as a son, a man, an African American, and an artist. The self- and race-assured artist Michael challenges her temporarily broken lover. Sean soon responds to this and to a poetic story danced and told by Michael with his own story and assurances:

> yes. that's right. me. i'ma be it. the photographer of all time.
> look out ansel/ . . . i can bring you the world shining grainy focused or shaking/ a godlike phenomenon/ sean david . . . i realize you're not accustomed to the visions of a man of color who has a gift/ but fear not/ I'll give it to ya a lil at a time. i am only beginning to startle/ to mesmerize and reverse the reality of all who can see. I gotta thing bout niggahs/ my folks/ that just wont stop/ & we are so correct for the photograph/ we profile

all the time/ styling/ giving angle & pattern/ shadows & still life. if somebody sides me cd see the line in niggahs/ the texture of our lives/ they wda done it/ but since nobody has stepped forward/ here I am . . .

Sean seems obviously representative of Shange the artist in his coming-into-his-own response to Michael, who is yet another representative of Shange the artist. This choreopoem seems a particularly significant statement made by Shange, poet and writer: She, like Sean, presents "the contours of life unnoticed" and she, like Michael, speaks "for everybody burdened."

Boogie Woogie Landscapes

After examining the identity of isolated young black women in *for colored girls who have considered suicide/ when the rainbow is enuf* and of couples in *A Photograph,* Shange concentrates on one woman's visions, dreams, and memories in *Boogie Woogie Landscapes,* which was first produced as a one-woman poetry piece in 1978 and then cast as a play in 1979, with music and dance. Layla, a young black woman, entertains in her dreams a series of nightlife companions who exemplify her perceptions of herself and her memories. "Layla" in Arabic means "born at night," and the entire drama exists in Layla's nighttime subconscious. Layla's dreams of Fidel Castro's Cuba, of primitive cruelties to African women, and of rock and roll and blues interweave with her feelings about growing up, family, brothers and sisters, parents, maids (some of which appear later in Shange's semiautobiographical novel *Betsey Brown*).

Spell #7

Shange's 1979 play *Spell #7,* like her first play, is structured like a highly electric poetry reading, but this time the cast is mixed male and female. A huge blackface mask forms the backdrop for actors and actresses of an imitation old-time minstrel show, where actors did skits, recited, and joked, all under the direction of a Mr. Interlocutor. The actors come offstage, relax at an actors' bar, and gradually remove their masks, revealing their true selves. Lou, the "practicing magician," reveals that his father gave up his role as magician when a colored child asked for a spell to make her white. The actors tell each other and the audience tall stories. One of these involves a child who thought blacks were immune to dread diseases and disease-ridden passions such as polio and pedophilia. She is disillusioned when, as an adult, she finds that blacks not only can but also do hurt one another, so she buys South African gold "to remind the black people that it cost a lot for us to be here/ our value/ can be known instinctively/ but since so many black people are having a hard time not being like white folks/ i wear these gold pieces to protest their ignorance/ their disconnect from history." Another woman loves her baby, which she names "myself," while it is in the womb but kills it after it is born. Still another girl vows to brush her "nappy" hair constantly so that she can toss it like white girls. By these contrasts and by wry lists and surprising parallels, Shange shows the pain and difficulty, as well as the hopefulness, of being black. Lou refers to the spell that caused his father to give up magic as he (Lou) casts the final spell of Spell #7:

> aint no colored magician in his right mind
> gonna make you white
> cuz this is blk magic you lookin at
> & i'm fixin you up good/ fixin you up good & colored
> & you gonna be colored all yr life
> & you gonna love it/ bein colored

The others join him in celebration of "bein colored"; but the minstrel mask drops down and Lou's final words contain anger as well as celebration:

> crackers are born with the right to be
> alive/ i'm making ours up right here
> in yr face/ & we gonna be
> colored & love it

From Okra to Greens

Shange's *From Okra to Greens* draws together and expands on the themes of her earlier theater pieces. The discovery by the lovers Okra and Greens of the beauty and strength—the god—within the individual is like that of the women who populate *for colored girls who have considered suicide/ when the rainbow is enuf.* Similarly, the lovers' discovery of what is sacred—of the fullness and color of life versus the "skinny life" of black and white—is the goal of Layla in *Boogie Woogie Landscapes,* of the actors in *Spell #7,* and of the artists of *A Photograph.* The love between two fully realized human beings, like that experienced by Sean and Michael in *A Photograph,* is fully expanded on in this two-character drama of Okra and Greens. The theme of the responsibility of the artist touched on by Sean and by Michael is also fully developed by the poets Okra and Greens.

In the opening scenes of *From Okra to Greens,* Greens speaks of Okra's plight as single black woman as Okra acts/dances the role. This scene is reminiscent of Sean and Michael speaking in unison about Sean's and then Michael's art in the final scene of *A Photograph* and Ross's talking while Maxine acts out the role that the two are creating together, on the spot, in *Spell #7.* In *From Okra to Greens,* as in her other choreopoems, Shange turns her dramatic poetry into staged drama. She presents verbatim much of the poetry of her collection *A Daughter's Geography.* Although her feminist protests are dramatized in this play as in *for colored girls who have considered suicide/ when the rainbow is enuf* and in *Boogie Woogie Landscapes,* here her feminist protest is given voice by the male character Greens. That both Okra and Greens are poets allows them to have an understanding of one another and of the roles forced on too many African American women and men as well as an understanding of the role that human be-ings *should* play in the world.

Okra first dances as "the crooked woman" as Greens speaks, showing his and society's distorted view of black women. Okra's dance reflects both her pain and her potential strength and beauty. As the two come together, Greens admits his own crook-edness in telling Okra that before their encounter he had not known "what a stood/up straight man felt like." Together the two characters create and present portraits of "some men" who degrade women (as they are encouraged to do by the patriar-chy). Once married, the two continue their dialogue, which in-cludes their consideration of one another and of the sociopolitical climate in which they and, later, their daughter, must reside.

Shange's *Okra and Greens* celebrates, as do Sean and Michael in *A Photograph*, the richness of African American life. Her love story extends to the poor of not only her own country but also the world. Okra pleads for the return of Haitian liberators Dessalines, Petion, and L'Ouverture with their visions of *"la liberte, l'egalite, la fraternite."* As in her other theater pieces, Shange calls here, too, for the return of American visionaries, among them monologues.

As the hope of the world's visionaries is shown to have dimmed, so the relationship between the lovers Okra and Greens dims momentarily. Abandoned by Greens, Okra says that "the moon cracked in a ugly rupture." Joined once more, the two encourage each other and others to "rise up" and to "dance with the universe." This story of the love between two poets is a love song to a universe in sad need of hope.

The refrain of *Boogie Woogie Landscapes*, that "we dont recognize what's sacred anymore," is revealed in *From Okra to Greens* in the portrait of the "pretty man" whose pretty floors are covered with the kind of rug that "little girls spend whole/ lives tying." Lack of recognition of the sacred is a theme repeated throughout the work. However, the love between Okra and Greens and their hope for their daughter and for the oppressed peoples of the world shows that recognition of the sacred is possible for aware, thinking, and caring individuals. The memory of other visionaries also shows the poets' and others' recognition of the sacred. It is clear here and throughout her writing that Shange would have her audience recognize the sacred in themselves and in others and do their part in telling the story—in spreading the word—and in fighting for liberty, equality, and fraternity for all.

Betsey Brown and The Love Space Demands

In 1991, Shange adapted her novel *Betsey Brown* into a play. The semiautobiographical work tells the story of a thirteen-year-old African American girl growing up in a middle-class household in 1950's St. Louis. *The Love Space Demands*, a loosely connected series of poems and monologues Shange herself performs with musical accompaniment, revolves around sexual relations in the age of AIDS (acquired immunodeficiency syndrome).

Other Literary Forms

Ntozake Shange's three genres—plays, poems, and novels—so overlap that one might say she has invented a new genre, which she has named the "choreopoem." She has published several volumes of poetry, including *Nappy Edges*, parts of which were included in her 1975 play *for colored girls who have considered suicide/ when the rainbow is enuf*, *Natural Disasters and Other Festive Occasions*; *A Daughter's Geography*; *Ridin' the Moon in Texas: Word Paintings*; and *I Live in Music*. Among her novels are *Sassafrass, Cypress, and Indigo* and *Betsey Brown*. She has gathered writings about her work from 1976 to 1984 into *See No Evil: Prefaces, Essays, and Accounts, 1976-1983*, the study of which is essential to an understanding of her art.

Shange has also distinguished herself as a director, of both her own work and that of others, notably Richard Wesley's *The Mighty Gents* in 1979. In 1980, Shange adapted Bertolt Brecht's *Mutter Courage und ihre Kinder* (1941; *Mother Courage and Her Children*, 1941), changing the scene from mid-seventeenth century Europe to post-Civil War America, making the protagonist an emancipated slave doing business with the army oppressing the Western Indians, and changing the language to black English.

Bibliography

Austin, Gayle. "Black Women Playwrights Exorcizing Myths." *Phylon* 48 (Fall, 1997): 229-239. Examines the work of Alice Childress, Lorraine Hansberry, and Shange in dispelling stereotypical myths of African American characters, such as the tragic mulatto and the comic Negro, and in presenting new constructions, such as the black militant and the evolving black woman.

Barrios, Olga. "From Seeking One's Voice to Uttering the Scream: The Pioneering Journey of African American Women

Playwrights Through the 1960s and 1970s." *African American Review* 37, no. 4 (Winter, 2003): 611-619. An examination of pioneering African American women playwrights. Primarily concerned with the pain these writers have experienced and the voyages of self-discovery they undergo through artistic creation.

Brown-Guillory, Elizabeth. *Their Place on the Stage: Black Women Playwrights in America.* New York: Greenwood Press, 1988. A good study of Shange, along with Alice Childress and Lorraine Hansberry. Analyzes *for colored girls who have considered suicide/ when the rainbow is enuf* at considerable length, as well as the 1979 trilogy, *Spell #7, Boogie Woogie Landscapes,* and *A Photograph.*

Cashin, Joan E. "William Faulkner Meets Ntozake Shange: A Special Issue on the American South." *Journal of Family History* 28, no. 4 (October, 2003): 463-465. An exploration of different conceptions of the family and on the roles its members play in traditional and contemporary life.

Effiong, Philip Uko. *In Search of a Model for African American Drama: A Study of Selected Plays by Lorraine Hansberry, Amiri Baraka, and Ntozake Shange.* New York: University Press of America, 2000. Analyzes the historical and sociopolitical considerations that determine the choices made by each dramatist. Considers the ritualization of black theater by each dramatist.

Lester, Neal A. *Ntozake Shange: A Critical Study of the Plays.* New York: Garland, 1995. Lester examines critically Shange's contributions to the American stage, suggests aspects of her work for further study, and contextualizes Shange's drama within appropriate literary traditions. A thorough and insightful study of Shange's *for colored girls who have considered suicide/ when the rainbow is enuf, Spell #7, A Photograph, Boogie Woogie Landscapes,* and *From Okra to Greens.*

Mullen, Harryette. "Artistic Expression Was Flowing Everywhere." *Meridians: Feminism, Race, Transnationalism* 4, no. 2 (April, 2004): 205-236. An article that explores the work of poet Alison Mills and Shange. Takes a look at the poets' influences, Mills's religious beliefs, and their conceptions of feminism.

Russell, Sandi. *Render Me My Song: African American Women Writers from Slavery to the Present.* New York: St. Martin's Press, 1990. Supplies a list of Shange's work up to *Betsey Brown.* Good biography and comments on the "choreopoem" format. Discusses the trilogy of plays ending with *A Photograph* and examines Shange's version of Bertolt Brecht's *Mother Courage and Her Children.* Puts Shange in context with Alexis De Veaux, Rita Dove, and Toni Cade Bambara, writers using blues styles fed by oral traditions, of which *for colored girls who have considered suicide/ when the rainbow is enuf* is exemplary.

Shange, Ntozake, and Emily Mann. "The Birth of an R&B Musical." Interview by Douglas J. Keating. *The Philadelphia Inquirer,* March 26, 1989. Follows the story of how Emily Mann and Shange took Shange's *Betsey Brown* from book to stage, in a long interview with both playwrights to mark the opening of the play at the Forum Theater in Philadelphia, as part of the American Music Theater Festival.

Sommers, Michael. "Rays of Hope in a Sky of Blues." Review of *The Love Space Demands* by Ntozake Shange. *The Newark Star-Ledger,* March 12, 1992. This appreciative review of *The Love Space Demands* provides an insightful overview of how Shange takes her poetry to the stage. Sommers finds the work "[a] very accessible, dramatically gripping and altogether handsomely-done theater piece."

"*Spell #7* Takes Us on Magical Trip." Review of *Spell #7,* by Ntozake Shange. *The Washington Times,* May 9, 1991. This descriptive review of *Spell #7* places the piece in the context of a continuing struggle of black women for a dignified place in society: "After all the tribulations and outpourings of feeling, the lingering message is one of racial pride."

— *Anne Mills King; Judith K. Taylor; Thomas J. Taylor*

Jean Toomer

Poet

Born: Washington, D.C.; December 26, 1894
Died: Doylestown, Pennsylvania; March 30, 1967

SHORT FICTION: "Mr. Costyve Duditch," 1928; "Winter on Earth," 1929; "York Beach," 1929.
DRAMA: *Balo*, pb. 1927.
POETRY: "Banking Coal," 1922; "Blue Meridian," 1936; *The Collected Poems of Jean Toomer*, 1988.
NONFICTION: "Race Problems and Modern Society," 1929; *Essentials: Definitions and Aphorisms*, 1931; "The Flavor of Man," 1949.
MISCELLANEOUS: *Cane*, 1923 (prose and poetry); *The Wayward and the Seeking*, 1980 (prose and poetry; Darwin T. Turner, editor).

Achievements

Cane is one of the most memorable and appealing books in African American literature, conveying a vivid sense of the life of southern blacks around 1920 (though little changed since the time of slavery) and showing clearly the conflicts between the feelings of black people and the desensitizing and spirit-diminishing urban life they found in the North. Yet *Cane* is significant not merely for its content but for its innovative form and style as well. Its combination of prose and verse, stories and poems, produces a unified impression, with poems foreshadowing or commenting on adjacent stories and the stories and sketches exploring a multitude of perspectives on black life, rural and urban.

Jean Toomer's impressionistic style, his seductive but not mechanical rhythms, his brilliant imagery and figurative language, his manipulation of language to produce a wide range of emotional and literary effects, were refreshing to many black writers during and after the Harlem Renaissance of the 1920's. Instead of adhering strictly to traditional European models of form and meter (like that of his major black contemporaries Claude McKay and Countée Cullen) or the literary realism and straightforward narrative style of black fiction to that date, he joined the progression of revolutionary poets and fiction writers who were creating literary Modernism, from Walt Whitman on through James Joyce, D. H. Lawrence, Gertrude Stein, Sherwood Anderson, and T. S. Eliot, up to Toomer's friend and contemporary Hart Crane.

Very few of Toomer's other works come even close to the towering achievement of *Cane*, but its poems and poetic prose provided later writers a successful means of evoking the feel of the black experience. A reader can still sense echoes of its style in the evocative prose of novelist Toni Morrison.

Biography

Jean Toomer (born Nathan Eugene) spent most of his life resisting a specific racial label for himself. His childhood and youth were spent in white or racially mixed middle-class neighborhoods in Washington, and his parents were both light-skinned. Jean's father left shortly after his birth and his mother died after remarrying, so that the most potent adult influences on his life were his maternal grandparents, with whom he lived until his twenties. His grandfather, P. B. S. Pinchback, had been elected Lieutenant-Governor in Reconstruction Louisiana and served as Acting Governor in 1873. Toomer believed that his victory was helped by his announcement that he had black blood, although Toomer denied knowing whether it was true. One thing is clear: Pinchback had indeed served the Union cause in the "Corps d'Afrique."

Later in life Toomer denied that he was a Negro—an acceptable statement if one understands his definition of "Negro" as one who identifies solely with the black race, for he, with certainly a great deal of nonblack ancestry, saw himself as not white, either, but "American," a member of a new race which would unify the heretofore conflicting racial groups through a mix-

(The Beinecke Rare Book and Manuscript Library, Yale University Library)

ture of racial strains. The attainment of such an "American" race remained his goal throughout most of his life after *Cane.*

Toomer's education after high school was varied, from agriculture at the University of Wisconsin to the American College of Physical Training in Chicago. Rather than completing courses toward a formal degree, however, he pursued his own reading in literature and social issues while working at assorted jobs until he decided to devote all his efforts to writing. He began writing and was published in a few magazines before moving South to become a schoolteacher in rural Georgia, an experience which he uses in "Kabnis," the final part of *Cane.*

The real nudge came in the form of a three-month stint as substitute principal of a school in a small Georgia town in the fall of 1921. He returned to Washington in November with material for a whole book. He published several poems and stories in assorted periodicals the following year and then gathered most of them and many new ones into a carefully structured book called *Cane*, published in 1923 by Boni and Liveright. The book caused a considerable stir among the influential white literati with whom he associated (such as Waldo Frank, Sherwood Anderson, and Hart Crane) and among black writers and intellectuals as well. Yet in its two printings (the second in 1927) it sold fewer than a thousand copies.

That same year, Toomer met the Russian mystic George Gurdjieff and embraced his philosophy of higher consciousness. After studying with him in France, Toomer returned to spread his teachings in America. A ten-month marriage to a white poet, Margery Latimer, ended with her death in childbirth in 1932. Two years later he married another white woman, Marjorie Content, and spent the rest of his life with her. This period in Toomer's life was largely devoted to self-improvement for himself and others, as he lectured and continued to write primarily philosophical and spiritually oriented work. He continued to publish some literary works until 1936, when his career came virtually to an end, despite attempts to have other works published. He became a Quaker and maintained no further identity with the black race, dying in 1967 largely forgotten.

Analysis: Short Fiction

Divided into three parts, Jean Toomer's *Cane* consists of short stories, sketches, poems, and a novella. The first section focuses on women; the second on relationships between men and women; and the third on one man. Although capable of being read discretely, these works achieve their full power when read together, coalescing to create a novel, unified by theme and symbol.

Cane

Like all of Toomer's work, *Cane* describes characters who have within a buried life, a dream that seeks expression and fulfillment; *Cane* is a record of the destruction of those dreams. Sometimes the dreams explode, the fire within manifesting itself violently; more often, however, the world implodes within the dreamer's mind. These failures have external causes, like the inadequacy or refusal of the society to allow expression, the restrictions by what Toomer calls the herd. They also have internal causes, primarily due to fears and divisions within the dreamer himself as he struggles unsuccessfully to unite will and mind, passion and intellect. In the later story "York Beach," Toomer describes this as the conflict between the wish for brilliant experience and the wish for difficult experience.

The one limitation on the otherwise thoroughgoing romanticism of this vision is Toomer's rigorous separation of humankind into those who dream, who are worth bothering about, and those who do not. While the struggle of Toomer's characters is for unity, it is to unify themselves or to find union with one other dreamer, never to merge with humankind in general. Like Kabnis, many find their true identity in recognizing their differences, uniqueness, and superiority. At the end of "York Beach," the protagonist tells his listeners that the best government would be an empire ruled by one who recognized his own greatness.

Toomer's dreamers find themselves in the first and third sections of *Cane* in a southern society which, although poor in compassion and understanding, is rich in supportive imagery. In the second part, set in the North, that imagery is absent, so the return of the protagonist to the South in part 3 is logical, since the North has not provided a nurturing setting. Although the return may be a plunge back into hell, it is also a journey to an underground where Kabnis attains the vision that sets him free.

The imagery is unified by a common theme: ascent. Kabnis says, "But its the soul of me that needs the risin," and all the imagery portrays the buried life smoldering within, fighting upward, seeking release. The dominant image of the book, the one that supplies the title, is the rising sap of the sugarcane. Cane whispers enigmatic messages to the characters, and it is to cane fields that people seeking escape and release flee. Sap rises, too, in pines, which also whisper and sing; and at the mill of part 1, wood burns, its smoke rising. The moon in "Blood-Burning

Moon" is said to "sink upward," an oxymoronic yoking that implies the difficulty of the rising in this book.

A second pattern of imagery is that of flowing blood or water, although generally in the pessimistic *Cane*, water is not abundant. In "November Cotton Flower," dead birds are found in the wells, and when water is present, the characters, threatened by the life it represents, often fear it. Rhobert, in a sketch of that name, wears a diver's helmet to protect him from water, life which is being drawn off. Dreams denied, blood flows more freely than water.

"Esther"

"Esther," the most successful story in *Cane*, comes early and embodies many of the book's major themes. It opens with a series of four sentences describing Esther as a girl of nine. In each, the first clause compliments her beauty, the second takes the praise away; the first clauses of each are progressively less strong. Esther represents the destruction of potential by a combination of inner and outer forces. On the outside there is her father, "the richest colored man in town," who reduces Esther to a drab and obsequious life behind a counter in his dry goods store. "Her hair thins. It looks like the dull silk on puny corn ears." Then there is King Barlo, a black giant, who has a vision in the corner of town known as the Spittoon. There, while townspeople gather to watch (and black and white preachers find momentary unity in working out ways to rid themselves of one who threatens their power), Barlo sees a strong black man arise. While the man's head is in the clouds, however, "little white-ant biddies come and tie his feet to chains." The herd in Barlo's vision, as in Toomer's, may destroy the dreamer.

Many, however, are affected by what Barlo has seen, none more so than Esther, who decides that she loves him. The fire begins to burn within. As she stands dreaming in her store, the sun on the windows across the street reflect her inner fire, and, wanting to make it real, Esther calls the fire department. For the next eighteen years, Esther, the saddest of all Toomer's women, lives only on dreams, inventing a baby, conceived, she thinks, immaculately. Sometimes, like many of his characters, sensing that life may be too much for her, knowing that "emptiness is a thing that grows by being moved," she tries not to dream, sets her mind against dreaming, but the dreams continue.

At the end of the story, Esther, then twenty-seven, decides to visit Barlo, who has returned to town. She finds the object of her dream in a room full of prostitutes; what rises is only the fumes of liquor. "Conception with a drunken man must be a mighty sin," she thinks, and, when she attempts to return to reality, she, like many Toomer characters, finds that the world has overwhelmed her. Crushed from without, she has neither life nor dreams. "There is no air, no street, and the town has completely disappeared."

"Blood-Burning Moon"

The main character undergoes a similar emotional destruction in "Blood-Burning Moon," Toomer's most widely anthologized short story (also found in the woman-centered first section). Here, however, the destructive force is primarily internal. Among the most conventional of Toomer's stories, "Blood-Burning Moon" has both a carefully delineated plot and a familiar one at that: a love triangle. What is inventional is the way Toomer manages the reader's feelings about the woman whom two men love. Both men are stereotypes. Bob Stone is white and repulsively so. Himself divided and content to be, he makes his mind consciously white and approaches Louisa "as a master should." The black, Tom Burwell, is a stereotype too: Having dreams, he expresses his love sincerely, but inarticulately; denied or threatened, he expresses himself violently.

The first two sections open with rhythmic sentences beginning with the word "up"; Louisa sings songs against the omen the rising moon portends, seeking charms and spells, but refusing the simple act of choosing between the two men. Because Louisa does not choose, the story comes to its inevitable violent climax and the death of both men. There is more, however: When Louisa is last seen she too has been destroyed, mentally, if not physically. She sings again to the full moon as an omen, hoping that people will join her, hoping that Tom Burwell will come; but her choice is too late. Burwell is dead, and the late-ness of her decision marks the end of her dreams. Like Esther, she is separated from even appropriate mental contact with the world that is.

Cane, Section 2

Barlo's vision (in "Esther"), then, is accurate but incomplete as a description of what happens to Toomer's protagonists. While it is true that the herd will often destroy the dreamer, it is just as likely that the dreamer, from inaction, fear, and division, will destroy himself. The four stories of section 2 all focus on pairs of dreamers who can isolate themselves from the rest of society but who cannot get their dreams to merge. In "Avey" it is the man who, focused on his own dreams, refuses to listen to and accept the value of Avey's dreams. In "Bona and Paul," Paul takes Bona away from the dance, not, as everyone assumes, to make love to her, but to know her; but knowing a human is denied him because Bona assumes she already knows him, "a priori," as he has said. Knowing he is black, she "knows" that he will be passionate. When he is interested in knowledge before passion, she discovers that to know *a priori* is not to know at all and flees him, denying his dream of knowing her.

In "Theater" the divided main character, sitting half in light, half in shadow, watches another dreamer, the dancer on stage, Dorris. She is dreaming of him, but, although "mind pulls him upward into dream," suspicion is stronger than desire, and by the end of the story John has moved wholly into shadow. When Dorris looks at him, "She finds it a dead thing in the shadow which is his dream." Likewise, in "Box Seat" Muriel is torn between the dreamer Dan, who stands with one hand lying on the wall, feeling from below the house the deep underground rumbling of the subway, literal buried life, and Mrs. Pribby, the landlady, rattling her newspaper, its thin noise contrasting with the powerful below-ground sound. Muriel chooses respectability. At the theater, to which Dan has followed her, she is repelled by a dwarf who offers her a rose; Dan rises to his feet to proclaim that Jesus was once a leper. This last, insistent image, suggesting the maimed sources of beauty that Muriel is too timid to accept, also indicates the overexplicit inflation of claims that damages some of Toomer's fiction. Although in *Cane* most of the stories are under control, some seem rather too sketchy; "Box Seat," however, foreshadows the fault that mars all of Toomer's later fiction: the sacrifice of dramatic ideas in favor of often pallid, philosophical ones.

"Kabnis"

The last and longest story in *Cane* integrates the themes, making explicit the nature of the destructive forces. The story is "Kabnis," a novella, and the force is sin, a word contained backward in Kabnis's name. It is the story of a black man out of place in the rural South, threatened not so much by whites as by his own people, by his environment, and by his sense of himself.

As the story opens, Kabnis is trying to sleep, but he is not allowed this source of dream; instead, chickens and rats, nature itself, keep him awake. He wants to curse it, wants it to be consistent in its ugliness, but he senses too the beauty of nature, and, because that prevents him from hating it entirely, he feels that even beauty is a curse. Intimidated by nature, Kabnis is also attacked by society, by the local black church, from which the shouting acclamations of faith torture Kabnis, and by the black school superintendent who fires him for drinking. As in "Box Seat," the protagonist is thus caught between expressions of life, which are yet too strong for him, and its repression, which traps him. So positioned, Kabnis, like Rhobert, is a man drowning, trying vainly to avoid the source of life. From this low point, for the only time in the book, Toomer describes the way up, and Kabnis gains enough strength to throw off his oppression.

He has three friends: Halsey, an educated black man who has been playing Uncle Tom; Layman, a preacher, whose low voice suggests a canebrake; and Lewis, a doppelgänger who suggests a version of what a stronger Kabnis might have become and who drops out of the story when Kabnis does indeed become stronger. Once fired, Kabnis takes up residence with Halsey, a Vulcan-like blacksmith who gives him work repairing implements, work for which Kabnis is ill-suited. In his basement, however, Halsey has his own buried life, an old man, Father John, and in the climactic scene, the three men descend into the underground for a dark night of the soul, for the *Walpurgisnacht* on which Kabnis confronts his own demons. Prefiguring the descents in such black fiction as Richard Wright's "Man Who Lived Underground" and Ralph Ellison's *Invisible Man* (1952), this is likewise a descent during which the values of the world above, met on unfamiliar terrain, are rethought. It is a night of debauchery, but also the night when the destructive illusions and fears of the men are exposed.

Father John represents those fears; when he speaks, his message is sin; but Kabnis knows, and for the first time can say, that because of sin the old man has never seen the beauty of the world. Kabnis has, and as he says, "No eyes that have seen beauty ever lose their sight." Kabnis then proclaims a new role for himself: If he is not a blacksmith, he may be, having known beauty, a wordsmith. "I've been shapin words after a design that branded here. Know whats here? M soul." If sin is what is done against the soul and if the soul of Kabnis is what needs the rising, then, as Kabnis says, the world has conspired against him. Now, however, Kabnis acknowledges and confronts that conspiracy, no longer fearing it or Father John. Exhausted by his effort, Kabnis sinks back, but Halsey's sister, Carrie K, does indeed carry K. She lifts him up, and together they ascend the stairs into the daylight, as the risen sun sings a "birth-song" down the streets of the town.

The end is not unequivocally optimistic: It is too small and too tentative a note in this large catalog of the defeated and destroyed. *Cane* does, however, suggest finally that as destructive as dreams may be, once one has seen beauty, if he can free himself from repression, from sin, he may re-create himself. "Kabnis is me," wrote Toomer to Waldo Frank, and he had more in mind than just his use of his experiences. For what Toomer has done in *Cane* is to chart the varieties of sin that society has done to people and, more important, since individuals are always more interesting than society to Toomer, that people have done to themselves. Wholeness is the aim, a wholeness that breaks down barriers between mind and will, man and woman, object and subject, and that allows the potential of dreams to be fulfilled. That the wholeness is so difficult to achieve is the substance of Toomer's short fiction; that Toomer achieves it, both for a character in "Kabnis" and more permanently in his only successful work, a book uniting fiction and poetry, songs and narration, images of fire and water, of descent and ascent, is his testimony that wholeness can be achieved by those who dream of it.

Analysis: Poetry

Jean Toomer was the writer of one book; no matter how often the phrase is used to disparage him, it cannot be denied. Beyond *Cane*, his only other works of value are the long poem "Blue Meridian," a small amount of short fiction, and his autobiographical writings. His plays, most of his other poetry, and his nonfiction are negligible. Yet even had he written only *Cane*, he would always be remembered as a major African American author—and primarily as a poet.

Cane

Whether prose, drama, or verse, all of *Cane* is imbued with a poet's sensibility: precise depiction of details using all the senses vividly, a rhythmic quality without slavish adherence to metrics, a sensitivity to words, phrasing, variations of theme, a fine ear for sound, and a polished sense of organic structure. Few books, whether prose or verse, have less of the prosaic than this one, which can put readers in an almost unabated state of intensity and exaltation, drawing them in by language, sound, rhythm, and form.

Toomer's purpose in this work is to embody what he sees as the dying folk spirit of the South by depicting the lives of its people and re-creating their feelings through language and rhythm. *Cane* achieves a vivid sense of the sensuality of its women, the alternating anguish and joy of life in the South, the toughness and beauty of the land of Georgia. These themes appear primarily in the first third of the book; the second third moves North into the city, where blacks from the South have difficulty fitting into the white-dominated social patterns while retaining roots in the South; in the final third, Ralph Kabnis, a Northern black man, comes South and the focus is on his conflict with the South, looking ahead to William Faulkner's *Absalom, Absalom!* (1936)

and Quentin Compson's climactic cry "I don't hate the South!" Throughout the book, Toomer shows both attraction to the South and a sense of holding back from it—on the part of a narrator in the first third, of Kabnis in the last third, and of assorted Northern-based characters in the middle third, who are losing touch with their black roots. The book, however, is hardly a glorification of the way of life of southern blacks: Kabnis notes that things are not so bad as the North thinks; yet the South still hosts an occasional lynching, as Toomer several times reminds his readers. Still, Toomer appreciates a vitality in southern blacks which disappears when they are removed from the land, a process that Toomer views as unfortunately inevitable in the modern world.

To create this sense of vitality and closeness to the land and the natural world, Toomer uses a vast array of references to nature—the pines, the cane fields, the sky at dusk, the red soil—as images themselves, as similes or metaphors in connection with his characters, or as recurring leitmotifs in the operatic development of his sketches. He uses rhythm and repetition to engage the reader in the immediacy of these sensory experiences. A close analysis of one of his pieces—"Karintha," the opening sketch in *Cane*—will illustrate Toomer's typical methods.

"Karintha"

Like other pieces in the book, "Karintha" opens with an epigraph, a song-like refrain of four lines that recurs throughout the sketch as a unifying device. The first of four paragraphs of varying lengths then introduces Karintha as a child, summing her up in the first sentence, which is poetically accretive rather than prosaically structured; the final adjective cluster echoes words from the epigraph's refrain. Two sentences in parallel construction follow, dealing with the actions the old men and the young men take with her, followed by two sentences in response to these, describing their respective feelings about her. The final sentence sums up the paragraph and "this interest of the male," with a metaphoric interpretation of it and a note of foreboding.

The second paragraph re-creates her girlhood in terms of

concrete actions and images: visual (color, shape, light), auditory (sounds of feet, voice, silence), kinetic (running, wind), tactile (stoning the cows, touching the earth). It sums up her sexual nature as well and ends with two sentences referring to the wishes of the old and young men from the first paragraph, regarding Karintha as she matures. Before Karintha is shown as a woman, the refrain of the epigraph is repeated, the first three lines each being cut by a few words. The new rhythm creates a pace appropriately faster than the wondering, more meditative earlier version.

The third paragraph makes assorted references to the subject matter and phrasing of earlier paragraphs. Repetitions of actual sentences and phrases and of sentence structure (in a series of short sentences showing what young men do for Karintha) evoke the sense of poetry, as does the second half of the paragraph, which, through indirection, reveals Karintha's murder of her infant. The birth is presented as a kind of emotionless miracle unconnected with Karintha herself, while the scene is given sensory richness. Juxtaposed, after ellipses, is the description of a nearby sawmill, its smoldering sawdust pile, and the heaviness of the smoke after Karintha's return. Ending this paragraph is a short song that someone makes up about smoke rising to "take my soul to Jesus," an unconsciously appropriate elegy for the unwanted baby.

The final paragraph begins as the third did—"Karintha is a woman"—and then echoes the last sentence of the first paragraph: "Men do not know that the soul of her was a growing thing ripened too soon." Toomer then suggests her unbreachable remoteness from men; the last sentence recalls the first in this sketch, describing her at twenty in the phrases used to describe her as a child. After a last repetition of her name, followed by ellipses, comes a repetition of the epigraph, followed by an ominous repetition of its last two words, "Goes down," and then more ellipses, hinting at the inevitable descent and defeat of this beautiful, vital creature, brought to maturity too soon through misuse by men.

Though printed as prose, this piece is essentially poetic; the outer details of Karintha's life are merely hinted, but Toomer's poetic prose gives a full sense of Karintha's person and appeal through the precise sensory details of the second paragraph, the recurring patterns of the old and young men's responses to her, and the use of songs as commentary. The echoes and repetitions of images and phrases act as leitmotifs, and Toomer's careful arrangement of them gives the piece a satisfying structure and a strong sense of Karintha's doom, trapped in an unchanging pattern.

Form, Style, and Tone
Such leitmotifs, along with vivid imagery and sentence patterns that are short, repeated, often fragmentary, are used throughout the prose pieces of *Cane* in place of rhyme and meter and line division to produce the quality of poetry. Indeed, many of these pieces (including "Rhobert," "Calling Jesus," "Seventh Street") must be read, like "Karintha," more as poetry than as fiction.

In the pieces clearly printed as poetry, Toomer is less experimental. Many of his poems use orthodox rhyme schemes and meters that a Henry Wadsworth Longfellow or James Russell Lowell would approve. Yet scarce as the poems in *Cane* are, they cover a variety of forms that few single books of poetry display. "Song of the Son," for example, is skillfully rhymed, beautifully evoking in five stanzas of flowing iambic pentameter the southern music which the poet is trying to capture in literature—as he says in this poem, before it vanishes. There are poems of rhymed couplets and brief pieces such as the Imagists might produce. There is a "Cotton Song," such as the work songs that slaves or free but poor farmhands might sing. There is much free verse, notably in "Harvest Song." Toomer's choices are not arbitrary; they suit the moods and subjects of their respective poems, conveying the spectrum of feelings that the writer wishes to present, from joy and exaltation to bitterness and despair.

Toomer also varies style and tone, as well as form, to suit theme and mood. Grim and laconic irony flavors "Conversion," as the African succumbs to "a white-faced sardonic god." "Georgia Dusk" offers lush images both of Southern life and of the African past (a recurring motif throughout the book). "Portrait in Georgia," with its short free-verse lines, reads like a catalog of bodily parts, such as an auctioneer would have prepared. Each is described through images of southern white violence: "lyncher's rope," "fagots," "scars," "blisters," "the ash of black flesh after flame." This poem makes no explicit statement, but the juxtaposition of human parts with these images, presented so simply and concisely, evokes a subtle sense of horror and sets up an appropriately ominous mood for the following story, "Blood-Burning Moon," which ends with an actual lynching. However attractive may be the Georgia of pines, red soil, sweet-smelling cane, and beauteous dusks, Toomer insists on reminding his reader of the dangers there as well, even without explicit condemnation of the bigoted whites or the oppressive social system. Toomer works by indirection, but without diminished effect.

"Harvest Song"
A similarly strong but quite different effect is achieved in "Harvest Song," which presents a field worker suffering at the end of a long day from chill, hunger, thirst, and fatigue. Each poetic "line" is made up of one or more sentences and takes up between one and five lines of print on the page. These sentences are generally short, simple statements that the speaker can barely utter, and they are often repeated, emphasizing his basic human needs, which remain unsatisfied. Toomer's words may not be those that the worker would actually use, but they mirror his thoughts closely, just as the prose pieces of *Cane* give a clear sense of their characters' minds and lives without using their actual language. The simple sentences and their repetition give an accurate sense of the worker's numbness. The poem's last long line (five sentences) is a more exalted outburst, though still despairing: The harvester beats his soft palms against the stubble in his field, causing himself pain that takes away his awareness of hunger, as the last sentence makes shockingly clear. "Harvest Song" indeed! The speaker hardly feels like singing with his throat parched from thirst; and what he harvests for himself means only more pain. Through the use of first-person narration and a simple style, Toomer evokes not pity for the poor

worker, not an external look as in Edwin Markham's "The Man with the Hoe," but rather an empathy from within, allowing the reader to participate fully in the experience.

Spiritual and Philosophical Beliefs

Too often, unfortunately, Toomer's later poetry drops the effective devices used in *Cane* and becomes didactic, explicitly philosophical, lacking *Cane*'s brilliantly realized images of concrete reality or its sharp, often startling metaphors. Toomer was mightily inspired by his few months in Georgia, and his sojourn even affected his interpretations of his own more familiar Washington and New York life; but after he had said what he had to say about the South, and the North in relation to the South, he seems to have exhausted his inspiration, except for his more "universal" themes, with only a little sense of poetry left, to be used in "Blue Meridian" and his stories "Winter on Earth" and "Withered Skin of Berries." The latter story returned Toomer to the lyrical style and poetic sense of structure of the *Cane* stories, but for the most part, Toomer preferred to ignore stylistic and literary matters and chose to express his spiritual and philosophical beliefs, largely influenced by George Gurdjieff's teachings, urging a regeneration of humanity that would eliminate the differences imposed by racial and other categories and bring people closer to God, one another, and the natural world.

"Blue Meridian"

This is the point that Toomer makes explicitly in his last major work, the long poem "Blue Meridian," first published in full in *New American Caravan* (1936) after a selection from an earlier version had appeared in *Adelphi* and *Pagany*. A further revised version is printed in Langston Hughes and Arna Bontemps's anthology *The Poetry of the Negro, 1746-1949* (1949), which places more emphasis on God and more clearly reveals Toomer's notion of the transformed America. A few of the more minor revisions are for the better. This is the version published in *The Wayward and the Seeking*, with some incidental changes.

"Blue Meridian" follows a structure much like that of Whitman's longer poems, such as "Passage to India" or "Crossing

Brooklyn Ferry," with recurring phrases or stanzas, often significantly altered. While it is not divided into individual sections, as
Eliot's *The Waste Land* (1922) and Crane's *The Bridge* (1930)
are—nor does it use the range of poetic forms of which Eliot
and Crane availed themselves—it nevertheless follows those poems in being an examination and criticism of the twentieth century world, achieving a multifaceted view by varying tone and
form.

Written largely in a hortatory, exalted style in an effort to invoke Toomer's higher spiritual goals for a better world and unified humankind, "Blue Meridian" explores the past and current
conditions of America. The European, African, and "red" races
are presented in appropriate images—even stereotypes—each
being shown as incomplete. Toomer's goal, as in much of his
prose, is to achieve a new race beyond individual racial identities, a "universal human being" to be called the "blue meridian,"
the highest stage of development beyond white and black, beyond divisions of East and West, of religion, race, class, sex, and
occupational classification, and transcending the materialism of
a commercial culture and the private concerns of individuals.
The message is not so different from that of Whitman, except
for greater criticism of modern business and the insistence on
the mingling of the races.

Detractions of Later Work
Racial themes and the black experience are missing from
Toomer's later poems—and even some of his earlier ones, such
as "Banking Coal" (*Crisis*, 1922). He was living with a white wife,
quite isolated from the African American literary world, or from
any literary world at all. Certainly one should not say that a black
writer (even one with so little black ancestry as Toomer) should
write only on black themes, but any writer should write out of direct experience; too much of Toomer's poetry aside from *Cane*
is vague and didactic, too intentionally "universal," too generally spiritualized, and essentially prosaic, like his aphorisms,
which lack the bite of Ralph Waldo Emerson's.

Unfortunately, Toomer's vocabulary in this later poetry—
including "Blue Meridian"—too often emulates that of Whit-

man at his most inflated moments, even when Toomer has a true poetic idea, as in "The Lost Dancer," which opens: "Spatial depths of being survive/ The birth to death recurrences . . . ." It is not so much the Latinate vocabulary, which Toomer's great contemporaries Crane and Stevens also used, but rather that, while they made much of the orotund, sensual sounds and suggestiveness of Latinate words, Toomer's word-choices are flat and vague, words made familiar through bombastic social-science jargon. Whereas the *Cane* poems stand out particularly for the vitality of their imagery, the apt metaphors and similes in "Face" and "Portrait in Georgia," the richness of language and sensory detail in "Song of the Son" and "Georgia Dusk," the harshness of the concrete nouns, verbs, and adjectives in "Harvest Song," images in the later poetry are greatly minimized. Here Toomer abandons the exalted Romantic eloquence of "Song of the Son," the verbal and emotional starkness of "Harvest Song," in favor of making philosophical statements.

At his best, Toomer was a brilliant artist in words, a sensitive portrayer of the life he lived and observed, as well as a sincere and concerned member of the human race. *Cane* will forever keep his name alive and arouse an interest in his other work, however inferior most of it has turned out to be. The musical quality of his best poetry and prose will be admired, not for its mere beauty but for its aptness to its subjects: the beauty and appeal as well as the tragedy of the life of the South.

Other Literary Forms

Toomer published several pieces of fiction after *Cane*, generally quite experimental inasmuch as they lacked plot, often included philosophical meditations, and indeed often worked more like poetry, with impressionistic scenes and descriptions and an emphasis on developing a theme through juxtaposition of sections rather than an overall sequence of action. Among these are "Winter on Earth" (*The Second American Caravan*, 1929), "Mr. Costyve Duditch" (*The Dial*, 1928), and "York Beach" (*New American Caravan*, 1929). The first two were collected in the posthumous volume *The Wayward and the Seeking*, edited by

Darwin T. Turner, along with a previously unpublished story from 1930, "Withered Skin of Berries," which is more in the style of *Cane*, though much longer than most of the pieces in that book. Toomer published one short, fragmentary play during his lifetime, *Balo*, in Alain Locke's collection *Plays of Negro Life* (1927), and two of several other plays which he wrote in *The Wayward and the Seeking*.

Nonfiction predominates in Toomer's work, indicating his concerns with philosophical and spiritual goals, as in "Race Problems and Modern Society," "The Flavor of Man," and *Essentials: Definitions and Aphorisms* (privately printed in 1931, some of its aphorisms having been printed earlier in *The Dial* and *Crisis*, with many appearing much later in *The Wayward and the Seeking*). These aphorisms are occasionally poetic and certainly worthy of contemplation, but they might be stronger if incorporated into actual poems. Portions of several versions of Toomer's autobiography appear in *The Wayward and the Seeking*. The rest of his many unpublished works, including many poems, remain in the Toomer Collection of the Fisk University Library.

Bibliography

Banks, Kimberly. "'Like a Violin for the Wind to Play': Lyrical Approaches to Lynching by Hughes, Du Bois, and Toomer." *African American Review* 38, no. 3 (Fall, 2004): 451-466. Contrasts the cruelty of lynching with the poetic way in which it has been described by the three authors and draws conclusions on lynching's effects.

Benson, Joseph, and Mabel Mayle Dillard. *Jean Toomer.* Boston: Twayne, 1980. The first book-length study of Toomer, this volume is an excellent introduction to Toomer's life, work, and place in American literature. After a biographical chapter, the book examines Toomer's novel *Cane* and representative later works. The bibliography includes unpublished works by Toomer and an annotated list of secondary sources.

Bone, Robert. *Down Home: A History of Afro-American Short Fiction from Its Beginnings to the End of the Harlem Renaissance.* New York: Capricorn Books, 1975. Argues that the theater in Toomer's story "The Theater" is an emblem of the two-way, reciprocal relationship of life and art, for there is an osmotic relationship between the life outside and the show inside. "Art-as-transfiguration" is Toomer's theme here; he is concerned with the death of experience and its rebirth as art.

Byrd, Rudolph P. "Jean Toomer and the Writers of the Harlem Renaissance: Was He There with Them?" In *The Harlem Renaissance: Revaluations*, edited by Amritjit Singh, William S. Shiver, and Stanley Brodwin. New York: Garland, 1989. In this article, Byrd argues that Toomer should not be considered part of the Harlem Renaissance because he was not in Harlem for many of the Renaissance's most important years, he did not associate himself with other Harlem writers, and he refused to be labeled as a "Negro" writer.

_____. *Jean Toomer's Years with Gurdjieff: Portrait of an Artist, 1923-1936*. Athens: University of Georgia Press, 1990. A good introduction to Toomer's years of studying orientalism and the mystical philosophy of George Ivanovitch Gurdjieff. It indicates that, although Toomer was an African American writer, his concerns were primarily spiritual and philosophical rather than social and ethnic. It is a fascinating account of one part of Jean Toomer's life.

Durham, Frank, ed. *The Merrill Studies in "Cane."* Columbus, Ohio: Charles E. Merrill, 1971. This volume is a collection of documents that reveal the history of Toomer's most important work, his novel *Cane*. Includes biographical essays, contemporary and more recent introductions to the novel, contemporary reviews, and critical essays.

Edmunds, Susan. "The Race Question and the 'Question of the Home': Revisiting the Lynching Plot in Jean Toomer's *Cane*." *American Literature* 75, no. 1 (March, 2003): 141-169. Compares *Cane* with Toomer's 1922 play *Natalie Mann*, paying particular attention to the role of horror in the two works.

Fabre, Geneviève, and Michel Feith, eds. *Jean Toomer and the Harlem Renaissance*. New Brunswick, N.J.: Rutgers University Press, 2001. A collection of essays by European and American scholars highlighting Toomer's bold experimentations, as well as his often ambiguous responses to the questions of his time.

Hajek, Friederike. "The Change of Literary Authority in the

Harlem Renaissance: Jean Toomer's *Cane.*" In *The Black Co-lumbiad: Defining Moments in African American Literature and Culture,* edited by Werner Sollos and Maria Diedrich. Cambridge, Mass.: Harvard University Press, 1994. Argues that one of the main unifying elements in *Cane* is the concept of changing authority, which occurs in three phrases corresponding to the three sections of the text. Asserts that the work is a swan song for a dying folk culture and a birth chant for a new black aesthetic.

Hawkins, Stephanie L. "Building the 'Blue' Race: Miscegenation, Mysticism, and the Language of Cognitive Evolution in Jean Toomer's 'The Blue Meridian.'" *Texas Studies in Literature & Language* 46, no. 2 (Summer, 2004): 149-182. Explores the intersection of science and mysticism in "The Blue Meridian" and explains Toomer's concept of the "blue" race.

Jones, Robert B. Introduction to *The Collected Poems of Jean Toomer,* edited by Robert B. Jones and Margery Toomer Latimer. Chapel Hill: University of North Carolina Press, 1988. Although this book is not about Toomer's fiction, the introduction gives an excellent account of Toomer's life and work within the context of the various phases of his writing and philosophical studies. In addition, it discusses the authors and poets who influenced Toomer's life and writings.

_____. *Jean Toomer and the Prison-House of Thought: A Phenomenology of the Spirit.* Amherst: University of Massachusetts Press, 1993. A short study of the philosophical aspects of Toomer's work. Includes bibliographical references and index.

Kerman, Cynthia Earl, and Richard Eldridge. *The Lives of Jean Toomer: A Hunger for Wholeness.* Baton Rouge: Louisiana State University Press, 1987. One of the most comprehensive biographies of Toomer yet written, this volume traces in careful detail how the writer was influenced by his unstable childhood, his fascination with mysticism, and his brief career among the literary elite of the 1920's. Includes a chronology, nearly thirty illustrations, and an extensive bibliography.

Larson, Charles R. *Invisible Darkness: Jean Toomer and Nella Larsen.* Iowa City: University of Iowa Press, 1993. Arranged in four sections, each split between Larsen and Toomer. Treats each author's relation to the publishing practices of the Harlem Renaissance, offering critical-biographical readings of Toomer's *Cane* and stories, and examining both authors' formative years and their negotiation of their racial identity. Bibliography, index.

McKay, Nellie Y. *Jean Toomer, Artist: A Study of His Literary Life and Work, 1894-1936.* Chapel Hill: University of North Carolina Press, 1984. Primarily a literary analysis, this book examines Toomer's major published works, especially *Cane*, and places them in the contexts of American and African American literature. The relationship between Toomer's work and his life is also examined, drawing heavily on his autobiographical writings.

Moore, Lewis D. "Kabnis and the Reality of Hope: Jean Toomer's *Cane*." *North Dakota Quarterly* 54 (Spring, 1986): 30-39. Moore's article discusses the elements of "hope" within the context of the characters in *Cane*. In particular, he indicates that despite the repressive aspects of the society in which they live, Toomer's characters are redeemed and indeed triumph over that society by virtue of the positive aspects of their humanity.

O'Daniel, Therman B., ed. *Jean Toomer: A Critical Evaluation.* Washington, D.C.: Howard University Press, 1988. This large volume contains forty-six essays and an extensive bibliography. The essays are arranged thematically and cover Toomer's life; his work as novelist, short-story writer, poet, and playwright; his friendships with other writers; religious and male-female themes; and various interpretations of *Cane*. An excellent and accessible collection.

Ramsey, William M. "Jean Toomer's Eternal South." *Southern Literary Journal* 36, no. 1 (Fall, 2003): 74-90. A new exploration of the American South as it is portrayed in *Cane*. Places the work in the context of the author's life, summarizes the plot, and theorizes about possible influences on modern readers.

Scruggs, Charles, and Lee VanDemarr. *Jean Toomer and the Terrors of American History.* Philadelphia: University of Pennsylvania Press, 1998. Scruggs and VanDemarr examine sources such as Toomer's early writings on politics and race, his extensive correspondence with Waldo Frank, and unpublished portions of his autobiographies to illustrate the ways in which the cultural wars of the 1920's influenced Toomer's *Cane* and his later attempt to escape from the racial definitions of American society.

Taylor, Paul Beekman. *Shadows of Heaven.* York Beach, Maine: S. Weiser, 1998. Examines the lives and works of Toomer, George Ivanovitch Gurdjieff, and A. R. Orage.

Wagner-Martin, Linda. "Toomer's *Cane* as Narrative Sequence." In *Modern American Short Story Sequences,* edited by J. Gerald Kennedy. Cambridge, England: Cambridge University Press, 1995. Discusses *Cane* as a modernist tour de force of mixed genre. Examines "Blood-Burning Moon" as Toomer's ideal fiction construct that provides insight into the structural and thematic radicalism of the collection.

Whalan, Mark. "'Taking Myself in Hand': Jean Toomer and Physical Culture." *Modernism/Modernity* 10, no. 4 (December, 2003): 597-616. Looks at the role played by the Physical Culture line of consumer products during the turn of the last century and explains its influence in Toomer's "Bona and Paul."

— *Howard Faulkner; Scott Giantvalley; Earl Paulus Murphy*

Alice Walker

Novelist, short-story writer, poet, and essayist

Born: Eatonton, Georgia; February 9, 1944

LONG FICTION: *The Third Life of Grange Copeland,* 1970; *Meridian,* 1976; *The Color Purple,* 1982; *The Temple of My Familiar,* 1989; *Possessing the Secret of Joy,* 1992; *By the Light of My Father's Smile,* 1998; *Now Is the Time to Open Your Heart,* 2004.

SHORT FICTION: *In Love and Trouble: Stories of Black Women,* 1973; *You Can't Keep a Good Woman Down,* 1981; *The Complete Stories,* 1994; *Alice Walker Banned,* 1996 (stories and commentary).

POETRY: *Once: Poems,* 1968; *Five Poems,* 1972; *Revolutionary Petunias, and Other Poems,* 1973; *Goodnight, Willie Lee, I'll See You in the Morning: Poems,* 1979; *Horses Make a Landscape Look More Beautiful,* 1984; *Her Blue Body Everything We Know: Earthling Poems, 1965-1990 Complete,* 1991; *Absolute Trust in the Goodness of the Earth: New Poems,* 2003; *A Poem Traveled Down My Arm,* 2003.

NONFICTION: *In Search of Our Mothers' Gardens: Womanist Prose,* 1983; *Living by the Word: Selected Writings, 1973-1987,* 1988; *Warrior Marks: Female Genital Mutilation and the Sexual Blinding of Women,* 1993 (with Pratibha Parmar); *The Same River Twice: Honoring the Difficult,* 1996; *Anything We Love Can Be Saved: A Writer's Activism,* 1997; *The Way Forward Is with a Broken Heart,* 2000; *Sent by Earth: A Message from the Grandmother Spirit After the Attacks on the World Trade Center and Pentagon,* 2001.

CHILDREN'S/YOUNG ADULT LITERATURE: *Langston Hughes: American Poet,* 1974; *To Hell with Dying,* 1988; *Finding the Green Stone,* 1991.

EDITED TEXTS: *I Love Myself When I Am Laughing . . . and Then Again When I Am Looking Mean and Impressive: A Zora Neale Hurston Reader,* 1979.

Achievements

Alice Walker's literary reputation is based primarily on her fiction, although her second book of poetry, *Revolutionary Petunias, and Other Poems*, received the Lillian Smith Award and a nomination for a National Book Award. Her first short-story collection, *In Love and Trouble: Stories of Black Women*, won the Rosenthal Award of the National Institute of Arts and Letters. In addition, she received a Charles Merrill writing fellowship, an award for fiction from the National Endowment for the Arts, and a Guggenheim Fellowship. She was also a Bread Loaf Scholar and a fellow at the Radcliffe Institute.

The Third Life of Grange Copeland was widely and enthusiastically reviewed in publications as varied as *The New Yorker, The New Republic,* and *The New York Times Book Review,* although journals aimed primarily at a black readership were often silent or critical of the violence and graphic depiction of rural black life. With the publication of *Meridian,* Walker's second novel, her work as a poet, novelist, essayist, editor, teacher, scholar, and political activist came together. *Meridian* was universally praised in scholarly journals, literary magazines, popular magazines, and black-oriented journals. Some critics, mainly black male reviewers, objected again to the honest, straightforward portrayals of black life in the South and to Walker's growing feminism, which they saw in conflict with her commitment to her race. Walker's third novel, *The Color Purple,* was widely acclaimed; feminist and *Ms.* editor Gloria Steinem wrote that this novel "could be the kind of popular and literary event that transforms an intense reputation into a national one," and Peter Prescott's review in *Newsweek* began by saying "I want to say at once that *The Color Purple* is an American novel of permanent importance."

These accolades were substantiated when Walker received both the American Book Award and the 1983 Pulitzer Prize in fiction. In 1984, she received a Best Books for Young Adults citation from the American Library Association for *In Search of Our Mothers' Gardens*. She has also won the O. Henry Award (1986), the Langston Hughes Award (1989), the Nora Astorga Leadership Award (1989), the Fred Cody Award for lifetime achievement (1990), the Freedom to Write Award (1990), the California Governor's Arts Award (1994), and the Literary Ambassador Award (1998).

At numerous colleges, as a teacher and writer-in-residence, Alice Walker established herself as a mentor, particularly to young African American women. Her crusades became international. To alert the world to the problem of female circumcision in Africa, she collaborated with an Anglo-Indian filmmaker on a book and film. She was a voice for artistic freedom, defending her own controversial writings and those of others, such as Salman Rushdie. In her writings and later open lifestyle, she affirmed lesbian and bisexual experience. Yet the accomplishment in which she took most pride was her resurrection of the reputation of Zora Neale Hurston, a germinal African American anthropologist and novelist, whose books had gone out of print.

Biography

Alice Malsenior Walker was born in Eatonton, Georgia, on February 9, 1944, the last of eight children of Willie Lee and Minnie Lou Grant Walker, sharecroppers in rural Georgia. Her relationship with her father, at first strong and valuable, became strained as she became involved in the civil rights and feminist movements. A moving depiction of her estrangement from her father occurs in her essay "My Father's Country Is the Poor," which appeared in *The New York Times* in 1977. For Walker, a loving and healthy mother-daughter relationship has endured over the years. An account of that relationship is central to her essays "In Search of Our Mothers' Gardens" and "Lulls—A Native Daughter Returns to the Black South" and in Mary Helen Washington's article "Her Mother's Gifts," in which Walker acknowledges that she often writes with her mother's voice—"Just as you have certain physical characteristics of your mother . . . when you're compelled to write her stories, it's because you recognize and prize those qualities of her in yourself."

One of the central events in Walker's childhood was a BB gun accident which left her, at age eight, blind in one eye. Scar tissue from that wound, both physical and psychological, seems to

(Jeff Reinking/Picture Group)

have left her with a compensating acuteness of vision, despite the conviction that she was permanently disfigured. Walker was affected enough by the accident to say in a 1974 interview with John O'Brien, "I have always been a solitary person, and since I was eight years old (and the recipient of a disfiguring scar, since corrected, somewhat), I have daydreamed—not of fairy-tales— but of falling on swords, of putting guns to my heart or head, and of slashing my wrists with a razor." Walker's partial blindness allowed her to attend Spelman College in Atlanta on a scholarship for the handicapped, following her graduation from Butler-Baker High School in 1961. She left Spelman after two years— which included summer trips to the Soviet Union and to Africa

as part of a group called Experiment in International Living—
to attend Sarah Lawrence College, from which she graduated in
1965. At Sarah Lawrence College she came under the influence
of the poet Muriel Rukeyser, who recognized her talent and arranged for her first publications. She also took a summer off for
a trip to her "spiritual home," Africa. She returned depressed
and pregnant, contemplated suicide for a time, but instead underwent an abortion and poured her emotions into writing.

Walker's political activity governed her movements during
the years immediately following her college graduation: She
spent the summer of 1965 in the Soviet Union and also worked
for civil rights in Liberty County, Georgia. The next year she was
a caseworker for New York City's Department of Social Services,
and then a voter-registration worker in Mississippi. In 1967, she
married Melvyn Leventhal, a civil rights lawyer, and moved to
Jackson, Mississippi, where she continued her civil rights work,
lived in the heart of the South as part of an interracial couple,
and taught at Jackson State University, while continuing to write
stories, poems, and essays. She taught at Tougaloo College in
Mississippi for a year before returning to the East, where she was
a lecturer in writing and literature at Wellesley College, an editor at *Ms.* magazine, and an instructor at the University of Massachusetts at Boston. By 1977, she had divorced her husband,
accepted a position as associate professor of English at Yale University, and written six books.

After *The Color Purple* won critical acclaim, in 1986, Walker
and her family shared the success with Eatonton. Walker's sister
established The Color Purple Educational Scholarship Fund,
and Walker adopted three elementary schools to help provide
needed supplies for students who maintained above-average
grades. Walker continued her activities in political forums as
well, working for civil rights and protesting against nuclear
weapons. She became an avid objector to female genital mutilation ("female circumcision") in Africa through public speaking
and through her novel *Possessing the Secret of Joy* and her nonfiction book *Warrior Marks: Female Genital Mutilation and the Sexual
Blinding of Women* (1993), which focus on the horrors and scars
of this practice.

Walker also used her success to help other female writers. She advocated women's literature classes and helped promote neglected female and black writers. In 1984, Walker began her own publishing company, Wild Trees Press. In the 1980's and 1990's she lived in Northern California, where she continued to write stories, essays, poems, and novels. Walker continued to write, though she did not recapture the acclaim or the notoriety that *The Color Purple* brought her. Critics complained of her stridency, the factual inaccuracies in her writings, and her tendency to turn her works of fiction into polemics. Many African Americans felt that her writings cast their society in a grim light. Walker lived for several years with Robert Allen, the editor of *Black Scholar.* Times had changed; the motto was no longer "black and white together," marriages between Jews and African Americans were out, and black-black relationships were in. As the millennium neared its close, Walker became more alert to the problems women of color faced throughout the world. Taking a female partner, she decided to devote her time and talents to celebrating women and rectifying wrongs committed against them.

Analysis: Long Fiction

The story of Alice Walker's childhood scar provides the most basic metaphor of her novels: the idea that radical change is possible even under the worst conditions. Although she was never able to regain the sight in one eye, Walker's disfigurement was considerably lessened:

> I used to pray every night that I would wake up and somehow it would be gone. I couldn't look at people directly because I thought I was ugly. . . . Then when I was fourteen, I visited my brother Bill [who] took me to a hospital where they removed most of the scar tissue—and I was a *changed person.* I promptly went home, scooped up the best-looking guy, and by the time I graduated from high school, I was valedictorian, voted "Most Popular," and crowned queen!

The idea that change and personal triumph are possible despite the odds is central to all of Walker's writing. Her work focuses directly or indirectly on the ways of survival adopted by black women, usually in the South, and is presented in a prose style characterized by a distinctive combination of lyricism and unflinching realism. Walker's women attempt not merely to survive, but to survive completely with some sense of stability, despite the constant thread of family violence, physical and mental abuse, and a lack of responsibility on the part of the men in their lives. Walker is simultaneously a feminist and a supporter of civil rights, not only for black Americans, but also for minorities everywhere.

The Third Life of Grange Copeland

Writing in 1973, Walker observed that her first novel, *The Third Life of Grange Copeland,* "though sometimes humorous and celebrative of life, is a grave book in which the characters see the world as almost entirely menacing." This dark view of life is common to Grange Copeland, the patriarch of a family farming on shares in rural Georgia, his son Brownfield, and the wives and daughters of both men. For all these characters, the world is menacing because of the socioeconomic position they occupy at the bottom of the scale of the sharecropping system. Father and son menace each other in this novel because they are in turn menaced by rage born out of the frustration of the system. Although the white people of the book are nearly always vague, nameless, and impersonal, they and the system they represent have the ability to render both Grange and Brownfield powerless.

It is not accidental that these characters' names have agricultural connotations. "Grange" suggests a late nineteenth century association of farmers, a feudal farm and grain storage building, and a combination of graze and range, while "Brownfield" and "Copeland" are self-explanatory—for the inability to cope with the land is what leads both male characters along virtually parallel paths. For the father, the mere appearance of the white farm boss's truck is enough to turn his face "into a unnaturally bland mask, curious and unsettling to see." The appearance of the truck causes the son to be "filled with terror of this man who could, by his presence alone, turn his father into something that might as well have been a pebble or a post or a piece of dirt." Although Grange is, in this same image, literally a piece of land, he eventually returns to the South and learns to live self-sufficiently, farming a section of soil he tricked his second wife into giving to him. Brownfield, in contrast, is never able to escape the share-cropping system, although he sees that, like his father, he is "destined to be no more than overseer, on the white man's plantation, of his own children." Brownfield is able to live obliviously on a farm in Georgia, content to blame all of his problems on others. The poor rural black workers of this novel are themselves little more than a crop, rotated from farm to farm, producing a harvest of shame and hunger, cruelty and violence.

Unlike the men of the novel, the women are menaced by both blacks and whites, by both the agricultural system and the "strange fruit" it produces. Margaret, Grange's first wife, is both physically and mentally degraded by her husband and then sexually exploited by a white truck driver, resulting in her second pregnancy. Unable to cope with this situation, Grange deserts his family, after which his wife poisons both her child and herself. Following his father's pattern, Brownfield marries and begins to work the land, but after "a year when endless sunup to sundown work on fifty rich bottom acres of cotton land and a good crop brought them two diseased shoats for winter meat," he too begins to abuse his wife. Although Brownfield's wife, Mem, is a schoolteacher intelligent enough to try to break the cycle of raising others people's crops, her brief rebellion against her husband's malevolent beatings and mental tortures is a failure: He is able to subjugate her through repeated pregnancies that sap her rebellion as they turn her once rich and strong body into a virtual wasteland of emaciation. Because her body, which represents the land of the South, is still able to produce children despite its depleted condition, Brownfield is enraged enough to murder her in retaliation for her physical shape: "he had murdered his wife because she had become skinny and had not, with much irritation to him, reverted, even when well-fed, to her former plumpness. . . . Plumpness and freedom from the

land, from cows and skinniness, went all together in his mind."
Despite his irrational abuse of her, Mem is not ashamed "of being black though, no matter what he said. . . . Color was something the ground did to the flowers, and that was an end to it."

What the ground did to these generations of southern black
people is the subject of Walker's novel—the whole lurid history
of violence, hatred, and guilt that she chronicles in this story of
one family's griefs. By the book's end, Brownfield Copeland has
murdered his wife and an unnamed albino baby, while Grange
Copeland has murdered his son Brownfield—first spiritually,
then physically—and indirectly has killed his first wife and her
infant.

Walker's characters are allegorical representations of the
classic modes of survival historically adopted by black Americans in dealing with their oppression. Brownfield identifies with
whites by daydreaming of himself on a southern plantation, sip-
ping mint juleps, and then by bargaining for his freedom with
the sexual favors of black women. Both of Grange's wives attempt to be true to the white stereotype of black women as promiscuous sexual beings, free of any moral restraints. Brownfield's wife, Mem, attempts the passive resistance advocated
by Martin Luther King, Jr., but she is destroyed by what her
husband calls "her weakness . . . forgiveness, a stupid belief
that kindness can convert the enemy." Brownfield's daughter,
Daphne, who calls herself the Copeland Family Secret Keeper,
tries the strategy of inventing a falsely romantic history of the
past, of the good old days when her father was kind, echoing
those historical revisionists who try to argue that slavery was not
that bad. Brownfield's other daughters try to stay away from
their father altogether, regarding him "as a human devil" of
whom they were afraid "in a more distant, impersonal way. He
was like bad weather, a toothache, daily bad news."

Each of the title character's three lives (at home in the South
as a sharecropper married to Margaret; in the North as a hustler
of alcohol, drugs, and women; and finally back in the South as a
farmer married to Josie and rearing his granddaughter Ruth)
parallels a traditional survival strategy, which Grange summarizes as follows, "The white folks hated me and I hated myself

until I started hating them in return and loving myself. Then I tried just loving me, and then you, and *ignoring* them much as I could." To put it another way, Grange tries at first to adapt to the system by believing what whites say about blacks; then he turns to the classic escape of the runaway slave—heading North to freedom; finally, he tries the technique of praising black life while ignoring whites altogether. A large part of the novel's devastation is caused by the repeated use of these techniques, not against whites, but against other members of the Copeland family. Only Ruth, the granddaughter through whom Grange seeks redemption, is able to deal with whites in an intelligent, balanced, nondestructive yet independent way. She has learned from her grandfather, and from her family history, that pure hatred becomes self-hatred, and violence begets self-violence; she therefore becomes the novel's symbol of the new black woman, ready to assume her place in black history as a courageous worker in the Civil Rights movement which the rest of her family has been groping to discover.

Meridian
Walker's second novel, *Meridian*, picks up chronologically and thematically at the point where her first novel ended. *Meridian* describes the struggles of a young black woman, Meridian Hill, about the same age as Ruth Copeland, who comes to an awareness of power and feminism during the Civil Rights movement, and whose whole life's meaning is centered in the cycles of guilt, violence, hope, and change characteristic of that dramatic time. Thematically, *Meridian* picks up the first novel's theme of self-sacrificial murder as a way out of desperate political oppression in the form of the constant question that drives Meridian Hill— "Will you kill for the Revolution?" Meridian's lifelong attempt to answer that question affirmatively (as her college friends so easily do), while remaining true to her sense of responsibility to the past, her sense of ethics, and her sense of guilt of having given to her mother the child of her teenage pregnancy, constitutes the section of the novel entitled "Meridian." The second third of the novel, "Truman Held," is named for the major male character in the narrative. The third major section of the novel, "End-

ing," looks back at the turmoil of the Civil Rights movement from the perspective of the 1970's. Long after others have given up intellectual arguments about the morality of killing for revolution, Meridian is still debating the question, still actively involved in voter registration, political activism, and civil rights organization, as though the movement had never lost momentum. Worrying that her actions, now seen as eccentric rather than revolutionary, will cause her "to be left, listening to the old music, beside the highway," Meridian achieves release and atonement through the realization that her role will be to "come forward and sing from memory songs they will need once more to hear. For it is the song of the people, transformed by the experiences of each generation, that holds them together."

In 1978, Walker described *Meridian* as "a book 'about' the Civil Rights movement, feminism, socialism, the shakiness of revolutionaries and the radicalization of saints." Her word "about" is exact, for all of these topics revolve not chronologically but thematically around a central point—the protagonist, Meridian Hill. In some ways, Meridian *is* a saint; by the book's end she has sustained her belief in the Civil Rights movement without losing faith in feminism and socialism, despite family pressures, guilt, literally paralyzing self-doubts, the history of the movement, and the sexism of many of its leaders. In contrast, Truman Held represents those males who were reported to have said that "the only position for a woman in the movement is prone." Although Truman Held is Meridian's initial teacher in the movement, she eventually leaves him behind because of his inability to sustain his initial revolutionary fervor, and because of his misogyny. Unlike Brownfield Copeland, Truman argues that women are of less value than they should be, not because of skinniness, but because "Black women let themselves go . . . they are so fat." Later in the novel, Truman marries a white civil rights worker whose rape by another black man produces disgust in him, as much at his wife as at his friend. When Truman seeks out Meridian in a series of small southern hamlets where she continues to persuade black people to register to vote and to struggle for civil rights, he tells her that the movement is ended and that he grieves in a different way than she.

Meridian answers, "I know how you grieve by running away. By pretending you were never there." Like Grange Copeland, Truman Held refuses to take responsibility for his own problems, preferring to run away to the North.

Meridian's sacrificial dedication to the movement becomes a model for atonement and release, words that once formed the working title of the book. *Meridian* could also have been called "The Third Life of Meridian Hill" because of similarities between Meridian's life and Grange Copeland's. Meridian leads three lives: as an uneducated child in rural Georgia who follows the traditional pattern of early pregnancy and aimless marriage, as a college student actively participating in political demonstrations, and as an eccentric agitator—a performer, she calls herself—unaware that the movement is ended. Like Grange Copeland in another sense, Meridian Hill is solid proof of the ability of any human to change dramatically by sheer will and desire.

Meridian is always different from her friends, who, filled with angry rhetoric, ask her repeatedly if she is willing to kill for the revolution, the same question that Grange asked himself when he lived in the North. This question haunts Meridian, because she does not know if she can or if she should kill, and because it reminds her of a similar request, posed in a similar way by her mother: "Say it now, Meridian, and be saved. All He asks is that we acknowledge Him as our Master. Say you believe in Him . . . don't go against your heart." In neither case is Meridian able to answer yes without going against her heart. Unlike her college friends and Truman Held, who see the movement only in terms of future gains for themselves, Meridian is involved with militancy because of her past: "But what none of them seemed to understand was that she felt herself to be, not holding on to something from the past, but *held* by something in the past."

Part of the past's hold on her is the sense of guilt she feels about her relationships with her parents. Although her father taught her the nature of the oppression of minorities through his knowledge of American Indians, her strongest source of guilt comes from her mother, who argues, like Brownfield Copeland, that the responsibility for *all* problems stems from outside oneself: "The answer to everything," said Meridian's mother, "is

we live in America and we're not rich." Meridian's strongest
sense of past guilt comes from the knowledge she gains when
she becomes pregnant: "it was for stealing her mother's serenity,
for shattering her mother's emerging self, that Meridian felt
guilty from the very first, though she was unable to understand
how this could possibly be her fault."

Meridian takes the form of a series of nonchronological sections, some consisting of only a paragraph, some four or five
pages long, that circle around the events of Meridian's life. The
writing is clear, powerful, violent, lyrical, and often symbolic.
Spelman College, for example, is here called Saxon College.
The large magnolia tree in the center of the campus, described
with specific folkloric detail, is destroyed by angry students during a demonstration: "Though Meridian begged them to dis-
mantle the president's house instead, in a fury of confusion and
frustration they worked all night, and chopped and sawed
down, level to the ground, that mighty, ancient, sheltering music tree." This tree (named The Sojourner, perhaps for Sojourner Truth) expands symbolically to suggest both the senseless destruction of black ghettos by blacks during the turmoil of
the 1960's, and also Meridian Hill herself, who receives a photograph years later of The Sojourner, now "a gigantic tree stump"
with "a tiny branch, no larger than a finger, growing out of one
side." That picture, suggesting as it does the rebirth of hope despite despair, also evokes the last vision of Meridian expressed
by the now-shamed Truman Held: "He would never see 'his' Meridian again. The new part had grown out of the old, though,
and that was reassuring. This part of her, new, sure and ready,
even eager, for the world, he knew he must meet again and recognize for its true value at some future time."

The Color Purple

Like her first two novels, *The Color Purple* has an unusual form.
The Color Purple presents the author's familiar and yet fresh
themes—survival and redemption—in epistolary form. Most of
the novel's letters are written by Celie, an uneducated, unloved,
black woman living in rural Georgia in the 1920's; Celie's letters
are written in what Walker calls "black folk English," a language

of wit, strength, and natural humor. Ashamed of having been raped by her stepfather, a man whom Celie thinks at the time is her father, she begins to send letters to God, in the way that children send letters to Santa Claus, because her rapist told her to tell nobody but God. Although her early letters tell of rape, degradation, and pain, of her stepfather's getting rid of the two children born of his cruelty, the tone is nevertheless captivating, ironic, and even humorous. Soon the despair turns into acceptance, then into understanding, anger, rebellion, and finally triumph and loving forgiveness as the fourteen-year-old Celie continues to write until she reaches an audience, some thirty years later. Like the author, who began writing at the age of eight, and who has turned her childhood experience in rural Georgia into three novels of violence, hatred, understanding, love, and profound hope for the future, Celie is a writer, a listener, a thinker, and a promoter of Walker's constant theme: "Love redeems, meanness kills."

Like Meridian Hill, Celie compares herself to a tree. After her stepfather's repeated rapes, Celie is sold into a virtual state of slavery to a man who beats her, a man she neither knows, loves, nor talks to, a man she can never call anything but Mr. ——, an ironic throwback to the eighteenth century English epistolary novel. Celie tries to endure by withholding all emotion: "I make myself wood. I say to myself, Celie, you a tree. That's how come I know trees fear man." Like The Sojourner, or like the kudzu vine of the deep South that thrives despite repeated attempts to beat it back, Celie continues to express her fears and hopes in a series of letters written in a form of black English that is anything but wooden. The contrast between the richly eccentric prose of Celie's letters and the educated yet often lifeless sentences of her sister Nettie's return letters supports Walker's statement that "writing *The Color Purple* was writing in my first language." The language of the letters is at first awkward, but never difficult to follow. As Celie grows in experience, in contact with the outside world, and in confidence, her writing gradually becomes more sophisticated and more like standard written English, but it never loses its originality of rhythm and phrase.

Based on Walker's great-grandmother, a slave who was raped at twelve by her owner, Celie works her way from ignorance about her body and her living situation all the way through to an awakening of her self-worth, as well as to an understanding of the existence of God, the relations between men and women, and the power of forgiveness in uniting family and friends. Much of this transformation is brought about through the magic of a blues singer named Shug Avery, who guides Celie in understanding sexuality, men, and religion without causing her to lose her own fresh insights, naïve though they are.

The letters that make up the novel are something like the missives that the protagonist of Saul Bellow's novel *Herzog* (1964) writes but never sends, in that they are often addressed to God and written in an ironic but not self-conscious manner. Because of the combination of dark humor and despair, the letters also evoke memories of the desperate letters from the physically and spiritually maimed addressed to the hero of Nathanael West's *Miss Lonelyhearts* (1933). Although Celie is unlettered in a traditional sense, her ability to carry the complicated plot forward and to continue to write—first without an earthly audience, and then to her sister, whom she has not seen for more than twenty years—testifies to the human potential for self-transformation.

Discussing Celie's attempts to confirm her existence by writing to someone she is not certain exists, Gloria Steinem says, "Clearly, the author is telling us something about the origin of Gods: about when we need to invent them and when we don't." In a sense, Shug Avery becomes a god for Celie because of her ability to control the evil in the world and her power to change the sordid conditions of Celie's life. Early in the book, when Celie is worrying about survival, about rape, incest, beatings, and the murder of her children, her only source of hope is the name "Shug Avery," a name with a magical power to control her husband. Not even aware that Shug is a person, Celie writes "I ast our new mammy bout Shug Avery. What it is?" Finding a picture of Shug, Celie transfers her prayers to what is at that point only an image: "I see her there in furs. Her face rouge. Her hair like somethin tail. She grinning with her foot up on somebody motocar. Her eyes serious tho. Sad some. . . . An all night long I stare at it. An now when I dream, I dream of Shug Avery. She be dress to kill, whirling an laughing." Shug Avery becomes a god to Celie not only because she is pictured in the first photograph Celie has ever seen, but also because she is dressed in a style that shows a sense of pride and freedom.

Once Celie's sister's letters begin to appear, mailed from Africa, where Nettie is a missionary, the ironic connection between the primitive animism of the Africans and Celie's equally primitive reaction to Shug's picture becomes clear. Although Nettie has crossed the ocean to minister to a tribe of primitive people, her own sister is living in inhuman conditions in Georgia: ignorance, disease, sexism, lack of control of the environment, and the ever-increasing march of white people. When Shug explains her own animistic religious beliefs—which include the notion that God is not a he or a she, but an it (just as Celie once thought Shug Avery was an it)—Celie is converted to a pantheistic worship that makes her early identification with trees seem less naïve.

When the narrator of Herman Melville's "Bartleby the Scrivener" tries to explain Bartleby's withdrawal from life, he thinks of the dead letter office in which the scrivener was rumored to have worked, and says, "On errands of life, these letters speed to death." In contrast, Celie's and Nettie's letters, ostensibly written to people long thought to be dead, speed across the ocean on errands of life, where they grow to sustain not merely the sisters in the book, but all those lucky enough to read them. As the author says of *The Color Purple*, "It's my happiest book . . . I had to do all the other writing to get to this point." For the reader who has gotten to this point in Walker's career by reading all of her other books, there is no question that Alice Walker's name could be substituted for Celie's in the author's statement about her most recent novel: "Let's hope people can hear Celie's voice. There are so many people like Celie who make it, who come out of nothing. People who triumph."

Possessing the Secret of Joy
The novels *By the Light of My Father's Smile* and *Possessing the Secret of Joy* share strong characters whose sexual identities suffer in

order to conform to the society in which they live. Only through death can Tashi and Mad Dog become complete and escape the male-dominated world and its restrictions.

Walker combines fact and fiction in *Possessing the Secret of Joy* to illustrate the effects that female genital mutilation has on the women who are subjected to the procedure. The main character, Tashi, an African tribal woman, willingly undergoes the tribal ritual of genital mutilation in a desire to conform to her culture and feel complete. This procedure leaves her physically and mentally scarred. Tashi realizes that the procedure destroyed her emotionally and made her feel as if she were something other than her true self. After her mutilation, she marries Adam Johnson and moves to America. She is renamed Evelyn Johnson, and her chapter headings shift from "Tashi" to "Evelyn" in order to demonstrate the conflict within her as she struggles to find her true identity. The conflict leads her to madness.

Tashi strives to understand her insanity and to interpret her recurring nightmares of a tower. With the help of her therapists, Mzee and Raye, and the members of her family, Tashi realizes the reasons for her insanity and gradually becomes stronger and able to face her nightmares and what they represent. The chapters are told through the eyes of all the main characters, a technique that provides insight into the effect that Tashi has on those around her. Through its main characters, Tashi, Olivia, and Adam, *Possessing the Secret of Joy* is connected to, but is not a sequel to, Walker's previous novels *The Color Purple* and *The Temple of My Familiar.*

By the Light of My Father's Smile

Walker's sixth novel, *By the Light of My Father's Smile,* follows the Johnson family on a journey through life, and to rebirth through death. Magdalena, referred to as Mad Dog, discovers her sensuality and its connection with her spirituality while living with her parents in Mexico. Her parents are pretending to be missionaries in order to do an anthropological study of the Mundo people. Magdalena is acutely aware of her emotions and sensuality, but she is severely beaten by her father when he discovers her sexual activity.

Magdalena's sister Susannah, shadowed by Magdalena's anger and frustration, is awakened to her true desires by her friend Irene, who is able to survive and accept life on her own terms despite the restrictions placed on her by her society. Susannah realizes that her unhappiness is the result of having been "sucked into the black cloth" and hypocrisy of the world. Each member of the Johnson family suffers through life searching for true love and happiness, which they find only in death. The story moves between the spiritual world and physical world as the father watches his two daughters come to terms with their anger and their true spirits. As characters pass into the spiritual world, they are enlightened to their failings in the physical world and make amends with those they have injured. Only when acceptance of each soul is obtained can the four family members cross the river and live in eternity.

Analysis: Short Fiction

The heroism of black women in the face of turmoil of all kinds rings from both volumes of Alice Walker's short stories like the refrain of a protest song. *In Love and Trouble* reveals the extremes of cruelty and violence to which poor black women are often subjected in their personal relationships, while the struggles in *You Can't Keep a Good Woman Down* reflect the social upheavals of the 1970's.

In Love and Trouble: Stories of Black Women

Such subjects and themes lend themselves to a kind of narrative that is filled with tension. The words "love" and "trouble," for example, in the title of the first collection, identify a connection that is both unexpected and inevitable. Each of the thirteen stories in this collection is a vivid confirmation that every kind of love known to woman brings its own kind of suffering. Walker is adept at pairing such elements so as to create pronounced and revealing contrasts or intense conflicts. One such pair that appears in many of these short stories is a stylistic one and easy to see: the poetry and prose that alternate on the page. Another unusual combination at work throughout the short fiction may be called the lyrical and the sociological. Like the protest song, Walker's stories make a plea for justice made more memorable by its poetic form. She breathes rhythmic, eloquent language into the most brutish and banal abuses.

These two elements—similarity of subject matter and the balance of highly charged contraries—produce a certain unity within each volume. Yet beyond this common ground, the stories have been arranged so as to convey a progression of interconnected pieces whose circumstances and themes repeat, alternate, and overlap rather like a musical composition. The first three stories of *In Love and Trouble,* for example, are all about married love; the next two are about love between parent and child; then come three stories in which black-white conflict is central; the fourth group concerns religious expression; and the last three stories focus on initiation. Other themes emerge and run through this five-set sequence, linking individual motifs and strengthening the whole. Jealousy is one of those motifs, as is the drive for self-respect, black folkways, and flowers, in particular the rose and the black-eyed Susan.

Four stories suggest the breadth of Walker's imagination and narrative skills. "Roselily" strikes an anticipatory note of foreboding. "The Child Who Favored Daughter" is an equally representative selection, this time of the horrific destruction of the black woman. "The Revenge of Hannah Kemhuff" is as cool and clear as "The Child Who Favored Daughter" is dark and fevered. The narrator recounts a tale of Voodoo justice, specifically crediting Zora Neale Hurston, author of *Mules and Men* (1935). The final story in this collection, "To Hell with Dying," is an affirmative treatment of many themes Walker has developed elsewhere more darkly.

You Can't Keep a Good Woman Down

You Can't Keep a Good Woman Down is Walker's salute to black women who are pushing ahead, those who have crossed some barriers and are in some sense champions. There are black women who are songwriters, artists, writers, students in exclusive Eastern schools; they are having abortions, teaching their men the meaning of pornography, coming to terms with the death of a father, on one hand, or with the meaning of black men raping white women, on the other. Always, they are caught up short by the notions of whites. In other words, all the political, sexual, racial, countercultural issues of the 1970's are in these stories, developed from what Walker calls the "womanist" point of view.

This set of stories, then, is somewhat more explicitly sociological than the first and somewhat less lyrical, and it is also more apparently autobiographical, but in a special sense. Walker herself is a champion, so her life is a natural, even an inescapable, source of material. Walker-the-artist plays with Walker-the-college-student and Walker-the-idealistic-teacher, as well as with some of the other roles she sees herself as having occupied during that decade of social upheaval. Once a writer's experience has become transformed within a fictive world, it becomes next to impossible to think of the story's events as either simply autobiography or simply invention. The distinction has been deliberately blurred. It is because Walker wants to unite her public and private worlds, her politics and her art, life as lived and life as imagined, that, instead of poetry, these stories are interspersed with autobiographical parallels, journal entries, letters, and other expressions of her personality.

Analysis: Poetry

Alice Walker writes free verse, employing concrete images. She resorts to few of the conceits, the extended metaphors, the latinate language, and other affectations often found in poetry. Readers frequently say that her verses hardly seem like poetry at all; they resemble the conversation of a highly articulate, observant woman. While her poetry often seems like prose, her fiction is highly poetic. The thoughts of Miss Celie, the first-person narrator of *The Color Purple*, would not have been out of place in a book of poetry. Boundaries between prose and poetry remain thin in the work of Walker. Her verse, like her prose, is always rhythmic; if she rhymes or alliterates, it seems only by accident. The poetry appears so effortless that its precision, its choice of exact image or word to convey the nuance the poet wishes, is not

971

immediately evident. Only close scrutiny reveals the skill with which this highly lettered poet has assimilated her influences, chiefly E. E. Cummings, Emily Dickinson, Robert Graves, Japanese haiku poems, Li Bo, Ovid, Zen epigrams, and William Carlos Williams.

Walker's poetry is personal and generally didactic, generated by events in her life, causes she has advocated, and injustices over which she has agonized. The reader feels that it is the message that counts, before realizing that the medium is part of the message. Several of her poems echo traumatic events in her own life, such as her abortion. She remembers the words her mother uttered over the casket of her father, and makes a poem of them. Other poems recall ambivalent emotions of childhood: Sunday school lessons which, even then, were filled with discrepancies. Some poems deal with the creative process itself: She calls herself a medium through whom the Old Ones, formerly mute, find their voice at last.

Some readers are surprised to discover that Walker's poems are both mystical and socially revolutionary, one moment exuberant and the next reeking with despair. Her mysticism is tied to reverence for the earth, a sense of unity with all living creatures, a bond of sisterhood with women throughout the world, and a joyous celebration of the female principle in the divine. On the other hand, she may lament that injustice reigns in society: Poor black people toil so that white men may savor the jewels that adorn heads of state.

Once: Poems
Walker's first collection of poetry communicates her youthful impressions of Africa and her state of mind during her early travels there, as well as the melancholy she felt upon her return to a racist United States, when thoughts of death, particularly by suicide, tormented her. Perhaps the epigram from French philosopher Albert Camus, which prefaces the book, expresses its mood best: "Misery kept me from believing that all was well under the sun, and the sun taught me that history wasn't everything."

The title poem of the collection contains several loosely connected scenes of injustice in the American South, small black children run down by vans, because "they were in the way," Jewish Civil Rights workers who cannot be cremated according to their requests because their remains cannot be found, and finally a black child waving an American flag, but from "the very/ *tips*/ of her/ fingers," an image perhaps of irony or perhaps of hope.

There are meditations on white lovers—blond, Teutonic, golden—who dare kiss this poet who is "brown-er/ Than a jew." There are memories of black churches, where her mother shouts, her father snores, and she feels uncomfortable.

The most striking poem is certainly "African Images," an assortment of vignettes from the ancestral homeland: shy gazelles, the bluish peaks of Mount Kenya, the sound of elephants trumpeting, rain forests with red orchids. Yet even glimpsed in the idealism of youth, Africa is not total paradise. The leg of a slain elephant is fashioned into an umbrella holder in a shop; a rhinoceros is killed so that its horn may be fashioned into an aphrodisiac.

Revolutionary Petunias, and Other Poems

Walker's third collection of poems is divided into two parts. The first is titled "In These Dissenting Times . . . Surrounding Ground and Autobiography." She proposes to write "of the old men I knew/ And the young men/ I loved/ And of the gold toothed women/ Mighty of arm/ Who dragged us all/ To church." She writes also "To acknowledge our ancestors" with the awareness that "we did not make/ ourselves, that the line stretches/ all the way back, perhaps, to God; or/ to Gods." She recalls her baptism "dunked . . . in the creek," with "gooey . . . rotting leaves,/ a greenish mold floating." She was a slight figure, "All in white./ With God's mud ruining my snowy/ socks and his bullfrog spoors/ gluing up my face."

The last half of the collection, "Revolutionary Petunias . . . the Living Through," begins with yet another epigram from Camus, reminding the reader that there will come a time when revolutions, though not made by beauty, will discover the need for beauty. The poems, especially those referred to as "Crucifixions," become more anguished, more angered. Walker becomes skeptical of the doctrine of nonviolence, hinting that the time for more direct action may have come. The tone of the last poems in the collection may be expressed best by the opening lines to the verse Walker called "Rage." "In me, " she wrote, "there is a rage to defy/ the order of the stars/ despite their pretty patterns."

Good Night, Willie Lee, I'll See You in the Morning
The fourth poetry collection expands on earlier themes and further exploits personal and family experiences for lessons in living. The title poem is perhaps the most moving and characteristic of the collection. Walker shared it again on May 22, 1995, in a commencement day speech delivered at Spelman College. As a lesson in forgiveness, she recalled the words her mother, who had much to endure and much to forgive, uttered above her father's casket. Her last words to the man with whom she had lived for so many years, beside whom she had labored in the fields, and with whom she had raised so many children were, "Good night, Willie Lee, I'll see you in the morning." This gentle instinctive act of her mother taught Walker the enduring lesson that "the healing of all our wounds is forgiveness/ that permits a promise/ of our return/ at the end."

Other Literary Forms
Walker was an early editor at *Ms.* magazine, in which many of her essays first appeared. Her interest in the then little-known writer Zora Neale Hurston led to her pilgrimage to Florida to place a tombstone on Hurston's unmarked grave, to Walker's editing of *I Love Myself When I Am Laughing . . . and Then Again When I Am Looking Mean and Impressive: A Zora Neale Hurston Reader,* and to her introduction to Robert Hemenway's *Zora Neale Hurston: A Literary Biography.* Later novels, *The Temple of My Familiar, Possessing the Secret of Joy,* and *By the Light of My Father's Smile* have employed narrative as little more than a vehicle for ideas on racial and sexual exploitation, abuse of animals and the earth, and New Age spirituality. *In Love and Trouble: Stories of Black Women* and *You Can't Keep a Good Woman Down* revealed

Walker to be one of the finest of late twentieth century American short-story writers. There was also time for an occasional children's book (*To Hell with Dying* is particularly notable) and several collections of essays (*In Search of Our Mothers' Gardens: Womanist Prose* is the most lyrical) that present impassioned pleas for the causes Walker espoused.

Bibliography

Bauer, Margaret D. "Alice Walker: Another Southern Writer Criticizing Codes Not Put to 'Everyday Use.'" *Studies in Short Fiction* 29 (Spring, 1992): 143-151. Discusses parallels between Walker's *In Love and Trouble* and stories by William Faulkner, Katherine Anne Porter, Eudora Welty, and Flannery O'Connor. Argues that Walker, like these other southern writers, examines the tendency to support social and religious codes at the expense of individual fulfillment.

Bloom, Harold, ed. *Alice Walker: Modern Critical Views*. New York: Chelsea House, 1989. A book-length compilation of the best of criticism on Walker. Authors Diane F. Dadoff and Deborah E. McDowell explore the resonant Zora Neale Hurston/ Alice Walker relationship. Radical feminism is addressed in this study, and Bloom discusses the mother/daughter motif in Walker's works.

Bloxham, Laura J. "Alice [Malsenior] Walker." In *Contemporary Fiction Writers of the South*, edited by Joseph M. Flora and Robert Bain. Westport, Conn.: Greenwood Press, 1993. A general introduction to Walker's "womanist" themes of oppression of black women and change through affirmation of self. Provides a brief summary and critique of previous criticism of Walker's work.

Borgmeier, Raimund. "Alice Walker: 'Everyday Use.'" In *The African-American Short Story: 1970 to 1990*, edited by Wolfgang Karrer and Barbara Puschmann-Nalenz. Trier, Germany: Wissenschaftlicher Verlag Trier, 1993. A detailed discussion of the generic characteristics of one of Walker's best-known stories. Analyzes the tension between the typical unheard-of occurrence and everyday reality as well as the story's use of a central structural symbol.

Butler-Evans, Elliott. *Race, Gender, and Desire: Narrative Strategies in the Fiction of Toni Cade Bambara, Toni Morrison, and Alice Walker.* Philadelphia: Temple University Press, 1989. Focusing on the connections between gender, race, and desire, and their relationship to the narrative strategies in the fiction of these three contemporary writers, Butler-Evans argues that Walker's works are "structured by a complex ideological position" oscillating between "her identity as 'Black feminist' or 'woman-of-color' and a generalized feminist position in which race is subordinated."

Davis, Thadious M. "Alice Walker's Celebration of Self in Southern Generations." *Southern Quarterly* 21 (1983): 39-53. Reprinted in *Women Writers of the Contemporary South,* edited by Peggy Whitman Prenshaw. Jackson: University Press of Mississippi, 1984. An early but still-useful general introduction to the works and themes of Walker, emphasizing particularly her concern for a sense of identity/self and her folk heritage. Davis discusses most significant works briefly, points out the sense of outrage at injustice in Walker's fiction, including several short stories, and also makes frequent references to her essays.

Dieke, Ikenna, ed. *Critical Essays on Alice Walker.* Contributions in Afro-American and African Studies 189. New York: Greenwood Press, 1999. Especially well suited for use in college literature classrooms, this collection gives particular attention to Walker's poetry and her developing ecofeminism.

Gates, Henry Louis, Jr., and Kwame Anthony Appiah, eds. *Alice Walker: Critical Perspectives Past and Present.* New York: Amistad, 1993. Contains reviews of Walker's first five novels and critical analyses of several of her works of short and long fiction. Also includes two interviews with Walker, a chronology of her works, and an extensive bibliography of essays and texts.

Gentry, Tony. *Alice Walker.* New York: Chelsea House, 1993. This biography is geared toward the high school student. The text is simple to read but thorough in providing biographical information about Walker and discussing her writing. A chronology and brief bibliography are also included.

Hooker, Deborah Anne. "Reanimating the Trope of the Talking

Book in Alice Walker's 'Strong Horse Tea.'" *Southern Literary Journal* 37, no. 2 (Spring, 2005): 81-103. Discusses the concept of the talking book as it is portrayed in Walker's story. Also analyzes the story's bias against rural traditions.

Lauret, Maria. *Alice Walker.* New York: St. Martin's Press, 2000. Provocative discussions of Walker's ideas on politics, race, feminism, and literary theory. Of special interest is the exploration of Walker's literary debt to Zora Neale Hurston, Virginia Woolf, and even Bessie Smith.

McKay, Nellie. "Alice Walker's 'Advancing Luna'—and Ida B. Wells: 'A Struggle Toward Sisterhood.'" In *Rape and Representation*, edited by Lynn A. Higgins and Brenda R. Silver. New York: Columbia University Press, 1991. Shows how the story allows readers to see how women's cross-racial relationships are controlled by systems of white male power. The story helps its audience understand why black women fail to provide group support for feminists of the antirape movement in spite of their own historical oppression by rape.

McMillan, Laurie. "Telling a Critical Story: Alice Walker's *In Search of Our Mothers' Gardens.*" *Journal of Modern Literature* 28, no. 1 (Fall, 2004): 107-124. Views Walker's 1983 book as a method for leveling political critiques. Draws on the essays "Beyond the Peacock," "Looking for Zora," and "In Search of Our Mothers' Gardens" to show how autobiography and literary criticism can be joined in ways that offer solutions to complex problems.

Mickelsen, Dawd J. "'You Ain't Never Caught a Rabbit': Covering and Signifyin' in Alice Walker's 'Nineteen Fifty-Five.'" *Southern Quarterly* 42, no. 3 (Spring, 2004): 5-21. Studies the importance of imitation—specifically, the imitation by African Americans of certain European American tendencies— in Walker's work.

Montelaro, Janet J. *Producing a Womanist Text: The Maternal as Signifier in Alice Walker's "The Color Purple."* Victoria, B.C.: English Literary Studies, University of Victoria, 1996. Examines themes of feminism, motherhood, and African American women in literature.

Petry, Alice Hall. "Walker: The Achievement of the Short Fiction." In *Alice Walker: Critical Perspectives Past and Present,* edited by Henry Louis Gates, Jr., and Kwame Anthony Appiah. New York: Amistad, 1993. A skeptical analysis of Walker's short fiction that contrasts the successful and focused achievement of *In Love and Trouble* (1973) with the less satisfying *You Can't Keep a Good Woman Down* (1981). Petry argues that the latter collection suffers in many places from unfortunate unintentional humor, trite and clichéd writing, and reductionism, and a confusion of genres that perhaps owe much to her being a "cross-generic writer."

Wade-Gayles, Gloria. "Black, Southern, Womanist: The Genius of Alice Walker." In *Southern Women Writers: The New Generation,* edited by Tonette Bond Inge. Tuscaloosa: University of Alabama Press, 1990. An excellent, thorough introduction to the life and literary career of Walker. Placing emphasis on Walker's voice as a black, southern woman throughout her works and arguing that Walker's commitment is to the spiritual wholeness of her people, Wade-Gayles examines several essays that are important to an understanding of her fiction and beliefs, her first three novels, both collections of short stories, and her collections of poetry. Supplemented by a bibliography of Walker's works, endnotes, and a useful secondary bibliography.

Walker, Rebecca. *Black, White, and Jewish: Autobiography of a Shifting Self.* New York: Riverhead, 2001. A self-indulgent but nevertheless insightful memoir by Alice Walker's daughter. Rebecca Walker, who describes herself as "a movement child," grew up torn between two families, two races, and two traditions, always in the shadow of an increasingly famous and absorbed mother.

Watson, Reginald. "The Power of the 'Milk' and Motherhood: Images of Deconstruction and Reconstruction in Toni Morrison's *Beloved* and Alice Walker's *The Third Life of Grange Copeland.*" *CLA Journal* 48, no. 2 (December, 2004): 156-183. Discusses the importance of maternity and maternal images in the two works. Also comments on the general nature of sexual relationships between African American men and African American women in the books.

White, Evelyn C. *Alice Walker: A Life.* New York: W. W. Norton, 2004. A well-reviewed biography balancing interviews with analysis and placement in historical context.

Winchell, Donna Haisty. *Alice Walker.* New York: Twayne, 1992. Provides a comprehensive analysis of Walker's short and long fiction. A brief biography and chronology precede the main text of the book. Each chapter refers to specific ideas and themes within Walker's works and focuses on how Walker's own experiences define her characters and themes. Following the narrative is a useful annotated bibliography.

— *Timothy Dow Adams; Mary A. Blackmon; Rebecca R. Butler; Theodore C. Humphrey; Allene Phy-Olsen; D. Dean Shackelford*

Joseph A. Walker

Playwright, actor, and educator

Born: Washington, D.C.; February 23, 1935
Died: Washington, D.C.; January 25, 2003

DRAMA: *The Believers*, pr., pb. 1968 (with Josephine Jackson); *The Harangues*, pr. 1969, revised pb. 1971 (as *Tribal Harangue Two*); *Ododo*, pr. 1970, pb. 1972; *Yin Yang*, pr. 1972; *The River Niger*, pr. 1972, pb. 1973; *Antigone Africanus*, pr. 1975; *The Lion Is a Soul Brother*, pr. 1976; *District Line*, pr. 1984; *The Absolution of Willie Mae*, pr. 1999.

SCREENPLAYS: *The River Niger*, 1976 (adaptation of his play).

NONFICTION: "Broadway's Vitality," 1973; "The Hiss," 1978; "Black Magnificance," 1980; "Themes of the Black Struggle," 1982.

Achievements

Joseph A. Walker began his association with the stage as an actor in theater productions of *The Believers, Cities of Beziques, Once in a Lifetime, A Raisin in the Sun,* and *Purlie Victorious;* then appeared on the screen in *April Fools* (1969) and Woody Allen's *Bananas* (1971); and acted in the 1960's television series *N.Y.P.D.* The lessons he learned as an actor helped him understand the fundamentals of dramatic production. In 1969, Walker became playwright, director, and choreographer for the Negro Ensemble Company in New York City. He served as playwright-in-residence for Yale University for 1970-1971 and as an instructor of advanced acting and playwriting for Howard University.

Walker won a number of prestigious awards, many of them for *The River Niger*, which was recognized with an Obie Award (1973), an Antoinette Perry (Tony) Award (1973), the Dramatist Guild's Elizabeth Hull-Kate Award (1973), the first Annual Audelco Award (1973), a John Gassner Award from Outer Circle (1973), a Drama Desk Award (1973), and the Black Rose Award (1973). This remarkable outpouring of critical approval culminated, also in 1973, with Walker being awarded a Guggenheim Fellowship. Also, in recognition for his years of work in drama, Walker was granted a Rockefeller Foundation grant (1979).

Biography

Joseph A. Walker was born in Washington, D.C., in 1935. His father, Joseph Walker, was a house painter and his mother, Florine Walker, a housewife. Walker graduated from Howard University in 1956 with a B.A. in philosophy and a minor in drama, having acted in several student productions (he portrayed Luke in James Baldwin's *Amen Corner* in May of 1955). Although he had realized that his real love was the theater, his fear of poverty drew him, after graduation, to the United States Air Force, where he enlisted as a second lieutenant and reached the rank of first lieutenant by the time of his discharge in 1960. His desire to become a high-ranking officer caused Walker to initially pursue navigators' training, but he later quit when he found himself spending more time writing poetry than studying for his navigator's exams. This dramatic shift of career was the source for a famous scene in *The River Niger* when navigator school student Jeff Williams is belittled by a white airman for his poetry writing in exactly the same way as Walker himself described being insulted during his military career. Trying to establish a balance between his fear of financial dependence and his inner desire to compose poetry, Walker decided to devote his full attention to the study of drama and poetry rather than to achieving high rank in the military. Further education gave him time to clarify his goals. Walker received an M.F.A. from Catholic University in 1963 and began teaching in a Washington, D.C., high school.

Walker followed this teaching position with one at City College of New York. He combined the role of instructor and playwright during his year as a playwright-in-residence at Yale University and then returned to Howard University, where he became a full professor of drama. While teaching, Walker continued his study of the stage and film by continuing to act. This personal line of study had a profound effect on the young actor-playwright. In 1969, the Negro Ensemble Company produced *The Harangues*. This was a personal milestone for the young Walker, who had, at this point, been studying other people's dramatic work for more than a decade. In 1970, Walker and his second wife, Dorothy Dinroe, started the acting troupe The Demi-Gods, a professional music-dance repertory company with Walker serving as artistic director. Walker's play *Ododo*, which The Demi-Gods later presented at Howard University in 1973, opened the Negro Ensemble Company's 1970 season. This work further examined racial strife and prepared audiences for the African American history that would be so vehemently elucidated in *The River Niger* and his later writings.

After the 1970's, Walker continued to write, albeit infrequently, about minority issues derived from his own personal experiences. One play, *District Line*, used his personal experience as a cab driver to demonstrate universal themes of racial strife and harmony. Essays submitted to *The New York Times*—"Themes of the Black Struggle" (1982) and "Black Magnificence" (1980), for example—and interviews conducted during the 1980's documented more recent difficulties that minorities faced in the mainstream world of the theater. Walker said that mainstream theaters were not willing to produce works from minority authors and there had not been adequate funding of minority-interest theater companies to make up for the lack of mainstream interest. According to Michele DiGirolamo in *Afro-American*, Walker stated that he had little success in getting his plays produced in the 1980's and 1990's because of shrinking budgets and an apathetic public. In 1995, he made an appearance at the National Black Theatre Festival in Winston-Salem, North Carolina, to encourage more young African American authors to write for the stage in the hope that the number of minority-run theater groups would continue to grow and present greater numbers of minority-interest plays. He died in 2003 following a stroke.

Analysis: Drama

Like many other African American authors, Joseph A. Walker examined issues close to the black community and, in particular, those dealing with black American men. Issues of personal identity, relationship strife, and racism play dominant roles in influencing both the thinking and the actions of the black male characters portrayed in his dramas. Lacking a homeland and history, repressed by both whites and assimilationist blacks, and dissociated from the comforts of stable male-female relationships, Walker's black protagonists lead desperate and often destructive lives.

Walker's critical success derived from his realistic portrayals of African American men. Working from his own, personal experiences as a black man in the United States, Walker examined interracial relationships, conflicts between people and society, and the struggle that many blacks have in achieving inner peace and acceptance.

The Harangues

The Harangues is made up of two closely paired one-act plays, each introduced by an episode designed purely to serve as the media for the author's invective. In the first episode, a fifteenth century West African man observes the presence of slave traders' ships sitting in the nearby harbor and, foreseeing a life of slavery for his newborn son, chooses to drown him rather than have him captured by the traders.

The one-act that follows this violent episode presents the story of a young interracial couple. A young black man wishes to marry a young white woman who has fallen deeply in love with him and become pregnant with his child. Because the woman's wealthy father opposes the match and threatens to disinherit his daughter, the young man decides that he and his fiancé must kill her father. Seemingly lacking any familial feeling, the white woman agrees to assist her lover in the murder of her father. However, the plan backfires while still in the planning stages. A traitorous black "friend" reveals the couple's intentions to the girlfriend's father and causes the death of the young black man, bringing an end to his plan to marry his white girlfriend and, with her, inherit her father's estate.

The second episode, echoing the first in theme and purpose, presents a contemporary black American revolutionary who, depressed by his vision of the repression inherent in modern society, decides that he has no future. Knowing that he himself will die, he nevertheless convinces his wife not to die with him but to live on to raise their son as a freedom fighter.

The one-act play that follows centers on a deranged black man in a bar who has taken captive three people—a white liberal man, a black conservative man sympathetic to white society, and the black man's white girlfriend—and has threatened to kill them unless they can justify their existence. After the captives are subjected to numerous humiliations, it becomes apparent that, according to the protagonist's ideas of "worthiness," only the white woman may be allowed to live. When the "executions" take place, however, the woman takes a bullet meant for her black lover. In the ensuing struggle, the black conservative gains control of his captor's gun and kills him. Once again, Walker demonstrates that the black man who resorts to violence to achieve his goals is destroyed by his own violence.

Yin Yang

Walker's play *Yin Yang*, first produced in 1972, was his least traditional. Walker designed the play to represent the age-old struggle between good and evil. In an article published in *The New York Times*, Walker said that "Good is represented by God, a hip swinging, fast-talking black mama . . . in conflict with Miss Satan, who is also a black female swinger." Although the play may seem to have been directed for a children's audience, with its reliance on archetypical figures and simple language, Walker claimed that the play draws on the biblical books of Job and Revelation. Walker had long seen a symbolic parallel between Job and blacks because, he said, both believe in their society and their religion even when such institutions seemingly cause them to suffer.

Yin Yang operates on the Chinese philosophy that everything in existence is the result of the combination of two opposing principles: the yin, the feminine, "evil," passive principle; and the yang, the masculine, "good," active principle. Thus, the characters of *Yin Yang* themselves represent the balance of good and evil, masculine and feminine.

The River Niger

Walker wrote four major plays before writing *The River Niger,* but it is this work that brought Walker nationwide recognition and revealed both his strengths and his weaknesses as a playwright. *The River Niger,* rather than being an entirely original work, is more a reworking and refinement of the ideas and issues developed in his earlier plays for a broader audience.

Although the plot and themes of *The River Niger* deal with African American life and issues, the play has been seen as having a far more universal relevance. Mel Gussow, in *Time* magazine, said that the play was powerful and compassionate and has an appeal beyond the borders of black experience. Both the play's realism and this global appeal arise from the fact that it is derived in part from Walker's own experiences and family—experiences that many outside the black community can also appreciate. As Gussow noted, "The playwright knows his people and we grow to know them, too, to understand their fears, appetites, frustrations, and vulnerabilities."

In *The River Niger,* Jeff Williams, who has dropped out of U.S. Air Force navigators' school because of the racist comments of a colleague, returns home to determine what to do with the rest of his life. Everyone has a different opinion on the direction he should take. His friends demand that he join them in defying the established order of white society and take part in the "revolution," while his family is disappointed that he ended his promising military career (his father's first question is "Where is your uniform?") and wants him to continue becoming an officer. Williams, however, is starting to recognize his own, inner desire to become a lawyer. Williams's hesitation and ambivalence can be readily understood by anyone who has had to make dramatic changes in his or her life.

District Line

District Line is an interesting discussion of how individuals of differing viewpoints and backgrounds can find common ground. A Washington, D.C., taxi stand serves as the setting for *District Line*, which depicts a day in the lives of six cab drivers: two white men, three black men, and one black woman. Each of the drivers comes from a different background, but each has similar hopes for the future and similar reactions to his or her past experiences. The issues and concerns of the black male characters, however, dominate this play, as they had most of Walker's earlier plays. The scenes concerning two of the black drivers (who are, by far, the most developed characters)—Doc, a moonlighting Howard University professor, another of Walker's alter egos, and Zilikazi, an exiled South African revolutionary—are the ones that receive the greatest amount of attention. Despite this focus on black men's issues, in *District Line*, Walker's presentation of the white characters—the two white drivers—seems more balanced. These white men, compared with white characters in Walker's earlier plays, are complex individuals rather than stereotypical white liberals or oppressors.

Other Literary Forms

Joseph A. Walker's reputation rests almost exclusively on his dramatic works, but he made numerous successful forays into the television and film industries. Primarily a stage dramatist, he expanded his literary horizons during the 1970's and the 1980's by regularly contributing essays to *The New York Times*, including "Broadway's Vitality" (1973), "The Hiss" (1978), "Black Magnificence," and "Themes of the Black Struggle." In 1976, he rewrote his three-act play *The River Niger* into a screenplay for New Line Cinema. The resulting film, starring Cicely Tyson and James Earl Jones, received considerable critical acclaim both at the time and in subsequent years.

Bibliography

Andrews, Laura. "Harlem Classic Revived at NBT." Review of *The River Niger*, by Joseph A. Walker. *Amsterdam News*, May 10,

2001, pp. 21-23. An overview of *The River Niger* and a discussion of its revival at the National Black Theater (NBT).

Barthelemy, Anthony. "Mother, Sister, Wife: A Dramatic Perspective." *Southern Review* 21, no. 3 (1985). Barthelemy compares and analyzes the dysfunctions of male-female relationships in three of Walker's plays. He presents Walker's repetitive use of stereotypical female roles in defining the positions and roles forced on black women by both their families and society in general.

Clurman, Harold. "The River Niger." *The Nation* 215, no. 21 (1972): 668. Although Clurman praises Walker's technique in *The River Niger*, he finds fault with Walker's use of symbolism in *Ododo*. He suggests that Walker is not sure which historical truths about black-white relationships he wants to tell, so he tries to make the play tell them all. This lack of focus, Clurman states, distorts and creates internal contradiction within both plays.

Gates, Anita. "She's a Can't-Help-It Kind of Person." Review of *The Absolution of Willie Mae*, by Joseph A. Walker. *The New York Times*, November 26, 1999, p. E3. A review of the play as staged by the Negro Ensemble Company.

Kauffmann, Stanley. "The River Niger." *The New Republic* 169, no. 12 (1973): 22. Kauffmann criticizes many of Walker's techniques in *The River Niger*, in particular his lack of subtlety with character motivations and dialogue, but appreciates both the real affection shown by his characters for one another and the recognition with which black audiences have responded to the play.

Lee, Dorothy. "Three Black Plays: Alienation and Paths to Recovery." *Modern Drama* 19, no. 4 (1975): 397-404. Lee argues that the alienation theme, when addressed in the context of African American concerns, is also a metaphor for the human condition. Lee describes Walker as seeking definitions of a sense of community or its telling absence both uniquely black and universally relevant.

— *Julia M. Meyers*

Booker T. Washington

Essayist and educator

Born: Near Hale's Ford, Virginia; April 5, 1856
Died: Tuskegee, Alabama; November 14, 1915

NONFICTION: *The Future of the American Negro,* 1899; *The Story of My Life and Work,* 1900; *Up from Slavery,* 1901; *The Negro Problem,* 1903; *Working with the Hands,* 1904; *Putting the Most into Life,* 1906; *The Story of the Negro,* 1909; *My Larger Education,* 1911.

Achievements

Booker T. Washington rose from slavery to become the founder and principal of the Tuskegee Institute in Alabama, an institution established to serve the needs of blacks in the South. Having gained the approbation of numerous white people who helped him receive an education, Washington became adept at dealing tactfully and effectively with influential whites while simultaneously attempting to advance the interests of blacks. He became an adviser to presidents of the United States in matters of race relations and was influential in gaining financial support from such industrial scions as Andrew Carnegie, George Eastman, and John D. Rockefeller. Support from these moguls helped build the endowment of Tuskegee, initially established with a two thousand dollar grant from the Alabama legislature, to more than two million dollars before his death in 1915.

Biography

Booker T. Washington was born into slavery on a plantation in Virginia. His mother, Jane, never revealed the identity of his father, although he was presumably a white man and probably a member of the family on a plantation near where Washington was born. Washington's mother clandestinely gave him the name Taliferro, the name of a prominent white family in the area where she lived, suggesting his possible paternity. Jane had an older son, John. In 1860, Jane married a slave named Washington who lived on a nearby plantation, and together they had a daughter named Amanda.

Washington was pressed into service at age five. His task was to turn the wheel on a contraption in his master's dining room that agitated a number of paper fans and kept flies away from the family table during meals. Meanwhile, Washington, his mother, and his siblings lived in a one-room cabin that had a dirt floor, an ill-fitting door, windows with no glass, and few pieces of furniture.

Though President Abraham Lincoln signed the Emancipation Proclamation in 1863, freeing all slaves, news of this act was slow to reach most slaves in the Deep South. Not until 1865, at the end of the Civil War, did most slaves learn that they had been emancipated. When the war ended, Booker T. Washington was nine.

In that year, Washington's stepfather moved his family to Malden, West Virginia, where the young Washington joined his stepfather in a job at a salt furnace. His stepfather boiled the salt out of water brought from underground, while Washington and his brother shoveled it into barrels. Soon a school for black children opened, so Washington had his first educational opportunity. At that time, he did not have a last name, so when his teacher asked what his name was, he gave his stepfather's surname, Washington, which became his name for life.

Soon Washington was working in the coal mines near Malden; the labor caused his school attendance to be sporadic. A turning point came, however, when he was hired by General Lewis Ruffner, a Malden industrialist, as a houseboy. Ruffner's wife, Viola, who insisted on meticulous cleanliness in her residence, taught Washington to keep her house spotless. She encouraged him to read, lent him books from her collection, and urged him to continue his education. In 1872, Washington first heard of the Hampton Institute in Virginia. It was five hundred miles from Malden, and Washington walked, caught rides on wagons, and stowed away on freight trains to get to Virginia.

(Library of Congress)

When Washington arrived at Hampton, the head teacher, Mary Mackie, informed him that her classes were full. She then asked Washington to sweep her floor. He did it so well that she bent the rules and admitted him. In 1875, he was graduated from Hampton Institute and returned to Malden to teach. By 1879, however, he had returned to Hampton as a teacher. Two years later, when Hampton's principal, General Samuel Armstrong, was approached by a group from Tuskegee, Alabama, to recommend someone to establish there an institute something like Hampton, Armstrong recommended Washington for the job.

At that point, the Tuskegee Institute was a dream rather than a reality. Washington arrived in Tuskegee and found neither campus nor buildings. Undaunted, he set up shop in an abandoned church, and the Tuskegee Institute was born. Washington spent the rest of his life in the service of that school, working closely with influential white people who helped increase the school's endowment to more than two million dollars by the time of Washington's death.

Washington's emphasis was on teaching black students such trades as carpentry and bricklaying. Tuskegee's emphasis was on vocational programs, which frustrated many blacks, who thought that their race would best be served by receiving a mainstream education comparable to that offered by white colleges and universities.

Washington had three wives. The first two died before he was forty. His third wife, Margaret, survived him, as did his two sons, Ernest Davidson, and Booker, Jr., and his adopted daughter, Laura. Washington fell ill while on one of his frequent speaking and fundraising tours. His wife rushed to New York City, where he was hospitalized, and brought him back to Tuskegee, arriving there on November 13, 1915. Washington died early the next morning.

Analysis: Nonfiction

Although much of Washington's writing has autobiographical elements, his two most notable autobiographies are *The Story of My Life and Work*, aimed primarily at black readers, and *Up from Slavery: An Autobiography*, which was written with white readers in mind. These books were collaborative efforts: the first was written with Edgar Webber, the second with Max Bennett Thrasher. Washington himself probably did little of the actual writing, although clearly he provided most of the detailed information. Washington was a riveting speaker. Many oratorical flourishes are found in his autobiographies, both of which have been published and republished, often with significant revision.

The Story of My Life and Work

This autobiography is not among Washington's most notable works. His collaborator presumably did most of the writing. It has been speculated that the book went to press when Washington was too occupied with other concerns to reread it and revise it for publication.

Written with a black audience in mind, this book contains episodes designed to establish a rapport between the author and his black audience. For example, Washington includes in this book an account of how he witnessed the beating of his uncle by his white master and of how the uncle cried out for help. Scenes like this are clearly designed to create empathy with the book's intended audience.

The book presents the details of Washington's early life. Homage is paid to the white people who were most instrumental in helping him receive an education and in aiding him in his rise to becoming the founder and principal of Tuskegee.

Among his white patrons were the Ruffners. General Ruffner owned the salt factory in which Washington's father worked, as well as the coal mines in which Washington himself was employed before he became the Ruffners' house servant. Viola Ruffner encouraged Washington to sharpen his literacy skills and to read as widely as possible. Her faith in him provided the youth with an underpinning that enabled him to continue his education against great odds.

Because Viola Ruffner had insisted on Washington's keeping her house immaculate, he developed an appreciation for cleanliness. He also became concerned with personal hygiene and, throughout his early years at Tuskegee, insisted that students pay close attention to washing their bodies.

When he arrived at Hampton, the head teacher, Mary F. Mackie, had already admitted as many students as she could, but, when Washington expertly swept her floor, she allowed him to enter and enabled him to pay for his education by doing janitorial work, which he did with great dedication.

Washington returned to Malden to teach after completing his studies at Hampton, but soon went to Washington, D.C., for additional training. When Washington completed these studies,

General Samuel Chapman Armstrong, Hampton Institute's principal, employed him to teach a group of Native American students at Hampton. So well did he succeed in this endeavor that Armstrong appointed him director of the night school for adults.

Therefore, it is not surprising that when a civic group from Tuskegee, Alabama, asked Armstrong to recommend someone to establish an institute in their town, Armstrong recommended Washington, even though the group making the request had not expected that Armstrong would consider a black person suitable for such a job.

The Story of My Life and Work emphasizes the need for blacks, many of them former slaves whose formal education had been prohibited, to make themselves indispensable to the dominant white society. Whereas some of the era's black reformers urged equality for blacks, Washington thought that such demands were unrealistic. He sincerely believed that if blacks could make themselves useful to society, the matter of gaining equality would eventually resolve itself.

In this book, Washington expands on a memorable analogy he used in one of his most celebrated speeches, delivered before the Atlanta Cotton Exposition in 1895. In this speech, which many attacked because of its implied support of the concept of separate but equal societies, Washington likened the races to the fingers of the hand. These fingers are separate, but they are all part of the same entity, so that in time of need, they form themselves into a fist. He was convinced that the races could work together in some critical situations, but that they could also remain separate.

Up from Slavery: An Autobiography
Certainly the more significant of Washington's two autobiographies is *Up from Slavery: An Autobiography.* The book was a bestseller and greatly influenced the thinking of many highly influential white people regarding matters of race and of the integration of freed slaves into society. This book has consistently been regarded as a major contribution to American as well as to African American literature.

993

In the years immediately before the publication of *Up from Slavery*, Washington had been one of President William McKinley's major advisors on matters of race. Upon McKinley's assassination in 1901, his successor, President Theodore Roosevelt, reached out to Washington for guidance, going so far as to invite Washington to join him and his family for an intimate dinner at the White House. This invitation caused considerable controversy; it marked the first time a black person had been a guest at such a dinner.

Washington's emphasis on teaching vocational subjects to blacks caused many black activists, including W. E. B. Du Bois, to consider him an Uncle Tom. Du Bois thought that Washington had naively sold out to influential northern industrialists in ways that he viewed as detrimental to the advancement of people of color. Washington's reputation at times was sullied by those who considered him primarily in the context of Du Bois's objections to his stands on the best methods for educating blacks.

Recent Booker T. Washington scholars have noted that his emphasis on hygiene in *Up from Slavery* must be read in the context of his broader goal of promoting black economic development. Grooming is a concomitant of success in the broader society, and Washington clearly recognized that ignoring the issue was unrealistic. Furthermore, his insistence that blacks adhere to values that promote economic growth is best viewed as a product of Washington's desire to more fully entrench (and thereby improve) the position of blacks within the broader society. Writing about *Up from Slavery*, Washington scholar Peter A. Coclanis calls Washington's teachings more "opportune than opportunistic."

Washington recounts how, even as a very young child, he was occupied constantly, first in providing motive power for the fans that kept flies from the family table, and soon afterward in hauling large gunny sacks of corn to market, a task that troubled Washington for two reasons.

First, in taking the corn to market, he passed a school and longed to be a student in it, but at that time it was illegal for slave children to attend school and for slaves to seek literacy. Second, the young boy had to make sure that the sacks of corn were properly balanced on the back of a horse, but the jarring motions of the horse's advance usually disturbed the balance, causing the sack to fall to the ground. The boy was not strong enough to reposition the sacks on the horse's back, so he had to wait, often for hours, for someone to come along and help him.

Washington's emphasis on bathing, keeping one's clothing clean, and using a toothbrush recur throughout *Up from Slavery* and has often been mocked, although the advice Washington gives is practical and sensible. Perhaps Washington rhapsodized too much on the toothbrush as one of the most far-reaching agencies of civilization.

Up from Slavery had considerable influence and prompted substantial financial contributions to the Tuskegee Institute by such industrialists as George Eastman, Andrew Carnegie, and John D. Rockefeller, all of whom not only made initial contributions but pledged continuing support on an annual basis.

Other Literary Forms

Aside from his autobiographies, Booker T. Washington is credited with many other titles, including *The Future of the American Negro*, a collection of his speeches and essays; *The Negro Problem*, a collection of his articles; *Putting the Most into Life*, a collection of his addresses; and at least twenty additional books, drawn mostly from Washington's public speeches. These books are intended to be inspirational and to promote the idea of enhancing the economic and political development of black society.

Bibliography

Brundage, W. Fitzhugh, ed. *Booker T. Washington and Black Progress: "Up from Slavery" One Hundred Years Later.* Gainesville: University of Florida Press, 2003. This collection of essays on various aspects of Washington's most celebrated work offers a comprehensive and varied view of his contributions. One of the most important considerations of Washington to date. Particularly cogent are essays by Peter A. Coclanis, Wilson J. Moses, and Robert J. Norell.

Gleiter, Jan. *Booker T. Washington*. Austin, Tex.: Raintree Steck-Vaughn, 1995. A reasonable starting point for those unfamiliar with Washington's work. Well written and direct.

Kikas, Gabriel. "Bush and Booker T. Washington's 'Compassionate Conservatism.'" *Contemporary Review* 285, no. 1664 (September, 2004): 157-160. Explores George W. Bush's implementation of Washington's ideas in U.S. policies.

McKissack, Patricia, and Frederick McKissack. *Booker T. Washington: Leader and Educator.* Rev. ed. Berkeley Heights, N.J.: Enslow, 2001. Directed toward juvenile readers, this short assessment covers the high points of Washington's life and contributions.

Moses, Wilson Jeremiah. *Creative Conflict in African American Thought: Frederick Douglass, Alexander Crummell, Booker T. Washington, W. E. B. Du Bois, and Marcus Garvey.* New York: Cambridge University Press, 2004. An excellent book; analyzes the writings of these important authors in the contexts of Jeffersonian and Jacksonian democracies as well as through the philosophy of social Darwinism.

Neyland, James. *Booker T. Washington: Educator.* Los Angeles: Melrose Square, 1992. A well-written, easily accessible consideration of Washington as an educator. In fewer than two hundred pages, Neyland captures a great deal of Washington's charisma.

Staub, Nancy M. "Booker T[aliferro] Washington." In *Encyclopedia of American Literature*, edited by Steven R. Serafin. New York: Continuum, 1999. Staub's brief overview of *Up from Slavery* is well informed and lucid. Her comments on *The Story of My Life and Work*, although not detailed, are carefully considered.

— *R. Baird Shuman*

Cornel West
Essayist and critic

Born: Tulsa, Oklahoma; June 2, 1953

NONFICTION: *Prophesy Deliverance! An Afro-American Revolutionary Christianity*, 1982; *Prophetic Fragments*, 1988; *The American Evasion of Philosophy: A Genealogy of Pragmatism*, 1989; *Breaking Bread: Insurgent Black Intellectual Life*, 1991 (with Bell Hooks); *The Ethical Dimensions of Marxist Thought*, 1991; *Beyond Eurocentrism and Multiculturalism*, 1993 (2 volumes); *Keeping Faith: Philosophy and Race in America*, 1993; *Race Matters*, 1993; *Jews and Blacks: Let the Healing Begin*, 1995 (with Michael Lerner; revised as *Jews and Blacks: A Dialogue on Race, Religion, and Culture in America*, 1996); *The Future of the Race*, 1996 (with Henry Louis Gates, Jr.); *Restoring Hope: Conversations on the Future of Black America*, 1997 (Kelvin Shawn Sealey, editor); *The Future of American Progressivism: An Initiative for Political and Economic Reform*, 1998 (with Roberto Mangabeira Unger); *The War Against Parents: What We Can Do for America's Beleaguered Moms and Dads*, 1998 (with Sylvia Ann Hewlett); *The Cornel West Reader*, 1999; *The African-American Century: How Black Americans Have Shaped Our Country*, 2000 (with Gates); *Cornel West: A Critical Reader*, 2001 (George Yancy, editor); *Democracy Matters: Winning the Fight Against Imperialism*, 2004.

EDITED TEXTS: *Theology in the Americas: Detroit II Conference Papers*, 1982 (with Caridad Guidote and Margaret Coakley); *Post-Analytic Philosophy*, 1985 (with John Rajchman); *Out There: Marginalization and Contemporary Cultures*, 1991; *White Screens, Black Images: Hollywood from the Dark Side*, 1994 (with James Snead and Colin MacCabe); *Encyclopedia of African-American Culture and History*, 1996 (with Jack Salzman and David Lionel Smith); *Struggles in the Promised Land: Towards a History of Black-Jewish Relations in the United States*, 1997 (with Jack Salzman); *The Courage to Hope: From Black Suffering to Human Redemption*, 1999 (with Quinton Hosford Dixie); *Taking Par-*

enting Public: The Case for a New Social Movement, 2002 (with Sylvia Ann Hewlett and Nancy Rankin); *Racist Traces and Other Writings: European Pedigrees/African Contagions,* 2003 (by James Sneak; with Kera Keeling and Colin MacCabe).

Achievements

Cornel West was an early achiever: He was student body president of both his junior and senior high schools and was a violinist in his school orchestra. He placed first in the two-mile track contest at the all-city meet and was on his school's seventh-grade football team. Upon graduation from John F. Kennedy High School in Sacramento, California, he entered Harvard University, where, in 1973, he received his bachelor's degree magna cum laude after three years. He continued his education at Princeton University, receiving his master's degree in 1975 and his doctorate in 1980. West has taught and administered programs at Princeton and Harvard Universities, and has also taught at Williams, the Union Theological Seminary, the University of Paris, and Yale's Divinity School. He is, however, best known for his prolific writing, and he has written, edited, or been coauthor of almost twenty books, some among the most challenging in contemporary philosophical writing. West is unquestionably among the most significant public intellectuals in the United States.

Biography

Cornel Ronald West is the son of a civilian Air Force administrator Clifton L. West, Jr., and his wife, Irene Bias West, a teacher and school principal after whom an elementary school in Sacramento, California, is named. Upon completing high school, he entered Harvard University as a philosophy major, but soon switched to a major in Near Eastern languages so that he could read the biblical languages Hebrew and Aramaic. West studied history extensively and pursued both formal course work and independent reading in social thought. At Harvard, West was surrounded by exciting intellectuals, and he drew fully upon the intellectual resources they offered.

After graduating from Harvard, West entered the philosophy program at Princeton University. He continued his studies there, receiving the Ph.D. in 1980, after having taken one year out to return to Harvard. During that year he married his first wife, the mother of his only child, Clifton L. West III. West is currently married to Elleni Gebre Amlak.

Richard Rorty, generally considered the most significant philosophical pragmatist in the United States, became one of West's mentors at Princeton and taught him a great deal about American pragmatism. West contrived his own version of what he termed "prophetic pragmatism," creating a new pragmatism that avoided Rorty's ethnocentricity and the conservatism that was inherent in Rorty's political pessimism.

While he was completing his doctoral studies, West was appointed assistant professor of the history of religion at New York City's Union Theological Seminary. At that time, Union was considered by many the most intellectually exciting seminary in the United States. West remained there for six years and spent another year affiliated with the school in 1988. In 1984, he joined the staff of Yale University's Divinity School, where he remained until 1987. He spent the spring semester of 1988 teaching at the University of Paris.

The following year, Princeton University appointed West professor of religion and made him director of its African American studies program. He served in that capacity from 1988 to 1994, when he was appointed professor of African American studies and the philosophy of religion at Harvard. In 2002, after a dispute with Harvard's president, Lawrence Summers, West returned to Princeton, this time as Class of 1943 University Professor of Religion.

West's religious posture, which postulates a union between Christianity and Marxism, has been truly ecumenical. Although clinging to his Baptist roots, he has reached out to people of other faiths in his attempts to understand the roots of religious divisions. In 1982, he collaborated with two Roman Catholic nuns in editing *Theology in the Americas: Detroit II Conference Papers.* He also has been extremely interested in the relationship between Jewish and African Americans, and has collaborated with two Jewish scholars on books that address this issue: *Jews and Blacks: A Dialogue on Race, Religion, and Culture in America*, with Michael Lerner, and *Struggles in the Promised Land: Towards a History of Black-Jewish Relations in the United States*, with Jack Salzman.

Analysis: Nonfiction

Much of West's writing is devoted to the development of a new pragmatism that runs somewhat counter to that of his Princeton mentor, Richard Rorty. West has read the work of the most significant philosophers of Western civilization—Immanuel Kant, David Hume, Ludwig Wittgenstein, Karl Marx, Leon Trotsky, Blaise Pascal, and Søren Kierkegaard—all of whom have influenced his thinking and led him to original insights. West's writing is essentially a quest to understand the position and role of African Americans in society and to analyze their roles in relation to the roles of other groups.

Prophesy Deliverance! An Afro-American Revolutionary Christianity

West made his publishing debut in 1982 with *Prophesy Deliverance!*, a collection of addresses he delivered at Brooklyn's Lord Pentecostal Church. In these addresses, West stresses the inherent value of all humanity regardless of race, class, gender, and other arbitrary distinctions. The prophetic Christianity that West espouses views knowledge as being communally created, a view that certainly speaks to the unity of all humans despite their obvious individual differences.

West outlines the steps prophetic Christianity must take in order to affect society. He recognizes and encourages the significant role that individualism plays, but he tempers it by insisting upon an acceptance of the supremacy of divine grace. He contends that prophetic Christianity must critically examine and seek to redirect the prevailing supremacy of a white society, which he believes is undermining African American society. He calls on blacks to honestly and objectively assess their responses to white domination and oppression.

Perhaps the most startling of West's proposals is his call for "thoughtful engagement" between prophetic Christianity and progressive Marxism. He calls on blacks to construct a model for advancing the progress and liberation of black Americans. His linking of Christianity and Marxism may seem a drastic alliance, but West's contention here and in much of his later writing is that a redistribution of wealth is essential to reforming society equitably. Certainly nothing could challenge white supremacy more pointedly than a move toward the Marxism that West champions.

Perhaps the most challenging insight in this book is West's understanding of where African Americans stand in relation to other immigrants in American society. During the nineteenth century, waves of immigrants from Europe flooded the United States, but, unlike American blacks, they were free.

West asserts that European modernity was in decline from 1871 until 1950 and that this decline resulted in postmodernism. He finds that African Americans were becoming a part of the modern world at precisely the time that European immigrants to America and their progeny were being drawn into the postmodern world. West's reasoning goes far in explaining and illuminating some of the black-white conflicts that have led to considerable racial strife in the United States, particularly in the decade immediately preceding the publication of this book.

The American Evasion of Philosophy: A Genealogy of Pragmatism

Having studied at Princeton with a man reputed to be America's greatest living pragmatic philosopher, Richard Rorty, and having a profound understanding of the works of such other American pragmatists as C. S. Peirce, William James, and John Dewey, it is not surprising that in 1989 West turned his attention to presenting his own take on pragmatism. Although he greatly admires Rorty, he is unable to unquestioningly accept Rorty's version of pragmatism, which espouses many ideals with which West can agree but some that he cannot.

Although Rorty is appalled by human cruelty and argues for a pluralistic society in which racial harmony exists, he argues from a white perspective and is unable to view racism the way West can, having been exposed to racism throughout his life. West's book is cautionary, arguing, however gently, against the new pragmatism that Rorty espouses. He argues that American pragmatism has evaded important aspects of its Cartesian predecessors.

West asserts that once we begin to demythologize philosophy, the result is the introduction of the complexities of both politics and culture. He takes Rorty to task for his reading of the pragmatism of John Dewey, who is in many respects the most significant pragmatic philosopher of the twentieth century. He faults Rorty's Dewey as being much more intellectually playful and politically tame than the Dewey West has gleaned from his extensive reading of Dewey's work. This book is essentially an argument in favor of West's prophetic pragmatism, which is a vital concomitant of his Christianity.

Race Matters

Race Matters was published in April, 1993, one year following the Los Angeles riots sparked by the trials of four police officers who had participated in the beating of Rodney King. To West, the case and its aftermath demonstrated the pain and distress the public feels in dealing seriously with any matter involving race. People would rather sweep such matters under the carpet than consider them with an eye toward bringing about much-needed change.

This collection presents essays with such titles as "Nihilism in Black America," "The Pitfalls of Racial Reasoning," "The Crisis of Black Leadership," "Demystifying the New Black Conservatism," "Beyond Affirmative Action: Equality and Identity," "On Black-Jewish Relations," and "Malcolm X and Black Rage." Throughout his text, West urges readers to work toward building a communal spirit.

West contends that the way people deal with situations determines their response to these situations, suggestive of Marshall McLuhan's contention in the mid 1960's that the medium is the message. Blacks and whites, liberals and conservatives have, according to West, been responsible for the failure of race relations in the United States. The white community appears limited to viewing the black community from a white perspective.

West urges the building of black-white coalitions, a more equitable distribution of resources, public intervention to provide for the needs of all citizens (particularly their health and educational needs), and the implementation of a system that prepares people, especially young people, to assume the leadership roles that will make his ideal society a reality.

West chides intellectually gifted blacks who choose to attend prestigious, predominantly white institutions of higher learning, suggesting that they do so for their own betterment rather than for the betterment of their race. He questions why they do not attend predominantly black schools and help to elevate the quality of such institutions. Coming from a writer whose degrees are from Harvard and Princeton, this suggestion has struck many readers as disingenuous.

The Rodney King debacle certainly brought racial tensions in Los Angeles to the boiling point, but West contends, probably quite validly, that race was the obvious and visible cause of the eruption, but not the fundamental cause. Rather, he blames a combination of economic decline, cultural decay, and political lethargy.

Democracy Matters: Winning the Fight Against Imperialism
In this sequel to *Race Matters*, published in 2004, eleven years after that best-selling collection of essays, Cornel West scrutinizes the democratic tradition in the United States and America's attempts to impose democracy upon sovereign Middle Eastern countries. His democracy would emphasize justice and love, would foster a worldwide sense of community built on Socratic dialogue and prophetic practices.

West decries America's attempts to impose a political system on the Middle East through military force and authoritarianism on the part of the United States government. As in much of his work, he cringes at the narrow perspectives through which America views the world. He recalls some of the greatest thinkers of the past, citing their historical, religious, and philosophical ideas, and he then compares their ideals with the current leadership of the United States.

Nine pages of this book are devoted to West's account of why he, after locking horns with Harvard president Lawrence Summers, resigned from his tenured professorship and, in 2002, returned to Princeton. His move from Harvard was highly controversial and resulted in other departures among some notable black scholars.

In this book, West writes analytically about America's youth culture and about hip-hop, in which he has a considerable interest. This interest was in part responsible for his rift with Summers and his departure from Harvard. He also analyzes American Christianity and somewhat softens but does not abandon his early contention that Christianity and Marxism must combine for the betterment of society.

Other Literary Forms

Cornel West's chief means of expression is oratory. He is a gripping speaker who has often been compared to Martin Luther King, Jr., for his ability to hold audiences spellbound. Fortunately, much of the verve that characterizes his speeches spills over into his writing, which can be quite intellectually challenging—some might say dense—but generally makes for rewarding reading. It engages the mind in exciting ways. In 1979, when West returned to Harvard for a year before completing his doctoral studies at Princeton, he wrote a novel, which remains unpublished. This has been, apparently, his only effort to do any major writing aside from the essays and books on philosophy that have established his reputation.

Bibliography

Dyson, Eric Michael. *Making Malcolm: The Myth and Meaning of Malcolm X.* New York: Oxford University Press, 1995. Dyson's view of Malcolm X is interesting when read in the light of West's essay, "Malcolm X and Black Rage," which is included in his collection of essays *Race Matters.*

Johnson, Clarence Shole. *Cornel West and Philosophy: The Quest for Social Justice.* New York: Routledge, 2003. Particularly relevant are chapter 3 on Marxism and Christianity and chapter 4 on black-Jewish relations. This source is quite specialized.

Rorty, Richard. "The Professor and the Prophet." *Transition: An*

International Review 58 (1991): 78. Reflections about pragmatism and about Cornel West by the Princeton professor who so strongly influenced him.

Sanoff, Alvin P. "Cornel West: A Theology for the Streets." *U.S. News & World Report,* December 18, 1992-January 4, 1993, p. 94. Largely focuses on *The American Evasion of Philosophy.* Questions West on his interpretation of American pragmatism.

West, Cornel. "Interview with Cornel West." Interview by Anders Stephanson. In *Universal Abandon,* edited by Andrew Ross. Minneapolis: University of Minnesota Press, 1988. One of the earliest interviews with West, largely focusing on the publication of his *Prophetic Fragments.* Stephanson discusses the controversial matter of West's considerations of Christianity and Marxism.

————. "Sketches of My Culture." http://www.cornelwest .com/. Accessed September 1, 2005. West's page contains a short biography and samples of the two-CD set he has produced with three colleagues, which is based on the idea that the power of African American culture comes from its music.

————, ed. *The Cornel West Reader.* New York: Basic Civitas Books, 1999. This collection of some of West's most important writing presents, in one volume, the broad range of his thinking. Excellent for readers who wish to assess the intellectual progression of this important intellectual.

Wood, Mark David. *Cornel West and the Politics of Prophetic Pragmatism.* Urbana: University of Illinois Press, 2000. Wood deals with such matters as the end of liberation theology, racism and the struggle for working-class democracy, the status of American pragmatism, and the future of revolutionary democratic politics. The presentation is specialized, but is recommended for serious students of West's writing.

Yancy, George, ed. *Cornel West: A Critical Reader.* Malden, Mass.: Blackwell, 2001. The eighteen contributions to this book are arranged under four headings: Pragmatism; Philosophy of Religion; Political Philosophy; and Cultural Studies. An excellent starting point for West enthusiasts.

— *R. Baird Shuman*

Phillis Wheatley

Poet

Born: West Coast of Africa (possibly the Senegal-
Gambia region); 1753(?)
Died: Boston, Massachusetts; December 5, 1784

POETRY: *Poems on Various Subjects, Religious and Moral,* 1773; *The
Poems of Phillis Wheatley,* 1966, 1989 (Julian D. Mason, Jr.,
editor).
MISCELLANEOUS: *Memoir and Poems of Phillis Wheatley: A Native African and a Slave,* 1833; *The Collected Works of Phillis Wheatley,*
1988 (John Shields, editor).

Achievements

From the time of her first published piece to the present day, controversy has surrounded the life and work of America's first black
poet, and only its second published woman poet (after Anne
Bradstreet). Few poets of any age have been so scornfully ma-
ligned, so passionately defended, so fervently celebrated, and so
patronizingly tolerated. Yet, during the years of her young adulthood, Phillis Wheatley was the toast of England and the colonies.
For years before she attempted to find a Boston publisher for her
poems, she had published numerous elegies celebrating the
deaths of many of the city's most prominent citizens. In 1770, she
wrote her most famous and most often-reprinted elegy, on the
death of "the voice of the Great Awakening," George Whitefield,
chaplain to the countess of Huntingdon, who was one of the leading benefactors of the Methodist evangelical movement in England and the colonies.

Not finding Boston to be in sympathy with her 1772 proposal
for a volume, Wheatley found substantial support the following
year in the countess of Huntingdon, whose interest had been
stirred by the young poet's noble tribute to her chaplain. Subse-

quently, Wheatley was sent to London, ostensibly for her health; this trip curiously accords, however, with the very weeks that her book was being printed. It is likely that she proofread the galleys herself. At any rate, she was much sought after among the intellectual, literary set of London, and Sir Brook Watson, who was to become Lord Mayor of London within a year, presented her with a copy of John Milton's *Paradise Lost* (1667) in folio. The earl of Dartmouth, who was at the time secretary of state for the colonies and president of the board of Trade and Foreign Plantations, gave her a copy of Tobias Smollett's translation of *Don Quixote* (1755). Benjamin Franklin, to whom she would later inscribe her second book of poetry (never published), has even recorded that, while in London briefly, he called on Wheatley to see whether "there were any service I could do her."

In the opening pages of her 1773 volume appears a letter of authentication of Wheatley's authorship which is signed by still another of the signatories of the Declaration of Independence, John Hancock. Added to the list of attesters are other outstanding Bostonians, including Thomas Hutchinson, then governor of Massachusetts, and James Bowdoin, one of the founders of Bowdoin College. Later, during the early months of the Revolution, Wheatley wrote a poem in praise of General George Washington titled "To His Excellency General Washington." As a result, she received an invitation to visit the general at his headquarters, and her poem was published by Tom Paine in *The Pennsylvania Magazine.* John Paul Jones, who also appreciated Wheatley's celebration of freedom, even asked one of his officers to secure him a copy of her *Poems.*

Nevertheless, she did not continue to enjoy such fame. A country ravaged by war has little time, finally, for poetry, and Wheatley regrettably, perhaps tragically, faced the rejection of two more proposals for a volume of new poems. Thwarted by the vicissitudes of war and poverty, Wheatley died from complications resulting from childbirth. Even so, her poetry has survived and is now considered to be among the best of its period produced in America or in England. It is just beginning to be recognized that, contrary to the opinion of those who would dispose of Wheatley as a mere imitator, she produced sophisticated, original poems whose creative theories of the imagination and the sublime anticipate the Romantic movement.

Biography

The known details of Phillis Wheatley's life are few. According to her master, John Wheatley of Boston, she "was brought from Africa to America in the Year 1761, between Seven and Eight Years of Age [sic]." Her parents were apparently sun-worshipers, for she is supposed to have recalled to her white captors that she remembered seeing her mother pouring out water to the sun every morning. If such be the case, it would help to explain why the sun is predominant as an image in her poetry.

(Library of Congress)

Her life with the Wheatleys, John and Susanna and their two children, the twins Mary and Nathaniel, was probably not too demanding for one whose disposition toward asthma (brought on or no doubt exacerbated by the horrible "middle passage") greatly weakened her. The Wheatleys' son attended Harvard, so it is likely that Nathaniel served as the eager young girl's Latin tutor. At any rate, it is certain that Wheatley knew Latin well; her translation of the Niobe episode from Ovid's *Metamorphoses* (before 8 C.E.), book 6, displays a learned knowledge and appreciation of the Latin original. Wheatley's classical learning is evident throughout her poetry, which is thick with allusions to ancient historical and mythological figures.

The turning point of Wheatley's career, not only as an author but also as a human being, came when her *Poems on Various Subjects, Religious and Moral* was published in London in 1773. After she returned from England, having been recalled because of Susanna Wheatley's growing illness, she was manumitted sometime during September, 1773. It is probable that Wheatley was freed because of the severe censure that some English reviewers of her *Poems* had directed at the owners of a learned author who "still remained a slave." At this very point, however, the poet's fortunes began a slow decline. In 1778, at the height of the war and after the deaths of both John and Susanna Wheatley, she married John Peters, a black man of some learning who failed to rescue the poet from poverty.

Wheatley died alone and unattended in a hovel somewhere in the back streets of the Boston slums in 1784, truly an ignominious end for one who had enjoyed such favor. She was preceded in death by two of her children, as well as by the third, to whom she had just given birth. She was at most only thirty-one years old. Given Wheatley's vision of the world "Oppress'd with woes, a painful endless train," it should not be surprising that her most frequently adopted poetic form is the elegy, in which she always celebrates death as the achievement of ultimate freedom—suggesting the thanatos-eros (desire for death) motif of Romanticism.

Analysis: Poetry

Beginning in the 1970's, Phillis Wheatley began to receive the attention she deserves. George McMichael and others, editors of the influential two-volume *Anthology of American Literature* (1974, 1980), observe that she and Philip Freneau were "the most important poets" of America's Revolutionary War era. To be sure, one of the major subjects of her poetry is the American struggle for independence. Temporal freedom is not her only subject, however; she is also much concerned with the quest for spiritual freedom. Consequently, the elegy, in which she celebrates the Christian rewards of eternal life and absolute freedom after death, is her favorite poetic form. In addition, she delights in describing God's creation of nature's splendors and sometimes appears to enjoy the beauties of nature for their own sake and not simply as acts of God's providence. It is in her poem "On Imagination," however, that Wheatley waxes most eloquent; in this poem, perhaps her most important single work, she articulates a theory of the imagination which strikingly anticipates that of Samuel Taylor Coleridge. Indeed, Wheatley's affinities with Romanticism, which run throughout her poetry, may come to be seen as her surest claim to a place in literary history.

Such an approach to this early American poet contradicts the widespread critical view that Wheatley was a highly derivative poet, inextricably mired in the neoclassical tradition. Her preference for the heroic couplet, one of the hallmarks of neoclassicism, has deceived many into immediately classifying her as neoclassical. One must recall, however, that George Gordon, Lord Byron also had a passion for the couplet. Surely, then, one must not be satisfied with a cursory glance at Wheatley's adoption of the heroic couplet; one must go on to explore the content of her poetry.

The Political Poems

Her political poems document major incidents of the American struggle for independence. In 1768, she wrote "To the King's Most Excellent Majesty on His Repealing the American Stamp Act." When it appeared, much revised, in *Poems on Various Sub-*

jects, Religious and Moral, the poet diplomatically deleted the last two lines of the original, which read, "When wars came on [against George] the proudest rebel fled/ God thunder'd fury on their guilty head." By that time, the threat of the King's retaliation did not seem so forbidding nor the injustice of rebellion against him so grave.

"America," a poem probably written about the same time but published only recently, admonishes Britain to treat "americus," the British child, with more deference. According to the poem, the child, now a growing seat of "Liberty," is no mere adorer of an overwhelming "Majesty," but has acquired strength of his own: "Fearing his strength which she [Britain] undoubted knew/ She laid some taxes on her darling son." Recognizing her mistake, "great Britannia" promised to lift the burden, but the promise proved only "seeming Sympathy and Love." Now the Child "weeps afresh to feel this Iron chain." The urge to draw an analogy here between the poem's "Iron chain" and Wheatley's own predicament is irresistible; while America longs for its own independence, Wheatley no doubt yearns for hers.

The year 1770 marked the beginning of armed resistance against Britain. Wheatley chronicles such resistance in two poems, the second of which is now lost. The first, "On the Death of Mr. Snider Murder'd by Richardson," appeared initially along with "America." The poem tells how Ebenezer Richardson, an informer on American traders involved in circumventing British taxation, found his home surrounded on the evening of February 22, 1770, by an angry mob of colonial sympathizers. Much alarmed, Richardson emerged from his house armed with a musket and fired indiscriminately into the mob, killing the eleven- or twelve-year-old son of Snider, a poor German colonist. Wheatley calls young Christopher Snider, of whose death Richardson was later found guilty in a trial by jury, "the first martyr for the common good," rather than those men killed less than two weeks later in the Boston Massacre. The poem's fine closing couplet suggests that even those not in sympathy with the quest for freedom can grasp the nobility of that quest and are made indignant by its sacrifice: "With Secret rage fair freedom's foes beneath/ See in thy corse ev'n Majesty in Death."

Wheatley does not, however, ignore the Boston Massacre. In a proposal for a volume which was to have been published in Boston in 1772, she lists, among twenty-seven titles of poems (the 1773 volume had thirty-nine), "On the Affray in King Street, on the Evening of the 5th of March." This title, naming the time and place of the Massacre, suggests that the poet probably celebrated the martyrdom of Crispus Attucks, the first black man to lose his life in the American struggle, along with the deaths of two white men. Regrettably, the poem has not yet been recovered. Even so, the title alone confirms Wheatley's continued recording of America's struggle for freedom. This concern shifted in tone from obedient praise for the British regime to supplicatory admonition and then to guarded defiance. Since she finally found a publisher not in Boston but in London, she prudently omitted "America" and the poems about Christopher Snider and the Boston Massacre from her 1773 volume.

She chose to include, however, a poem dedicated to the earl of Dartmouth, who was appointed secretary of state for the colonies in August, 1772. In this poem, "To the Right Honourable William, Earl of Dartmouth, His Majesty's Principal Secretary of State for North America," she gives the earl extravagant praise as one who will lay to rest "hatred faction." She knew of the earl's reputation as a humanitarian through the London contacts of her mistress, Susanna. When the earl proved to support oppressive British policies, the poet's expectations were not realized; within four years of the poem's date, America had declared its independence. Since her optimism was undaunted by foreknowledge, Wheatley wrote a poem which was even more laudatory than "To the King's Most Excellent Majesty on His Repealing the American Stamp Act." Perhaps she was not totally convinced, however; the poem contains some unusually bold passages for a colonist who is also both a woman and a slave.

For example, she remarks that, with Dartmouth's secretaryship, America need no longer "dread the iron chain,/ Which wanton *Tyranny* with lawless hand/ Had made, and with it meant t'enslave the land." Once again Wheatley uses the slave metaphor of the iron chain. Quite clearly she also accuses the

Crown of "wanton *Tyranny*," which it had wielded illegally and with the basest of motives—to reduce the colonies to the inhuman condition of slave states. Here rebellious defiance, no longer guarded, is unmistakable; the tone matches that of the Declaration of Independence. It is a mystery how these lines could have gone unnoticed in the London reviews, all of them positive, of her 1773 volume. Perhaps the reviewers were too bedazzled by the "improbability" that a black woman could produce such a volume to take the content of her poetry seriously.

In this poem, Wheatley also presents a rare autobiographical portrait describing the manner in which she was taken from her native Africa. The manuscript version of this passage is more spontaneous and direct than the more formally correct one printed in the 1773 volume, and thus is closer to the poet's true feelings. It was "Seeming cruel fate" which snatched her "from Afric's fancy'd happy seat." Fate here is only apparently cruel, since her capture has enabled her to become a Christian; the young poet's piety resounds throughout her poetry and letters. Her days in her native land were, nevertheless, happy ones, and her abduction at the hands of ruthless slavers doubtless left behind inconsolable parents. Such a bitter memory of the circumstances of her abduction fully qualifies her to "deplore the day/ When Britons weep beneath Tyrannic sway"; the later version reads: "And can I then but pray/ Others may never feel tyrannic sway?" Besides toning down the diction, this passage alters her statement to a question and replaces "Britons" with the neutral "others." The question might suggest uncertainty, but it more probably reflects the author's polite deportment toward a London audience. Since, in the earlier version, she believed Dartmouth to be sympathetic with her cause, she had no reason to exercise deference toward him; she thought she could be frank. The shift from "Britons" to "others" provokes a more compelling explanation. In the fall of 1772, Wheatley could still think of herself as a British subject. Later, however, after rejoicing that the earl's administration had given way to restive disillusionment, perhaps the poet was less certain about her citizenship.

Three years after the publication of her 1773 volume, Wheatley unabashedly celebrated the opposition to the "tyrannic sway" of Britain in "To His Excellency General Washington," newly appointed commander in chief of the Continental Army; the war of ideas had become one of arms. In this piece, which is more a paean to freedom than a eulogy to Washington, she describes freedom as "divinely fair,/ Olive and laurel bind her golden hair"; yet "She flashes dreadful in refulgent arms." The poet accents this image of martial glory with an epic simile, comparing the American forces to the power of the fierce king of the winds:

> As when Eolus heaven's fair face deforms,
> Enwrapp'd in tempest and a night of storms;
> Astonish'd ocean feels the wild uproar,
> The refluent surges beat the sounding shore.

For the young poet, America is now "The land of freedom's heaven-defended race!" While the eyes of the world's nations are fixed "on the scales,/ For in their hopes Columbia's arm prevails," the poet records Britain's regret over her loss: "Ah! cruel blindness to Columbia's state!/ Lament thy thirst of boundless power too late." The temper of this couplet is in keeping with Wheatley's earlier attitudes toward oppression. The piece closes as the poet urges Washington to pursue his objective with the knowledge that virtue is on his side. If he allows the fair goddess Freedom to be his guide, Washington will surely emerge not only as the leader of a victorious army but also as the head of the newly established state.

In Wheatley's last political poem, "freedom's heaven-defended race" has won its battle. Written in 1784 within a year after the Treaty of Paris, "Liberty and Peace" is a demonstrative celebration of American independence. British tyranny, the agent of American oppression, has now been taught to fear "americus" her child, "And new-born *Rome* shall give *Britannia* Law." Wheatley concludes this piece with two pleasing couplets in praise of America, whose future is assured by heaven's approval:

> Auspicious Heaven shall fill with favoring Gales,
> Where e'er *Columbia* spreads her swelling Sails:
> To every Realm shall *Peace* her Charms display,
> And Heavenly *Freedom* spread her golden Ray.

Personified as Peace and Freedom, Columbia (America) will act as a world emissary, an emanating force like the rays of the sun. In this last couplet, Wheatley has captured, perhaps for the first time in poetry, America's ideal mission to the rest of the world.

The fact that Wheatley so energetically proclaims America's success in the political arena certainly attests her sympathies—not with the neoclassic obsession never to challenge the established order nor to breach the rules of political and social decorum—but with the Romantic notion that a people who find themselves unable to accept a present, unsatisfactory government have the right to change that government, even if such a change can be accomplished only through armed revolt. The American Revolution against Britain was the first successful such revolt and was one of the sparks of the French Revolution. Wheatley's steadfast literary participation in the American Revolution clearly aligns her with such politically active English Romantic poets as Percy Bysshe Shelley and Lord Byron.

The Elegies
In her elegies, on the other hand, Wheatley displays her devotion to spiritual freedom. As do her political poems, her elegies exalt specific occasions, the deaths of people usually known to her within the social and religious community of the poet's Old South Congregational Church of Boston. Also in the manner of her poems on political events, her elegies exceed the boundaries of occasional verse. The early, but most famous of her elegies, "On the Death of the Rev. Mr. George Whitefield, 1770," both illustrates the general structure in which she cast all seventeen of her extant elegies and indicates her recurring ideological concerns.

Wheatley's elegies conform for the most part to the Puritan funeral elegy. They include two major divisions: First comes the portrait, in which the poet pictures the life of the subject, then follows the exhortation, encouraging the reader to seek the heavenly rewards gained by the subject in death. The portrait usually comprises three biographical steps: vocation or conversion; sanctification, or evidence of good works; and glorification, or joyous treatment of the deceased's reception into heaven. Wheatley's elegy on Whitefield surprisingly opens with the glorification of the Great Awakener, already in heaven and occupying his "immortal throne." She celebrates the minister's conversion or vocation in an alliterative line as "The greatest gift that ev'n a God can give." Of course, she writes many lines describing the good works of a man wholly devoted to the winning of souls during the seven visits which he made to America during and after the period of the Great Awakening.

Whitefield died in Newburyport, Massachusetts, on September 30, 1770, having left Boston only a week or so before, where he had apparently lodged with the Wheatley family. Indeed, the young poet of sixteen or seventeen appears to recollect from personal experience when she observes that the minister "long'd to see *America* excel" and "charg'd its youth that ev'ry grace divine/ Should with full lustre in their conduct shine." She also seizes this opportunity to proclaim to the world Whitefield's assertion that even Africans would find Jesus of Nazareth an *"Impartial Saviour."* The poem closes with a ten-line exhortation to the living to aspire toward Whitefield's example: "Let ev'ry heart to this bright vision rise."

As one can see, Wheatley's elegies are not sad affairs; quite to the contrary, they enact joyful occasions after which deceased believers may hope to unite, as she states in "On the Death of the Rev. Dr. Sewell, 1769," with "Great God, incomprehensible, unknown/ By sense." Although one's senses may limit a firsthand acquaintance with God, these same senses do enable one to learn *about* God, especially about God's works in nature. The poem in the extant Wheatley canon which most pointedly addresses God's works in nature is "Thoughts on the Works of Providence." This poem of 131 lines opens with a ten-line invocation to the "Celestial muse," resembling Milton's heavenly muse of *Paradise Lost.*

Identifying God as the force behind planetary movement, she writes, "Ador'd [is] the God that whirls surrounding spheres" which rotate ceaselessly about "the monarch of the earth and skies." From this sublime image she moves to yet another: "'Let there be light,' he said: from his profound/ Old chaos heard and trembled at the sound." It should not go unremarked that Wheatley could, indeed, find much in nature to foster her belief, but little in the mundane world of ordinary men to sustain her spiritually. The frequency of nature imagery but the relative lack of scenes drawn from human society (with the exception of her political poems, and even these are occasions for abstract departures into the investigation of political ideologies) probably reflects the poet's insecurity and uncertainty about a world which first made her a slave and then gave her, at best, only second-class citizenship.

In "An Hymn to the Morning," one of her most lyrical poems, Wheatley interprets the morn (recall her mother's morning ritual of pouring out water to the rising sun) as the source of poetic afflatus or inspiration. The speaker of the poem, Wheatley herself, first perceives the light of the rising sun as a reflection in the eye of one of the "feather'd race." After she hears the song of the bird which welcomes the day, she turns to find the source of melody and sees the bird "Dart the bright eye, and shake the painted plume." Here the poet captures with great precision the bird's rapid eye movement. The bird, archetypal symbol of poetic song, has received the dawn's warm rays which stimulate it to sing. When the poet turns to discover the source of melody, however, what she sees first is not Aurora, the dawning sun, but Aurora the stimulus of song reflected within the "bright eye" of the bird.

In the next stanza the poet identifies the dawn as the ultimate source of poetic inspiration when she remarks that the sun has awakened Calliope, here the personification of inspiration, while her sisters, the other Muses, "fan the pleasing fire" of the stimulus to create. Hence both the song of the bird and the light reflected in its eye have instructed her to acknowledge the source of the bird's melody; for she aspires to sing with the same pleasing fire which animates the song of the bird. Like many of the Romantics who followed her, Wheatley perceives nature both as a means to know ultimate freedom and as an inspiration to create, to make art.

It is in her superlative poem, "On Imagination," however, that Wheatley most forcefully brings both aspirations, to know God and to create fine poetry, into clear focus. To the young black poet, the imagination was sufficiently important to demand from her pen a fifty-three-line poem. The piece opens with this four-line apostrophe:

> Thy various works, imperial queen, we see,
> How bright their forms! how deck'd with pomp by thee!
> Thy wond'rous acts in beauteous order stand,
> And all attest how potent is thine hand.

Clearly, Wheatley's imagination is a regal presence in full control of her poetic world, a world in which her "wond'rous acts" of creation stand in harmony, capturing a "beauteous order." These acts themselves testify to the queen's creative power. Following a four-line invocation to the Muse, however, the poet distinguishes the imagination from its subordinate fancy:

> Now, here, now there, the roving Fancy flies;
> Till some lov'd object strikes her wand'ring eyes,
> Whose silken fetters all the senses bind,
> And soft captivity involves the mind.

Unlike the controlled, harmonious imagination, the subordinate fancy flies about here and there, searching for some appropriate and desired object worthy of setting into motion the creative powers of her superior.

Fancy and Memory

In "Thoughts on the Works of Providence," the poet describes the psychology of sleep in similar fashion. Having entered the world of dreams, the mind discovers a realm where "ideas range/ Licentious and unbounded o'er the plains/ Where Fancy's queen in giddy triumph reigns." Wheatley maintains that in sleep the imagination, once again "Fancy's queen," creates worlds which lack the "beauteous order" of the poet sitting before a writing desk; nevertheless, these dream worlds provoke memorable images. In "On Recollection" Wheatley describes the memory as the repository on which the mind draws to create its dreams. What may be "long-forgotten," the memory "calls from night" and "plays before the fancy's sight." By analogy, Wheatley maintains, the memory provides the poet "ample treasure" from her "secret stores" to create poetry: "in her pomp of images display'd,/ To the high-raptur'd poet gives her aid." "On Recollection" asserts a strong affinity between the poet's memory, analogous to the world of dreams, and the fancy, the associative faculty subordinate to the imagination. Recollection for Wheatley functions as the poet's storehouse of images, while the fancy channels the force of the imagination through its associative powers. Both the memory and the fancy, then, serve the imagination.

Wheatley's description of fancy and memory departs markedly from what eighteenth century aestheticians, including John Locke and Joseph Addison, generally understood as the imagination. The faculty of mind which they termed "imagination" Wheatley relegates to recollection (memory) and fancy. Her description of recollection and fancy closely parallels Coleridge's in the famous thirteenth chapter of *Biographia Literaria* (1817), where he states that fancy "is indeed no other than a mode of Memory emancipated from the order of time and space." Wheatley's identification of the fancy as roving "Now here, now there" whose movement is analogous to the dream state, where "ideas range/ Licentious and unbounded," certainly frees it from the limits of time and space. Coleridge further limits the fancy to the capacity of choice. "But equally with the ordinary memory," he insists, "the Fancy must receive all its materials ready made from the law of association." Like Coleridge's, Wheatley's fancy exercises choice by association as it finally settles upon "some lov'd object."

If fancy and memory are the imagination's subordinates, then how does the imagination function in the poet's creative process? Following her description of fancy in "On Imagination," Wheatley details the role the imagination plays in her poetry. According to her, the power of the imagination enables her to soar "through air to find the bright abode,/ Th' empyreal palace of the thund'ring God." The central focus of her poetry remains contemplation of God. Foreshadowing William Wordsworth's "winds that will be howling at all hours," Wheatley exclaims that on the wings of the imagination she "can surpass the wind/ And leave the rolling universe behind." In the realm of the imagination, the poet can "with new worlds amaze th' unbounded soul."

Immediately following this arresting line, Wheatley illustrates in a ten-line stanza the power of the imagination to create new worlds. Even though winter and the "frozen deeps" prevail in the real world, the imagination can take one out of unpleasant reality and build a pleasant, mythic world of fragrant flowers and verdant groves where "Fair Flora" spreads "her fragrant reign," where Sylvanus crowns the forest with leaves, and where "Show'rs may descend, and dews their gems disclose,/ And nectar sparkle on the blooming rose." Such is the power of imagination to promote poetic creation and to release one from an unsatisfactory world. Unfortunately, like reality's painful intrusion upon the delicate, unsustainable song of John Keats's immortal bird, gelid winter and its severe "northern tempests damp the rising fire," cut short the indulgence of her poetic world, and lamentably force Wheatley to end her short-lived lyric: "Cease then, my song, cease the unequal lay." Her lyric must end because no poet can indefinitely sustain a mythic world.

In her use of the imagination to create "new worlds," Wheatley's departure from eighteenth century theories of this faculty is radical and once again points toward Coleridge. Although she does not distinguish between "primary" and "secondary" imagination as he does, Wheatley nevertheless constructs a theory which approaches his "secondary" imagination. According to Coleridge, the secondary imagination, which attends the creative faculty, intensifies the primary imagination common to all men. Coleridge describes how the secondary imagination operates in this well-known passage: "It dissolves, diffuses, dissipates, in order to recreate;/ or where this process is rendered impossible, yet still at all/ events it struggles to idealize and to unify." In spite of the fact that Wheatley's attempt to dissolve, diffuse, and dissipate is assuredly more modest than Coleridge's "swift half-intermitted burst" in "Kubla Khan," she does, nevertheless, like the apocalyptic Romantics, idealize, unify, and shape a mythopoeic world. Proceeding in a systematic fashion, she first constructs a theory of mental faculty which, when assisted by the associative fancy, builds, out of an act of the mind, a new world which does indeed stand in "beauteous order." This faculty, which she identifies as the imagination, she uses as a tool to achieve freedom, however momentary.

Wheatley was, then, an innovator who used the imagination as a means to transcend an unacceptable present and even to construct "new worlds [to] amaze the unbounded soul"; this practice, along with her celebration of death, her loyalty to the American struggle for political independence, and her consistent praise of nature, places her firmly in that flow of thought which culminated in nineteenth century Romanticism. Her diction may strike a modern audience as occasionally "got up" and stiff, and her reliance on the heroic couplet may appear outdated and worn, but the content of her poetry is innovative, refreshing, and even, for her times, revolutionary. She wrote during the pre-Revolutionary and Revolutionary War eras in America, when little poetry of great merit was produced. Phillis Wheatley, laboring under the disadvantages of being not only a black slave but also a woman, nevertheless did find the time to depict that political struggle for freedom and to trace her personal battle for release. If one looks beyond the limitations of her sincere if dogmatic piety and her frequent dependence on what Wordsworth called poetic diction, one is sure to discover in her works a fine mind engaged in creating some of the best early American poetry.

Other Literary Forms

Phillis Wheatley's cultivation of the letter as a literary form is attested by her inclusion of the titles of several letters in each of her proposals for future volumes subsequent to the publication of her *Poems on Various Subjects, Religious and Moral.* Regrettably, none of these proposals provoked enough response to secure publication of any new volumes. Scholars continue to discover both poems and letters that Wheatley names in these proposals. The letters mentioned in them are addressed to such noted persons as William Legge, second earl of Dartmouth; Selina Hastings, Countess of Huntingdon; Dr. Benjamin Rush; and George Washington. They display a graceful style and articulate some of Wheatley's strongest protestations in support of the cause of American independence and in condemnation of Christian hypocrisy regarding slavery.

Bibliography

Barker-Benfield, G. J., and Catherine Clinton, comps. *Portraits of American Women: From Settlement to the Present.* New York: St. Martin's Press, 1991. A collection of essays that locate the histories of women and men together by period. Includes portraits of Phillis Wheatley and others designed to appeal to a wide range of readers. Includes bibliographical references.

Bassard, Katherine Clay. *Spiritual Interrogations: Culture, Gender, and Community in Early African American Women's Writing.* Princeton, N.J.: Princeton University Press, 1999. A historical analysis that includes a discussion of the works of Wheatley. Includes bibliographical references and index.

Franke, Astrid. "Phillis Wheatley, Melancholy Muse." *New England Quarterly* 77, no. 2 (June, 2004): 224-254. Examines the impact that Wheatley's work had on her personality, as well as her use of political and religious imagery in pursuit of a neoclassicist aesthetic.

Gates, Henry Louis, Jr. "Beautiful Words: Phillis Wheatley 1753-1784." *Current Events*, February 7, 2003, pp. 2-4. A brief analysis of Wheatley's life, work, experiences as a slave, and poetic accomplishments.

_____. "Phillis Wheatley on Trial." *New Yorker* 78, no. 43 (January, 2003): 82-88. An interesting critique of Wheatley's poetry and on her importance as a poet. Also contains information about Wheatley's life and career.

Jones, Jacqueline. "Anglo-American Racism and Phillis Wheatley's 'Sable Veil,' 'Length'ned Chain,' and 'Knitted Heart.'"

In *Women in the Age of the American Revolution*, edited by Ronald Hoffman and Peter J. Albert. Charlottesville: University Press of Virginia, 1989. This sometimes difficult study includes fascinating biographical information and offers a close reading of dozens of poems. Jones delineates the importance of *Poems on Various Subjects, Religious and Moral* as an early commentary on slavery and on American female thought.

Richmond, Merle. *Phillis Wheatley.* American Women of Achievement. New York: Chelsea House, 1988. Written for young adults, this biography is lively and informative. The dozens of illustrations include a portrait of Wheatley and a sample of her handwriting. Contains suggestions for further reading, a chronology, and an index.

Rinaldi, Ann. *Hang a Thousand Trees with Ribbons: The Story of Phillis Wheatley.* New York: Harcourt, 1996. This fictionalized biography is aimed at younger readers and is written in the style Wheatley might have used to write her own autobiography between young childhood and majority. In addition to relating the fateful events of her life, starting with her abduction from Senegal, she discusses writing and its significance. Rinaldi appends a note explaining issues of fact and fiction in her work.

Robinson, William H. *Phillis Wheatley: A Bio-bibliography.* Boston: G. K. Hall, 1981. After a brief biography and review of the critical reception, this volume presents an annotated list of representative writings about Wheatley from 1761 to 1979. Includes reprinted appendixes commenting on two of the poems, and an extensive index.

_____. *Phillis Wheatley and Her Writings.* New York: Garland, 1984. This is by far the finest introduction to Wheatley by the preeminent Wheatley scholar. Presents a brief biography, the text of all the poems and surviving letters (several in facsimile) with an analysis, nine appendixes providing background information, a bibliography, and an index.

_____, ed. *Critical Essays on Phillis Wheatley.* Boston: G. K. Hall, 1982. This fascinating collection of sixty-five essays contains early comments and reviews, including several by Wheatley herself, important reprinted essays from 1834 to 1975, and five critical evaluations original to this book. An editor's introduction provides a biographical and critical overview. Supplemented by a chronology and an index.

Thompson, Gordon E. "Methodism and the Consolation of Heavenly Bliss in Phillis Wheatley's Funeral Elegies." *CLA Journal* 48, no. 1 (September, 2004): 34-51. Studies Wheatley's departure from Puritan pessimism and analyzes the more uplifting and egalitarian tone of her Methodist-oriented elegies.

—John C. Shields

John Edgar Wideman

Novelist and short-story writer

Born: Washington, D.C.; June 14, 1941

LONG FICTION: *A Glance Away*, 1967; *Hurry Home*, 1970; *The Lynchers*, 1973; *Hiding Place*, 1981; *Sent for You Yesterday*, 1983; *The Homewood Trilogy*, 1985 (includes *Damballah, Hiding Place*, and *Sent for You Yesterday*); *Reuben*, 1987; *Philadelphia Fire*, 1990; *The Cattle Killing*, 1996; *Two Cities*, 1998.

SHORT FICTION: *Damballah*, 1981; *Fever: Twelve Stories*, 1989; *All Stories Are True*, 1992; *The Stories of John Edgar Wideman*, 1992; *God's Gym*, 2005.

NONFICTION: *Brothers and Keepers*, 1984; *Fatheralong: A Meditation on Fathers and Sons, Race and Society*, 1994; *Conversations with John Edgar Wideman*, 1998 (Bonnie TuSmith, editor); *Hoop Roots*, 2001; *The Island: Martinique*, 2003.

EDITED TEXTS: *My Soul Has Grown Deep: Classics of Early African-American Literature*, 2001; *Twenty: The Best of the Drue Heinz Literature Prize*, 2001.

Achievements

When he emerged upon the literary scene in the late 1960's, John Edgar Wideman stood out from his peers as a black American writer who did not address exclusively themes of racial conflict and militant nationalism. He concentrated instead on individual psychological struggles that transcend color lines. His earliest novels were enthusiastically received, and he was lauded as a successor to William Faulkner.

After being asked to teach African American literature and essentially having to "teach himself" the field, Wideman began to overtly centralize racial themes in his writing, most radically with the publication of *The Lynchers*, which begins with a chronology of 116 historically documented lynchings. His primary critical acclaim, however, came with the publications of the Homewood series, engendered by the death of his grand-mother, Freeda French, in 1973. *Sent for You Yesterday*, the final work of the Homewood trilogy, received the 1984 PEN/Faulk-ner Award for Fiction, the International Association of Poets, Playwrights, Editors, Essayists, and Novelists. Wideman set a new precedent when he received his second PEN/Faulkner Award for *Philadelphia Fire*. In addition, he was awarded the Lannan Lit-erary Fellowship for Fiction in 1991 and a MacArthur Founda-tion Award (a "genius grant") in 1993.

In spite of favorable reviews of his fiction, some critics have accused Wideman of indulging in an unconventional style at the expense of theme. More often than not, though, his experi-mentation extends meaning by illustrating the impact of the past in addition to the inextricable bonds among generations. His autobiographical *Brothers and Keepers*, which displays some of his innovative techniques, earned a National Book Critics Circle Award nomination. In 1998, Wideman won the prestigious Rea Award, sponsored by the Dungannon Foundation and estab-lished to honor a short story author "for literary power, original-ity, and influence on the genre." Wideman's critical accolades have been profuse, but it is his range of style, continual for-malistic innovation, and his powerful prose that warrant his consideration as one of the best American writers of his genera-tion.

Biography

John Edgar Wideman was the first of five children born to Bette French and Edgar Wideman. His youth was spent in the African American community of Homewood, within the city of Pitts-burgh, Pennsylvania, and his fiction draws heavily upon the ex-periences of his family across a century of Homewood history. As a youth, Wideman demonstrated the same blend of athletic and academic ambition that often distinguishes his fictional characters and dramatizes their divided allegiances. Upon grad-uation as Peabody High School valedictorian, Wideman re-ceived a Benjamin Franklin scholarship to the University of

(University of Wyoming)

Pennsylvania and subsequently played for its basketball team, hoping someday to be drafted by the National Basketball Association. Selected for the Philadelphia Big Five Basketball Hall of Fame and tapped for Phi Beta Kappa, Wideman also won a Rhodes scholarship (and was only the second African American to do so); upon completion of his B.A. at the University of Pennsylvania in 1963, he attended Oxford University, where, in 1966, he earned a B.Phil. as a Thouron Fellow in the eighteenth century novel. Having been an active writer since his undergraduate years, Wideman secured a Kent Fellowship from the University of Iowa Writers' Workshop in 1966. His first novel, *A Glance*

Away, appeared in 1967, winning for him immediate attention as a significant new voice in contemporary American letters.

Alongside his creative endeavors, Wideman steadily pursued an academic career. In 1966, he accepted a teaching position at the University of Pennsylvania, where he later headed the African American studies program from 1971 to 1973 and rose to the rank of professor of English; he was also assistant basketball coach from 1968 to 1972. Academic appointments brought him to Howard University, the University of Wyoming at Laramie, and the University of Massachusetts at Amherst. The National Endowment for the Humanities in 1975 named him a Young Humanist Fellow; in 1976, the U.S. State Department selected him for a lecture tour of Europe and the Near East. That same year, he held a Phi Beta Kappa lectureship. Wideman married Judith Ann Goldman in 1965, and together they had three children: Daniel, Jacob, and Jamila. The family tragedy of his youngest brother, Rob, who was convicted in 1978 of armed robbery and murder, was grimly reiterated in 1988, when Wideman's son Jacob received a life sentence for the 1986 murder in Arizona of a teenage traveling companion. His daughter Jamila, having inherited her father's basketball prowess, garnered a position playing in the Women's National Basketball Association (WNBA) professional league. In the 1980's and 1990's he frequently contributed articles and review essays to *The New York Times Book Review* and to popular magazines such as *TV Guide, Life,* and *Esquire.*

In speaking about the formative influences upon his writing, Wideman asserts that his creative inclinations underwent a transformation upon his arrival as a new faculty member at the University of Pennsylvania, where students of color assumed him to be as well versed in the African American literary legacy as he was in the Anglo-American tradition. His responsiveness to their concerns prompted him not only to create the university's African American studies program but also to recover the cultural identity that he had self-consciously minimized in pursuit of the dominant culture's standards of academic excellence. His subsequent writing, fiction and nonfiction alike, repeatedly sounds the autobiographical theme of "coming home," and

Wideman not only dissects the obstacles that thwart such return but also espouses the belief that art can at least make possible a temporary reconciliation between past and present. By paralleling his own multigenerational family history and the community history of Homewood, Wideman fuses personal and collective memory to create a mythology of the human condition at once particular and universal.

Analysis: Long Fiction

The recurring thematic emphasis in John Edgar Wideman's novels is on the way history, both collective and personal, and the stories that arise from that history, shape notions of reality. From homosexual college professors to ghetto junkies, Wideman's characters are often uncomfortable with their places in history and unsure that they even understand those few traditions that they do observe. Therefore, they shuttle between the imaginary and the real in order to rediscover the past, revive it, or at least preserve whatever parts they do recall. Despite Wideman's literary beginnings in the racially turbulent 1960's, when blacks in America articulated their estrangement from Africa, his white as well as black characters crave the rootedness that distinguishes those who have come to terms with their backgrounds. Shifting from the anonymous northern cities of his first three novels to the clearly delineated Homewood of *Hiding Place* and *Sent for You Yesterday*, Wideman nevertheless consistently indicates that ignorance of heritage results in isolation and psychological turmoil. The same observation is later applied to Philadelphia, specifically Osage Avenue.

Wideman forgoes strictly chronological plot development, adopting instead an intricate experimental style consisting of stream-of-consciousness narrative, long interior monologues, dream sequences, surrealistic descriptions, and abrupt shifts in time, diction, and points of view. Beginning each novel almost exclusively in medias res, he employs a technique influenced by the works of T. S. Eliot, James Joyce, and Jean Toomer, yet indisputably original. In *The Lynchers*, for example, he illustrates the traditionally victimized status of black Americans with a preface that cites more than one hundred documented lynchings. Reeling between their own ravaged communities and impenetrable white ones, the black protagonists of his first two novels, *A Glance Away* and *Hurry Home,* occupy a jumbled landscape where blues clubs coexist with biblical icons. Similarly, in *Hiding Place* and *Sent for You Yesterday,* Wideman retells the stories of his ancestors until a shack or a cape acquires the same expressive quality as a cross. As the author himself explains, "You can call it experimentation, or you can call it ringing the changes. . . . I value spontaneity, flexibility, a unique response to a given situation. . . . Getting too close to the edge but then recovering like the heroes of the Saturday matinee serials. That's excitement."

A Glance Away
Dedicated to "Homes," Wideman's first novel, *A Glance Away,* creates thematic excitement with its treatment of two drifting men coming to terms with their pasts. After a year spent at a rehabilitation center for drug addicts, Eddie Lawson, a disillusioned young black man, returns to his listless, decaying urban neighborhood. Rather than celebrating, however, he spends his gloomy homecoming confronting the goblins that drove him to the brink in the first place: his mother Martha Lawson's idealization of his dead older brother, his girlfriend Alice Smalls's rejection of him for sleeping with a white woman, and his own self-disgust over abandoning a secure postal job for menial, marginal employment. Dejected and defeated by nightfall, he drags himself to grimy Harry's Place in order to cloak his memories in a narcotic haze. There, he is reconciled by his albino friend Brother Smalls with another outcast named Robert Thurley, a white college professor struggling with his own record of divorce, alcoholism, and homosexuality. Though discrepancies between wealth and power divide the two homeless men, each manages to urge the other to maintain his faith in people despite his guilt-ridden history.

 A Glance Away generated much favorable critical response in particular for Wideman's depiction of the alienated Thurley. In trying to disavow his personal past, this connoisseur of food and art embraces a surfeit of creeds and cultures. "In religion an aesthetic Catholic, in politics a passive Communist, in sex a re-signed anarchist," he surrounds himself with treasures from both East and West and indulges in a smorgasbord of the globe's delicacies. Yet as a real measure of the displacement that these extravagances so futilely conceal, he quotes lines from T. S. Eliot's "The Love Song of J. Alfred Prufrock" (1917), in which a similarly solitary speaker searches for intimacy in a world bereft of its cultural moorings.

Emphasizing his protagonists' self-absorption and the es-trangement of their family members and friends, Wideman abandons strictly chronological plot development in favor of lengthy interior monologues. Conversations tend to be short; more likely than not they are interrupted by unspoken flash-backs and asides. Using speech to measure isolation, the author portrays both Eddie and Thurley as incapable of communicat-ing adequately. Eddie, for example, becomes tongue-tied around a group of southern travelers, shuddering in his bus seat instead of warning them as he wishes for the reality of the Northern mecca that they seek. Similarly, despite the empowering quali-ties of a gulp of Southern Comfort, Thurley delivers a lecture on Sophocles' *Oedipus Tyrannus* (c. 429 B.C.E.) fraught with "futility and detachment, . . . introspection and blindness." In one bril-liant play on this speechlessness, both men suddenly converse as if they were actors on a stage. This abrupt emphasis on what is spoken—to the exclusion of private thoughts—stresses each person's imprisonment within him- or herself. Flowing from a weaker artist's pen, *A Glance Away* would have become a mere exercise in allusive technique and stream-of-consciousness style. On the contrary, it reads with the effortless ease of a masterfully crafted lyrical poem. Key to its success is Wideman's careful alli-ance of form and content, not to mention his insightful treat-ment of a rootlessness that transcends the barriers of race.

Hurry Home

The same compact length as the novel that precedes it, *Hurry Home* similarly focuses upon the theme of rootlessness. Its ambi-tious protagonist, the honors graduate Cecil Otis Braithwaite, is in many ways an upscale Eddie Lawson with a wife and an advanced degree. After slaving through law school, supporting himself with a meager scholarship and his earnings as a janitor, Cecil has lost his aspirations and his love for his girlfriend, Esther Brown. In search of something more, he escapes from his wedding bed to Europe, where he roams indiscriminately for three years among its brothels as well as its art galleries. In the tradition of Robert Thurley of *A Glance Away,* two white men as displaced as Cecil attempt to guide him: Charles Webb, belatedly in search of an illegitimate son, and Albert, a mercenary in Webb's employ who has also abandoned a wife. Too lost to save themselves, however, this pair can offer no enduring words of solace to Cecil.

Hurry Home is more sophisticated than *A Glance Away* in its treatment of the isolation theme. It suggests, for example, that the upwardly mobile Cecil is not merely disturbed by his personal past; he is estranged as well from his African and European cultures of origin. On the other hand, nowhere does *Hurry Home* convey the hope that pervades its predecessor. Cecil travels more extensively than does Eddie to reclaim his past, yet he gains no key to it to speak of. Confronting his European heritage merely confirms his status as "a stranger in all . . . tongues." He flees to the African continent by boat, "satisfied to be forever possessed," only to be forever rebuffed from a past that "melts like . . . wax . . . as I am nearer . . . the flame." When he returns at last to his Washington, D.C., tenement, the fruitlessness of his journey is underscored. There, he finds all the same as when he first entered following his miserable nuptials. Symbolically limning his rootlessness, he switches vocations, abandoning the tradition-steeped protocol of the bar for the faddish repertoire of a hairdresser. Thus, "hurry home," the catchphrase for his odyssey, is an ironic one. Cecil really can claim no place where a heritage nurtures and sustains him, no history that he can truly call his own.

Hurry Home displays a masterful style commensurate with that of the later Homewood novels. In addition to a more controlled stream-of-consciousness technique, recurring Christian symbols, icons of Renaissance art, and fragments from Moorish legend powerfully indicate Cecil's fractured lineage. This second novel being a more refined paradigm than the first, Wideman seemed next inclined to break new ground, to address intently the racial polarization that had unsettled American society by the early 1970's, producing that period's most influential published works.

Hiding Place

After an eight-year interval during which he researched black American literature and culture, Wideman applied folk sources more fully than ever before in *Hiding Place,* one of the three works of fiction that make up *The Homewood Trilogy.* Challenged to enlarge his black readership without limiting the universal relevance of his themes, he chose to emphasize one black family based largely on his own Homewood clan. In this novel's swift, uncomplicated plot, Tommy Lawson, a tough, wisecracking youth from the black neighborhood of Homewood, is running from the police after his involvement in a robbery and killing. He seeks refuge among the weedy plots and garbage piles of desolate Bruston Hill, a once-fertile area to which his ancestor Sybela Owens fled from the South and slavery with Charlie Bell, her white owner's recalcitrant son. In the lone residence at the crest of the Hill, a rotting wooden shack sardonically known as "that doghouse," the reclusive "Mother" Bess Owens reluctantly offers her sister's great-grandson a temporary haven. After Tommy regains the courage to elude the authorities eager to convict him for a murder that he did not commit, Bess reaffirms her ties to her kin and ends her self-imposed isolation. Not knowing whether Tommy is dead, has escaped, or has been captured, she burns her shack and prepares to reenter Homewood to retell Tommy's tragic story so that another like it might never happen again.

Though Bess does not leave her longtime home until the novel's final chapter, *Hiding Place* is as much the story of her isolation from family as it is Tommy's story. Just as Tommy has shirked his responsibilities as a husband, father, and son, Bess has turned her back upon the younger generations of kin whose ways are alien to her. Widowed and childless, she has retreated into an archaic lifestyle, shunning the twentieth century amenities of electricity and phones in order to avoid intimacy with others. Physically rooting herself among Bruston Hill's ruins, she has been running from the present in her mind by focusing her thoughts on the past, especially the deaths of loved ones that have occurred. Only when she becomes involved in Tommy's affairs does she rekindle her active commitment to the family.

In *Hiding Place*, Wideman's style dramatically differs from those of the canonized white writers who were his early models. With a method many reviewers have compared to jazz, his characters unfold the histories of five generations of Lawsons and Frenches. Bess herself repeats certain key events in the family history several times; one of her favorites is the one in which Mary Hollinger revives her cousin Freeda French's stillborn baby by plunging it into the snow. Yet like a jazz improvisation, where instruments alternately play solo and play together, she retells the tale each time in a different way, varying her approach to it with different bits of superstition, mysticism, and folklore. Even Wideman's Clement, an inarticulate orphan similar to Benjy Compson in William Faulkner's *The Sound and the Fury* (1929), bears the unique stamp of the black American experience. As the author himself avows, Clement's assimilation into Homewood reflects the nature of the black community as a tolerant extended family.

Its legacy of songs, tales, and superstitions notwithstanding, the Homewood that finally draws Bess back is a model of urban blight, a "bombed out" no-man's-land of "pieces of buildings standing here and there and fire scars and places ripped and kicked down and cars stripped and dead at the curb." This dying landscape, and in a similar way Bess's ramshackle Bruston Hill homestead, proclaims the present descendants' dissociation from their ancestors and one another. In *Sent for You Yesterday*, the final installment of *The Homewood Trilogy* and the 1984 PEN/ Faulkner Award winner for outstanding fiction, this undercurrent becomes the novel's predominant theme. Carl French and his lover Lucy Tate relate the stories of a Homewood gone by to the latest generation of listeners, as if the recovery of the past is integral for the entire community's survival and solidarity.

Sent for You Yesterday

Sent for You Yesterday cannot be divided easily into main story and subplots. All the episodes in it are major in scope and significance. The most memorable ones include the saga of the piano player Albert Wilkes, who slept with a white woman and murdered a white policeman; the tragedy of Samantha, whose college education could not shield her from grief and madness; and the bittersweet adventures of the resilient Brother Tate, an albino and best friend of Carl, who communicates only with gestures and scat sounds. Retold by Carl's nephew Doot, a former Homewood resident modeled largely after Wideman himself, each tale conveys a lesson to a younger generation. More than mere exempla, however, the stories emphasize the cyclic nature of the human condition: Each generation rises to further, alter, and often reenact the accomplishments of its predecessors. Thus, Uncle Carl's street in Homewood becomes to Doot "a narrow, cobbled alley *teeming* with life. Like a wooden-walled ship in the middle of the city, like the ark on which Noah packed two of everything and prayed for land." This determination to survive that the ark imagery calls to mind impels Carl and Lucy to share Homewood's history. By remembering past lives, by preserving traditions, they ensure their own enduring places in the memories of their heirs.

Reuben

Traditions preserved and memories presented from black America's African past form the backbeat of *Reuben*, Wideman's next novel of community and interracial struggle. From a rusting trailer that his clients describe as part office, part altar to the gods, the dwarf Reuben serves the poor of Homewood in need of a lawyer, a psychologist, a warrior, or a priest. Like West African *griots* or oral scribes, who commit to unerring memory genealogies, triumphs, faults, and names, Reuben relies upon a mix of law and bureaucratic legerdemain that he has heard from his own employers and remembered. Like an obliging ancestral spirit shuttling prayers from this world to the next, Reuben negotiates pacts between the ghetto's bombed-out streets and the oak, plush, and marble interiors of City Hall. As he prescribes legal strategies and bestows grandfatherly advice, he also steers his clients to confront and abandon the views that have overturned their lives. When words and contracts alone will not do, Reuben rustles deep within collective memory and knots a charm: "A rag, a bone, a hank of hair. Ancient grains of rice. . . . " Reuben transforms garbage into power, excrement into nourishment, gristle into life. He preaches reincarnation and the nature of things dead to rise again, and he catalyzes his clients to seek similar transformations in themselves.

Infused with magic and spiritualism, *Reuben* also is illustrated by the ravaged images of the inner city. Wideman likens ghetto buildings to the rat-infested holds of slave ships and the people in those buildings to roles of both predator and prey. Much of the Homewood population resembles a coffle of freshly branded slaves, slaves who are bound by laws instead of chains, by the welfare system or underworld crime instead of a plantation economy. Others are human versions of rats—snitching, beating, starving, stealing, and otherwise pestering their neighbors with an eat-or-be-eaten mentality. "There were historical precedents, parallels," Reuben understands. "Indian scouts leading longhairs to the hiding places of their red brethren. FBI informers, double agents, infiltrators of the sixties. An unsubtle variation of divide and conquer." In this bleak landscape, the game of divide and conquer has changed little since enslavement.

Philadelphia Fire

Philadelphia Fire, The Cattle Killing, and *Two Cities* are framed within a geographic shift from Pittsburgh to Philadelphia. In keeping with Wideman's fluid notion of history and myth as mutually interlocking categories of representation, *Philadelphia Fire* recasts the 1985 police bombing of the building occupied by the radical MOVE organization. John Africa, MOVE's leader, is represented as Reverend King, who is described as "a nouveau Rousseau." King leads a rebellion against the infringement on African American individual and communal rights couched in the guises of "urbanization" and "integration" by espousing an ideology that embraces a return to nature and a rejection of modern material values. Elsewhere, Wideman asserts that "the craziness of MOVE is their sanity; they were saying no to the system . . . it makes perfect sense. So the myth of integration is analogous to the prophecy of the cattle killing."

The Cattle Killing

This prophecy serves as the guiding metaphor for the novel *The Cattle Killing*, and it refers to the lies told to the African Xhosa people in order to make them believe that to combat European oppression they must kill their cattle. The cattle are their life force, and their destruction leads to the near annihilation of Xhosa culture. The people die as their cattle die, struck down because they believed the lie of the prophecy: "The cattle are the people. The people are the cattle." Wideman subtly extends this metaphor to consider the problem of intraracial crime ravaging American inner cities and connects contemporary circumstances with the diseased and disintegrating conditions surrounding the yellow fever outbreak of eighteenth century Philadelphia.

In all three instances—in Africa, in Philadelphia, in black urbania—there is a potential for annihilation because of an epidemic fueled by hysteria, exacerbated by racist ideology and carried out by those who believe the "lie" and perpetrate their self-destruction. The narrator of *Cattle Killing*, Isaiah, called "Eye," is an obvious recasting of the biblical figure who prophesies the downfall of the nation of Israel. He is a prophet who warns of false prophecies—in this case, the lie of integration, which is, intricately entwined with modernization and its attenuating conspicuous consumption, the theme foregrounded in *Philadelphia Fire*. This text's distinction from *Philadelphia Fire*, however, lies in the vision of hope with which readers are left; *The Cattle Killing* is also a love story.

Two Cities

The Cattle Killing and the following novel, *Two Cities*, mark a thematic shift for Wideman. Though harkening back to the theme of love (a kind of communal love) inherent in the Homewood trilogy, the novels transcend that representation, exploring the healing potential of intimate, spiritual love. *Two Cities*, which links Philadelphia and Pittsburgh, Cassina Way and Osage Avenue, explores the difficulty of loving in troubled times. It overwhelmingly endorses the embracing of love, not merely physical love but also self-love, love of community, and love of life, as the only viable means of refusing and subverting the lies which have threatened to destroy the African American community.

From the beginning of his extensive literary career, critics have often compared Wideman's prose to the experimental fictions of the eighteenth century English writer Laurence Sterne. The sociable Sterne had befriended Ignatius Sancho, a gregarious former slave, a prodigious correspondent, and host of one of London's most popular salons. Sancho admired Sterne's mock humility and imitated his wit and playful style. In turn, Sterne admired the double entendre, self-scrutiny, and flair for detail in the letters of his African friend.

In Wideman's novels, the voices of the African Sancho and the Englishman Sterne converge. These works present black America from the perspectives of the enslaved and the descendants of the enslaved, as well as from the vantage of those whites who served as either tormentors and oppressors or benefactors and friends. These works warn of the potholes where our elders slipped before, and they expose the reader to the vistas that one often fails to notice and enjoy. They achieve Wideman's goal of "expanding our notions of reality, creating hard, crisp edges you can't swallow without a gulp."

Analysis: Short Fiction

John Edgar Wideman's avowed artistic end is the creation of characters whose rich inner lives testify to a "sense of themselves as spiritual beings" that challenges the deterministic simplicities often dominant in literary depictions of the African American sensibility. Like Richard Wright, Ralph Ellison, and James Baldwin before him, Wideman insistently links naturalistic detail to an existential quest for meaning and integrity that is complicated by the peculiar difficulties of sustaining one's humanity under the degradations of racism. While the material consequences of racist injustice are ever-present in his stories, Wideman makes clear that his most pressing concern is the threat posed to the souls of its victims. In turn, he suggests that the renewal of contemporary African American society, increasingly ravaged by hopelessness and self-destructiveness, lies in a self-conscious recovery of, and healing through, the cultural identity he so rigorously documents in his evocation of Homewood. Thus in Wideman's fiction the struggle of individual souls in an absurd and dehumanizing world does not unfold in a completely existential void; his characters move within a community whose past vitality derived from history, traditions, language, and relationships linking generations back beyond the darkness of slavery. The imaginative architecture that unifies the Homewood Trilogy employs interpenetrating plot lines, family trees, and community legends to make clear that Wideman's real subject is the communal survival once made possible by its citizens' heroic decency against great odds.

Damballah

Damballah, the collection of twelve short stories that begins *The Homewood Trilogy,* announces Wideman's intentions aesthetically as well as thematically. The fuguelike polyphony of voices achieved by bringing together separate narratives drawn from a wide spectrum of Homewood personalities and historical moments captures not only the community's diversity but also the power of oral culture in all of its forms—speech, music, storytelling—to nourish and sustain it in the midst of unrelenting racial hostility. In "The Chinaman," a narrative "I" identified elsewhere as John (and quite evidently an autobiographical presence) explains that the funeral of his maternal grandmother, Freeda, had reconnected him with old family legends that he had years earlier set aside as unworthy of serious literary treatment. Listening months later to his own mother describe Freeda's death and thereby complete a story he had been unable to finish alone, he concludes, "The shape of the story is the shape of my mother's voice." Wideman's narrator repeatedly explains that this text is a collaborative project in which narratives culled from the collective memory of his family are woven together through the mediating agency of his own consciousness to reveal a design that affirms the faith in human possibility now leaching away in the ruins that were once Homewood.

Wideman's preoccupation with the crisis of black men in modern America—a crisis vividly depicted in his own estrangement from his origins and his brother Rob's criminality and imprisonment—explains the placement of his maternal grandfather, John French, at the center of these stories. French's defiant courage, loyalty, quick wit, tough-minded devotion to his family, and acute survival instincts make him a model of masculine virtue for a new generation desperately in need of his example. He stands in seemingly obvious contrast to his equally talented but blighted grandson Tommy Lawson, the narrator's drug-addicted brother, whose crimes destroy his future and who is the counterbalancing focus of the last third of the collection. Yet French lives on in Tommy's rebellious energy and probing mind, making the youth's current circumstances all the more tragic.

Wideman also records the voices of the strong women who have sustained the community throughout the crises surrounding their men and whose emotional anguish reflects the complex emotional dynamic between black men and women in Wideman's fiction. Freeda Hollinger French, the text's matriarch, proves herself capable of swift, violent intervention to safeguard her child or her husband in "Lizabeth: The Caterpillar Story." Lizabeth French Lawson actually gives birth to the narrator in "Daddy Garbage," within a story line juxtaposed to the grim discovery of another infant's frozen corpse and the moral imperative of the two old men who find it and insist upon a decent burial. As the future is denied to one child and extended to another, one perceives a subtle echo of the divergent paths Lizabeth's own sons will pursue in later years.

Wideman's sensitivity to the orality of African American culture leads him to seek linguistic approximations for the music and talk-story patterns at the heart of African American imaginative expression. His prose resonates with the jazz rhythms of African American vernacular and often quotes directly from the musical yoking of human misery and triumph in what is called the blues. In "The Songs of Reba Love Jackson," a successful

Gospel singer admits that her artistry expresses emotional nuances beyond the power of language alone: "Couldn't speak about some things. She could only sing them. Put her stories in the songs she had heard all her life so the songs became her stories." In the closing piece of the volume, "The Beginning of Homewood," the narrator creates a wall of sound from the voices he has unloosed in the preceding stories; writing to his brother Tommy in prison, he acknowledges that his real task as a writer has been to hear and synthesize those women's testimonials to the community's history of defeat and transcendence:

> The chorus wailing and then Reba Love Jackson soloing. I heard May singing and heard Mother Bess telling what she remembers and what she had heard about Sybela Owens. I was thinking the way Aunt May talks. . . . her stories exist because of their parts and each part is a story worth telling . . . the voice seeks to recover everything, that the voice proclaims *nothing is lost*, that the listener is not passive but lives like everything else within the story.

Wideman's most immediate purpose here is to tell the story of the slave woman Sybela Owens who, together with her white master/lover, fled the South, settled on Bruston Hill, the symbolic navel of Homewood, and began the family line that has produced his own family. By embedding Sybela's story of physical and spiritual redemption within a mediation on his brother's grim circumstances, the narrator conveys the continued urgency of such issues for African Americans; he also engages in the metafictional self-reflexiveness that characterizes his generation of American writers as he muses over the act of writing and its problematic relationship to lived events. Wideman has even bigger aims with Sybela, however, for his imaginative energy also transforms her into a mythic female progenitor who becomes a thematic counterpart to the African slave Orion ("Ryan") introduced in the first (and title) story, "Damballah." Like Sybela, Orion resists the degradation of his circumstances, so much so that his unyielding integrity leads to his execution by enraged whites who accuse him of sexual crimes. Before his death, however, he inspires an American-born slave boy with the mysterious power of his native religious beliefs, having taught him to chant to Damballah, the "good serpent of the sky" and a paternal deity whose wisdom and benign oversight make of the cosmos one transcendent family. Despite Wideman's sophisticated postmodernist affinity for refracting illusions of "reality" through multiple conflicting subjectivities, he seeks, finally, an integrative vision in which the mythical and the historical coalesce to offer the hope of spiritual renewal.

Fever

While *Damballah* draws its cumulative power from its unifying narrative sensibility and its consistent focus upon the citizens past and present of Homewood, *Fever: Twelve Stories* demonstrates a much looser internal logic grounded in thematic rather than storytelling interlacings. Once again, Wideman uses the short story to escape the constraints of novelistic continuity and reconfigure—this time through unrelated voices—motifs that assume international proportions. His most striking theme correlates the historical catastrophes of American slavery, the Holocaust, and modern international terrorism, thereby suggesting a common pattern of scapegoating and racist antagonism that transcends the experience of any single group of victims.

"The Statue of Liberty" and "Valaida," for example, both demonstrate how episodes of interracial miscommunication and self-indulgent fantasizing about the imaginary "Other" continually compromise the possibility of real human engagement. Moreover, in the latter story, a Jewish Holocaust survivor relates to his black maid a story of the jazz performer, whose actions in a wartime concentration camp saved his life; her droll response resists the empathy he has attempted to build between them: "Always thought it was just you people over there doing those terrible things to each other." In "Hostages," an Israeli expatriate and daughter of Auschwitz survivors reflects on her first marriage to an Israeli Arab and her current marriage to a wealthy businessman who offers a prime target for Muslim terrorists; finally she sees herself as a hostage to the comfortable but isolated life she leads and meditates on the Talmudic lesson of the Lamed-Vov, or "God's hostages," predestined "sponges drawing mankind's suffering into themselves."

"Fever," the volume's title story—and one of its most accomplished—depicts the 1793 yellow fever epidemic in Philadelphia, a crisis attributed to African slaves brought up north from the Caribbean but in fact resulting from the internally bred corruption of the swamp-ridden city. A metaphor for the pervasive racial contagions of this ironically dubbed "City of Brotherly Love," the fever levels all distinctions of race, gender, and class even as it triggers responses affirming them. The story's protagonist, Richard Allen, is a minister exhausting himself in Christian service to dying whites and blacks alike. Eventually confronted by the angry monologue of an infected Jewish merchant unimpressed by his humanity, he too is told of the Lamed-Vov, the implication being that Allen has been arbitrarily selected "to suffer the reality humankind cannot bear," enduring an unimaginable and unrelieved burden of "earth, grief and misery." A nihilistic voice in the text, Abraham deconstructs Allen's faith and further magnifies the din of conflicting perspectives—past and present, conciliatory and confrontational—that make the story the touchstone of the volume's exploration of compassion as a limited but essential response to incomprehensible suffering, be its origins cosmic or human—or both.

Elsewhere, Wideman contrasts vision versus blindness ("Doc's Story" and "When It's Time to Go") to illustrate very different positionings by African Americans within the racially charged dominant culture through which they try to move. Wideman's attunement to the musical textures of African American culture again asserts itself, as does his interest in the drama of the individual alienated from his root culture by his ambitions. "Surfiction" offers an exercise in postmodern pastiche that is both a self-conscious parody of the imaginative stasis to which contemporary critical and aesthetic practice can lead and a serious study of the ways in which human determination to communicate across the void poignantly subverts even the most sophisticated intellectual distancing devices. Finally, then, the reader of this volume is left musing on the cultural incompatibilities institutionalized by ideologies of difference—racial, gender, ethnic, nationalistic—and the heroic folly of the Richard Allens of the world, who resist them against all odds.

Other Literary Forms

An intensely lyrical novelist and short story writer, John Edgar Wideman has also written works of autobiographical nonfiction. *Brothers and Keepers* blends facts with fictionalized characters and incidents as the author scrutinizes his own relationship to his brother Robert. Wideman is also the author of *Fatheralong: A Meditation on Fathers and Sons, Race and Society.* He has also written regularly on African American topics for *The New York Times Book Review* and has published scholarly work on African American predecessors such as Charles Waddell Chesnutt and W. E. B. Du Bois.

Bibliography

Bell, Bernard W. *The Afro-American Novel and Its Tradition.* Amherst: University of Massachusetts Press, 1987. Bell provides a short but incisive overview of Wideman's evolving concerns as an African American as well as a postmodernist innovator. He also notes Wideman's evocative uses of history as an imaginative paradigm and identifies as his major theme "the conflict between [his protagonists'] ascribed and achieved identities as black men."

Bennion, John. "The Shape of Memory in John Edgar Wideman's *Sent for You Yesterday.*" *Black American Literature Forum* 20, nos. 1/2 (Spring/Summer, 1986): 143-150. Bennion argues that the reader's struggle to grasp the "foreign and familiar" aspects of Wideman's *Sent for You Yesterday* mirrors the struggle the characters undergo to apprehend their experiences. One's ordering of reality is made possible only through a complex negotiation between order and chaos.

Berben, Jacqueline. "Beyond Discourse: The Unspoken Versus Words in the Fiction of John Edgar Wideman." *Callaloo* 8 (1985): 525-534. Although this essay is primarily a study of the novel *Hiding Place*, the second volume in the Homewood Trilogy, Berben also discusses the mythic character of Homewood as it unfolds in *Damballah*. Berben's argument that Wideman regularly evaluates his characters according to their ability to deal with truth and break free from self-delusion offers useful insight into all Wideman's writing.

Byerman, Keith Eldon. *John Edgar Wideman: A Study of the Short Fiction*. New York: Twayne, 1998. A critical look at Wideman's short fiction, including interview material. Includes a bibliography and an index.

Carden, Mary Paniccia. "'If the City Is a Man': Founders and Fathers, Cities and Sons in John Edgar Wideman's *Philadelphia Fire*." *Contemporary Literature* 44, no. 3 (Fall, 2003): 472-501. Reexamines the impact of African American activism during the 1960's and 1970's. Argues that Philadelphia represents both the history of colonialism and slavery as well as the uncertain future of African American men in the novel.

Coleman, James W. *Blackness and Modernism: The Literary Career of John Edgar Wideman*. Jackson: University Press of Mississippi, 1989. The book contends that Wideman's fiction has evolved from a modernist emphasis on alienation and despair to a postmodernist portrayal of black communities that are strong and sustaining. Coleman evaluates the fiction for its fantasy, surrealism, magic, ritual, folklore, and mainstream influences. He appends an interview with Wideman on changes in the fiction.

_____. "Going Back Home: The Literary Development of John Edgar Wideman." *CLA Journal* 27 (March, 1985): 326-343. Coleman considers how Wideman transforms his childhood neighborhood into myth that unifies and directs *The Homewood Trilogy*. Once they can connect to their ancestors' lives, alienated and isolated characters in the books can revitalize themselves and rejoin their communities. Important is Wideman's use of gospel music, scat songs, dreams, oral stories, blues, the numbers game, street vernacular, and other aspects of black American folk culture.

Dreiser, Petra. "Black, Not Blank: Photography's (Invisible) Archives in John Edgar Wideman's *Two Cities*." *A Journal for the Interdisciplinary Study of Literature* 37, no. 4 (December, 2004):

185-202. Explores the crucial role assumed by photography in Wideman's novel and explains its power as a transforming agent.

Dubey, Madhu. "Literature and Urban Crisis: John Edgar Wideman's *Philadelphia Fire.*" *African American Review* 32 (Winter, 1998): 579-595. Dubey examines *Philadelphia Fire* in relation to its implicit critique of urban renewal and its attenuating glorification of consumption and excess, legitimation of law and order, and the resulting dispossession, displacement, and segregation of the city's inhabitants.

Gysin, Fritz. "John Edgar Wideman: 'Fever.'" In *The African-American Short Story: 1970 to 1990*, edited by Wolfgang Karrer and Barbara Puschmann-Nalenz. Trier, Germany: Wissenschaftlicher Verlag, 1993. A detailed discussion of the title story of Wideman's 1989 collection. Provides historical background for the 1793 Philadelphia yellow fever epidemic and the part African American citizens played in fighting the epidemic. Analyzes the collage structure of the story and Wideman's use of formal narrative devices of compression, repetition, and telescoping of experiences.

Hume, Kathryn. "Black Urban Utopia in Wideman's Later Fiction." *Race & Class* 45, no. 3 (January-March, 2004): 19-35. Discusses the importance of utopian ideals in *Philadelphia Fire, Two Cities*, and *Hoop Roots*.

Literary Cavalcade. "John Edgar Wideman: A Return to His Roots." 57, no. 8 (May, 2005): 39-40. Provides a brief overview of Wideman's extraordinary achievements as a scholar and author.

Mbalia, Doreatha D. *John Edgar Wideman: Reclaiming the African Personality.* London: Associated University Presses, 1995. Examines the African influences on Wideman's work. Includes bibliographical references and an index.

O'Brien, John, ed. *Interviews with Black Writers.* New York: Liveright, 1973. In this early interview, Wideman sets forth his interest in aesthetic experimentation at the expense of fictional realism, his penchant for fabulation, and the relationship between his racial subjects and his artistic choices in rendering them.

Pinckney, Darryl. "The Hunted." Review of *God's Gym*, by John Edgar Wideman. *The New York Review of Books*, March 24, 2005, 59-62. A review of Wideman's recent book.

Rafferty, Terrence. "Pumping Irony." Review of *God's Gym*, by John Edgar Wideman. *The New York Times Book Review*, March 20, 2005, 20-21. A second *New York Times* review of Wideman's book.

Rushdy, Ashraf. "Fraternal Blues: John Edgar Wideman's Homewood Trilogy." *Contemporary Literature* 32, no. 3 (Fall, 1991): 312-345. Rushdy begins by suggesting that the narrator of the trilogy utilizes three modes of narrating which are depicted in the three texts, *Damballah*, *Hiding Place*, and *Sent for You Yesterday*, respectively: letters, stories, and "the blues." He argues that the narrative voice gains an understanding of self when it finds a "blues voice." Rushdy discusses "achieving a blues mind," which, he asserts, is based upon impulses borrowed from blues, jazz, and gospel music.

Wideman, John Edgar. "The Black Writer and the Magic of the Word." *The New York Times Book Review*, January 24, 1988, 1, 27-28. Wideman explains his commitment to preserving black American patterns of speech. He shows that the double entendre and sound variation in the English of black American speakers are conscious attempts to establish self-esteem and respond to the manipulations of whites. He contends that black writers have been frustrated by publishers and critics who measure their worth according to fluctuating standards of literate speech.

_____. *Conversations with John Edgar Wideman*. Edited by Bonnie TuSmith. Jackson: University Press of Mississippi, 1998. Compiles interviews with Wideman that span thirty-five years. The interviews are framed around the publication of his various novels, short stories and autobiographical works. In her introduction, TuSmith represents Wideman as a man committed to his craft, compassionate about his subjects, and engaged in refining and revising his acts of representation.

_____. "Going Home: A Conversation with John Edgar Wideman." Interview by Wilfred D. Samuels. *Callaloo* 6 (February, 1983): 40-59. This interview investigates how Wideman has found creative inspiration in his family history, African heritage, and black American folk culture. He discusses his concern for reaching black American readers and his transition from mainstream academic pursuits to the study of black American literature.

_____. *Hoop Roots.* Boston: Houghton Mifflin, 2001. Wideman's reflection on his enduring relationship to the game of basketball. Basketball frequently appears in the author's fiction and has played a pivotal role in Wideman's personal life. Wideman uses the game to explore issues of aging, love, race, and even music.

_____. "John Edgar Wideman." In *Conversations with American Novelists,* edited by Kay Bonetti, Greg Michaelson, Speer Morgan, Jo Sapp, and Sam Stowers. Columbia: University of Missouri Press, 1997. In this interview by Kay Bonetti, Wideman discusses the oral tales told to him by his aunt, which he developed into the stories in the Homewood Trilogy. Talks about the politics of writing in America, the risks writers have to take to write truthfully about themselves and those they love, and his fiction's concern with brotherhood and sisterhood.

Wilson, Matthew. "The Circles of History in John Edgar Wideman's *The Homewood Trilogy.*" *CLA Journal* 33 (March, 1990): 239-259. Wilson argues the Homewood sequence as a nontraditional family chronicle. The essay examines interconnections among individual family histories, events from American enslavement, and the histories of the Fon and Kongo cultures. A central theme of the trilogy is that black Americans resist annihilation and vanquish the oppressive acts of whites by telling their own stories and exposing their authentic histories.

— Heather Russell Andrade; Margaret Boe Birns;
Barbara A. McCaskill; Barbara Kitt Seidman

John A. Williams

Novelist

Born: Jackson, Mississippi; December 5, 1925

LONG FICTION: *The Angry Ones,* 1960 (also known as *One for New York*); *Night Song,* 1961; *Sissie,* 1963; *The Man Who Cried I Am,* 1967; *Sons of Darkness, Sons of Light: A Novel of Some Probability,* 1969; *Captain Blackman,* 1972; *Mothersill and the Foxes,* 1975; *The Junior Bachelor Society,* 1976; *!Click Song,* 1982; *The Berhama Account,* 1985; *Jacob's Ladder,* 1987; *Clifford's Blues,* 1998.

DRAMA: *Last Flight from Ambo Ber,* pr. 1981; *Vanqui,* pr. 1999 (libretto).

POETRY: *Safari West,* 1998.

NONFICTION: *Africa: Her History, Lands, and People,* 1962; *The Protectors: The Heroic Story of the Narcotics Agents, Citizens, and Officials in Their Unending, Unsuing Battles Against Organized Crime in America and Abroad,* 1964 (as J. Dennis Gregory, with Harry J. Ansliger); *This Is My Country Too,* 1965; *The Most Native of Sons: A Biography of Richard Wright,* 1970; *The King God Didn't Save: Reflections on the Life and Death of Martin Luther King, Jr.,* 1970; *Flashbacks: A Twenty-Year Diary of Article Writing,* 1973; *Minorities in the City,* 1975; *If I Stop I'll Die: The Comedy and Tragedy of Richard Pryor,* 1991 (with Dennis A. Williams).

EDITED TEXTS: *The Angry Black,* 1962; *Beyond the Angry Black,* 1966; *Amistad 1,* 1970 (with Charles F. Harris); *Amistad 2,* 1971 (with Harris); *The McGraw-Hill Introduction to Literature,* 1985 (with Gilbert H. Muller); *Way B(l)ack Then and Now: A Street Guide to African Americans in Paris,* 1992 (with Michel Fabré); *Bridges: Literature Across Cultures,* 1994 (with Muller, author).

Achievements

One of the most prolific and influential writers of his era, John A. Williams infused his works with self-exploration, reflecting the collective social experience of African Americans. He lectured widely, contributed extensively to anthologies, and edited numerous collections, such as *The Angry Black, Beyond the Angry Black, Amistad 1, Amistad 2, The McGraw-Hill Introduction to Literature, Way B(l)ack Then and Now: A Street Guide to African Americans in Paris,* and *Bridges: Literature Across Cultures.* In the 1970's, he was a contributing editor for such publications as *American Journal* and *Politicks,* and in the 1980's he served in a similar capacity for the distinguished, groundbreaking publication *Journal of African Civilizations.*

Williams was the recipient of numerous awards, beginning with his recognition in 1962 by the National Institute of Arts and Letters. His other honors and achievements include the Richard Wright-Jacques Roumain Award (1973), the National Endowment for the Arts award (1977), the Lindback Award for Distinguished Teaching, Rutgers University (1982), the American Book Award for *!Click Song* (1983), the New Jersey Literary Hall of Fame Michael Award (1987), the American Book Award for *Safari West* (1998), and induction into the National Literary Hall of Fame (1998).

Biography

John Alfred Williams was born near Jackson, Mississippi, in Hinds County, to Ola and John Henry Williams. Williams's mother, whose African name means "Keeper of the Beautiful House" or "He Who Wants to Be Chief," had been born in Mississippi; his father's roots were in Syracuse, New York, where the couple met. When Williams was six months old, he returned with his mother to Syracuse. The family resided in the multiethnic Fifteenth Ward, and Williams attended Washington Irving Elementary, Madison Junior High, and Central High School. Joining the Navy in 1943, Williams served in the Pacific, and after discharge in 1946 and his return to Syracuse he completed his secondary education, followed by a brief term at Morris Brown College in Atlanta and then enrollment at Syracuse University, where he studied creative writing. In 1947, he married Carolyn Clopton, with whom he had two sons, Gregory and

(Library of Congress)

Dennis. In 1950, Williams earned his B.A. and continued at Syracuse to pursue graduate study. During this period, he worked at a variety of jobs—foundry work, social work, public relations, insurance, radio and television—while developing as a journalist. Following the failure of his marriage in 1952 and a brief stay in California in 1954, he was determined to become a professional writer. In 1946, he contributed pieces to the Syracuse newspaper, the *Progressive Herald,* continuing through 1955 as a reporter for the *Chicago Defender,* the *Pittsburgh Courier,* the *Los Angeles Tribune,* and the *Village Voice.*

After moving to New York in 1954, he worked for a vanity publisher, Comet Press, in 1955-1956 and at Abelard-Schuman in 1957-1958. In 1958, Williams was director of information for the American Committee on Africa, a reporter for *Jet* magazine, and a stringer for the Associated Negro Press. Based in Barcelona for a period, he was employed in 1959 by WOV Radio in New York; his first published novel, *The Angry Ones*, appeared in 1960.

Though Williams was nominated in 1962 for the Prix de Rome by the American Academy of Arts and Letters, his name was withdrawn for reasons that Williams attributed to his upcoming interracial marriage. In 1963 Williams contributed an article to *Ebony* magazine and began writing for *Holiday*. He became an Africa correspondent for *Newsweek* in 1964, and in 1965 he married Lorrain Isaac, with whom he had a son, Adam. Williams began his career in higher education in 1968, teaching at the College of the Virgin Islands and the City College of New York. He held positions at the University of California at Santa Barbara, University of Hawaii, Boston University, New York University, University of Houston, and Bard College. From 1979 to 1994 he taught at Rutgers University while continuing his literary activities. Following the publication of *Safari West* in 1998, his long-awaited novel—his first in twelve years—*Clifford's Blues*, was published.

Analysis: Long Fiction

Williams's novels draw on personal experience, though they are not strictly autobiographical; they reflect the racial issues facing American society, especially during the civil rights period. Williams writes in the clear, readable prose of the journalist; his plot structures mix linear time with flashback passages to achieve a seamless continuity. His characters have been writers, jazz musicians, black mothers, and military veterans, and his themes have addressed the hardships of the black writer, the expatriate in Europe, black family life, interracial relationships, and political conspiracy. The presentation of jazz is a frequent element, and New York City is a repeated setting, though Williams has also depicted the Caribbean and Africa.

The Angry Ones
Williams's initial novel is a first-person narrative drawing on autobiographical elements. Like Williams, Stephen Hill, the African American main character, is a World War II veteran who works for a vanity press in New York. Early in the novel, Williams refers to African and Native American origins and jazz contexts. The novel is principally about Steve's relationships with his employer, coworkers, and friends. One of Steve's closest associates is Linton Mason, a white former collegemate and editor at McGraw-Hill. The novel uses Lint's success in publishing to indicate the racial divide, sexual jealousy, and the benefits of being white in America. Another theme is the search for a meaningful relationship, the choice between interracial and intraracial love. The causes of black "anger" are linked to Steve's frustrating attempts to rise within the company run by Rollie Culver and, generally, the treatment of black men in New York's publishing world, symbolized by the suicide of Steve's black friend Obie Roberts. The novel presents racism through the day-to-day experiences of the main character.

Night Song
Set in Greenwich Village, New York, in the 1950's, *Night Song* is a "jazz novel" that mirrors the life of famed alto saxophonist Charlie Parker through the portrayal of Eagle (Richie Stokes), a drug-addicted musician who retains the capabilities of jazz performance despite his debilitation. Eagle befriends the alcoholic David Hillary, an out-of-work white college professor employed in the jazz café run by Keel Robinson, a former black preacher and Harvard graduate involved in an interracial relationship with Della. Each of the characters is fractured, most notably Eagle, whose alcoholism and addiction are implicitly the result of the racist treatment of the black artist. Williams portrays David as a savior and betrayer of Eagle; David's "healing" is the ironic result of his association with Eagle, Keel, and Della.

Sissie
Titled after the mother of two principal characters, Iris and Ralph, *Sissie* is divided into four parts. Through memories, the

novel presents the stories of Iris, Ralph, and Sissie Joplin, with Sissie's history revealed in parts 3 and 4, resulting in a Joplin family saga. Iris's story, her failed marriage, her career in Europe, and her relationship with the jazz musician called Time, is the first extended flashback. Ralph's recollections, his experiences in the military, and his struggle as a writer in New York are presented through psychoanalysis, a device that reveals racial issues from the viewpoint of a white psychologist, a symbol of societal norms. Sissie Joplin, a matriarchal figure, has an affair that threatens the stability of her marriage, which undergoes numerous challenges, such as the difficulty of surviving economic hard times and the struggle to find personal fulfillment through love. Sissie is ultimately the catalyst for Ralph and Iris's recognition of their family's conflicted yet sustaining experiences.

The Man Who Cried I Am

Williams's best-received and perhaps most influential work, *The Man Who Cried I Am* revolves around Max Reddick, an African American writer reunited in Amsterdam with his Dutch former wife, Margrit. Williams presents, within a twenty-four-hour time period, the downward spiral of Reddick, a Chester Himes figure, who is suffering from colon cancer. Through flashbacks, Reddick's recollections of a thirty-year past present the social experience of black Americans through the civil rights era. The novel portrays Reddick's association with Harry Ames, a character based on black novelist Richard Wright, who has uncovered the King Alfred Plan, a plot to place America's black population in concentration camps. Other characters in the novel also resemble actual black writers or political figures, such as Marion Dawes, a James Baldwin type; Paul Durrell, a Martin Luther King, Jr., replica; and Minister Q, a Malcolm X parallel. Furthermore, Williams develops African characters, such as Jaja Enzkwu, who reveals the King Alfred Plan to Harry Ames. The involvement of the Central Intelligence Agency (CIA) in Reddick's death points to an international conspiracy against black people, demonstrating Williams's tragic vision of global race relations.

Captain Blackman
An exploration of black contributions in American wars, this novel employs a narrative strategy in which time is fluid. At the outset, Captain Blackman, a Vietnam soldier who teaches his troops the history of black Americans in the military, is wounded and trapped by the Viet Cong. His hallucinations are used to develop scenes in various periods of American wars, from the American Revolution through Vietnam. In these settings, Blackman experiences battle and the racial circumstances affecting black troops. The novel mixes fictional characterizations with historical fact, as in the reference to the Battle of Bunker Hill in the American Revolution. Williams portrays a possible nuclear armageddon, in which black people become the forces of control, though the reversal of power from black to white is itself part of the dream visions of Blackman.

!Click Song
Considered by Williams at the time to be the novel in which he achieved the most effective coalescence of his literary intentions, *!Click Song*, titled after a vocal sound found in the Xhosa language of South Africa, parallels two writers, one black, the other white and Jewish. Using flashbacks, manipulating linear time, the narrative develops the literary careers of Cato Douglass and Paul Cummings. Divided into three sections, "Beginnings," "Middle," and "Endings," *!Click Song* uses the first-person narrator, Cato, as a representation of the journey of the black American writer. Beginning with the funeral of Paul, who committed suicide, the novel returns to the undergraduate experiences of the two veterans pursuing creative writing, circumstances that suggest the author's biography. Parallels to Williams's life are inescapable, especially in the treatment of Cato's career. However, Williams goes beyond mere autobiography by using Cato to symbolize the black artist who resists cultural falsehood, as in the closing section in which Cato in the 1960's offers a countertext to the withholding of information about black culture by major museums.

Jacob's Ladder

Jacob's Ladder explores the predicament of an African American military attaché, Jacob Henry (Jake), caught in the turmoil of American destabilizing efforts in Pandemi, a fictitious West African country, where he had spent part of his youth as the son of a black American missionary. Resembling Liberia, Pandemi is ruled by Chuma Fasseke, Jake's childhood friend. The government of Chuma Fasseke has replaced that of the Franklins, a family descended from nineteenth century repatriated African Americans. The novel also offers a parallel to Nigeria in the portrayal of Taiwo Shaguri, the head of state of Temian. Containing elements of an espionage thriller, *Jacob's Ladder* proposes that an African country can attain nuclear capabilities. Williams humanizes Jake and Fasseke, creating a work deeper than clandestine intrigue. The final sections describe the fall of Fasseke and the takeover of the nuclear power plant by his opposition, assisted by the CIA. The epilogue uses the ironic device of the press release to show the perspective of the international press.

Other Literary Forms

Known primarily as a novelist but also a short-story writer, John A. Williams has produced an extraordinary number of nonfiction pieces, many of them journalistic. He was among the first African Americans of his generation to write a fact book about Africa, *Africa: Her History, Lands, and People*. His treatment of 1960's social issues can be found in *The Protectors*, containing stories about narcotics agents. *This Is My Country Too* documents Williams's travels throughout the United States in 1963-1964, from articles serialized in *Holiday* magazine. A controversial work, *The King God Didn't Save* is a critical look at civil rights leader Martin Luther King, Jr.'s public and private life, and *The Most Native of Sons* treats the life of the famed black novelist Richard Wright. A comprehensive compilation of articles, some autobiographical, was published in *Flashbacks: A Twenty-Year Diary of Article Writing*. Williams also produced an award-winning book of poetry, *Safari West*, the play *Last Flight from Ambo Ber*, dealing with the Falashas in Ethiopia, and the libretto for the opera *Vanqui.*

Bibliography

Campbell, James. "Black American in Paris." Review of *The Man Who Cried I Am,* by John A. Williams. *The Nation,* September 27, 2004, 29-33. A recent review of Williams's 1967 book.

Cash, Earl A. *John A. Williams: The Evolution of a Black Writer.* New York: Third Press, 1975. This text is the first book-length study of Williams's works, covering the nonfiction and the novels through *Captain Blackman.*

Evans, Mari. Review of *Clifford's Blues,* by John A. Williams. *The New Crisis* 108, no. 2 (March/April, 2001): 41-42. A review of one of Williams's more recent books.

Fleming, Robert. "John A. Williams: A Writer Beyond 'isms.'" *Black Issues Book Review* 4, no. 4 (July/August, 2002): 46-49. A profile of the author that discusses his literary style and reputation and provides samples of his work.

Gayle, Addison, Jr. *The Way of the New World: The Black Novel in America.* Garden City, N.Y.: Doubleday, 1975. Gayle addresses the shift from protest to history in *The Man Who Cried I Am* and *Captain Blackman.*

Muller, Gilbert H. *John A. Williams.* Boston: Twayne, 1984. Containing a chronology and thematic approach, this study is a comprehensive treatment of Williams's life and work through *!Click Song.*

Nadel, Alan. "My Country Too: Time, Place, and Afro-American Identity in the Work of John Williams." *Obsidian II* 2, no. 3 (1987): 25-41. This article examines selected nonfiction and fiction, showing political orientation and modernist patterns.

Ramsey, Priscilla R. "John A. Williams: The Black American Narrative and the City." In *The City in African-American Literature,* edited by Yoshinobu Hakutani and Robert Butler. Madison, N.J.: Fairleigh Dickinson University Press, 1995. Focusing on urban realities, this study offers an overview of selected Williams novels.

Reilly, John M. "Thinking History in *The Man Who Cried I Am.*" *Black American Literature Forum* 21, nos. 1/2 (1987): 25-42.

Reilly considers Williams's novel in relation to naturalism and history.

Ro, Sigmund. "Toward the Post-Protest Novel: The Fiction of John A. Williams." In *Rage and Celebration: Essays on Contemporary Afro-American Writing*. Atlantic Highlands, N.J.: Humanities Press, 1984. This essay argues that Williams's novels develop from protest fiction to novelistic treatments of 1960's racial issues.

Rogers, Michael. Review of *The Man Who Cried I Am*, by John A. Williams. *Library Journal* 129, no. 11 (June, 2004): 111-117. A thorough review of Williams's book.

— Joseph McLaren

August Wilson

Playwright

Born: Pittsburgh, Pennsylvania; April 27, 1945
Died: Seattle, Washington; October 2, 2005

DRAMA: *Ma Rainey's Black Bottom,* pr. 1984, pb. 1985; *Fences,* pr., pb. 1985; *Joe Turner's Come and Gone,* pr. 1986, pb. 1988; *The Piano Lesson,* pr. 1987, pb. 1990; *Two Trains Running,* pr. 1990, pb. 1992; *Three Plays,* pb. 1991; *Seven Guitars,* pr. 1995, pb. 1996; *Jitney,* pr. 2000, pb. 2001; *King Hedley II,* pr. 2001; *Gem of the Ocean,* pr. 2003; *How I Learned What I Learned,* pr. 2003; *Radio Golf,* pr. 2005.
TELEPLAYS: *The Piano Lesson,* 1995 (adaptation of his play).
NONFICTION: *The Ground on Which I Stand,* 2000.

Achievements

Critics have hailed August Wilson as an authentic voice of African American culture. His plays explore the black experience historically and in the context of deeper metaphysical roots in African culture. His major plays have been successfully produced by regional theaters and on Broadway; in fact, he became the first African American playwright to have two plays running on Broadway simultaneously.

Wilson received an impressive array of fellowships, awards, and honorary degrees: the Jerome Fellowship in 1980, the Bush Foundation Fellowship in 1982, membership in the New Dramatists starting in 1983, and the Rockefeller Fellowship in 1984. He was also an associate of Playwrights Center, Minneapolis, and received the McKnight Fellowship in 1985, the Guggenheim Fellowship in 1986, six New York Drama Critics Circle Awards from 1985 to 2001, the Whiting Foundation Award in 1986, the Pulitzer Prize in drama in 1987 (for *Fences*) and 1990 (for *The Piano Lesson*), the Tony Award by the League of New York Theatres and Producers (for *Fences*), the American Theatre Critics Award in 1986, the Outer Circle Award in 1987, and the Drama Desk Award and John Gassner Award in 1987.

Wilson's goals were "to concretize the black cultural response to the world, to place that response in loud action, so as to create a dramatic literature as powerful and sustaining as black American music." While the form of his plays breaks no new ground, the substance and language produce powerful emotional responses. Rooted in the black experience, Wilson's plays touch universal chords.

Biography

August Wilson was born in Pittsburgh, Pennsylvania, on April 27, 1945, in the Hill District, a black neighborhood. He was one of six children born to Daisy Wilson from North Carolina, and a German baker, Frederick August Kittel, who eventually abandoned the family. Wilson left school at fifteen when a teacher refused to take his word that a twenty-page paper on Napoleon was his own work. He spent the next few weeks in the library, pretending to be at school. It was through reading, especially all the books he could find in the "Negro" subject section, that Wilson educated himself.

Later, he worked at odd jobs and spent time on street corners and at a cigar store called Pat's Place, listening to old men tell stories. Coming into adulthood during the Black Power movement of the 1960's, Wilson was influenced by it and participated in the Black Arts movement in Pittsburgh, writing and publishing poetry in black journals. With longtime friend Rob Penny, he founded the Black Horizons Theatre Company in Pittsburgh in 1968. He produced and directed plays, but his efforts at playwriting in those years failed, he later recalled, because he "didn't respect the way blacks talked" so he "always tried to alter it." He formed a connection with the Penumbra company in St. Paul and moved there in 1978. It was in this much smaller black community that he learned to regard the "voices I had been brought up with all my life" with greater respect.

Married in 1981 to Judy Oliver (he had a daughter, Sakina

Ansari, from an earlier marriage), Wilson began to write scripts for the children's theater of a local science museum. This effort led him to submit his scripts to the National Playwrights Conference at the Eugene O'Neill Center in Waterford, Connecticut. His work caught the attention of conference director Lloyd Richards, who was also the dean of the Yale School of Drama and the artistic director of the Yale Repertory Company. Under Richards's direction, a staged reading of *Ma Rainey's Black Bottom* was performed in 1982 at the Eugene O'Neill Center, followed by a production at Yale and a Broadway success. The succeeding plays by Wilson followed the same pattern, with intervening production at regional theaters. Wilson eventually dissolved his relationship with Richards and turned to director Marion McClinton to stage *Jitney* and *King Hedley II*.

Divorced in 1990, Wilson moved to Seattle, Washington, where he continued to write his cycle of plays. He also participated as a dramaturge at the Eugene O'Neill Center when one of his own works was not being produced. After *Seven Guitars*,

(AP/Wide World Photos)

Wilson and his coproducer, Ben Mordecai, formed a joint venture called Sageworks, which gave Wilson artistic and financial control of his plays both as a writer and producer. Wilson refined his plays through a series of separate productions, writing and editing through each production's rehearsal process. Before reaching its New York run, *King Hedley II* received six regional productions. Wilson married Constanza Romero, and they had a daughter, Azula. In 2005, as his play *Radio Golf* was being completed, Wilson announced that he had advanced liver cancer. He died within a few months, at the age of sixty.

Analysis: Drama

Each of August Wilson's major plays dramatizes the African American experience in a different decade of the twentieth century, and the action of each play is driven by the arrival or presence of a character who has what Wilson called the "warrior spirit," the quality that makes a man dissatisfied and determined to change or disrupt the status quo. Each of the plays is affected by Wilson's feeling for the blues, music that he called the "flag bearer of self-definition" for African Americans. Characters sing the blues, music is called for in scene transitions, and the rhythms of the dialogue reflect the blues. His plays are written to be performed on a single setting with action that is chronological. While he wrote within the genre of psychological realism, each play displays a different degree of adherence to structure and plotting. His characters, mostly men, are African Americans uncertain of their own places in the world.

One of Wilson's greatest strengths was with language: The authenticity and rhythms of the dialogue and the colorful vitality of metaphor and storytelling connect him to the oral tradition of the African American and African cultures. He discussed in an interview the indirect quality of black speech, with its circling of issues and answers that are not answers. Characters answer the question they think is intended, not necessarily the one that is expressed. This language, in fact, often becomes the unique poetry of his drama. The language is full of implied meanings and dependent on tonal quality for interpretation.

Wilson also placed increasing emphasis with each play on the superstitions and beliefs that affect his characters. These superstitions seem to come from a mixture of Christianity, ancient African religions, and street wisdom.

Ma Rainey's Black Bottom

In *Ma Rainey's Black Bottom*, Wilson uses a historical figure, "Mother of the Blues" singer Ma Rainey, and invents a story around her. The setting is a simultaneous representation of a 1927 recording studio and a band-rehearsal room. Overlooking the studio from the control booth are Ma's white producer and white agent, their presence and location a graphic symbol of white society's control over black music.

The dialogue seems to meander through silly and inconsequential matters. The underlying seriousness of these matters becomes apparent as the characters reveal their ways of coping with the white world. Ma Rainey plays the prima donna (note the pun in the play's title) while she acknowledges to her band that, like all black artists, she is exploited. Her music is her "way of understanding life." Wilson centers her in the play, a dynamic and colorful presence, but the character central to the action is Levee.

Levee has that warrior spirit. The tragic irony is that when he lashes out and kills, he kills the only educated band member in the play. His urge for self-sufficiency (to have his own band and make his own music) becomes self-destructive. By application, Wilson suggests that the misplaced rage of his race can result in self-destruction. The grimly serious resolution to this play does not describe the tone of lightness and humor in much that precedes it. It is Levee's appetite that drives the play, sometimes comically, and it is his frustrated hunger that causes an unnecessary death.

Fences

Wilson's second major work, *Fences*, won a Pulitzer Prize in drama as well as Tony Awards for Wilson, the director, and two actors. It centers on the dynamic, volatile character Troy Maxson and takes place primarily in 1957. Troy is the warrior character whose spirit disrupts his own life as well as those of his sons and wife. Often inviting comparison with Arthur Miller's *Death of a Salesman* (pr., pb. 1949), the play dramatizes the life of a baseball player prevented from realizing his big-league dreams by the color barrier, overcome too late for him. *Fences* is about a man's battle with life and his emotional, sometimes irrational way of facing unfairness, pain, love, and hate. The fence that Troy built around his life, like that built around his home, could neither shut out the world's injustice nor protect his family or himself from his shortcomings. The final scene occurs after Troy's death in 1965, when others can express feelings about Troy that were not articulated before. This scene provides a quietly emotional contrast to the intensely alive Troy of the previous eight scenes. It is a necessary scene and yet points up the failure of father and son to express directly what they felt in their earlier confrontation.

Troy's brother, Gabriel, whose head injury from the war has made him believe himself to be God's angel Gabriel, provides a kind of mystical presence. Wilson uses his madness for a theatrically effective closing to the play. When Gabriel discovers that his horn will not blow to open the gates of heaven for Troy, he performs a weird "dance of atavistic signature and ritual" and howls a kind of song to open the gates. This marked the beginning of Wilson's increasing use of ritual, myth, and superstition in his plays.

Joe Turner's Come and Gone

In *Joe Turner's Come and Gone*, Wilson reaches farther back into the historical black experience. As in the old blues song of the same title, the brother of the governor of Tennessee, Joe Turner, found and enslaved groups of black men. Herald Loomis, the mysterious central character in this play, was so enslaved in 1901 and not released for seven years. The play dramatizes his search for his wife, which is actually a search for himself. His arrival at a Pittsburgh boardinghouse in 1911 disrupts and disturbs, creating the tension and significance of the drama.

Another boardinghouse resident, Bynum, establishes his identity as a "conjure man" or "rootworker" early in the play.

Bynum's search for his "shiny man" becomes a thematic and structural tie for the play. At the end of the first act, during a joyous African call-and-response dance, Loomis has a sort of ecstatic fit, ending with his being unable to stand and walk. Some kind of dramatic resolution must relate Bynum's vision and Loomis's quest. It comes in the final scene when wife Martha returns and Loomis learns that his quest is still unrealized. Wilson describes Loomis's transformation in actions rather than words. His wife does not restore him, nor does her religion restore him. In desperation, he turns a knife on himself, rubs his hands and face in his own blood, looks down at his hands, and says, "I'm standing. My legs stood up! I'm standing now!" It is at this point that he has found his "song of self-sufficiency." Wilson's rather poetic stage directions articulate a redemption that Loomis cannot verbalize, risking audience misinterpretation.

Bynum's final line of the play recognizes Loomis as a shiny man, the shiny man who can tell him the meaning of life. The suggestion of a Christ figure is unmistakable, and yet Loomis's soul is not cleansed through religious belief. He has denied the Christ of the white man, despite Martha's pleading. His epiphany is in finding himself. Joe Turner has come but he has also gone. Herald Loomis finds his identity in his own African roots, not in the slave identity that the white Joe Turner had given him.

The Piano Lesson
With his fourth major play, Wilson crafted a more tightly structured plot. In fact, *The Piano Lesson* is stronger thematically and structurally than it is in character development. The characters serve to dramatize the conflict between the practical use of a family heritage to create a future, and a symbolic treasuring of that heritage to honor the past. The piano, which bears the blood of their slave ancestors, is the focus of the conflict between Boy Willie and his sister, Berniece. Its exotic carvings, made by their great-grandfather, tell the story of their slave ancestors who were sold in exchange for the piano. Its presence in the northern home of Berniece and her Uncle Doaker represents the life of their father who died stealing it back from Sutter.

Berniece is embittered and troubled not only by the piano and her father's death but also by her mother's blood and tears that followed that death and by the loss of her own husband. In contrast, Boy Willie is upbeat and funny, an optimistic, ambitious, and boyish man who is sure he is right in wanting to sell the piano to buy Sutter's land. He has the warrior spirit. Throughout the play, the presence of Sutter's ghost is seen or felt. Sutter's ghost seems to represent the control that the white man still exerts over this family in 1937. Boy Willie chooses to ignore the ghost, to accuse his sister of imagining it, but ultimately it is Boy Willie who must wrestle with the ghost.

Wilson said that this play had five endings because Berniece and Boy Willie are both right. The conflict is indeed unresolved as Boy Willie leaves, telling Berniece that she had better keep playing that piano or he and Sutter could both come back. The lesson of the piano is twofold: Berniece has learned that she should use her heritage, rather than let it fester in bitterness, and Boy Willie has learned that he cannot ignore the significance of this piano, which symbolizes the pain and suffering of all of his ancestors. There is little in the play that deviates from the central conflict. The skill of Wilson's writing is seen in the interplay of characters bantering and arguing, in the indirect quality of questions that are not answered, and in the storytelling. While characters may serve primarily as symbols and plot devices, they are nevertheless vivid and credible.

Two Trains Running
The disruptive character in Wilson's fifth play is Sterling, but the theme of *Two Trains Running*, set in 1969, is found in the character Memphis, the owner of the restaurant in which the action occurs. Memphis came north in 1936, driven away by white violence. He has always meant to return and reclaim his land. In the course of the play, he learns that he has to go back and "pick up the ball" so as not to arrive in the end zone empty handed. He must catch one of those two trains running south every day. He must not surrender.

The major characters in the play represent varying degrees of tenacity. Wilson skillfully builds a plot around two threads:

Memphis's determination to get the city to pay his price for his property, and Sterling's determination to find a place for himself and gain the love of Risa. Hambone is a crazy character, driven mad almost ten years ago when the butcher Lutz across the street refused to pay him a ham for doing a good job of painting his fence. Hollaway, a commentator character, observes that Hambone may be the smartest of them all in his refusal to give up—each day going to Lutz and asking for his ham. The unfortunate fact is, though, that his life has been reduced to this one action; all he can say is "I want my ham. He gonna give me my ham." Risa, a woman determined not to be dependent on a sexual attachment, has scarred her own attractive legs to make herself less desirable. In spite of herself, she is attracted to the vitality and optimism of Sterling, and Sterling is most tenacious of all. His warrior spirit has landed him in prison and may do so again, but his zeal and good humor are compelling.

The constant reminders and presence of death give resonance to the lives and efforts of these people. When the play opens, the Prophet Samuel has already died and the offstage mayhem surrounding the viewing of his body is evident. Characters talk about several other deaths, and no sooner is Prophet Samuel buried than Hambone is discovered dead (again offstage). The reactions to his death make up the ending of the play. Memphis and Sterling, trusting in the prophecies of the 322-year-old seer Aunt Ester, both triumph. Sterling runs across the street, steals a ham, and presents it to Mr. West, the undertaker, to put in Hambone's coffin. This final flourish of the play is an assertion of character identity and life. *Two Trains Running* may be Wilson's most accomplished work in blending character, plot, and theme.

Seven Guitars

Two Trains Running was followed in 1995 by *Seven Guitars*. Set in the 1940's, it tells the tragic story of blues guitarist Floyd Barton, whose funeral opens the play. The action flashes back to recreate the events of Floyd's last week of life. Floyd had arrived in Pittsburgh to try to get his guitar out of the pawnshop and to convince his former lover, Vera, to return with him to Chicago. A record he made years earlier has suddenly gained popularity, and he has been offered the opportunity to record more songs at a studio in Chicago.

The play's central conflicts are Floyd's struggle to move forward in his musical career and his personal strife with Vera and his bandmates. A subplot centers on Floyd's friend Hedley and his deteriorating physical and mental health as his friends attempt to place him in a tuberculosis sanatorium. The play contains some of Wilson's familiar character types, including the mentally aberrant Hedley; the troubled-by-the-law young black male protagonist, Floyd; the capable and independent woman, Louise; and the more needy, younger woman, Ruby. It also contains elements of music, dance, storytelling, violence, and food.

Jitney

Wilson reworked an earlier, short play *Jitney*. Becker, a retired steel-mill worker, runs a jitney station, serving the unofficial taxi needs of the black community of Pittsburgh's Hill district during early autumn of 1977. The jitney drivers are a rich collection of troubled but hard-working men. The station offers the men a living and a sense of independence that is threatened by the city's plans to tear down the neighborhood in the name of urban renewal. Becker also faces a personal crisis. His son, Booster, is about to leave prison after serving twenty years for murdering his well-to-do white girlfriend. Father and son have not spoken for two decades. Becker is bitter that his son threw away a promising career, and Booster sees his father's lifetime of hard work and submissiveness to white landlords and bosses as demeaning. Father and son never reconcile, but they indirectly attempt to redeem themselves to each other. Becker decides to organize the jitney drivers and fight the urban renewal. Yet, just as Becker begins the move to resistance, he falls victim to his rigorous work ethic and dies unexpectedly. As the dispirited drivers praise his father, Booster begins to respect his father's accomplishments and prepares to carry on Becker's mission to save the jitney station.

King Hedley II

King Hedley II takes place in the backyard of a few ramshackle houses in the Hill District of Pittsburgh in 1985. Its protagonist, King Hedley II, is a petty thief and a former convict engaged in selling stolen refrigerators. Believing that he is being held back while everybody else is moving forward, Hedley dreams of a better life. His partner in crime is a shady character named Mister. Hedley's wife, Tonya, is pregnant with a child she does not want to raise in the rough life she knows. Hedley's mother, Ruby, is a former jazz singer who is reunited with an old lover, the con man Elmore. The next-door neighbor, Stool Pigeon, is a crazy old man who stacks old newspapers in his hovel. He is the play's mystic messenger who buries a dead cat in the backyard and brings to its grave various tokens that he believes will bring the animal back to one of its nine lives. The yard, barren except for weeds and garbage, is a major symbol. Hedley tries to raise plants in it, even fencing off a small patch with barbed wire. However, like Hedley's efforts to better himself, the attempt to grow something is doomed.

Other Literary Forms

Although August Wilson is known primarily for his plays, some of his poetry was published in black literary journals, such as *Black World*, in 1969. He published a teleplay, *The Piano Lesson*, in 1995, and a nonfiction work, *The Ground on Which I Stand*, in 2000.

Bibliography

Bigsby, C. W. E. *Modern American Drama, 1945-1990*. Cambridge, England: Cambridge University Press, 1992. The author interviewed Wilson for pertinent biographical data and includes some in-depth analysis of the first four plays.

Bogumil, Mary L. *Understanding August Wilson*. Columbia: University of South Carolina Press, 1999. Bogumil provides readers with a comprehensive view of the thematic structure of Wilson's plays, the placement of his plays within the context of American drama, and the distinctively African American experiences and traditions that Wilson dramatizes.

Brustein, Robert. *Reimagining American Theatre*. New York: Hill & Wang, 1991. Brustein, critic and former artistic director of the Yale Repertory Theatre before Lloyd Richards, is one of the few negative voices criticizing Wilson's drama. He finds particular fault with the mechanisms and symbols of *The Piano Lesson*.

Elam, Harry J. *The Past as Present in the Drama of August Wilson*. Ann Arbor: University of Michigan Press, 2004. An interesting, wide-ranging, and largely positive analysis of Wilson's work.

Elkins, Marilyn, ed. *August Wilson: A Casebook*. New York: Garland, 1994. The essays investigate such thematic, artistic, and ideological concerns as Wilson's use of the South and the black human body as metaphors; his collaboration with Lloyd Richards; the influences of the blues and other writers on his work; his creative method; and his treatment of African American family life.

Herrington, Joan. *I Ain't Sorry for Nothin' I Done: August Wilson's Process of Playwriting*. New York: Limelight Editions, 1998. Herrington traces the roots of Wilson's drama to visual artists such as Romare Bearden and to the jazz musicians who inspire and energize him as a dramatist. She goes on to analyze his process of playwriting—how he brought his experiences and his ideas to stage life—by comparing successive drafts of his first three major plays.

Hill, Holly. "Black Theatre into the Mainstream." In *Contemporary American Theatre*, edited by Bruce King. New York: St. Martin's Press, 1991. Hill's analysis of the plays sets them in the context of their period.

Isherwood, Charles. "August Wilson's 100-Year Memory." *The New York Times*, April 27, 2005, p. E1. Discussion of Wilson's play *Radio Golf* in advance of its appearance at the Yale Repertory Theater. Elaborates on Wilson's writing technique, the play's plot, and some of Wilson's thoughts on the nature of the African American experience.

Miller, Darryl H. "On the Eighteenth Hole: August Wilson's *Radio Golf* Thoughtfully Finishes His Ten-Play Cycle." Review of

Radio Golf, by August Wilson. *Los Angeles Times,* August 12, 2005, p. E1. A very positive review of the play. Lauds the effective portrayal of the hopelessness engendered by postponing dreams.

Nadel, Alan. *May All Your Fences Have Gates.* Iowa City: University of Iowa Press, 1994. Nadel deals individually with five major plays and also addresses issues crucial to Wilson's canon: the role of history, the relationship of African ritual to African American drama, gender relations in the African American community, music and cultural identity, the influence of Romare Beardern's collages, and the politics of drama.

Theater 9 (Summer/Fall, 1988). This special issue includes the script of *The Piano Lesson* with an earlier version of the ending, production photographs, and two informative essays. The articles "Wrestling Against History" and "The Songs of a Marked Man" explore Wilson's themes, especially the importance of myths and superstitions.

Wilson, August. "Influences: August Wilson." Interview by Boris Kachka. *New York,* November 1, 2004, 72-73. An interesting interview that focuses on Wilson's love of reading and books, in particular the books of poet Dylan Thomas.

Wolfe, Peter. *August Wilson.* London: Macmillan, 1999. A comprehensive analysis of Wilson's theater. Wolfe sees the dramatist as exploding stereotypes of the ghetto poor, through his juxtapositions of the ordinary and the African American surreal, which evoke anger, affection, and sometimes hope.

— *Rhona Justice-Malloy; Sally Osborne Norton*

Jay Wright

Poet

Born: Albuquerque, New Mexico; May 25, 1935

POETRY: *Death as History,* 1967; *The Homecoming Singer,* 1971; *Soothsayers and Omens,* 1976; *Dimensions of History,* 1976; *The Double Invention of Komo,* 1980; *Explications/Interpretations,* 1984; *Elaine's Book,* 1986; *Selected Poems of Jay Wright,* 1987; *Boleros,* 1991; *Transfigurations: Collected Poems,* 2000.

Achievements

Jay Wright's poetic vision is unique in its cross-cultural approach to African American spiritual and intellectual history. He has been called one of the most original and powerful voices in contemporary American poetry. Though critical acclaim of his work has been slow in coming, he has received a number of prestigious awards: an Ingram Merrill Foundation Award and a Guggenheim Fellowship in 1974; an American Academy and Institute of Arts and Letters Literature Award in 1981; an Oscar Williams and Gene Derwood Writing Award in 1985; a MacArthur Fellowship that spanned the years 1986-1991; and the Academy of American Poets Fellowship in 1996.

Biography

Jay Wright was born in 1935 in Albuquerque, New Mexico, to Leona Dailey, a Virginian of black and Native American ancestry. His father, George Murphy, a light-complexioned African American construction worker, jitney driver, and handyman who later adopted the name of Mercer Murphy Wright, claimed both Cherokee and Irish descent. Wright remained with his mother until the age of three, when Leona gave the boy to the cook Frankie Faucett and his wife Daisy, a black Albuquerque couple known for taking in children. Daisy Faucett was as religious as her husband was proud and generous. Wright's early, intense exposure to the African American church was attributable to her. Mercer Wright, in the meantime, had relocated to California. It was not until his son was in his early teens that he went to live with his father, and later his stepmother Billie, in San Pedro. During his high school years in San Pedro, Wright began to play baseball. In the early 1950's, he worked as a minor-league catcher for the San Diego Padres, the Fresno Cardinals, and the Aguilars of Mexicali. He also learned to play the bass in those days. In 1954 he joined the Army, and he served in the medical corps until 1957. He was stationed in Germany for most of that time, which gave him the opportunity to travel throughout Europe.

A year after his return to the United States, Wright enrolled in the University of California at Berkeley under the G.I. Bill. At Berkeley, he devised his own major in comparative literature and was graduated after only three years. Before deciding to continue his literary studies, Wright considered studying theology and spent a semester at Union Theological Seminary in New York on a Rockefeller grant. He left Union for Rutgers University in 1962. In 1964, Wright interrupted his graduate studies to spend a year teaching English and medieval history at the Butler Institute in Guadalajara, Mexico. He returned to Rutgers in 1965. During the next three years, Wright completed all the requirements for his doctoral degree except the dissertation. While at Rutgers, Wright lived and worked part-time in Harlem, where he came into contact with a number of other young African American writers, among them Henry Dumas, Larry Neal, and LeRoi Jones (who later changed his name to Amiri Baraka).

In 1968, Wright married Lois Silber, who joined him during his second and longest sojourn in Mexico. The couple lived briefly in Guadalajara and then moved to Jalapa, where they maintained a residence until the autumn of 1971. Many of Wright's poems recall these and other Mexican settings. Wright returned to the United States from time to time, spending brief periods as a writer-in-residence at Tougaloo and Talladega colleges and at Texas Southern University, as well as several months as a Hodder Fellow at Princeton University. In early 1971, the Wrights departed for Scotland. During Wright's two-year tenure as Joseph Compton Creative Writing Fellow at Dundee University, they lived in Penicuik, outside Edinburgh. Upon their return to the United States in 1973, the Wrights moved first to Warren and then to Piermont, New Hampshire.

Wright has traveled extensively throughout Europe, the United States, Central and South America, and Canada. In 1988, he was part of a group of writers who visited the People's Republic of China under the auspices of the University of California at Los Angeles. Since 1975, he has taught at Yale University, at the universities of Utah, Kentucky, and North Carolina at Chapel Hill, and at Dartmouth College.

Analysis: Poetry

The most distinctive feature of Jay Wright's poetry is what he calls "a passion for what is hidden." This passion for sounding the depths of varied histories and mythologies—Western European, African, Caribbean, North and South American, and Asian—takes the poetic shape of a spiritual quest that is at once intensely personal and compellingly collective. The object of Wright's quest is to restore to African American literature a sense of the breadth, the complexity, and the coherence of its cultural, historical, social, artistic, intellectual, and emotional resources. Writing poetry is his way of uncovering and reinventing eclipsed linkages between cultural traditions often believed to be separate. "For me, multicultural is the fundamental process of human history," he explained in a 1983 interview in *Callaloo.*

Wright's work exemplifies what Guyanese novelist Wilson Harris, whom Wright acknowledges as a major source of inspiration, has termed a poetics of the cross-cultural imagination. Wright's autobiographical persona embarks on poetic journeys into uncharted territories where familiar temporal, political, and linguistic boundaries blur and dissolve. Fragmented voices from many different historical periods and cultural traditions emerge as the poet's (and the reader's) guides through a veritable maze of historical and mythological references and allusions that ultimately come together in a rather unorthodox vision of African American or black culture. It is unorthodox within a United States context because of Wright's sensitivity to and insistence on continuities across, not just within, cultures. No African American, Wright insists, "can have escaped grounding in other cultures."

Though his poetic vision is firmly grounded in African American historical experience and expressive culture, Wright's sense of what it means to be a black poet is distinctly different from that of most African American poets of his generation. Even if Wright's quest for creativity time and again leads him to specific African religions and folklore, mainly Akan, Nuer, Dogon, and Bambara, that quest is not predicated on a rejection of "Western" traditions. In that respect, Wright's poetics and cultural politics are more akin to those of Robert Hayden and even Melvin Tolson than to the work of Amiri Baraka and others who embraced black cultural nationalism in the late 1960's and early 1970's.

Wright's poetry is remarkable in its erudite and consistently innovative engagement with a wide variety of literary and cultural traditions. The scope of his vision and the depth of his perception can largely be attributed to Wright's extensive research in medieval and Renaissance literatures, music, anthropology, the history of religions, and the history of science. The notes appended to *Explications/Interpretations, Dimensions of History,* and especially *The Double Invention of Komo* point to some of the principal holdings of Wright's scholarly archives. The most important texts behind his poems are *The Akan Doctrine of God* (1944), by Ghanaian politician and philosopher J. B. Danquah, and the studies of Dogon and Bambara traditional societies conducted in the 1920's and 1930's by a team of French anthropologists under the direction of Marcel Griaule. Most consciously, Wright's poetry takes recourse to Griaule's *Conversations with Ogotemmêli: An Introduction to Dogon Religious Ideas* (1948) and his later collaboration with Germaine Dieterlen, *The Pale Fox* (1965). Yet annotations are atypical for Wright, who, though he yielded to the demands of his publishers in these instances, is usually adamant in his refusal to explicate his poetry to those who find it inaccessible. What lies behind this refusal is not arrogance or obscuration, as some critics have assumed, but what Wright sees as an abiding respect for the complexity and difficulty of the social, cultural, and historical processes his poetry tries to represent. An assimilation of a vast body of knowledge, his poetry demands rigorous intellectual and imaginative engagement from each reader.

The formal experiments in which he engages are as extravagant as the texture of his poetry is dense. A mixture of Italian, German, and Spanish interspersed with Dogon and Bambara ideograms, Wright's language is at times so unfamiliar that to describe it as "English" seems inadequate. Musical forms such as the blues and jazz, as well as a host of Caribbean and Latin American song and dance forms, are as integral to his poetic endeavors as are attempts at making English verse responsive to the "grammars" and metrics of other languages.

The Homecoming Singer

Semantic density and formal extravagance are particularly characteristic of the book-length poems that have followed Wright's first collection, *The Homecoming Singer,* which was preceded in 1967 by a chapbook, *Death as History.* These early poems, most of which are reprinted in *Selected Poems of Jay Wright,* tend to be more manageable from both a thematic and a linguistic point of view. *The Homecoming Singer* is important to Wright's canon not only as a record of his early artistic, spiritual, and intellectual development but also because it contains all the seeds of his later writing. The two opening poems, "Wednesday Night Prayer Meeting" and "The Baptism," inspired by the religious zeal of Daisy Faucett, lament the failure of institutionalized African American religions to provide spiritual resources for what Wright, with Harris, calls "the redefinition of the person." The tragic lack of "myths to scale your life upon" results in "the senseless, weightless,/ timedenying feeling of not being there" with which the poet is left at the end of "Reflections Before the Charity Hospital." Yet rather than leading to the despair and violence of LeRoi Jones's "A Poem for Willie Best," a text on which

Wright brilliantly meditates in "The Player at the Crossroads" and "Variations on a Theme by LeRoi Jones," this alienation and dispossession heighten the poet's awareness, as in "First Principles," of "the tongues of the exiled dead/ who live in the tongues of the living." In "Destination: Accomplished," this new awareness grows into an abiding emotional and intellectual desire for "something to put in place." It is the death-challenging search for "new categories for the soul/ of those I want to keep" that finally directs Wright toward traditional African societies, their rituals and mythologies, in "A Nuer Sacrifice" and "Death As History."

Like all of Wright's poetry, though more explicitly so, *The Homecoming Singer* draws on autobiographical experience as a catalyst for the persona's introspective inquiries into the possible nature of an African American cultural and literary tradition. Memories of his two fathers, in "A Non-Birthday Poem for My Father," "Origins," "First Principles," and "The Hunting-Trip Cook," become occasions for acknowledging and examining the responsibilities the dead confer upon the living. This is what connects these presences from Wright's personal past, which also include his alcoholic stepmother in "Billie's Blues," to "the intense communal daring" of Crispus Attucks and W. E. B. Du Bois.

The Homecoming Singer also acquaints the reader with geographies to which Wright returns throughout his poetic career. In "An Invitation to Madison County," one of the best poems in this collection, the black American South offers unexpected memories and visions of community to the displaced poet, whose journey in this instance follows that of so many other African American writers in search of their cultural origins. The Southwest, which, along with California, provides the setting for Wright's family remembrances, is another place of origin; its history also connects the persona with the Mexico of "Morning, Leaving Calle Gigantes," "Chapultepec Castle," "Jalapeña Gypsies," and "Bosques de Chapultepec." "A Month in the Country" offers a fleeting glimpse of the "New England reticence" of New Hampshire, to which the persona escapes after "The End of an Ethnic Dream" to soothe his "blistered" brain. In later poems, all these places evolve into full-fledged symbolic geographies. "Sketch for an Aesthetic Project" and "Beginning Again," the two poems that close *The Homecoming Singer,* are the initial attempts of the "aching prodigal" at weaving his memories and his discontent into a poetic design that transcends individual experience. These poems are preludes to *Soothsayers and Omens,* the first volume of a poetic cycle that continues with *Explications/Interpretations, Dimensions of History,* and *The Double Invention of Komo.* Each of these book-length poems is part of a carefully constructed pattern or dramatic movement, and this is the order in which Wright places them.

Soothsayers and Omens

The poem that opens the first of *Soothsayers and Omens* four parts is significantly titled "The Charge." Reminiscent of Wright's homages to paternal figures in *The Homecoming Singer,* this poem focuses on fathers and sons "gathered in the miracle/ of our own memories." With "The Appearance of a Lost Goddess" and the rise of a female principle to complement and balance the male presences, the poet identifies himself as an initiate who has accepted the charge to reconstruct neglected and severed ties. This reconstruction takes the initial shape of six short poems titled "Sources" with which Wright inaugurates his systematic exploration of African cosmologies. "Sources" draws heavily on West African precolonial mythologies, both of which become part of a collective memory. The two longer poems that follow and change the pace of the first part, "Benjamin Banneker Helps to Build a City" and "Benjamin Banneker Sends His 'Almanac' to Thomas Jefferson," weave elements of Dogon theology around quotations from the letters of the African American astronomer, an "uneasy" stranger in his own land who bemoans "the lost harmony" and the injustices of slavery.

Dogon ritual becomes even more significant in Part IV, whose title, "Second Conversations with Ogotemmêli," refers directly to Griaule's anthropological exploits. These are poems of apprenticeship that invoke different components and stages of the creation of the universe, represented by the water spirit Nommo, creator of the First Word (that is, language) and his twin Amma, Lébé, guardian of the dead, and the Pale Fox, agent of chaos. Wright's "Conversations" are characterized by exchanges and relationships very different from those that prevail between anthropologist and informer. For Wright's persona, Ogotemmêli is a spiritual guide or "nani" who "will lead me into the darkness" and whose silences promise the speech of redemption with which to mend "the crack in the universe." The terms and trajectory of Wright's journey into darkness, a sort of Middle Passage in reverse that leads back to Africa, are also indebted to Dante's search, even if the spiritual map (the "God") Wright's initiate "designs" is different. It is no coincidence, then, that "Homecoming," the poem that announces "a plan of transformations," is laced with quotations from *La divina commedia* (c. 1320; *The Divine Comedy*).

At the same time that *Soothsayers and Omens* initiates the reader into African mythologies, it also revisits Mexico and New Mexico, geographies already implicit in the pre-Columbian references of the opening poems. The most remarkable of the transitional poems in Parts II and III is "The Albuquerque Graveyard," a place to which Wright's persona returns to worry the dead, the "small heroes," with a quest for patterns that is as "uneasy" as Benjamin Banneker's. The poet's announcement that

> I am going back
> to the Black limbo,
> an unwritten history
> of our own tensions,

is a precise summary of his desire and purpose throughout *Soothsayers and Omens*: both to articulate a history that has not been written and to un-write a history that has neglected, even forgotten—the participation of Africans and African Americans in founding what is deceptively called "Western" civilization.

If *Soothsayers and Omens* is the "first design," the first step toward the articulation of a spiritual order, *Explications/Interpretations* marks the next logical stage in what Wright calls his "African-Hellenic-Judaic discourse." Dedicated to poet Robert

Hayden and critic Harold Bloom, this volume generates somewhat different patterns and principles of order and also introduces a set of new players on a new stage in "MacIntyre, The Captain, and the Saints." This central dramatic poem enacts Wright's personal and intellectual ties with Scotland. MacIntyre, the Irish-Scottish clan to which the names Murphy and Wright can be traced, is Wright's autobiographical persona who, instead of conversing with Ogotemmêli, now turns to astronomer David Hume, poet Hugh MacDiarmid, and anthropologist Robert Sutherland Rattray. A new element in this poem is the use of ideograms, a strategy indebted to Ezra Pound's works, which Wright explores more fully in *Dimensions of History* and *The Double Invention of Komo*. Yet dramatic poetry, a form for which Wright has an undoubted preference, is not the only important formal aspect of this volume. *Explications/Interpretations* is also energized by the vital rhythms of African American music. The poem is divided into three parts, "Polarity's Trio," "Harmony's Trio," and "Love's Dozen," titles that already indicate Wright's concern with music and number. "Tensions and Resolutions" introduces dualism or twinning and balance as concepts that inform the poem's thematic and structural organization: "Each act caresses/ the moment it remembers,/ and the moment it desires." This double "act" is of course the act of writing, which makes Wright's poem a "field of action" along the lines of Charles Olson's "projective verse."

Explications/Interpretations
That the rhythms of writing and speaking are formal articulations of the poet's being is crucial to understanding the dynamics of *Explications/Interpretations* and indeed of all of Wright's poems. The arrangement of the poems in groups of three, six, and twelve (plus one) already creates a sense of rhythm, which is rendered most explicit in "The Twenty-Two Tremblings of the Postulant," subtitled "Improvisations Surrounding the Body." This poem is a good example of Wright's kind of blues poetry, in which the compositional principle is derived not from the call-and-response structure of the blues lyrics, as is the case, for instance, in the poetry of Langston Hughes and Sterling Brown,

but from the arrangement of the twenty-two short poems across a sequence of chords. Each poem corresponds not only to a different part of the human body but also to a musical bar that belongs to a specific chord, I, IV, or V. The last two bars, we are told at the end of the poem, are "tacit," which makes for a total of twenty-four bars, whose musical equivalent is a (doubled) blues line. *Explications/Interpretations* as a whole is a poetic improvisation on this basic blues line, one of the most distinctive rhythms of African American culture. These are the sounds of flesh and bone that constitute the poem's and the poet's "grammar of being." For Wright, who insists on poetry's social and historical responsibilities, these schemes, "the god's elemental bones," are "a launch-pad/ into the actual" ("Inscrutability").

Wright's emphasis in *Explications/Interpretations* on the body as a site of knowledge and action is indicative of his rejection of dualisms. The spiritual does not exist in separation from the material any more than male exists without female. They are what Wright conceives of as "twins," and the desired relationship between them is one of balance. This is most clearly articulated in "The Continuing City: Spirit and Body" and "The Body," two poems that lay out aesthetic and philosophical principles indebted to Danquah's *The Akan Doctrine of God.* In his notes, Wright identifies *Explications/Interpretations* as an attempt "to claim this knowledge as part of the continuing creative life of the Americas"; the Americas are what comes into full view in *Dimensions of History.*

Dimensions of History

Though *Dimensions of History* is dedicated to the late Francis Ferguson, with whom Wright studied at Rutgers, the book owes perhaps its most significant debt to Harris's notion of "vision as historical dimension." This third volume of Wright's poetic cycle maintains the tripartite structure of *Explications/Interpretations,* a scheme now more explicitly associated with the three stages of an initiation ritual: separation, transition, (re)incorporation. Part 1, "The Second Eye of the World. The Dimension of Rites and Acts," announces this link not only by being itself divided into three poems but also by offering the reader a Dogon ideogram that, according to Griaule and Dieterlen, represents the separation of the twins, male and female, at the moment of circumcision. The historical dimension of separation within an African American context is (enforced) exile. This historical condition becomes the "special kinship" the poet's persona shares with his other selves, the dead to whose realm he descends and whose claims he seeks to understand in a spiritually barren land from which the god has retreated. Among them are once again Du Bois and Attucks, who are joined by the voices of and allusions to Frederick Douglass, St. Augustine, Toussaint Louverture and many others who congregate in a text brimming with references to Aztec, Mayan, Incaic, Egyptian, Arabic, Christian, Yoruba, Akan, and, of course, Dogon and Bambara mythologies. Ogotemmêli's return in the figure of the blind sage at the beginning of the second poem commences the process of healing: "Anochecí enfermo amanecí bueno" (I went to bed sick, I woke up well) are the words that open the third poem, at the end of which the persona names himself "a dark and dutiful dyēli,/ searching for the understanding of his deeds."

Part 2, titled "Modulations. The Aesthetic Dimension," consists of an assortment of poetic forms, many of them linked to Caribbean and Latin American musical forms and instruments such as the Cuban *son*, the *areito*, and the *bandola*, a fifteen-string Colombian guitar. The shorter poems in "Rhythms, Charts, and Changes," "The Body Adorned and Bare," a section reminiscent of the meditations on the body in *Explications/Interpretations*, and "Retablos" (votive paintings) lead up to Wright's "Log Book of Judgments," a series of ethical and aesthetic formulations distilled from the persona's historical and ritualistic experiences. They culminate in the following lines from "Meta-A and the A of Absolutes": "I am good when I know the darkness of all light,/ and accept the darkness, not as a sing, but as my body."

Dimensions of History closes with "Landscapes. The Physical Dimension," whose themes and poetic architecture return to the history of the conquest of the Americas and to Náhua (Aztec) mythology and poetry. The most notable formal aspects of this final part are the encyclopedic monoliths, block passages that list the vital statistics of five American nations: Venezuela,

Colombia, Panama, Mexico, and the United States. The spaces between these building blocks or "stones" are filled with Wright's own enchanted mortar, a possible translation of the Náhuatl-infused Spanish idiom *cal y canto* (literally, mortar and song) that joins Wright's compositional principles with his cross-cultural concerns. This syncretic idiom, which also conjures up such Latin American poets as Pablo Neruda and José María Arguedas, is a miniature representation of the rhizomes Wright's poem uncovers. It is one of his "emblems of the ecstatic connection." His poet's Middle Passages temporarily end with an image of the Great Gate of the ancient Mayan city Labná, a sole triumphal arc in a city without fortifications that is both "a gateway to the beautiful" and "the image of our lives among ourselves."

The Double Invention of Komo

The Double Invention of Komo, which is dedicated to the memory of Griaule, may well be called the most African of Wright's poems. Wright's most sustained and ambitious effort in the genre of dramatic poetry, *The Double Invention of Komo* is a poetic reenactment of the initiation ceremonies performed by the all-male Komo society among the Bambara. The object of these highly formalized ceremonies is to maintain the Bambara's traditional intellectual, religious, and social values. *The Double Invention of Komo* "risks ritual's arrogance" to the extent that the logic and the specifics of this ritualistic process inform the poem's conceptual and formal structures. Of special importance to Wright are the 266 great signs, a system of ideograms that organizes Bambara cosmology. Each sign inscribes a different "name" or aspect of the god and binds him to the material objects and substances associated with Komo's altars, as in "*Dyibi*—obscurity—gold." As is evident from "The Initiate Takes His First Six Signs, the Design of His Name," such naming is an exceedingly complex process. What Wright is after is the sacred "grammar" of names that, ultimately, evolve into a secular "alphabet" of creation. *The Double Invention of Komo* is quite explicitly and self-consciously a poem about the metaphysics of writing, and this accounts for much of its difficulty.

The central preoccupation of *The Double Invention of Komo* is how to achieve self-knowledge through writing, how to fashion a language that would redress loss and dispossession. Writing, for Wright, is a process of simultaneous dismemberment and reassembly of meaning and community: It is both "scalpel" and "suture," both excision and circumcision. Like the ritual scars on the body of the initiate, poetic writing confers not only knowledge of traditional values but also kinship. It is as if the poet's pen were a ritual knife "cutting" the initiates (and the readers) into kinship, marking them as members of a special community. As the persona's status changes from that of an initiate to that of a "delegate," the statements made in *Dimensions of History*'s "Meta-A and the A of Absolutes" are reformulated: "What is true is the incision./ What is true is the desire for the incision,/ and the signs' flaming in the wound." It is in this sense that the Middle Passage, which all of the persona's journeys reenact, becomes a rite of passage that compensates for the violent psychic dismemberment and the geographical dispersal of the members of Africa's traditional cultures. Wright's key metaphor, the limbo, refers to Harris, who regards this dance, created on the crowded slave ships, as a form of silent collective resistance. Harris's sense of the limbo as a "structure of freedom" has been an inspiration for Wright since "The Albuquerque Graveyard." It also encapsulates the main concerns that have motivated Wright's explorations of the poetic potential of music and dance.

Elaine's Book

Given the usually all-male composition of Wright's imaginary communities and especially the emphasis on male initiation rituals in *The Double Invention of Komo*, the foregrounding of female voices in *Elaine's Book* is almost startling. While women are never entirely absent from his poetry, which frequently identifies creativity as a female principle, this is the first book in which they assume historical, rather than exclusively mythological, stature. They are an integral part of the poetic geographies Wright's persona traverses in his fascinating explorations of female otherness. The female voices in *Elaine's Book* assume many different identities: that of Yemanjá, the Yoruba/Afro-Cuban Goddess of the waters; that of Hathor or Aphrodite; that of the Virgin of Guadalupe, whom Wright connects with the Aztec goddess Tonantzin; that of the African American poet Phillis Wheatley; and those of many others who take their places right next to Octavio Paz, Paul Celan, and Friedrich Hölderlin, who now merely provide epigraphs.

Wright's poetic language is as rich as his symbolic geography is varied and extensive. His journey into the night, which begins with the sunset of "Veil, I," not only leads the reader to pre-Columbian Mexico, Spain, Scotland, and back to the United States, but also guides the reader across an ever-changing linguistic surface in which even historical documents, such as letters by Wheatley, the former slave Judith Cocks, Louisa Alexander, and the Harvard astronomer Cecilia Payne Yaposchkin take on poetic qualities of their own. *Elaine's Book* can be said to achieve resonance as well as consonance: Each fragment sounds new depths as it becomes part of a "nation," which, like the "city," is also a figure for the poem itself.

That a poet who lives in uncertain multiplicities, who knows neither his actual birth date nor his real name, should be fascinated by names and dates is hardly surprising.

Boleros

In *Boleros*, a book dedicated to his wife Lois, Wright's preoccupation is with imagining the fictions that, like his own father's stories, lead to names—in this case, names of Greek muses, of saint's days adorned with "graces and the seasons," and of places. "All names," he writes, "are invocations, or curses." Reinventing these stories and histories of origins is the poetic project of *Boleros* and the point of departure for further journeys across far-flung geographies of the spirit. As in *Elaine's Book*, the poet's guides are mostly female: Erato, Calliope, Euterpe, Thalia, Polyhymnia, Clio, Terpsichore, Urania. Yet the familiar Greek identities of these muses are complicated by the association of each of their personalities with concepts taken from another of Wright's favorite archives, *The Egyptian Book of the Dead* (first published in English in 1894). The resulting Africanization of the muses recalls Martin Bernal's compelling speculations in *Black Athena: The Afro-Asiatic Roots of Classical Civilization* (1987). Many of the sites the poet's persona revisits in *Boleros* are familiar ones: Edinburgh, Guadalajara, Jalapa, New Hampshire, and always West Africa. The poet also takes up a number of new residences, however, most significant among them the city of Benares in Uttar Pradesh, one of the intellectual and cultural centers of traditional India. "Black spirits such as mine will always come/ to a crossroads such as this," the persona explains at the shores of the Ganges. As always, these geographic journeys become explorations of poetic form. Most striking in this regard are the six poems in "Sources and Roots" and "Coda," which are the title's most concrete reference points. The relatively brief poems in these final sections, many of which open with lines from popular Latin American songs, are daring in their use of Spanish meter and rhyme in an English-language environment. The results of such unexpected contact are wondrous formal hybrids, whose breaks with English accentuation are infused with Wright's wit and humor:

> Esta tierra da de todo.
> Oh, perhaps, you will see no sloe
> plum, or no white-tailed, ginger doe,
> break-dancing at sunset when snow
> shows us its blackberry wine skin.

Poems such as this are testimony to the transformations of vision and language at the many crossroads to which Wright's ceaseless poetic journeys lead. These transformations truly are Wright's "gift," for few poets have dared to bridge the troubled waters of cultural difference. Even fewer have succeeded so splendidly.

Transfigurations: Collected Poems

Transfigurations: Collected Poems collects Wright's work produced over the course of more than twenty-five years of poetic exploration. The volume is hefty, providing more than six hundred pages of densely textured verse, including sixty pages of new poetry. Detailed references to West African, Haitian, Mexican, and European and American Christian religious rituals abound, as well as to the various political and poetic genealogies in which Wright situates himself. Geographic journeys expose the earth itself to the questioning soul of the poet. In a single poem, Wright travels from North Africa to Jamaica to Boston and then on to Spain, dropping historical allusions at every step. The esoteric network of obscure signs and allusions he uses serves to trace his own development in which, for nearly three decades, he has determinedly initiated himself into the mysteries of language, history, and sense.

Transformation and transfiguration act as the axes of this collection. A bulk of the poems in the volume speak to initiation, the human ceremonial act that marks transformation: the Mexican boy to whom a god says, "You must prepare for my eruption/ and the guarded way I have of guarding you," or the West African Dogon boy who undergoes the trials and tribulations of coming into adulthood, "If I were the light's sacred buffoon,/ I could read this meaning and mount/ my own awakening" in the spectacular poem "The Double Invention of Komo." A transfiguration, similarly, is a change of appearance, one that is accompanied with a sense of revelation. A refinement of vision, put to the service of metamorphosis, is one of Wright's most potent forces. For example, in "The Abstract of Knowledge/the First Test," Wright transfigures the scene of the Dogon boy encountering the first phase of his initiation, in which he must undergo an hallucinatory vision of the universe in the light of the knowledge that he will obtain from his vision. That vision changes knowledge, transfiguring it and transforming it. In these lines, a number of the features of Wright's poetry are apparent: the tightly rhythmical free verse—which lacks enjambment for the most part, the voice of the dramatic persona, the physical details, and a cosmological reach.

Other Literary Forms

Jay Wright has published several plays in *Hambone, Callaloo,* and *The Southern Review.* He has also written essays on African American poetry and poetics, the most important of which is "Desire's Design, Vision's Resonance: Black Poetry's Ritual and Historical Voice," which appeared in *Callaloo* (volume 10, number 1, 1987).

Bibliography

Callaloo 6 (Fall, 1983). This special issue includes an excellent interview in which Wright outlines the theories behind his poetry. It also contains a general introduction to Wright's poetry by Robert B. Stepto, a rather superficial assessment of his early poetry by Gerald Barrax, and detailed commentary on the Benjamin Banneker poems by Vera M. Kutzinski.

Clifford, James. *The Predicament of Culture: Twentieth-Century Ethnography, Literature, and Art.* Cambridge, Mass.: Harvard University Press, 1988. This critical look at the rise of modern anthropology and its entwinement with literature is useful background reading for some of Wright's main sources, notably Marcel Griaule and his team. Equally relevant are Clifford's comments on the West's representation of other cultures and the negotiation of cultural differences.

Harris, Wilson. *The Womb of Space: The Cross-Cultural Imagination.* Westport, Conn.: Greenwood Press, 1983. While this study includes a brief discussion of *The Double Invention of Komo*, it is valuable primarily for its conceptualization of the literary dynamics of "the cross-cultural imagination." Though Wright's debt is to Harris's earlier writings, this book summarizes the main concepts and ideas that have guided Harris's thinking since the beginning of his career.

Kutzinski, Vera M. *Against the American Grain: Myth and History in William Carlos Williams, Jay Wright, and Nicolás Guillén.* Baltimore: Johns Hopkins University Press, 1987. The second part of this book, "The Black Limbo: Jay Wright's Mythology of Writing," provides the fullest available commentary on Wright's poetry. Focusing on *Dimensions of History* and its historical and theoretical sources, it places Wright's cross-cultural poetics within the context of the diverse cultural and literary histories of the Americas. Has detailed notes and a useful index.

Okpewho, Isidore. "Prodigal's Progress: Jay Wright's Focal Center." *MELUS* 23, no. 3 (Fall, 1998): 187-209. Wright's search for a satisfactory cultural identity through the successive volumes of his poetry is examined. Wright's movement from the autobiographical to the scholarly to a poetic self-creation through ritual and religion is traced.

O'Leary, Peter. Review of *Transfigurations*, by Jay Wright. *Chicago Review* 47, no. 2 (Summer, 2001): 71-75. Review's Wright's book of collected poems.

Stepto, Robert B. "After Modernism, After Hibernation: Michael Harper, Robert Hayden, and Jay Wright." In *Chant of Saints: A Gathering of Afro-American Literature, Arts, and Scholarship*, edited by Michael S. Harper and Robert B. Stepto. Urbana: University of Illinois Press, 1979. This article concentrates on portions of *Dimensions of History*. It is useful for situating Wright's poetry within the "call-and-response" structures of an African American literary tradition whose central concern, according to Stepto, is with "freedom and literacy."

Welburn, Ron. "Jay Wright's Poetics: An Appreciation." *MELUS* 18, no. 3 (Fall, 1993): 51. The historical and metaphysical codes that add energy to Wright's poetry are examined. In spite of his relative obscurity, Wright deserves appreciation for his creative intellect.

Wiman, Christian. Review of *Transfigurations*, by Jay Wright. *Poetry* 179, no. 2 (November, 2001): 102-105. A review of Wright's book by one of poetry's foremost thinkers.

— *Sarah Hilbert; Vera M. Kutzinski*

Richard Wright

Novelist, short-story writer, and memoirist

Born: Roxie, Mississippi; September 4, 1908
Died: Paris, France; November 28, 1960

LONG FICTION: *Native Son*, 1940; *The Outsider*, 1953; *Savage Holiday*, 1954; *The Long Dream*, 1958; *Lawd Today*, 1963.

SHORT FICTION: *Uncle Tom's Children: Four Novellas*, 1938 (expanded as *Uncle Tom's Children: Five Long Stories*, 1938); *Eight Men*, 1961.

DRAMA: *Native Son: The Biography of a Young American*, pr. 1941 (with Paul Green).

POETRY: *Haiku: This Other World*, 1998 (Yoshinobu Hakutani and Robert L. Tener, editors).

NONFICTION: *Twelve Million Black Voices: A Folk History of the Negro in the United States*, 1941 (photographs by Edwin Rosskam); *Black Boy: A Record of Childhood and Youth*, 1945; *Black Power: A Record of Reactions in a Land of Pathos*, 1954; *The Color Curtain*, 1956; *Pagan Spain*, 1957; *White Man, Listen!*, 1957; *American Hunger*, 1977; *Richard Wright Reader*, 1978 (Ellen Wright and Michel Fabré, editors); *Conversations with Richard Wright*, 1993 (Keneth Kinnamon and Fabré, editors).

MISCELLANEOUS: *Works*, 1991 (2 volumes).

Achievements

Richard Wright is often cited as being the father of the post-World War II African American novel. The works of James Baldwin and Ralph Ellison owe a direct debt to the work of Wright, and his role in inspiring the Black Arts movement of the 1960's is incalculable. Further, he was one of the first African American novelists of the first half of the twentieth century to capture a truly international audience. Among his many honors were a Guggenheim Fellowship in 1939 and the Spingarn Award from the National Association for the Advancement of Colored People (NAACP) in 1941 for his novel, *Native Son*. This novel, which Baldwin said was "unquestionably" the "most powerful and celebrated statement we have had yet of what it means to be a Negro in America," along with the first volume of his autobiography and the stories in *Uncle Tom's Children*, constitute Wright's most important lasting contributions to literature. His plots usually deal with how the harrowing experience of racial inequality transforms a person into a rebel—usually violent, and usually randomly so. The more subtle achievement of his fiction, however, is the psychological insight it provides into the experience of oppression and rebellion.

Biography

The poverty, racial hatred, and violence that Richard Nathaniel Wright dramatizes in fiction come directly from his own experience as the child of an illiterate Mississippi sharecropper. Richard was six years old when his father was driven off the land and the family moved to a two-room slum tenement in Memphis, Tennessee. The father deserted the family there. Richard's mother, Ella Wright, got a job as a cook, leaving Richard and his younger brother Alan alone in the apartment. When his mother became ill, the brothers were put in an orphanage. An invitation for Ella and the boys to stay with a more prosperous relative in Arkansas ended in panic and flight when white men shot Uncle Hoskins, who had offered the Wrights a home. The family lived for some time with Richard's grandparents, stern Seventh-day Adventists. Wright's grandmother believed that all fiction was "the devil's lies"; her chief goal was to force Wright into a religious conversion, a goal in which she was singularly unsuccessful. In this grim, repressive atmosphere, Richard became increasingly violent and rebellious.

Although he completed his formal education in the ninth grade, the young Richard read widely, especially Stephen Crane, Fyodor Dostoevski, Marcel Proust, T. S. Eliot, and Gertrude Stein. Wright moved from school to school, attempting to

(Library of Congress)

make friends and make his talents known. Though both tasks were difficult, he became valedictorian of his class. Even this accomplishment was spoiled when the principal insisted that Wright read a speech which the principal himself had written, and Wright refused. An uncle told Richard, "They're going to break you," and society, both black and white, seemed intent on doing so. Wright was determined to resist, not to be claimed by his environment as he felt so many blacks around him were.

Wright left Mississippi for Memphis, Tennessee, had little luck there, and—with money stolen from the film theater where he worked—moved to Chicago. When others stole, Wright disapproved—not for moral reasons, but because he felt stealing did not change the fundamental relationship of a person to his environment. When it offered a chance to change that environment, Wright accepted it. In Chicago, Wright became involved with others who viewed the country as he did, first in a federal theater project and then with the communist John Reed Club, which supported his writing until Wright's goals differed from their own. In 1937, he moved to New York City to become the editor of the *Daily Worker.* A year later, he published his first important work, *Uncle Tom's Children,* after which he won a Guggenheim Fellowship, which provided him with the time and funds to write *Native Son.* The novel was published to great acclaim and was followed by a second major work, *Black Boy.* Although his writing career was a success, Wright was arguing more frequently with the Communist Party, with which he finally broke in 1944, and was becoming less optimistic about the hope of racial progress in the United States.

In 1945, at the invitation of the French government, Wright went to France and became friends with Jean-Paul Sartre, Simone de Beauvoir, and other existentialists. His next novel, *The Outsider,* has been called the first existential novel by an American writer. Wright traveled widely, lectured in several countries, and wrote journalistic accounts of his experiences in Africa and Spain. He died unexpectedly in Paris of amoebic dysentery, probably contracted in Africa or Indonesia under conditions his friend and biographer Margaret Walker, in *Richard Wright: Daemonic Genius* (1988), believes indicate at least medically questionable decisions, or, possibly, homicide. After his death, three more works, *Eight Men, Lawd Today,* and *American Hunger,* were published.

Analysis: Long Fiction

Richard Wright's best work is always the story of one man's struggle to define himself and by so doing make himself free and responsible, fully human, a character worthy not of pity but of admiration and horror simultaneously. Typically, the character is an outsider, and Wright uses blackness as a representation of that alienation, though his characters are never as interested in defining their blackness as in defining their humanity. Although many characters in Wright's works are outsiders without being aware of their condition, Wright is never interested in them except as foils. Many of them avoid confronting themselves by fleeing to dreams; religion and liquor are two avoidance mechanisms for Wright's characters, narcotics that blind them to their surrounding world, to what they are and what they might be.

Even Wright's main characters must not think about that world too often: To let it touch them is to risk insanity or violence, and so his characters strive to keep the fire within in check, to keep the physical hunger satisfied. Thus, all of Wright's protagonists are initially trapped by desire and by fear—fear of what might happen to them, what they may do, if they risk venturing outside the confines of black life in America—and the desire to do so. The life outside may be glimpsed in films; for example, in *Native Son,* Bigger Thomas goes to a film and watches contrasting and artificial views of black and white society. Yet as untruthful as both views are, they remind Bigger of a reality beyond his present situation. Desire is often symbolized by flight; Bigger, like other Wright characters, dreams of flying above the world, unchained from its limitations.

Most of Wright's stories and novels examine what happens when the protagonist's fear is mastered for a moment when desires are met. The manifestation of desire in Wright is almost always through violence (and it is here, perhaps, that he is most pessimistic, for other, more positive, manifestations of desire, such as love, can come only later, after the protagonists have violently acted out their longings). Violence is central to Wright's fiction, for as important as sex may be to his characters, power is much more so, and power is often achieved through violence; in Wright's world, beatings and murders are frequent acts— central and occasionally creative.

Once the character has acted, he finds himself trapped again in a new set of oppositions, for in acting, he has left the old sureties behind, has made himself free, and has begun to define and create himself. With that new freedom comes a new awareness of responsibility. He is without excuses, and that awareness is as terrifying as—though more liberating than—the fears he has previously known. Although Wright does not always elaborate on what may follow, the characters open up new possibilities for themselves. If one may create one's self by violence, perhaps, Wright sometimes suggests, there are other, less destructive ways as well.

Some of Wright's novels end on this note of optimism, the characters tragically happy: tragic because they have committed violent and repulsive acts, but happy because for the first time they have *chosen* to commit them; they have freed themselves from their constraints, and the future, however short it may be, lies open. Others end simply with tragedy, the destruction achieving no purpose, the characters attaining no illumination.

Lawd Today

Lawd Today, written before *Native Son*, but not published until after Wright's death, tells the story of Jake Jackson from his awakening on the morning of February 12, 1936, to that day's violent conclusion. Jackson is Wright's most inarticulate protagonist: He has a banal life, undefined dreams, and a vague sense of discontent which he is unable to explain. Violent and prejudiced, he speaks in clichés, a language as meaningless as his life.

Technically, the book incorporates a montage of radio broadcasts, newspaper articles, and religious and political pamphlets into the narration of Jake's day. Divided into three sections, *Lawd Today* opens with Jake's dream of running up an endless staircase after a disappearing voice. That dream gives way to the reality of his life: hunger, anger, and recrimination. Tricked by Jake into an abortion for which Jake still owes five hundred dollars and now claiming to have a tumor which will cost another five hundred dollars to remove, Jake's wife represents his entrapment. In the first section, "Commonplace," Jake reveals his brutish and trivial character: his anger at his wife, a jealousy and resentment that lead him to bait her so he can hit her, a mock battle straightening his hair, and a meeting with friends who work with him at the post office. As they play bridge to pass the time until work, Wright presents without comment their stupid, cliché-ridden conversation.

Section 2, "Squirrel Cage," shows the men at work. They are all alienated in meaningless, routine jobs, but Jake's position is the most desperate, for his wife has been to see his boss, and he is now threatened with the loss of his job. Falling deeper into debt by borrowing more money and making mistakes on the job, Jake is trapped by his work—despite his own protestations, as a self-proclaimed Republican and capitalist, that work is liberating. This section, too, ends with a long, rambling, and banal conversation among the men at work.

In the concluding section, "Rat's Alley," the men go to a brothel for a good time on some of Jake's borrowed money. There, Jake is robbed and then beaten for his threats of revenge. Finally, Jake stumbles homeward, his day nearing an end. The February weather, pleasant when the book began, has turned bad. All of Jake's frustration and anger finally erupt; he beats his wife, whom he finds kneeling asleep by the bed in an attitude of prayer. As they struggle, he throws objects through the window. She grabs a shard of broken glass and slashes him three times. The book ends with Jake lying in a drunken stupor, bleeding, while his wife is on her knees, also bleeding, praying for death. Outside, the wind blows mercilessly.

Although some of the experimentalism of *Lawd Today* seems artificial, and although the protagonist is too limited to sustain the reader's interest, this early work is powerful and economical. The situation, if not the character, is typical of Wright's work, and the reader understands Jake's violent frustration. *Lawd Today* has its flaws, but it foreshadows the strengths of Wright's best work and in its own right is a daring and fascinating novel.

Native Son

Along with *Black Boy*, *Native Son* is one of Wright's finest achievements: a brilliant portrayal of, as Wright put it, the way the environment provides the instrumentalities through which one expresses oneself and the way that self becomes whole despite the environment's conspiring to keep it divided.

The book parallels Theodore Dreiser's *An American Tragedy* (1925): Both are three-part novels in which there is a murder, in part accidental, in part willed; an attempted flight; and a long concluding trial, in both cases somewhat anticlimactic. Both novels are concerned with the interplay of environment and heredity, of fate and accident, and both have protagonists who rebel against the world which would hold them back.

In the first part of *Native Son*, Bigger Thomas is a black man cut off from family and peers. Superficially like his friends, he is in fact possessed of a different consciousness. To think about that consciousness is for him to risk insanity or violence, so Bigger endeavors to keep his fears and uncertainty at a preconscious level. On the day of the first section, however, he is required by the welfare agency to apply for a job as a menial at the home of the rich Dalton family. Mr. Dalton is a ghetto landlord who soothes his conscience by donating sums of money for recreational purposes. That it is a minuscule part of the money he is deriving from blacks is an irony he overlooks. Mrs. Dalton is blind, a fact that is necessary to the plot as well as being symbolic. Their daughter, Mary, is a member of the Communist Party, and from the moment she sees Bigger, who wants nothing more than to be left alone, she begins to enlist his support.

The first evening, Bigger is to drive Mary to a university class. In reality, she is going with Jan Erlone, her communist boyfriend, to a party meeting. Afterward, they insist that Bigger take them to a bar in the black part of town. Jan and Mary are at this point satirized, for their attitudes toward blacks are as limited and stereotyped as any in the novel. Bigger does not want to be seen by his friends with whites, but that fact does not occur to Mary. After much drinking, Bigger must carry the drunken Mary to her bedroom. He puts her to bed, stands over her, attracted to the woman he sees. The door opens and Mrs. Dalton enters. When Mary makes drunken noises, Bigger becomes frightened that Mrs. Dalton will come close enough to discover him, so he puts a pillow over Mary's face to quiet her. By the time Mrs. Dalton leaves, Mary is dead.

Wright wanted to make Bigger a character it would be impossible to pity, and what follows is extremely grisly. Bigger tries to put Mary's body in the furnace and saws off her head to make her fit. However accidental Mary's death may appear to the reader, Bigger himself does not regard it as such. He has, he thinks, many times wanted to kill whites without ever having the opportunity to do so. This time there was the act without the desire, but rather than seeing himself as the victim of a chance occurrence, Bigger prefers to unite the earlier desire with the present act, to make himself whole by accepting responsibility for the killing. Indeed, he not only accepts the act but also determines to capitalize on it by sending a ransom note. Later, accused of raping Mary as well, an act he considered but did not commit, he reverses the process, accepting responsibility for this, too, even though here there was desire but no act. His only sign of conscience is that he cannot bring himself to shake the ashes in the furnace; this guilt is not redemptive, but his undoing, for, in an implausible scene in the Dalton basement, the room fills with smoke, the murder is revealed to newspaper reporters gathered there, and Bigger is forced to flee.

He runs with his girlfriend, Bessie Mears. She, like Bigger, has a hunger for sensation, which has initially attracted him to her. Now, however, as they flee together, she becomes a threat and a burden; huddled with her in an abandoned tenement, Bigger wants only to be rid of her. He picks up a brick and smashes her face, dumping her body down an airshaft. His only regret is not that he has killed her, but that he has forgotten to remove their money from her body.

The rest of the plot moves quickly: Bigger is soon arrested, the trial is turned into a political farce, and Bigger is convicted and sentenced to death. In the last part of the novel, after Bigger's arrest, the implications of the action are developed, largely through Bigger's relations to other characters. Some of the characters are worthy only of contempt, particularly the district attorney, who, in an attempt at reelection, is turning the trial into political capital. Bigger's mother relies on religion. In a scene in the jail cell, she falls on her knees in apology before Mrs. Dalton and urges Bigger to pray, but toughness is Bigger's code. He is embarrassed by his mother's self-abasement, and although he agrees to pray simply to end his discomfort, his attitude toward religion is shown when he throws away a cross a minister has given him and throws a cup of coffee in a priest's face. In his view, they want only to avoid the world and to force him to accept guilt without responsibility.

Bigger learns from two characters. The first is Boris Max, the lawyer the Communist Party provides. Max listens to Bigger, and for the first time in his life, Bigger exposes his ideas and feelings to another human. Max's plea to the court is that, just as Bigger must accept responsibility for what he has done, so must the society around him understand its responsibility for what Bigger has become and, if the court chooses to execute Bigger, understand the consequences that must flow from that action. He does not argue—nor does Wright believe—that Bigger is a victim of injustice. There is no injustice, because that would presume a world in which Bigger could hope for justice, and such a world does not exist; more important, Bigger is not a victim, for he has chosen his own fate. Max argues rather that all men are entitled to happiness. Like all of Wright's protagonists, Bigger has earlier been torn between the poles of dread and ecstasy. His ecstasy, his happiness, comes from the meaningfulness he creates in his existence, a product of self-realization. Unhappily for Bigger, he realizes himself through murder: It was, he feels, his highest creative act.

If Max articulates the intellectual presentation of Wright's beliefs about Bigger, it is Jan, Mary's lover, who is its dramatic representation. He visits Bigger in his cell and, having at last understood the futility and paucity of his own stereotypes, admits to Bigger that he too shares in the responsibility for what has happened. He, too, addresses Bigger as a human being, but from the unique position of being the one who is alive to remind Bigger of the consequences of his actions, for Bigger learns that Jan has suffered loss through what he has done and that, while Bigger has created himself, he has also destroyed another.

Native Son ends with the failure of Max's appeals on Bigger's behalf. He comes to the cell to confront Bigger before his execution, and the novel closes with Bigger Thomas smiling at Max as the prison door clangs shut. He will die happy because he will die fulfilled, having, however terribly, created a self. *Native Son* is Wright's most powerful work, because his theme, universal in nature, is given its fullest and most evocative embodiment. In the characterization of Bigger, alienated man at his least abstract and most genuine, of Bigger's exactly rendered mind and milieu, and of Bigger's working out of his destiny, *Native Son* is Wright's masterpiece.

The Outsider

Wright's next novel, *The Outsider,* written in France and published thirteen years after *Native Son,* suffers from a surfeit of internal explanation and a failure to provide a setting as rich as that of *Native Son.* Still, its portrayal of Cross Damon and his struggle to define himself, while too self-conscious, adds new dimensions to Wright's myth.

As the novel opens, Damon is trapped by his life. His post-office job is unfulfilling, his wife is threatening, and his underage mistress is pregnant. He "desires desire," but there is no way for that desire to be completed. "A man creates himself," he has told his wife, but the self Damon has created is a nightmare. He broods, his brooding as close as he comes to religion. Damon gets his chance for new life on the subway. Thought dead after his identification papers are found near the mangled body of another, Damon gets a chance to create himself anew. He must invent, he thinks, not only his future, but also a past to fit with his present; this new opportunity brings with it a different and more potent sense of dread.

From the beginning of this new life, Damon is remarkably successful at the mechanics of creating a past. He easily obtains a birth certificate and a draft card. At a deeper level, however, he traps himself as surely as he has been trapped in his old life, so that his new one becomes a continuous act of bad faith. Even before he leaves Chicago, he hides in a brothel where he encounters a coworker who recognizes him. Damon murders the man and throws his body out a window. The pattern of violence, so typical of Wright's characters, begins in earnest for Damon.

Taking a train to New York, Damon meets two people who will influence his new life, a black waiter who introduces him to the world of communist politics in New York City, and Ely Houston, the district attorney, who is the most articulate person in the novel and the only one to understand Damon fully. Houston asks Damon why, when all blacks are outsiders, so few seem conscious of this fact. Wright suggests that being human is too much to be borne by people, that the struggle to define oneself is too difficult; the novel is a testament to that suggestion.

The Communist Party members, too, are outsiders, and there is nothing unified about their company. Each one that Damon meets is playing god, hoping to protect and extend his personal power. Their awareness of their motives varies, but they are a threat to Damon, and the action of the book is propelled by a series of murders: Damon himself wants to act like a god. Near the end of the book, Houston comes to understand that Damon is the killer, but—rather than indicting and punishing him legally—Houston allows him to go free, alone with his knowledge of what he is. Damon is horrified by his fate, but he is robbed of even that when he is killed by two Communist Party members who fear him.

The Outsider is both an extension and a modification of Wright's earlier views; it is far more pessimistic than *Native Son,* and the influence of the French existentialists is more pervasive. Like earlier Wright heroes, Damon is engaged in defining the world and himself. "The moment we act 'as if' it's true, then it's true," he thinks, because each person, in the absence of a god, is able to create the world and its truth. From Fyodor Dostoevski, Wright borrows the notion of underground man and the idea that without a god, all is permitted. Yet as each man plays god, as each becomes criminal, policeman, judge, and executioner, there are no longer limits. People desire everything, and desire is described as a floating demon. People are jealous gods here— the worlds they create are petty, their jealousy destructive. Damon is loved in the novel, but that love, unlike the love in *Native Son,* which is held up as potentially meaningful, is here without promise. Although he creates himself and his world in *The Outsider,* all that is made is violent and brutal, a world without redemption even in the act of self-realization.

At the end of the novel, Cross Damon dies, not with Bigger Thomas's smile, but with the knowledge that alone, people are nothing. Searching in his last moments of freedom for a clean, well-lighted place in which to rest before he confronts the world again, Cross finds only death. Before he dies, he admits his final act of bad faith: He has thought that he could create a world and be different from other men, that he could remain innocent. Like Joseph Conrad's Kurtz in *Heart of Darkness* (1902), Damon dies realizing the futility of that hope; having looked into his own heart of darkness, he dies with the word *horror* on his lips.

It is Wright's bleakest conclusion, the book his most relentless examination of the consequences of his own philosophy. If *The Outsider* lacks the narrative drive of *Native Son*, it remains a strongly conceived and troubling piece of fiction.

Analysis: Short Fiction

"Fire and Cloud" in *Uncle Tom's Children* is perhaps the best representative of Richard Wright's early short fiction. It won first prize in the 1938 *Story* magazine contest which had more than four hundred entries, marking Wright's first triumph with American publishers. Charles K. O'Neill made a radio adaptation of the story after it appeared in *American Scenes*.

"Fire and Cloud"

Unlike the later works concerning black ghetto experience, "Fire and Cloud" has a pastoral quality, recognizing the strong bond of the southern black to the soil and the support he has drawn from religion. Wright reproduces faithfully the southern black dialect in both conversation and internal meditations. This use of dialect emphasizes the relative lack of sophistication of rural blacks. His protagonist, Reverend Taylor, is representative of the "old Negro," who has withstood centuries of oppression, sustained by hard work on the land and humble faith in a merciful God.

Wright's attitude toward religion, however, is ambivalent. Although he recognizes it as contributing to the quiet nobility of the hero, it also prevents Taylor from taking effective social action when his people are literally starving. The final triumph of Reverend Taylor is that he puts aside the conciliatory attitude which was part of his religious training and becomes a social activist. Instead of turning the other cheek after being humiliated and beaten by white men, he embraces the methods of his Marxist supporters, meeting oppression with mass demonstration. Strength of numbers proves more effective and appropriate for getting relief from the bigoted white establishment than all his piety and loving kindness. Early in the story Taylor exclaims "The good Lawds gonna clean up this ol worl some day! Hes gonna make a new Heaven n a new Earth!" His last words, however, are "Freedom belongs t the strong!"

The situation of the story no doubt reflects Wright's early experience when his sharecropper father was driven off the plantation. Taylor's people are starving because the white people, who own all the land, have prohibited the blacks from raising food on it. No matter how Taylor pleads for relief, the local white officials tell him to wait and see if federal aid may be forthcoming. When two communist agitators begin pushing Taylor to lead a mass demonstration against the local government, white officials have Taylor kidnapped and beaten, along with several deacons of his church. Instead of intimidating them, this suffering converts them to open confrontation. As the communists promised, the poor whites join the blacks in the march, which forces the white authorities to release food to those facing starvation.

The story's strength lies in revealing through three dialogues the psychological dilemma of the protagonist as opposing groups demand his support. He resists the communists initially because their methods employ threat of open war on the whites—"N tha ain Gawds way!" The agitators say he will be responsible if their demonstration fails through lack of numbers and participants are slaughtered. On the other hand, the mayor and chief of police threaten Taylor that they will hold him personally responsible if any of his church members join the march. After a humiliating and futile exchange with these men, Taylor faces his own church deacons, who are themselves divided and look to him for leadership. He knows that one of their number, who is just waiting for a chance to oust him from his church, will run to the mayor and police with any evidence of

Taylor's insubordination. In a pathetic attempt to shift the burden of responsibility that threatens to destroy him no matter what he does, he reiterates the stubborn stand he has maintained with all three groups: He will not order the demonstration, but he will march with his people if they choose to demonstrate. The brutal horse-whipping that Taylor endures as a result of this moderate stand convinces him of the futility of trying to placate everybody. The Uncle Tom becomes a rebel.

Critics sometimes deplore the episodes of raw brutality described in graphic detail in Wright's fiction, but violence is the clue here to his message. Behind the white man's paternalistic talk is the persuasion of whip and gun. Only superior force can cope with such an antagonist.

"The Man Who Lived Underground"

Wright's best piece of short fiction is "The Man Who Lived Underground." Although undoubtedly influenced by Dostoevski's underground man and by Franz Kafka's "K," the situation was based on a prisoner's story from *True Detective* magazine. The first version appeared in 1942 in *Accent* magazine under the subtitle "Two Excerpts from a Novel." This version began with a description of the life of a black servant, but Wright later discarded this opening in favor of the dramatic scene in which an unnamed fugitive hides from the police by descending into a sewer. This approach allowed the story to assume a more universal, symbolic quality. Although racist issues are still significant, the protagonist represents that larger class of all those alienated from their society. Eventually the fugitive's name is revealed as Fred Daniels, but so completely is he absorbed into his Everyman role that he cannot remember his name when he returns to the upper world. His progress through sewers and basements becomes a quest for the meaning of life, parodying classic descents into the underworld and ironically reversing Plato's allegory of the cave.

Although Plato's philosopher attains wisdom by climbing out of the cave where men respond to shadows on the cave wall, Wright's protagonist gains enlightenment because of his underground perspective. What he sees there speaks not to his rational understanding, however, but to his emotions. He moves among symbolic visions which arouse terror and pity—a dead baby floating on the slimy water whose "mouth gaped black in a soundless cry." In a black church service spied on through a crevice in the wall, the devout are singing "Jesus, take me to your home above." He is overwhelmed by a sense of guilt and intuits that there is something obscene about their "singing with the air of the sewer blowing in on them." In a meat locker with carcasses hanging from the ceiling, a butcher is hacking off a piece of meat with a bloody cleaver. When the store proprietor goes home, Fred emerges from the locker and gorges on fresh fruit, but he takes back with him into the sewer the bloody cleaver—why he does not know.

When Fred breaks through a wall into the basement of a movie house, the analogy to Plato's myth of the cave becomes explicit. He comes up a back stair and sees jerking shadows of a silver screen. The Platonic urge to enlighten the people in the theater, who are bound to a shadow world, merges with messianic images. In a dream he walks on water and saves a baby held up by a drowning woman, but the dream ends in terror and doubt as he loses the baby and his ability to emulate Christ. All is lost and he himself begins to drown.

Terror and pity are not the only emotions that enlarge his sensibilities in this underground odyssey. As he learns the peculiar advantages of his invisibility, he realizes that he can help himself to all kinds of gadgets valued by that shadow world above ground. He collects them like toys or symbols of an absurd world. He acquires a radio, a light bulb with an extension cord, a typewriter, a gun, and finally, through a chance observation of a safe being opened by combination, rolls of hundred dollar bills, containers of diamonds, watches, and rings. His motivation for stealing these articles is not greed but sheer hilarious fun at acquiring objects so long denied to persons of his class.

In one of the most striking, surrealist scenes in modern literature, Fred delightedly decorates his cave walls and floor with these tokens of a society which has rejected him. "They were the serious toys of the men who lived in the dead world of sunshine and rain he had left, the world that had condemned him, branded him guilty." He glues hundred dollar bills on his walls. He winds up all the watches but disdains to set them (for he is beyond time, freed from its tyranny). The watches hang on nails along with the diamond rings. He hangs up the bloody cleaver, too, and the gun. The loose diamonds he dumps in a glittering pile on the muddy floor. Then as he gaily tramps around, he accidentally/on purpose, stomps on the pile, scattering the pretty baubles over the floor. Here, indeed, is society's cave of shadows, and only he realizes how absurd it all is.

When the euphoria of these games begins to pall, Fred becomes more philosophical, perceiving the nihilistic implications of his experience. "Maybe *any*thing's right, he mumbled. Yes, if the world as men had made it was right, then anything else was right, any act a man took to satisfy himself, murder, theft, torture." In his unlettered, blundering way, he is groping toward Ivan Karamazov's dark meditation: "If there is no God, then all things are permissible." Fred becomes convinced of the reality of human guilt, however, when he witnesses the suicide of the jewelry store's night watchman, who has been blamed for the theft he himself committed. At first, the scene in which police torture the bewildered man to force a confession strikes Fred as hilariously funny, duplicating his own experience. When the wretched man shoots himself before Fred can offer him a means of escape, however, Fred is shocked into a realization of his own guilt.

The protagonist ultimately transcends his nihilism, and like Platonic realism's philosopher who returns to the cave out of compassion for those trapped there, Fred returns to the "dead world of sunshine and rain" to bear witness to the Truth. Like the philosopher who is blinded coming out of the light into cave darkness, Fred seems confused and stupid in the social world above ground. When he is thrown out of the black church, he tries inarticulately to explain his revelation at the police station where he had been tortured and condemned. The police think he is crazy, but because they now know they accused him unjustly, they find his return embarrassing. Fred euphorically insists that they accompany him into the sewer so that they too can experience the visions that enlightened him. When he shows them his entrance to the world underground, one of the policemen calmly shoots him and the murky waters of the sewer sweep him away.

This ironic story of symbolic death and resurrection is unparalleled in its unique treatment of existential themes. Guilt and alienation lead paradoxically to a tragic sense of human brotherhood, which seems unintelligible to "normal" people. The man who kills Fred Daniels is perhaps the only person who perceives even dimly what Daniels wants to do. "You've got to shoot this kind," he says. "They'd wreck things."

Other Literary Forms

Wright's nonfiction works, such as *Twelve Million Black Voices* and *White Man, Listen!*, have proven to be of lasting interest. He developed a Marxist ideology while writing for the Communist *Daily Worker*, which was very influential on his early fiction, notably *Native Son* and *Uncle Tom's Children*, but which culminated in an article, "I Tried to Be a Communist," first published by the *Atlantic Monthly* in 1944. Although he abandoned Marxist ideology, he never abandoned the idea that protest is and should be at the heart of great literature.

Even more important than these collections, however, is the first volume of Wright's autobiography, *Black Boy: A Record of Childhood and Youth*, which opens up a world of experience to the reader. It traces the first seventeen years of Wright's life— from his birth in Mississippi and the desertion of the family by his father, through years of displacement as he travels from one relative to another with his ill mother and religious grandmother. The early years find Wright, like his later protagonists, an outsider, cut off from family, from friends, from culture. He is as out of place among blacks as among whites, baffled by those blacks who play the roles whites expect of them, himself unable to dissimulate his feelings and thoughts.

Although the work is nonfiction, it is united by powerful metaphors: fire, hunger, and blindness. Wright's inner fire is mirrored throughout the work by actual fires; indeed, his first act is to set afire the curtains in his home. His physical hunger, a constant companion, is an image of his hunger for knowledge and connection, and his two jobs in optical factories suggest the blindness of society, a blindness given further representation in *Native Son.*

What Wright learns in *Black Boy* is the power of words. His early life is marked by physical violence: He witnesses murders and beatings, but it is the violence of words which offers liberation from his suffocating environment. Whether it is the profanity with which he shocks his grandmother, the literalness with which he takes his father's words, or the crude expressions with which he taunts Jewish shopkeepers, he discovers that words have a power which makes him an equal to those around him. When he feels unequal, as in his early school experiences, he is speechless. The culmination of this theme occurs when Wright acquires a library card and discovers through his readings of the American social critics of the early part of the twentieth century, such as H. L. Mencken and Sinclair Lewis, that he is not alone in his feelings and that there are others who share his alienation and discontent.

When Wright finally sees his father many years after his desertion, his hatred dissolves: He realizes that his father, trapped by his surroundings, with neither a cultural past nor an individual future, speaks a different language from his own, holds different thoughts, and is truly a victim and therefore not worthy even of his hatred. Wright's characters must never be victims, for as such they hold no interest. At the end of the book, he goes north, first to Memphis and, when that fails, north again to Chicago, pursuing the dream, having now the power of words to articulate it and to define himself.

The record of his years in Chicago is found in the posthumously published second autobiographical volume, *American Hunger* (written in 1944, published in 1977). Largely a record of his involvement and later disillusionment with the Communist Party, this book is interesting for its view of a later, mature Wright who is still struggling with institutions which would limit his freedom.

Bibliography

Baldwin, James. *The Price of the Ticket: Collected Nonfiction, 1948-1985.* New York: St. Martin's Press/Marek, 1985. The essays "Everybody's Protest Novel" and "Alas, Poor Richard" provide important and provocative insights into Wright and his art.

Basu, Biman. "The Genuflected Body of the Masochist in Richard Wright." *Public Culture* 16, no. 2 (2004): 239-264. An interesting comparison of Wright's *Black Boy* with works by Frederick Douglass and Booker T. Washington. Examines the role of power as embodied by slave and master.

Bérubé, Michael. "Disability and Narrative." *PMLA: Publications of the Modern Language Association of America* 120, no. 2 (March, 2005): 568-577. Examines the role of handicaps in Wright's work. Finds that their presence is common, despite a lack of intention on Wright's part.

Bloom, Harold, ed. *Richard Wright.* New York: Chelsea House, 1987. Essays on various aspects of Wright's work and career, with an introduction by Bloom.

Butler, Robert. *"Native Son": The Emergence of a New Black Hero.* Boston: Twayne, 1991. One of Twayne's Masterwork Studies, this is an accessible critical look at the seminal novel. Includes bibliographical references and an index.

Calloway, Catherine. "Fiction: The 1930s to the 1960s." *American Literature* 77, no. 2 (June, 2005): 349-368. This chapter examines Wright's work and compares it to that of four other major American authors: James Baldwin, Ralph Ellison, Chester Himes, and John Steinbeck.

Collum, Dany Duncan. "Pledging Allegiance to the Imagination." *Sojourners Magazine* 33, no. 12 (December, 2004): 39-40. Discusses Wright's interest in fellow writer H. L. Mencken and the origin of Wright's decision to pursue a writing career.

Fabré, Michel. *The Unfinished Quest of Richard Wright.* New York: William Morrow, 1973. Although this volume is one of the most important and authoritative biographies available on Wright, readers interested in Wright's life should consult Margaret Walker's biography as well (see below).

_____. *The World of Richard Wright.* Jackson: University Press of

Mississippi, 1985. A collection of Fabré's essays on Wright. A valuable resource, though not a sustained, full-length study. It contains two chapters on individual short stories by Wright, including the short story "Superstition." Supplemented by an appendix.

Felgar, Robert. *Richard Wright*. Boston: Twayne, 1980. A general biographical and critical source, this work devotes two chapters to the short fiction of Wright.

Hakutani, Yoshinobu. *Richard Wright and Racial Discourse*. Columbia: University of Missouri Press, 1996. Chapters on *Lawd Today, Uncle Tom's Children, Native Son, The Outsider,* and *Black Boy,* as well as discussions of later fiction, black power, and Wright's handling of sexuality. Includes an introduction and a bibliography.

Kinnamon, Keneth. *The Emergence of Richard Wright*. Urbana: University of Illinois Press, 1972. A study of Wright's background and development as a writer, up to the publication of *Native Son* in 1940.

_____, comp. *A Richard Wright Bibliography: Fifty Years of Criticism and Commentary: 1933-1982*. Westport, Conn.: Greenwood Press, 1988. A mammoth annotated bibliography (one of the largest annotated bibliographies ever assembled on an American writer), which traces the history of Wright criticism. This bibliography is invaluable as a research tool.

_____, ed. *Critical Essays on Richard Wright's "Native Son."* New York: Twayne, 1997. Divided into sections of reviews, reprinted essays, and new essays. Includes discussions of Wright's handling of race, voice, tone, novelistic structure, the city, and literary influences. Index but no bibliography.

Rand, William E. "The Structure of the Outsider in the Short Fiction of Richard Wright and F. Scott Fitzgerald." *CLA Journal* 40 (December, 1996): 230-245. Compares theme, imagery, and form of Fitzgerald's "The Diamond as Big as the Ritz" with Wright's "The Man Who Lived Underground" in terms of the treatment of the outsider. Argues that both Fitzgerald and Wright saw themselves as outsiders—Wright because of race and Fitzgerald because of economic class.

Walker, Margaret. *Richard Wright: Daemonic Genius*. New York:

Warner, 1988. A critically acclaimed study of Wright's life and work written by a friend and fellow novelist. Not a replacement for Michel Fabré's biography but written with the benefit of several more years of scholarship on issues that include the medical controversy over Wright's death. Walker is especially insightful on Wright's early life, and her comments on Wright's short fiction are short but pithy. Includes a useful bibliographic essay at the end.

Webb, Constance. *Richard Wright: A Biography.* New York: Putnam, 1968. A well-written biography that remains useful.

— *Thomas Cassidy; Howard Faulkner; Katherine Snipes*

Frank Yerby

Novelist

Born: Augusta, Georgia; September 5, 1916
Died: Madrid, Spain; November 29, 1991

LONG FICTION: *The Foxes of Harrow*, 1946; *The Vixens*, 1947; *The Golden Hawk*, 1948; *Pride's Castle*, 1949; *Floodtide*, 1950; *A Woman Called Fancy*, 1951; *The Saracen Blade*, 1952; *The Devil's Laughter*, 1953; *Bride of Liberty*, 1954; *Benton's Row*, 1954; *The Treasure of Pleasant Valley*, 1955; *Captain Rebel*, 1956; *Fairoaks*, 1957; *The Serpent and the Staff*, 1958; *Jarrett's Jade*, 1959; *Gillian*, 1960; *The Garfield Honor*, 1961; *Griffin's Way*, 1962; *The Old Gods Laugh: A Modern Romance*, 1964; *An Odor of Sanctity*, 1965; *Goat Song*, 1968; *Judas, My Brother*, 1968; *Speak Now: A Modern Novel*, 1969; *The Dahomean: An Historical Novel*, 1971; *The Girl from Storyville*, 1972; *The Voyage Unplanned*, 1974; *Tobias and the Angel*, 1975; *A Rose for Ana Maria*, 1976; *Hail the Conquering Hero*, 1978; *A Darkness at Ingraham's Crest*, 1979; *Western*, 1982; *Devilseed*, 1984; *McKenzie's Hundred*, 1985.
SHORT FICTION: "Health Card," 1944.

Achievements

Frank Yerby wrote many best-selling historical novels over a long career beginning in the 1940's. Most of his best work, however, dates from the 1960's, after he had established himself as a prolific popular novelist. Yerby excelled at creating complicated, fast-moving plots that give vivid impressions of historical eras and periods. Often the novels contradict myths and stereotypes of the periods in question. Almost every novel, too, suggests the futility of finding real truth in the universal confusion of the human condition. While Yerby's protagonists are flawed, often by ruthlessness and infidelity, they are also characterized by a fierce sense of dignity based on the worth of a human life.

Biography

Frank Garvin Yerby was born in Augusta, Georgia, on September 5, 1916. He received a B.A. at Paine College in 1937 and an M.A. at Fisk College in 1938. Subsequently, he did graduate work in education at the University of Chicago. From 1939 to 1941, Yerby taught English, first at Florida A&M and then at Southern University and Agricultural and Mechanical College. Married in 1941, he worked from 1941 to 1944 at the Ford Motor Company in Dearborn, Michigan, as a technician and then as an inspector at Fairchild Aircraft from 1944 to 1945. In 1944, he won an O. Henry Memorial Award for the short story "Health Card," a story that dealt sensitively with black issues. In 1945, he started work on a novel, *The Foxes of Harrow*, which he

(Library of Congress)

aimed to make a commercial success. Thereafter, Yerby wrote many similar melodramatic best-sellers. His books have sold millions of copies and have been translated into at least fourteen languages.

Divorced in the 1950's, Yerby moved to France and then to Spain, where he died in 1991. He had four children from his first marriage. His second wife was his researcher and general manager; some of his later novels give evidence of considerable research. He traveled widely, and sometimes his travels involved investigating locales of works in progress.

Analysis: Long Fiction

Frank Yerby was a best-selling author, and much of what he did has clear commercial appeal, a point on which Yerby made inconsistent remarks. His plots are intricate and involved, but in many of his novels, the characterizations are basically flat. His most-used era is that of the nineteenth century South, yet he wrote about many other places and times in his more than thirty novels. Occasionally, he set a novel in modern times. The superficial reader of best-sellers will find in Yerby's novels fast-paced narrative with appropriate amounts of violence and sex.

Yerby was more, however, than a mere best-selling writer. His short stories written early in his career show promise and develop radically different themes from those of his costume novels. In the 1960's, secure after many commercial successes, Yerby began to do his best work, dealing with larger issues of race and religion, which figure less prominently in his earlier novels. The characters in these later novels are no longer cardboard figures, while the backgrounds are as richly detailed and vividly recreated as ever. Yerby's historical novels must be evaluated within the context of that often unappreciated genre. His novels almost always show the conflict between two worlds or orders, as great historical novels do. Yerby rarely deals with actual historical figures but rather creates characters who have to deal with the essential conflicts of their eras. Often his novels, even the early ones, destroy widely held myths and stereotypes; critic Darwin Turner suggests that this revisionism might be Yerby's most significant contribution as a novelist. While extensive research is not evident in his early work, many of Yerby's later novels were thoroughly researched. Yerby was at his best in creating the color and movement of a particular era.

Yerby's typical protagonist is, in the words of his main character in *The Serpent and the Staff*, an *auslander* or outsider, excluded from the ruling social order. The protagonist experientially develops a philosophy that often approaches modern existentialism, an attitude that life has no answer but that people still must cope with the bleakness of human existence with both dignity and humanity. This pattern emerges in Yerby's first novel, *The Foxes of Harrow*, and is developed in three of his best novels: *Griffin's Way*, *An Odor of Sanctity*, and *The Dahomean*.

The Foxes of Harrow
The Foxes of Harrow, Yerby's first novel, is set in the South and covers the years from 1825 to just after the end of the Civil War. Superficially, it is a novel about a clever schemer who rises to own a plantation with a neoclassical mansion, Harrow, and who has marriages to beautiful white women and a liaison with a stunning mulatto. Much of the novel is composed of stock devices of pulp fiction, and Yerby himself said of *The Foxes of Harrow* that he set out to write a popular novel that would make him a lot of money, regardless of literary merit. Yerby added, however, that he became strangely involved with the writing of the novel and, despite himself, exceeded the ambitions of the pulp genre. Stephen Fox, the protagonist, is an outsider, originally shanty Irish. He is not merely the rogue that early reviewers took him for, whose success and eventual fall conform to a predictable pulp outline. Fox sees all values and ideals slip from him, so that at the end, he is a failure despite his humanity and perception. He is superior to the Southerners with whom he sympathetically deals. More than merely a novel of stock devices, *The Foxes of Harrow* is a story about the failure of a culture.

In the opening of the novel, Yerby's authorial voice establishes a pensive tone as he describes a visit to Harrow, now in ruins, in the twentieth century. Harrow is the symbol of a lost cause. Thus, for symbolic purposes, Harrow is cut off from the modern world. Bathed in moonlight, the ruins of Harrow have a decadent grandeur. The visitor feels driven from room to room and finally away from the house, never wanting to look back. The shortness of the opening, six brief paragraphs, makes the tone all the more striking, and the mood shifts quickly into the dialogue and description of the arrival of Stephen Fox in New Orleans in 1825.

Yerby was at his best in the novel in creating vivid images and scenes of the region during the forty or so years the novel spans. New Orleans appears as a lush feudalistic world where color is measured by degrees, given the novel's constant references to mulattos, quadroons, and octaroons, references which are historically true to the setting. New Orleans emerges as a backward society that refuses to drain the marshes where the mosquitoes carrying yellow fever breed and instead fires cannon to disperse the plague. The society also destroys the creativity of freed blacks. In one case, a thoroughly educated black returns from France and is killed for acting as if he were equal to whites. The most poignant scene occurs at the end of the novel, when the young heir to Harrow returns after the war to New Orleans to be confronted by a former slave of Harrow now in control. This former slave presents the heir's unknown half brother (by a beautiful mulatto) to his former master, who sees the image of his father as a young man—but the half brother is mentally retarded. As the scene concludes, Yerby deftly shows the social history of the next one hundred years of the South. The former slave, now the ruler, knows that power will again return to the whites but suggests that blacks and whites can live together and respect one another. The heir, a combination of the worst of his father's roguish tendencies and the excesses of New Orleans, emphatically denies that such equality and reconciliation between the races are possible.

Yerby was weakest in his creation of character in *The Foxes of Harrow,* for the characters are one-dimensional and move woodenly through a convoluted, overheated plot. Stephen Fox is the fox, the rogue set off from Southern society by his birth, whose goals are riches and the most beautiful woman in New Orleans, Odalie Arceneaux, a cold, haughty belle. Her sister Aurore is a foil to her, for she is warm and beautiful and in love with Stephen, who is too blind at first to see her love. As is common in pulp fiction, Odalie dies in childbirth, and Stephen then marries gentle Aurore, but only after having fathered a child by a beautiful mulatto when Odalie had spurned his strong sexual drives.

Underneath this claptrap, though, is an author working with social issues not to be found in the typical 1946 pulp novel. In one scene, a black woman recently inducted into slavery throws herself into the Mississippi rather than live in bondage. Old Calleen, a trusted slave at Harrow, later tells her grandson Inch (the son of the drowned slave) that someday, the rightness of their freedom will be made apparent. More significantly, in understated dialogue Stephen talks to his son Etienne about freeing slaves and says that the country must treat all people equally, including the blacks and the poorest whites. When his son dismisses the poor, white or black, Stephen uses history as a defense, mentioning the French Revolution, Haiti, and insurrectionist Nat Turner. It is in his sympathy and balance in treating social matters that Yerby's "moral mobility" appears, a phrase that a London *Times* writer used in reviewing a later Yerby novel.

Griffin's Way

Griffin's Way was published in 1962, sixteen years after *The Foxes of Harrow*, and is a departure in some respects from Yerby's work up to that time. It treats the Mississippi of the 1870's unglamorously, highlighting squalor, inbreeding among whites, and the violence of the Klan in a manner more characteristic of William Faulkner than of the standard best-selling author. The novel shows the paralysis of humane white society after the war, a paralysis symbolized by the central hero's amnesia and invalid status.

Much of the novel debunks the grandeur and opulence of the old South, which Yerby himself had occasionally exploited in earlier novels. The ruined South appears first through the eyes of a Northerner, Candace Trevor, a New England minister's daughter married to a paralyzed Southerner and hired as a nurse for Paris Griffin as the novel opens. She despises the Southern "courtesy" to which women are subjected, dismisses the neoclassical architecture in the poorly constructed homes, and comments on how most planters lived in squalor even before the war. Unlike her father, she believes in a Darwinian theory of evolution and sees the darker forces in herself as part of the ape still remaining in people. Candace knows that to cure Paris of his amnesia she must find the key to it from Paris's oversexed wife Laurel. Ferreting out answers with the right leading questions, she discovers the tawdry, twisted story that led to Paris's amnesia and emotional paralysis. It is only her austere moral upbringing that allows her to control her love for Paris to use her knowledge to help him.

When Candace does cure him, Paris tries to return to his home, Griffin's Way, and to his wife Laurel, but while his cure is a rebirth, it does not allow a return. To begin with, he has returned to a world changed by the war, a world of political corruption and violence, a world that has regressed, so that even a sixty-mile trip, once possible in three hours, now involves an arduous three-day journey because the railroads remain unrepaired even five years after the war. Three years later, with the railroad rebuilt, Paris and Laurel visit Vicksburg, where Paris, despite his humanity, appears troubled by the apparent ascendancy of blacks. Yerby balances the situation by having Paris also see the obvious corruption of the black superintendent of schools, who lives in the grand style of the old South on money intended for the schools. Paris is thus caught between two worlds: He rejects the Klan as apes but resents a black man wearing a suit as if he is accustomed to it. Even renewed, Paris still represents the paralysis of the humane white during the Reconstruction.

Yerby titled the last third of the novel "Apocalypse," and this part has unresolved elements, unresolved on account of Yerby's honesty in dealing with his material. Paris watches the new world tumble around him, powerless to do anything. Black militants and white Klansmen fight all over the South, but Paris can only catalog the battles; he cannot change events. His moment of action does allow him to rescue Samson, a former slave, and

Samson's wife by helping them escape to the North. He can do nothing to help his brother, his mulatto wife, and their children, who are burned in their house except for one daughter, who dies after being repeatedly raped, all of them victims of the Klan. He also helps a black minister escape, but only after the dynamiting of the minister's house, which killed a daughter. At his daughter's funeral, the minister delivers a stern sermon to the Klan members, who then threaten his life so that Paris must again help him. The Klan members finally back off from Paris's house when one accidentally shoots Laurel, still very much a symbol of Southern womanhood. The novel ends with dawn imagery, the night having been endured and the humane whites now waiting for the light of morning. Whether the whites threatened by the Klan can start anew is unclear. Given the implied parallel to modern events, Yerby seems to be saying that it is too soon to tell whether the twentieth century can rise above racial violence; nevertheless, the concluding imagery does suggest hope.

An Odor of Sanctity

In *An Odor of Sanctity,* Yerby is at his best as a historical novelist. It is a long, deftly paced novel which, while using many of the stock elements of Yerby's novels of the 1940's and 1950's, also deals intelligently with a religious theme. Once again, Yerby creates an outsider, Alaric Teudisson, as hero; he is set off by his odor of sanctity, a saintly force in him of which he is not fully aware for most of his life. Teudisson must deal with the complex culture of medieval Spain, a battleground for Christians, Moors, and numerous bands of marauding barbarians.

Like earlier Yerby protagonists, Teudisson is involved in many liaisons and several marriages. Teudisson is a striking blond of Visigoth extraction who, before the male hormones take effect, is so "beautiful" that at one point he is almost made a catamite. Thereafter, Teudisson has numerous sexual encounters, one unconsummated marriage, and finally a marriage to a woman who has been repeatedly raped by bandits, a marriage which shows Teudisson's magnanimity and one which also brings Teudisson genuine happiness and a family.

The religious motif of *An Odor of Sanctity* adds depth to what would otherwise be an entertaining but rather shallow melodrama. Despite himself, Teudisson becomes a saint by the end of the novel. As a man, Teudisson is handsome but scarred by battle, but as a boy, his beauty, so unlike the usual rough Goth face, led his mother and others to think he was marked for the priesthood. He turns from his religious impulses to lead a secular life, however, and while doing so, he finds his saintliness. In dealing with women, he shows a compassion and love that are the basis of his profound sexual appeal; at one point of seeming dissolution, he has numerous prostitutes loving him because he has talked to them and treated them as human beings and not merely as sex objects. Misused by a woman, he always responds with kindness. By the end of the novel, Teudisson becomes the arbiter between Moor and Christian factions when a certain group of fanatic Christians wants to destroy all tolerance for the predominant Moors. Throughout the novel, Teudisson has been a genuine ecumenist. At the end, Teudisson, doubting his saintly powers because he is unable to save his wife, willingly seeks crucifixion and thus enters sainthood and legend. In losing himself, he gains sainthood.

As in most of his novels, Yerby's greatest strength in *An Odor of Sanctity* is his re-creation of a time, a re-creation imbued with color and action. Again, a humane authorial voice speaks throughout the novel. The book shows that the diversity of medieval Spain is indeed its glory. While the Moorish culture encourages learning and recognizes Christ as a prophet, the contrasting Christian culture (except for Teudisson and a few Church fathers) is dark and intolerant. In showing the clash between these cultures, *An Odor of Sanctity* is first-rate historical fiction.

The Dahomean

If one of Yerby's novels is destined to last, it is *The Dahomean*, a novel unlike any of his others. It is a simple, moving tale of the life of a black man in his African culture before he was sold into slavery. Yerby neither idealizes nor sensationalizes his material but presents a story composed of love, envy, and hatred that reads as a legend, a story of characters and events drawn larger than life. The protagonist, Nyasanu, is like other Yerby protagonists because he is an alien or outsider: He is far less violent and far more handsome than most men of his society. Caught in the ugliness of the American slave system, he has the tragic quality of some of the great existentialist heroes.

Yerby begins the chronological narrative of Nyasanu as he is about to enter manhood, a passage marked by the painful ritual of circumcision. The early parts of the novel present such rituals in convincing detail. Yerby moves the reader from Nyasanu's initiation to an enemy's attempt to destroy his guardian tree to his wedding and the deflowering of his bride. In "A Note to the Reader," Yerby explains that the novel is based on research into the customs of the Dahomeans of the nineteenth century, but Yerby adds to his research his own respect of this African culture.

As Nyasanu moves through his period of manhood, Yerby depicts the society of the Dahomeans as a stage for the great primal emotions and forces of life. Nyasanu has encounters with numerous women, but his sexual experiences are never merely sensational, the stuff of popular fiction: Nyasanu has a reality which sets him apart from Yerby's typical protagonists. In addition to his sexual encounters, Nyasanu has the experience of real brotherhood, for his society expects each male to have his three closest friends identified in order. Battles with warring tribes give Nyasanu the chance to show bravery and also to distinguish himself as more sensitive to violence than the average Dahomean. In addition, Yerby shows the diversity of Dahomean society, which includes both male homosexuals and Amazonian warriors.

In a moving discussion with his number-one friend, Kpadunu, Nyasanu learns that the generations are all of one fabric. Each generation faces the same problems of love, the family, and death. The old priests, therefore, give answers based on the past to the young and the unsure, and—given the coherence of their society—the answers generally hold. Facing the problem of belief in the gods which these old priests try to inculcate in the young, Nyasanu realizes that their wisdom is not divine but experiential, that the past of his society answers the present needs. Ironically, his friend Kpadunu is trying to help Nyasanu rise above the control of priests by showing where their wisdom resides, yet he actually makes the skeptical Nyasanu believe more than he did, so that he must face the priestly prediction that his life will end in Dahomey but will begin again in another place.

Nyasanu does learn that he can count on the inexorability of fate and not the protection of the gods. In quick succession, he loses his friend Kpadunu, his wife in childbirth, and his father. He comes to see his heroism as mere foolishness in taking risks. Rather than listening to the gods, he simply faces life as chieftain and husband of Kpadunu's widow. Far more than the ritual of circumcision, his acceptance of life and his rejection of the illusion of divine protection mark Nyasanu's adulthood. When Nyasanu next appears in the novel, he is chieftain and has four wives. His life is successful until he is sold into slavery with the aid of his homosexual brother and rival.

The betrayal of Nyasanu has the archetypal pattern of tragedy, the hero fallen from great heights, undone by his own blindness in not facing the evil of his brother and his incestuous brother-in-law and by his pride in not following the past and living with his extended family in the same compound. He faces the guns of his attackers with his sword, only to be told to put his sword down, for in the modern era, swords are powerless against guns. First, he must watch the murder of his mother (the slavers see that she is too old to have children), the subsequent murder of all his children (the slavers know that they would die on the voyage across the Atlantic), and the subjugation of his wives, the rape of some and the suicide of one. His response is disassociation, a silence which lasts the rest of his life.

Like a classical tragedy, *The Dahomean* treats terrible despair in its conclusion but leads to an illumination, Nyasanu's enlightenment. He recognizes the evil of blacks selling blacks into American slavery, although they have no conception of the degradation of this foreign slavery, their domestic slavery being gentle and indulgent. Philosophically, Nyasanu faces the bleakness of life with the realization that there are no answers. Truth is only that there is no truth. Nyasanu acquits himself with honor; like a great tragic hero, he has his dignity, the dignity of silence in the face of the emptiness of the human condition.

Other Literary Forms

In addition to his novels, Frank Yerby wrote poetry and short stories that are often found in anthologies of black literature. One story, "Health Card," first published in *Harper's* magazine, won a special O. Henry Memorial Award in 1944.

Bibliography

Bone, Robert A. *The Negro Novel in America.* Rev. ed. New Haven, Conn.: Yale University Press, 1965. A general survey of black novels. Bone dismisses Yerby as the "prince of pulpsters."

Glasrud, Bruce A., and Laurie Champion. "'The Fishes and the Poet's Hands': Frank Yerby, A Black Author in White America." *Journal of American & Comparative Cultures* 23, no. 4 (Winter, 2000): 15-22. Analyzes Yerby's commercial success as a writer and explores some of the challenges faced by writers (particularly African American writers) during the mid-twentieth century.

Klotman, Phyllis. "A Harrowing Experience: Frank Yerby's First Novel to Film." *College Language Association Journal* 31 (December, 1987): 210-222. Focuses on the changes made to Yerby's story when *The Foxes of Harrow* was adapted to the screen.

Mendelson, Phyllis Carmel, and Dedria Bryfonski, eds. *Contemporary Literary Criticism.* Vol. 7. Detroit: Gale, 1977. Contains excerpts of positive criticism about Yerby's use of racial themes.

Metzger, Linda, and Deborah A. Straub, eds. *Contemporary Authors.* New Revision Series 16. Detroit: Gale, 1986. Contains a sympathetic look at Yerby's work. Also contains an interview with the novelist.

Osborne, Gwendolyn. "Romance: How Black Romance—Novels, That Is—Came to Be." *Black Issues Book Review* 4, no. 1 (January/February, 2003): 50-53. Details Yerby's contribution to African American romance novels and provides a profile of the genre.

Ryan, Bryan. *Major Twentieth-Century Authors.* Detroit: Gale, 1991. Contains a brief entry on Yerby.

Smiles, Robin V. "Uncovering Frank Yerby." *Black Issues in Higher Education* 21, no. 19 (November, 2004): 28-31. Provides some interesting biographical information, details on Yerby's second wife, and his strongest artistic influences.

Turner, Darwin. "Frank Yerby as Debunker." In *The Black Novelist,* edited by Robert Hemenway. Columbus, Ohio: Merrill, 1970. Turner comments on Yerby's "painful groping for meaning" behind a "soap-opera façade."

— Dennis Goldsberry

Al Young

Novelist and poet

Born: Ocean Springs, Mississippi; May 31, 1939

LONG FICTION: *Snakes*, 1970; *Who Is Angelina?*, 1975; *Sitting Pretty*, 1976; *Ask Me Now*, 1980; *Seduction by Light*, 1988.

POETRY: *Dancing*, 1969; *The Song Turning Back into Itself*, 1971; *Geography of the Near Past*, 1976; *The Blues Don't Change: New and Selected Poems*, 1982; *Heaven: Collected Poems, 1956-1990*, 1992; *Conjugal Visits, and Other Poems in Verse and Prose*, 1996; *The Sound of Dreams Remembered: Poems, 1990-2000*, 2001.

NONFICTION: *Bodies and Soul: Musical Memoirs*, 1981; *Kinds of Blue: Musical Memoirs*, 1984; *Things Ain't What They Used to Be: Musical Memoirs*, 1987; *Mingus/Mingus: Two Memoirs*, 1989 (with Janet Coleman); *Drowning in the Sea of Love: Musical Memoirs*, 1995.

EDITED TEXTS: *Changing All Those Changes*, 1976 (of James P. Girard); *Zeppelin Coming Down*, 1976 (of William Lawson); *Yardbird Lives!*, 1978 (with Ishmael Reed); *Calafia*, 1979 (with Reed and Shawn Hsu Wong); *Quilt*, 1981-1986 (with Reed; 5 volumes); *African American Literature: A Brief Introduction and Anthology*, 1996.

Achievements

For his first collection, *Dancing*, Al Young won the National Arts Council Award for poetry. In 1968, Young received a National Arts Council Award for editing. Young was a Wallace E. Stegner Fellow in 1966, and in 1969 he received a Joseph Henry Jackson Award from the San Francisco Foundation for *Dancing*. The next year, his first novel, *Snakes*, appeared and was praised for its authentic portrayal of a young man, addicted to jazz, growing up in urban America.

Young received a Guggenheim Fellowship in 1974 and a National Endowment for the Arts Fellowship in 1975. His considerable work on small literary magazines includes founding and editing *Loveletter* (an avant-garde review of the 1960's that has received awards from the National Arts Council), editing *Changes* (for the West Coast), and coediting, with Ishmael Reed, *Yardbird Reader.* He cofounded the Yardbird Publishing Cooperative and continues to work actively in small-press publishing.

In the 1980's, Young turned increasingly to writing nonfiction, often having to do with music and film. He earned an Outstanding Book of the Year citation from *The New York Times* in 1980 for *Ask Me Now,* a Pushcart Prize in 1980, an American Book Award from the Before Columbus Foundation in 1982 for *Bodies and Soul,* and a Fulbright Fellowship in 1984.

Biography

Albert James Young, the son of Mary (Campbell) and Albert James Young, was born in Ocean Springs, Mississippi, near Biloxi, on the Gulf of Mexico. His childhood, which he characterizes as happy, was divided between rural Mississippi and urban Detroit. Though he moved through several communities and schools, he values the flexibility that he gained by adapting to different subcultures. His father was an auto worker (in part, the model for Durwood Knight's father in *Ask Me Now*), and also a professional musician, like his son. For five years, Young sang and played the flute and guitar professionally, at first while attending the University of Michigan, then while working as a disc jockey at radio station KJAZ-FM, Alameda, California. The character M. C. in *Snakes* reflects some of Young's aspirations as a young jazz musician, and the poem "A Little More Traveling Music" reflects his divided roots in rural and urban music. American blues and jazz and their origins in African music have influenced the themes and the formal structures of Young's fiction and poetry.

Young has credited his interest in writing narratives to his early exposure to the art of southern storytelling, and his fictional and poetic use of regional and ethnic vernacular draws upon his memories of southern speech as well as his wide reading in American literature (especially the works of Zora Neale Hurston, Mark Twain, Langston Hughes, and Jesse Stuart) and British and European literature.

Young attended the University of Michigan from 1957 to 1961 before moving to the San Francisco Bay area in 1961. There he received his A.B. degree in Spanish from the University of California at Berkeley in 1969. He and his wife Arline June (Belch) were married in 1963 and have a son, Michael James Young. From 1966 to 1967, Young was a fellow in Advanced Fiction Writing at Stanford University; in 1969, he received his bachelor of arts degree in Spanish at the University of California, Berkeley. Young taught writing at the San Francisco Museum of Art during the late 1960's and was linguistic consultant for the Berkeley Neighborhood Youth Corps. From 1969 to 1973, he held Stanford University's Edward H. Jones Lectureship in Creative Writing. He was the 1979 director of Associated Writing Programs, an organization of graduate university administrators, teachers, and students of creative writing, was writer-in-residence at the University of Washington from 1981 to 1982, and served as consultant to the New York writer's organization Poets and Writers in 1974 and 1975.

Young also spent many years in the 1970's and 1980's working as a film screenwriter for various Los Angeles-area studios. He was a writer-in-residence at the University of Washington in Seattle from 1981 to 1982, and served as the vice president of Yardbird Publishing Cooperative. He became a familiar face on the lecture circuit at universities throughout the United States. In the 1990's, he continued writing, contributing to anthologies, and creating "musical memoirs." Though he has traveled widely—in Spain, France, Mexico, and the United States—he has made his home in Northern California. Many of his poems and novels record his sensitive observations on the diverse cultural lives of people in the San Francisco Bay area, and several of his works have been presented on KQED-TV San Francisco and by the Pacifica Radio Network.

Analysis: Long Fiction

Al Young's concern for language, a concern that embraces both mistrust and love, is clearly evinced in his prose. His second novel, *Who Is Angelina?*, and his fourth, *Ask Me Now*, have third-person narrative personae who stand distractingly close to their author; they appear hesitant to act freely for want of purpose. Readers of the first and third novels, however, will quickly recognize Young's ability to render in his first-person narrative personae a vibrant male voice of new adulthood (*Snakes*), or sagacious middle age (*Sitting Pretty*).

The author's background as a professional musician enables him to use music descriptively as well as metaphorically; the reader shares the experience of making music and feeling music make life known. The music of language also affects Young's style. He makes careful alterations to standard syntax and diction, sometimes punctuation, in order to set the speech closer to its natural human tone. His objective is not merely to create contemporary dialect, but also to create an enduring contemporaneity, to offer rhythmically, as the poet-musician should, the nonverbal meanings that language can carry in its sounds. Young creates this quality of speech through narrative personae who speak softly or stridently, sometimes too literally, yet with voices constant and sincere.

Love, like a curse or a whimper, extends most intensely from the individual to those nearby. The contemporary American social dilemma is thereby represented in Young's prose just as it appears in his poetry: Each person must somehow maintain the unity, fidelity, and consistency love requires while grappling for the freedom and oneness that American mythology promises. Although *Snakes* and *Sitting Pretty* are more successful, all Young's novels contain graphic portrayals of mainstream urban America—middle-class people who try to be good at being themselves. They emote, they dream, and they reason. At worst, they stand too large on the page; at best, they find purpose to complement the dignity they feel. Whether he narrates with commentary from a third-person point of view, or with the immediacy of first-person sensory experience, Young confronts the problems of individuals growing into their individuality, and the qualities of life central to the congregate American family.

Snakes

The narrative persona of Young's first novel, *Snakes*, is M. C. Moore, who recollects his youth and adolescence in the mature, seasoned voice of the novel's master of ceremonies. A novel of formation, *Snakes* is in the *Bildungsroman* tradition and is rendered in a tone of voice at once nostalgic and fatherly. Although he has only snapshots of his true parents by which to remember them, M. C. gradually finds their love implanted in his own initialed name, "so it sound[s] like you had some status," his first lover explains, "whether you did or not." For M. C., the process of learning who he is becomes the composition of his own music.

M. C. discovers music in his soul and he makes music the core of his world. He finds music everywhere, "in the streets, in the country, in people's voices," and "in the way they lead their lives." Providing counterpoint, M. C.'s grandmother Claude offers guidance and family history, and M. C. is her captive audience: "I could listen to Claude talk all day long, and did, many a time. Her voice was like music." The association expands as his views of love and music merge, and women ultimately become "lovable fields of musical energy."

While living with relatives in the South, M. C. learns at the age of ten that music will be his life. His Uncle Donald, a "night rambler" with a "talent for getting hold of a dollar," turns their impoverished household into a "blind pig," or a Meridian, Mississippi, version of a speakeasy. During his first exposure to the amoral world of adults, M. C. meets Tull, an itinerant jazz pianist who in effect provides the novel's premise: "You'll get it if you keep at it. Listen, just take your time, one note a time over here with your right hand. Just take your time, that's all it is to playin' the piano or anything else. Take your time and work it on out." The impression lasts; M. C. goes on to structure his life around his love of music and his faith that music will help him grow.

Literature also has a formative effect on him. It is not literature as found in the classroom or in books—M. C. attends high school in body only, and barely earns his diploma—rather, literature personified in Shakes, his closest friend, whose name is short for Shakespeare. Shakes has a "greedy memory and a razor tongue." He is bright, musical, and funny: "You hip to Cyrano de Bergerac? Talk about a joker could talk some trash! Cyrano got everybody told! Didn't nobody be messin with Cyrano, ugly as he was."

Yet there is more to know about life than its music and its literature; such knowledge appears in the person of Champ, who exposes M. C. to contemporary jazz and the business hemisphere of that musical world. In his bemusing, self-sacrificial way, Champ also demonstrates his worsening drug addiction and the consequential brutalization of his sensibilities. "Poor Champ," M. C. soon observes while he learns to jam, to feel his music come alive inside himself and issue forth, "who wanted to play an instrument so badly, would stand around working his arms and fingers for hours sometimes, shaping the smoky air in the room into some imaginary saxophone. . . . We all wanted to get good."

The evil to which Champ submits himself opposes the good that he gives M. C.—music as growth and expression. M. C.'s band, "The Masters of Ceremony," discover in their art a meaning that transcends the music they produce, and although the group separates after one demo and some local gigs, M. C.'s early success provides him with a clearer view of the possibilities of his life and a deep sense of wonder. He emerges from his plain, ordinary background complete, communicative, and capable of more, having also achieved his own narrative voice, that husky, now masculine voice the reader has heard maturing since the story's outset. He boards the New York bus a musician, grown: "I don't feel free . . . but I don't feel trapped." Awkwardly, painfully, naturally, M. C. has learned to look for the subtle ironies that enrich both life and art. Ready at last for the rest of what he will be, the young adult takes with him his guitar, his music, and precious recordings of his song "Snakes," which throughout the novel parallels his experience of youth: "The tune sounded simple the first time you heard it, but it wasn't all that simple to play."

Who Is Angelina?

While the narrative voice of *Snakes* provides contrast and consistency—a gradual merging of the maturing young man with his adult consciousness—the narrative voice of *Who Is Angelina?* accomplishes neither. Angelina is already grown, but her adult life has entered a phase of meaningless triviality. This she blames on the shifting cultural milieu of Berkeley, California. Life in Berkeley seems different now—dangerous—and the people's sense of freedom and fun, that community spirit of festivity, is gone. She uses the burglary of her apartment as the justification, and a friend's convenient cash as the means, to skip town—an act she considers the prerequisite for introspection. She flees not only her fictional problems but also her reader as well; a character with both brains and beauty who struggles with mere communal ennui is less than sympathetic. Moreover, even the reader who can overlook her escapist behavior needs to know more about her, and most of her background is provided through recollection and reminiscence. The novel's principal events—travel in Mexico, some romantic sex, an emergency trip home to Detroit, an encounter with a street thief—facilitate reflection by the viewpoint character, and the reader must simply accept her gradual appraisals. Dramatically, little takes place. Most of this novel is exposition; what little action there is consists of Angelina's consideration of an adaptation to what goes on around her.

The unifying thematic metaphor of *Who Is Angelina?* is the act of taking away: Angelina is robbed (her reaction is passive); her lover's mysterious occupation suggests more of the same; her father is robbed and nearly killed; a friend's purse is stolen (her reaction this time is spontaneous and violent). Eventually, Angelina's searching appears to reach some sort of resolution that makes her worthy of new self-esteem. Yet the reader can only observe, not participate in this search, because—unlike *Snakes*'s composer-narrator—Angelina does not experience within the narrative a process of growth.

Plainly, Angelina is a woman experiencing a crisis of self-identity during a series of events that propel her toward introspection. What she ultimately discovers within herself is a typical American complex of contradictions, such as the one she de-

scribes to a fellow traveler early in her journey, the contradiction Americans create by equating individuality with isolation:
"Angelina explained that in America it's the individual who matters most and that she and her family, such as it was, lived at separate ends of what's called reality. She too was lonely and fed up
with a kind of life she'd been leading."

Whether the narrator addresses the reader directly or
through the medium of a letter to a former lover, the exposition
continues: "Everyone nowadays is busy digging for roots. Well, I
know them well and it doesn't make a damn bit of difference
when it comes to making sense of who I am and why I make the
kinds of mistakes I do. In the end, I've discovered, it all comes
down to being in competition with yourself." At moments,
Angelina's concern waxes angry and the culturally contempla-
tive author intrudes: "I'm not so sure that all those chitlins,
hamhocks, hog maws, pigsfeet, spareribs and cooking with
lard—soulfood so-called—isn't contributing more toward
bringing about black genocide, as the phrasemongers would
have it, than Sickle Cell Anemia." An important discovery about
herself does take place, however, and this is what her wandering
is all about. The exploration has been a contemporary one that
many young, single Americans never complete: "The truth was
that, most of all, she loved open-hearted vulnerable strangers
for whom she wasn't strictly obliged to feel anything."

In the end, Angelina also learns that she has been changing
at the same time that her surroundings have been changing. Because she has confused one process with another, separation followed by a reassertion of self followed by a return to her point of
departure appears to be cathartic. If so, the reader hopes that
she also learns that life is and continues to be a process of
change, some small part of which is subject to each individual's
conscious control. Angelina's recognition of this consciousness
is both the special story and the ordinariness of Young's second
novel.

Sitting Pretty

Sidney J. Prettymon, the narrative persona of *Sitting Pretty*, is
streetwise, sardonic, and ironically self-conscious. He establishes

early a mock superstitious mentality—astronauts may mess up the moon so that it can no longer be full—and verbalizes "the integral aspects of [his] personal philosophy to be cool." Prettymon is dangerously learned: "I cut this article out of the *National Inquirer* that maintain how you can succeed and develop yourself and transformate your whole personality by the buildin' up your vocabulary." His inborn sense of linguistic sound combines comically with his interest in discovering associative meanings (*radical chic* connotes to him the concubine of a politically motivated Arab husband of many wives), but the best humor to be found in *Sitting Pretty* is derived from Prettymon's command of the text. The reader is at all times close to Prettymon, and he exploits the closeness. Having pondered his plot-situation at the story's outset, he describes himself to himself as being "on the threshold of destiny, temptation, and fate." Turning aside, he speaks directly to the reader: "Now, that's bad! [good] Let me run through that one again so y'all can savor it."

The narrative opens below the closing sentence of Mark Twain's *Adventures of Huckleberry Finn* (1884); in many ways, Sidney J. Prettymon is a contemporary, self-possessed Jim. As Twain's narrative control allowed him to elevate linguistic puns through burlesque to high satirical levels, Young's narrative is successful here by virtue of its consistently controlled authorial distance: "All I mean by imagination," Prettymon says, "is the way stuff look when you pull back from it and give it some reflection room." Prettymon as first-person narrative persona allows the author to work most effectively; because his imagination provides Prettymon with overview, it allows him to construct connotative ironies.

The incongruous coexistence of common insight and aesthetic misinterpretation (Huck does not misinterpret aesthetic qualities; he misses them entirely) works through sarcastic understatement: "Carpe Diem, like they say in Latin. Save the day." The author's hand moves subtly, characterizing by misquotation.

Like M. C.'s unknown parents, Prettymon has given his son an inspirational name with which to command respect—Aristotle: "He is a lawyer." Professionally successful, Aristotle is a son ungrateful for his name, and working-class Prettymon must struggle to disguise his pride as resentment: "He go around callin hisself A. Winfred Prettymon. I'm the one give him his first name and that's his way of gettin back at me. I wanted him to stand out and be distinguished and be the bearer of a name that smack of dignity." Telephoning his daughter, Prettymon again creates linguistic pandemonium, quoting Ralph Waldo Emerson in order to reinforce some fatherly advice, then addressing the reader as the individualistic, pro-consumer Henry David Thoreau: "I hung up fast, then taken the receiver back off the hook again so the operator couldn't ring me back for that extra ten cent. I ain't go nothing but the vastest contempt for the Phone Company. Leeches and rascals! Need to be investigated."

Sitting Pretty is Young's best novel in three ways: consistency of viewpoint, ingenuity of the narrative-persona, and control of the language. The last must be perfect for an author to choose suggestive, convincing variations consistent with popular speech. Young's rendering of black dialect for artistic purpose is found throughout his fiction, and it works effectively here. The novel's language is an unconcealed treasure:

> What with all that racket and commotion and the drink I'd just taken, I was startin to feel randy—a term the Professor use, British word for horney—randy for my own private bottle of sweet wine. Got a job lines up and just *know* Aristotle gon spring my Plymouth loose. Celebratin time! Time to do that quiet furlough down to Adamo's again.

Surprised, uniquely joyful, Sidney J. Prettymon rediscovers his treasure again and again.

Seduction by Light

For his fifth novel, Young again employs a first-person narrative persona, female and clairvoyant. Mamie Franklin is a woman in her forties, rich in impressions and experience. She grew up in Mississippi an admirer of her namesake and imaginary tutor/ yogi Benjamin Franklin, made those feelings real through writing, left home early to perform in the style of Dinah Washington with her husband's group, the Inklings, and married and had her son Benjie out of wedlock. She lives now in Santa Monica with Burley, the man she loves and whose love is returned until—cataclysmically—Mamie's past and future upheave into the narrative present.

As in *Snakes* and the adventures of Sidney J. Prettymon, there is a running commentary on situation and circumstance along with a steady stream of verbal ironies and satiric asides. Mamie works part-time in Beverly Hills as a domestic for Mr. Chrysler and his French wife Danielle, who live in "a big stockbroker Tudor" graced with eucalyptus, or "Noxema trees." Mamie has the confidence of her employers, in fact their favor, as she drives her Honda Civic (nicknamed Sweepea) up the front driveway and strolls into the house. There she discovers a strange, unclothed woman with toes and fingernails painted black who looks like "a bleached-out, fuzzy-headed raccoon," and a Monopoly board, which compromises Mr. Chrysler ("that man loves to play Monopoly . . . with real money").

This kind of fun—the world according to Mamie Franklin— enlivens the novel's complication. Regarding the 1970's, that too-short period when black consciousness merged with African American professional development and economic opportunity, Mamie says, "[I]t mighta looked to the public like anything black was gonna make money . . . but that wasn't nothin but an illusion."

More than witty, these quips come from a woman who made her living as a performer during the 1950's, when the business of entertainment reinstituted racial segregation, and who now sees further deterioration in the filmmaking business: "This old brotherhood junk, funny stuff and jive everybody use to be talkin—all that went out the minute the money started gettin shaky." With a tonal admonition for more education, she observes that the film industry is being run by young white men who "started readin *Variety* and *Billboard* when they were nine." For Mamie, age enables one to "ripen into know-how, or better yet, know-when." After all, she says, "The smarter you are, the harder you smart when you fall."

Throughout the novel, light and light imagery brighten the

reader's way like the sunlit flowers of Alice Walker's *The Color Purple* (1982) or the moonlit landscapes of Nathaniel Hawthorne's tales. Mamie's vision captures both the brilliance and the business of the California landscape while nuances of Eastern philosophy energize her sensibility and evoke a mood of resolution. Such evocations occur in dreams or dreamlike experiences, such as the surreal state of shock following the reality of an earthquake or the emotional upheaval of sexual renewal. "It was all done with light," Mamie says of cinematic production and marketing. Like the girl she "use to be" watching a film at the Grand Lux Theatre, Mamie learns that "pretty much every last one of us out here [in California] gettin seduced." As girl and as mother, as woman and as lover, Mamie looks over her shoulder to see "nothin but light, not a thing but light quiverin and makin patterns on a screen."

Throughout her life, Mamie has had enlightening experiences. She recalls a vision of sunlight playing over a leaf, how the light "shimmered all around it; then the leaf sends out this invisible feeler [and] suck up the light around it, drink it up, sip on it like you would a glassa buttermilk." Similarly, when Mamie's housemate Burley returns in spirit, he describes his passage from life: "It was like this hole opened up in the middle of my forehead and the light started pourin into it."

Moreover, Mamie contemplates the textuality of her life by the light of her contemplations, suggesting that this affects the storyteller, too:

> Where do you begin when you start tellin your story and rememberin as you go along? Do you start with the source of light itself, the sun? Or do you start with what the sun touches, the moon? Or do you only deal with what the moonlight touches?

We must consider the light by which we live our lives, Mamie suggests, as we rewrite the texts of our lives:

> It's actually possible in one lifetime to do so much and to get caught up in so many of your own illusions and lies and half lies

until it can finally come down to sun versus moon versus moonlight.

Celebratory and down-to-earth, Young's novels glow with human warmth. In the mode of vernacular speech, *Seduction by
Light* rings true with contemporary experience while transmut-
ing everyday life into the light of love.

Analysis: Poetry

Al Young's poetry originates in visual and aural memories and
in musical forms which are then developed through suitable
language and prosody. The music that inspires his poetry includes rhythm and blues and jazz, and he makes effective use of
various American dialects. The metaphor of dancing unites the
visual images and musical forms, and suggests both the formal-
ity and the spontaneity of design in his poetry.

Young also writes about family relationships and does so with
insight, humor, and affection. His fictional characters and poetic personas often center their identities in their family life,
which enables them, somehow, to cope with the meanness and
injustice of contemporary urban American society. The family
relationships are hardly idyllic, and characters habitually annoy
and occasionally hurt one another; nevertheless, the love they
feel for one another transforms their lives. Although his work
offers no simplistic ideological solutions, his poems and novels
clearly reflect his belief in the writer's function: to change society by expanding the reader's perception of reality.

Dancing

Dancing, Young's first collection, explores many forms of dance,
including "A Dance for Militant Dilettantes," "Dancing Day to
Day," "The John Coltrane Dance," "Reading Nijinsky's Diary,"
"Dancing Pierrot," "A Little More Traveling Music," and "Dancing." Young's rejection of "monocultural values, of whatever
hue," is reflected in the diverse cultural backgrounds of the poems in *Dancing*.

At the beginning of his collection, Young places an uncharacteristic poem, perhaps written after the manuscript of *Snakes* had been refused by a series of publishers interested only in black voices that were violently angry and bitter. "A Dance for Militant Dilettantes" implicitly rejects the advice of a friend who urges him to play the stereotypic role of a honky-hating African American activist, writing about bloodying "those fabled wine & urine-/ stained hallways." While modifying the Homeric cliché of wine-dark seas, Young's brilliant epithet exposes the contemporary racism of the publisher who wants to market "a furious nigrah" and of the militant dilettantes willing to sell out.

The poet in "Dancing Day to Day" lives in and writes about a multicultural world, in which people are fearful of violence and yet live, fairly contentedly, one day at a time. In the first four lines of this poem, Young echoes T. S. Eliot, in the "come and go" of his monotonous, trivial, habitual Prufrockian world, but, significantly, without Eliot's contempt:

> In my street
> the people mostly go.
> Very few come
> to what I'd call home.

The walking iambic meter of lines two and four alternates with the emphatic trochees of lines one and three, and his quatrain establishes the dominant metric pattern of the verse paragraphs that follow. This open design, built on no regular line length, perfectly expresses the speaker's relaxed attitude toward his neighbors, as well as the freedom of their daily natural movements.

"The John Coltrane Dance," a tribute to the music of John Coltrane, uses repetition, subtle assonance, and alliteration to suggest the emotional power of Coltrane's musical compositions and performances. The word "sound" occurs seven times, is echoed in "astound" and "surround," and introduces a pattern of sibilants. The line, "Mr Love Trane," occurs only twice (lines two and twenty-four), but its distinctive concluding spondee, lengthened by the long vowels, sets a metrical pattern that also occurs in lines eight ("tree dance"), fourteen ("smoothed stones"), sixteen ("hurt songs"), and eighteen ("sound cures"). Against the implied hesitation of this duple meter, Young syncopates rapidly moving feet of triple meter, such as the dactyl ("hovering," line six), the anapest ("where that sound," line fourteen) and the tribrach, or three unaccented syllables ("& cleansed the," line fifteen, and "on all the," line twenty-three). Traditional prosody offers these terms to describe lines of verse, but readers familiar with open forms in American poetry and listeners familiar with Coltrane's extended and complex rhythmic patterns may not need this abstract analysis to hear the musical phrases of Young's poem. The poem first invokes Coltrane as muse ("Fly on into my poem"), imitating both the sounds and the impact of one of his solo performances, then places his music within the social and political history of Black America (the migrations from Alabama, the confrontation over segregated schools in Little Rock, Arkansas, and the urban ghettos in the city of brotherly love, Philadelphia, Pennsylvania). Citing the function of the blues, expressing pain to soothe and heal it, Young identifies Coltrane's music as creating and keeping alive both collective and individual history. In a temporal metaphor moving from day to night, Young suggests that Coltrane's music also forecasts the future, as the "sunrise" of line nine is transformed into the "stars" of the final line. It is an optimistic poem, celebrating the growth of the spirit, through a history and an artistic form that recall dark nights of the soul.

In the playful "Dancing Pierrot," the speaking poet claims to have known the moons of China, Egypt, Mexico, Tokyo, Bahia, San Francisco, Tanzania, and the Moors; further, he claims to have known not merely fat and skinny moons (the lunar phases), but moons that shone "lifetimes ago." Clearly, he claims the international and timeless realm of the poet who speaks to all cultures, to all races, and to all ages. Like Jules Laforgue, whose Pierrot of *L'Imitation de Notre-Dame la Lune* (1886; "Imitation of Our Lady the Moon") appears in the title, Young imagines the poet as a kind of noble lunatic, drunk on moonlight. His dancing seems that of the marionette, jerkily bobbing at the end of his strings, an image reinforced by several short two- and three-syllable lines, and by the many one-syllable words; the lyrical fifth stanza, however, echoing "Drink to me only with thine eyes," breaks the confining strings and creates the feeling of freedom. The poet's function appears in the third of the poem's five stanzas, as he observes the effects of moonlight (imagination) on ordinary working people, whose aspirations the poet powerfully images as "armed to the eyes/ with star guns" (lines twenty-eight and twenty-nine). The workers, who might seem imprisoned by repetitive movements, have a vision of self-liberating power, which is articulated by the poet.

"Reading Nijinsky's Diary" also considers the madness of the artist, whose dance plays between the extremes of confinement ("bodily concern/ vinetangled nerve") and freedom ("—cut loose, freed/ to know ever for all"). The visual images that Young employs suggest the surviving photographs of Waslaw Nijinsky in costume for his roles as the faun in *Afternoon of a Faun* and as the rose in *Specter of the Rose*. The identification of the dancer with the dance, like that of the poet with the poem, carries the threat of insanity. For Young, unlike Nijinsky, the descent into madness is only temporary, and he is released by the incantation: "'My madness is my love/ for mankind.'"

"A Little More Traveling Music" is the autobiographical sketch of a poet and singer born in Mississippi, reared on the "Colored music, rhythmic & electrifying" broadcast over the radio, and on the music of a mother's recited family history. His move "up north" introduced him to the external, daily sounds of urban traffic and the internal music of moonlit dreams, and educated him in the sounds of written poetry. The third stanza narrates the return to "motherly music" and the poet's synthesis of that oral tradition with his formal education. The cycle of personal history culminates in his choice of vocation: "I turned to poetry & to singing." Performing and creating are made possible by listening to his "own background music."

The long poem "Dancing," which gives its title to the collection, responds personally and politically to the crises that Americans endured in the late 1960's. Admonitory rhetoric and judgmental images establish the poet as a cultural historian. The four sections of "Dancing," however, do not trace a chronology, since the work begins and ends in the night before a dawn, with the poet in the dark about his life, but hopeful. There are none of the theological issues that Eliot explores in *The Waste Land* (1922), and yet Young claims the same correlation between personal and cultural crises and records a spiritual descent followed by a mystical elevation. Writing in the oracular tradition of Walt Whitman, Allen Ginsberg, Amiri Baraka, and the Old Testament prophets, Young envisions a decade of personal experience in the context of his jeremiad on contemporary American culture. "Dancing" begins as the writer, struggling with his muse in the early evening, thinks of the world outside and of the roads he might have taken (heroin dealer, drunken bum, drifter).

Sobered by his thought that he "is capable of being assassinated/ at any moment" (as were Martin Luther King, Jr. and Robert Kennedy in 1968), and saddened that people continue to live trivial, habitual lives, that the younger generation seeks violent solutions, and that America's commercialism assigns little value to his grandfather's work on a farm, the poet laments the corruption of "Ahhhhhmerica!/ you old happy whore." Sections one and two present the poet's confusion and the decline of America, culminating in a descent "to these dark places/ to these waters"—but, significantly, the drowning is only apparent. The moon is associated with the heart pumping blood, "washing the way clear for new origins," and the blood that is ritually spattered is, symbolically, that of fish.

At the end of section two, the speaker recognizes that attempting to bring "the promiseland" to a chosen few by violent means has only polluted his mind: "the knife doubles back." After this self-inflicted death, section three offers a new beginning: "Be the mystic/ & wage ultimate revolution." All stereotypic revolutionary roles are rejected, and the short homily concludes with the admonition to "Be yourself." Section four makes the connection between the speaker's own past dreams and his projected life. The steps to this new life he learns from a stranger met in April (in Young's calendar, not the cruellest month, but the time of resurrection). The poem concludes where it began, at the writer's desk in early evening, but with a

new optimism. As he works, he envisions a people newly energized by the night, he hopes for the dawn, and he pronounces
a blessing of peace. The final hortatory line—"Let the revolutions proceed!"—rejects the tyranny of any one ideological
movement and advocates the proliferation of individual struggles.

The Song Turning Back into Itself

The Song Turning Back into Itself, a collection taking its name
from a long poem in seven parts, includes forty-four poems
grouped under the five headings "Loneliness," "The Song Turning Back into Itself," "The Prestidigitator," "Everywhere," and
"The Move Continuing." In an interview published in *New Orleans Review,* Young explained that *The Song Turning Back into Itself* has three levels of meaning: that history moves in cycles;
that American popular music is returning to its roots in folk, African, and other ethnic music; and that the individual, going
through changes, nevertheless returns to an original, unique
self.

These three returns are all explored in "The Old Fashioned
Cincinnati Blues," which appears in the first group of poems.
Dedicated to Jesse "Lone Cat" Fuller, and taking its form and its
train-ride setting from the blues, the poem is a nostalgic return
to the poet's past—to a trip made by rail from Cincinnati, Ohio,
to Meridian, Mississippi, by two young brothers, for a summer
visit with grandparents and relatives left behind in the South.
Vivid sensual images are fixed in his memory: "RC Cola coolers"
and "tin tub baths" and "swapping ghost stories." The adult sees
himself as essentially the same as the boy he was in 1949. The
poet experiences his journey not just as a personal reminiscence, but as part of the American tradition, for the voice of
Walt Whitman can be heard in Young's lines: "O Americana!/
United Statesiana!"

The seven numbered poems titled "The Song Turning Back
into Itself" are a spiritual autobiography of the poet, from the
baby's first breath through the adult shouting joyfully: "SING/
one sweet long song to undo/ all sickness & suffering." This persona draws on many sources for inspiration, including Billie

Holiday (who sings "variations on the theme/ of human love &/ its shadow/ loneliness") and Rainer Maria Rilke (whose eighteenth "Sonnet to Orpheus" may be heard in "Feel today/ vibrating/ in the throat"). Singing the blues becomes, in these poems, an exploration of the singer's identity and roots. Images from his personal memories merge with historical events to suggest recurring cycles, as in the speculation: "Consider Nazis & crackers/ on the same stage/ splitting the bill."

The Blues Don't Change

Young's unique blending of whimsy and social satire also appears in one of the twenty-seven new poems published in *The Blues Don't Change*. It is a poem written in memory of two men who died on the same day in 1973: "W. H. Auden and Mantan Moreland." Not only does Young violate snobbish propriety by considering a poet of high culture, W. H. Auden, in the same text with a popular comic motion-picture actor, Mantan Moreland, but he also overturns his readers' expectations about their speech patterns. The poem consists of a dialogue between these two, in paradise, with Moreland praising Auden's *The Age of Anxiety* (1947) for "doubtless" engaging "our/ innermost emotions & informed imagination," and Auden responding, "No shit!" One can imagine the curiosity of a fellow poet as Young arranges for Moreland to ask Auden why he cut the line "We must all love one another or die" from his poem "September 1, 1939." The line was superfluous, as Auden's reply declares, "We gon die anyway no matter/ how much we love." Having justified Auden's technique, Young also defends Moreland, whose role-playing was harshly judged by militant activists. Auden praises Moreland's technique, "the way you buck them eyes/ & make out like you running sked all the time." That fear, Auden notes, is the essence of "the black/ experience where you be in charge of the scene." Moreland did stop "shufflin'," and Young's poem reclaims with pride this actor's achievements.

Several of the poems in *The Blues Don't Change* are tributes to Black American musicians; most notable are "Billie," "The James Cotton Band at Keystone," "My Spanish Heart," and "Lester Leaps In." Each poem recreates the impact of their performances on a rapt listener. Listening to Holiday while drinking, he seems to take in her song through his mouth. The sexuality that Holiday projected in her singing is expressed metaphorically in the listener's fantasy of swallowing her delightful body. The song and his drink intoxicate, "whirling/ me through her throaty world and higher." The listener recognizes the seductress that Holiday enacted in his tribute to her "Cleopatric breath." In contrast to the dreamily slow movement of lines in "Billie," "The James Cotton Band at Keystone" plays with a livelier rhythm, demonstrating "Believe me, the blues can be volatile too,/ but the blues don't bruise; they only renew."

The return to cultural roots revitalizes both the individual and society. In "The Blues Don't Change," his apostrophe to the relentless rhythm and brilliant images of the blues, Young again pays tribute to the uniquely American expression of life's pain and sadness, and to the performers whose artistry lifts the spirit. Working within American forms of speech and music, this poet soars, defining his own voice and enriching America's cultural heritage.

The Sound of Dreams Remembered

Almost a decade passed between Young's 1992 collection titled *Heaven: Collected Poems, 1956-1990* and his 2001 volume *The Sound of Dreams Remembered: Poems, 1990-2000*. *Heaven* filled nearly three hundred pages, displayed an abundant affection for the ordinary world, and showcased several influences (noted in the collection's introduction) that included Amiri Baraka (LeRoi Jones), Vladimir Mayakovsky, and Federico García Lorca.

The work of Langston Hughes and Charles Bukowski makes its influential mark on *The Sound of Dreams Remembered*. Disjointed thoughts, full of mystique and sentiment, like those of Bukowski, are apparent here. The collection is a readable and topical history of the decade, providing meditations on love, travel, politics, and misbehavior. Casual blank verse gives way to fluid, rhyming iambic pentameter in poems like "The Old Country":

What is it want,
or need to haul or lug like Motorolas
of the blood? Beep! The mileage we squander
on these jumps from mayonnaise Minnesotas
to curry Calcuttas, from Tokyos you could wander.

Other Literary Forms

Al Young has published short stories in *Changes, Chicago Review, Encore, Essence, The Evergreen Review, Journal of Black Poetry, The Massachusetts Review, Place,* and *Rolling Stone.* He wrote the introduction to *Yardbird Lives!,* a collection of writings that he and Ishmael Reed compiled from the biennial *Yardbird Reader.* He has written several screenplays, including "Nigger" (unpublished) based on Dick Gregory's autobiography, a film script for his novel *Sitting Pretty,* and the script for *A Piece of the Action* (in collaboration with Bill Cosby and Sidney Poitier).

Young has also written a series of autobiographical anecdotes, in *Bodies and Soul: Musical Memoirs,* each of which is organized around his response to a specific song or musical performance. The title piece, for example, begins with his meditation on Coleman Hawkins's 1939 performance of "Body and Soul." *Bodies and Soul* was followed by other "musical memoirs," including *Kinds of Blue: Musical Memoirs, Mingus/Mingus: Two Memoirs* (with Janet Coleman), and *Drowning in a Sea of Love: Musical Memoirs.*

Bibliography

Bell, Bernard W. *The Afro-American Novel and Its Tradition.* Amherst: University of Massachusetts Press, 1987. Bell compares African American writers and their works. Especially useful is his comparison of Young's *Snakes* to 1960's novels by Gordon Parks, Kristin Hunter, Rosa Gunn, Barry Beckham, and Louise Meriwether. Because Bell classifies these works as *Bildungsromane* in the European literary tradition, his analysis helps establish Young as a viable black-experience author in the United States and abroad.

Broughton, Irv. *The Writer's Mind: Interviews with American Au-

thors. Vol. 3. Fayetteville: University of Arkansas Press, 1990. Contains a rare and enlightening interview with Young in which he explains his poetic philosophy. This source is widely available and is useful to undergraduate as well as graduate students. A good overview.

Coleman, Janet, and Al Young. *Mingus/Mingus: Two Memoirs*. Berkeley, Calif.: Creative Arts, 1989. Not much has been written about Young, therefore, Young's own memoir becomes essential for understanding his life and work.

Davis, Thadious M., and Trudier Harris, eds. *Dictionary of Literary Biography*. Vol. 33. In *Afro-American Fiction Writers After 1955*. Detroit: Gale, 1984. This reference provides a cursory glance at Young's career as a postmodernist writer on the American scene. The citation itself is brief yet helpful to place the author in the mainstream of contemporary writers of various ethnic backgrounds.

Draper, James P. *Black Literature Criticism: Excerpts from Criticism of the Most Significant Works of Black Authors over the Past Two Hundred Years*. Detroit: Gale, 1997. Contains a fifteen-page chapter on Young that includes criticism, interviews from 1976 to 1989, a short biography, and a bibliography.

Kirkpatrick, D. L., ed. *Contemporary Novelists*. 4th ed. New York: St. Martin's Press, 1986. This compilation features a condensed biography of Young plus an extensive listing of the author's works through 1982. A useful guide to Young as an emerging American artist, this reference profiles him among novelists of various ethnic backgrounds.

Lee, Don. "About Al Young." *Ploughshares* 19, no. 1 (Spring, 1993): 219. A short profile of Young's life as poet and screenwriter.

Matney, William C., ed. *Who's Who Among Black Americans*. 5th ed. Lake Forest, Ill.: Educational Communications, 1988. A collection of interviews and personal profiles, this presentation of the author considers his manifold interests as a young African American writer. Those who know Young as poet, musician, screenwriter, editor, or teacher will find useful material regarding the manifold interests of the novelist.

Nixon, Will. "Better Times for Black Writers?" *Publishers Weekly*

235 (February 17, 1989): 35-40. Young and several other African American writers and editors speak out regarding their reception in the publishing world.

_____. "Black Male Writers: Endangered Species?" *American Visions* 5, no. 1 (February, 1990): 24-29. An interesting study of the reasons why African American male writers were largely ignored during the 1980's. Also looks at the rise of African American female writers.

Ostendorf, Berndt. *Black Literature in White America.* Totowa, N.J.: Barnes and Noble Books, 1982. Considers black writers' roots and the influence of music on their lives and art as both expression and performance. While the references to Young are brief and pertain to his poetry, the musical context of this presentation will be useful for those researching Young's concern for music in American culture and literature.

Ross, Michael E. "Hollywood's Civil Servants." *The New York Times Book Review,* February 5, 1989, 12. Ross profiles Young and some other African American writers working in Hollywood, a town that is traditionally tough on its artists. A lively and interesting article for all students.

Scharf, Michael. Review of *The Sound of Dreams Remembered: Poems, 1990-2000,* by Al Young. *Publishers Weekly* 248, no. 20 (May 14, 2001): 78-80. A mixed review that suggests that Young might have benefited from a more severe editorial eye.

Schultz, Elizabeth. "Search for 'Soul Space': A Study of Al Young's *Who Is Angelina?* and the Dimensions of Freedom." In *The Afro-American Novel Since 1960,* edited by Peter Bruck and Wolfgang Karrer. Amsterdam: Gruner, 1982. Young's novel was written in 1975, a time when few fiction works by African Americans were being published. Schultz analyzes his work in terms of the quest for expression, especially when the speaker is out of the mainstream.

Shockley, Ann Allen, and Sue P. Chandler. *Living Black American Authors: A Biographical Directory.* New York: R. R. Bowker, 1973. Recognition of black writers was new during the early 1970's, especially in the overall context of American letters. This work contains extensive interpretive detail regarding

Young's early works, his achievements other than writing fiction, and his personal values and insights.

Young, Al. "Al Young's Net: Life Under Construction." http://www.alyoung.org/. Accessed September 1, 2005. The author's Web site contains information about his books, current projects, favorite poems (by other authors), images, audio clips, and reviews.

_____. "We Jazz/We Die Soon: Jazz Film Thoughts." *Antaeus* 71-72 (Fall, 1993): 122-130. An essay by Young that reveals some of the authors thoughts on the portrayal of jazz in recent films.

—*Joseph F. Battaglia; Sarah Hilbert;*
Judith L. Johnston; Daryl F. Mallett

Essays

African American Drama

Introduction

Seeking to extricate the power of African American music and dance from the stereotypes and trivializations of minstrelsy in its various forms, African American dramatists struggled during the twentieth century to locate or create an audience receptive to the full range of their thematic and theatrical concerns. The attempt to develop an autonomous style without sacrificing all access to production confronts African American playwrights, collectively and individually, with a paradoxical situation in which they must first demonstrate their mastery of traditionally European American themes and techniques to dispel stereotypes concerning African American ability and character.

Faced with tensions between their African and European American audiences, and with class tensions within the black audience, African American dramatists have followed three distinct paths. Some, concentrating on commercial success in the predominantly white mainstream American theater, have contributed to Broadway-style revues only tangentially concerned with challenging inherited conceptions of African American experience. More self-consciously literary playwrights, usually working on the margins of the commercial theater, have occasionally achieved some commercial success with plays designed to increase white awareness of the variety and complexities of the African American experience. Increasingly, however, serious African American dramatists have sought to address directly an African American audience, frequently but, given the cultural and economic realities of the United States, by no means exclusively in theaters located in the black communities.

Historical Development

Ed Bullins, a major figure in both contemporary and African American drama, describes this historical development and contemporary direction in a statement that has exerted a substantial impact on the subsequent development of the tradition:

1151

With the present Black Writers turned away from addressing an anticipated white readership and appealing the plight of Blackness in America to their masochistic delight, the literature has changed from a social-protest oriented form to one of a dialectical nature among Black people—Black dialectics—and this new thrust has two main branches—the dialectic of change and the dialectic of experience. The writers are attempting to answer questions concerning Black survival and future, one group through confronting the Black/white reality of America, the other, by heightening the dreadful white reality of being a modern Black captive and victim. These two major branches in the mainstream of the new Black creativity, the dialectic of change (once called protest writing, surely, when confronting whites directly and angrily, then altered to what was called Black revolutionary writing when it shifted . . . away from a white audience to a Black) and the dialectic of experience (or being), sometimes merge, but *variety* and *power* in the overall work are the general rule.

As Bullins suggests, early African American dramatists and performers did in fact anticipate a white audience or, in the rare case where the plays were published, a white readership. Complicating matters was that audience's familiarity with the minstrel shows, such as that of Thomas Rice, which developed in the South as early as the 1830's and enjoyed a vogue well into the twentieth century. Originally performed by whites in blackface imitating songs and dances they had witnessed in slave communities, the minstrel shows rapidly developed into travesties with no direct relationship to any actual African American culture. By the time blacks formed their own troupes after the Civil War, the minstrel stereotypes were so firmly established that black performers were forced to add the familiar blackface makeup if they wished to attract an audience.

Despite this pressure to correspond to preconceived stage images, however, several black dramatists, and especially black performers, established serious reputations during the nineteenth century. Actors such as Ira Aldridge and Victor Séjour, who performed primarily in Europe, also wrote plays on racial themes, as did William Wells Brown, whose abolitionist play *The Escape: Or, A Leap for Freedom* (pr. 1858) is generally credited as the first work of African American dramatic literature. Paul Laurence Dunbar, who frequently performed his own dialect poetry for white audiences grounded in the neo-minstrel stereotypes of the plantation tradition, collaborated with Will Marion Cook on *Clorindy: Or, The Origin of the Cakewalk* (pr. 1898), the first African American play to receive a full-scale commercial production. Although Bob Cole's *A Trip to Coontown* (pr. 1898) was produced by blacks, it was not until 1916 that a serious play written, acted, and produced by blacks was performed in the United States. Sponsored by the National Association for the Advancement of Colored People, Angelina Grimké's *Rachel* (pr. 1916), while addressed primarily to a white audience, did not pander to the stereotypes of tragic mulatto, black beast, or comic darky.

The Harlem Renaissance

The movement in African American drama from an exclusive address to the white audience toward Bullins's black dialectics began during the Harlem Renaissance of the 1920's. Responding to the growth of sizable African American communities in northern urban centers, black playwrights seriously envisioned for the first time a theater not predicated entirely on white expectations. Companies such as Cleveland's Karamu House and Gilpin Players (named after Charles Gilpin, one of the first black actors to earn a major reputation as an actor on American stages), Philadelphia's Dunbar Theatre, and New York's influential Lafayette Players, along with the Krigwa Little Theatre movement, which under the sponsorship of W. E. B. DuBois established theaters in many large cities, provided proving ground for black actors and playwrights. At about the same time, plays by European American dramatists, especially Ridgley Torrence (*The Rider of Dreams*, pr. 1917), DuBose Heyward and Dorothy Heyward (*Porgy*, pr. 1927), Paul Green (the Pulitzer Prize-winning *In Abraham's Bosom*, pr. 1926), Marc Connelly (*The Green Pastures: A Fable*, pb. 1929), and Eugene O'Neill (*The Em-*

1153

peror Jones, pr. 1920, and *All God's Chillun Got Wings*, pr. 1924), began to treat African American characters and themes more seriously than had their predecessors. The presence of a black-oriented, if not yet predominantly black, audience, accompanied by the partial abatement of minstrel stereotypes, encouraged a significant number of African American playwrights to begin working during the 1920's and 1930's.

Many, including Zora Neale Hurston (*Great Day*, pr. 1937), Wallace Thurman (*Harlem*, pr. 1929), Countée Cullen and Arna Bontemps (*God Sends Sunday*, pr. 1931), Georgia Douglas Johnson (*Plumes*, pb. 1927), Jean Toomer, and Langston Hughes, had previously worked and remain best known as poets and novelists. Others, including Frank Wilson (*Walk Together, Chillun*, pr. 1936), Hall Johnson (*Run Little Chillun*, pr. 1933), and especially Willis Richardson, established their reputations primarily as dramatists. Whatever their primary literary focus, however, the playwrights of the Harlem Renaissance responded to the call sounded by James Weldon Johnson in the preface to *The Book of American Negro Poetry* (1922) for a new type of artist who would do for African Americans "what [John Millington] Synge did for the Irish; he needs to find a form that will express the racial spirit by symbols from within rather than by symbols from without."

As Sterling A. Brown observed in *Negro Poetry and Drama* (1937), the plays written in response to this call were of two distinct types: the problem play, which extended the "political" tradition of Grimké and William Wells Brown, and the folk-life play, which to some extent attempted to reconstruct the materials that had been trivialized in the minstrel tradition. Among the most successful playwrights to work with both approaches was Richardson, who wrote a half-dozen plays of lasting interest, including *The Broken Banjo* (pr. 1925) and *The Chip Woman's Fortune* (pr. 1923), the first play by an African American produced on Broadway. More powerful as literature, Toomer's complex philosophical character study "Kabnis," published as section 3 of *Cane* (pb. 1923), a work incorporating prose and poetry as well as drama, presented insurmountable staging problems given the generic conventions of the era.

Depression Era

As the excitement of the Harlem Renaissance gave way to the political determination of African American writing of the Great Depression era, attention gradually shifted away from the optimistic aesthetics of the influential critic Alain Locke, cofounder along with Montgomery Gregory of the Howard University Players, whose anthology *Plays of Negro Life* (1927) included work by both black and white writers. Supported by programs such as the Federal Theatre Project, playwrights such as Hughes and Theodore Ward, whose *Big White Fog* (pr. 1938) is widely considered the most powerful African American play of the decade, contributed to the proletarian theater exemplified by European American dramatists such as Clifford Odets. Despite the shift away from mainstream political positions, much pressure remained on black playwrights to align their views with those of their radical white contemporaries. Hughes, who began writing plays in the 1920's and had the first Broadway hit by an African American playwright in *Mulatto,* which ran from 1935 to 1937, supported leftist political causes in plays such as *Scottsboro Limited* (pr. 1932), as did novelist Richard Wright, whose *Native Son* (1940) was a commercial success in a dramatic adaptation by Wright and white playwright Paul Green. Although best known as a poet, Hughes continued to work in theater throughout his career, although he abandoned the explicitly political focus in later plays such as *Simply Heavenly* (pr. 1957) and *Tambourines to Glory* (pr. 1963).

Postwar Developments

The transition from a drama addressed to an anticipated white audience to Bullins's black dialectics accelerated after World War II, proceeding in two major phases. The first phase, involving recognition of serious African American drama from a mainstream white audience, centered on the commercial and artistic success of a sequence of plays reinforcing the premises of the nonviolent Civil Rights movement of the 1950's and early 1960's. The second, heralded by Amiri Baraka's stunning *Dutchman* (pr. 1964) and culminating in the community theater movement frequently associated with black nationalist politics, redirected attention to the internal concerns of the African American community. By no means devoid of assertive political commitment, the plays of the first phase typically endorsed an integrationist philosophy, partially in deference to the anticipated white audience and partially as a result of the early successes and promise of Martin Luther King, Jr.'s interracial strategies. The first major success of the period, Louis Peterson's *Take a Giant Step* (pr. 1953), was followed rapidly by William Branch's *In Splendid Error* (pr. 1954), Alice Childress's *Trouble in Mind* (pr. 1955), and Ossie Davis's *Purlie Victorious* (pr. 1961).

The most significant plays of this phase were Lorraine Hansberry's *A Raisin in the Sun* (pr. 1959) and James Baldwin's *Blues for Mister Charlie* (pr. 1964). Although Baldwin's play drew substantial critical and political attention largely as a result of his position as a novelist and community spokesperson, *A Raisin in the Sun* is unarguably the first major contribution by an African American playwright to the dramatic literature of the United States. Focusing on the tensions between the members of an African American family seeking to realize their individual conceptions of the American Dream, the play possesses a variety and power equal to that of any play written in the dominant realistic mode of the mainstream stage of the 1950's.

Although *Blues for Mister Charlie* failed to match the 530-performance run of *A Raisin in the Sun*, which won the New York Drama Critics Circle Award for 1958-1959, the two plays established a lasting African American presence in American drama on Broadway, Off-Broadway, and Off-Off-Broadway as well as on community and regional stages previously devoted almost entirely to European American drama. Douglas Turner Ward's Negro Ensemble Company has maintained a continuing presence Off-Broadway with productions such as Ward's own *Day of Absence* (pr. 1965) and Charles Fuller's *A Soldier's Play* (pr. 1982), which was the second Pulitzer Prize-winning play by an African American dramatist. The first, Charles Gordone's brilliant absurdist work *No Place to Be Somebody* (pr. 1969), produced by leading Off-Broadway producer Joseph Papp, reflects the developing avant-garde tradition in black theater. Several plays by

Baraka, Bullins, and Adrienne Kennedy (*Funnyhouse of a Negro*, pr. 1964, and *A Rat's Mass*, pr. 1966) had substantial influence on experimental dramatists outside the African American community. Reflecting the continuing interaction of African and European American avant-garde theaters, *The Gospel at Collonus* (pr. 1983), an adaptation of Sophocles' work written by prominent white experimental playwright Lee Breuer but given its emotional power by the improvisational performance style of the all-black cast, followed *Dutchman* and several of Bullins's plays as winner of the Obie Award for best play. Other plays by African American dramatists that have made a notable impact on mainstream audiences during the 1960's and 1970's include Lonne Elder's *Ceremonies in Dark Old Men* (pr. 1969) and Joseph Walker's *The River Niger* (pr. 1972).

Community Theater Movement

Although these playwrights have made an impact in the mainstream theatrical world, the energy of African American drama since the mid-1960's derives in large part from the community theater movement spearheaded by Baraka and Bullins. Repudiating not only the focus on the white audience but also the emphasis of many earlier playwrights on the problems of the black middle class, these dramatists oriented their work toward the entire black community. In part, this shift can be attributed to the growing influence of the separatist philosophy of Malcolm X as the Civil Rights movement confronted a new set of problems in the North.

Baraka's *Dutchman* marked the major transition point in African American theater, emphasizing the common position of all blacks, however fully assimilated into the mainstream. The climactic murder of the articulate black protagonist by a white woman, who has manipulated his complex self-consciousness, provided a symbol that exerted a major impact on younger playwrights such as Ron Milner, Jimmy Garrett, Richard Wesley, Marvin X, Sonia Sanchez, and Ben Caldwell. Working in community theaters such as Baraka's Spirit House of Newark, Bullins's and Robert MacBeth's New Lafayette Theater, Woodie

King, Jr.'s New Federal Theatre of New York, John O'Neal's Free Southern Theatre of Mississippi and New Orleans, Val Gray Ward's Kuumba Theatre of Chicago, and the Black Arts/West of San Francisco, these playwrights struggled to create a theater designed specifically to reach an audience unlikely to attend traditional theatrical events.

Drawing heavily on traditions of African and African American music and dance, many of their plays, including Milner's *Who's Got His Own* (pr. 1966), Garrett's *And We Own the Night* (pr. 1967), and Wesley's *The Last Street Play* (pr. 1977), redirected "protests" intended for whites when presented in mainstream theaters toward the revolutionary, usually nationalist vision that Bullins associates with the "dialectic of change." Particularly in his Obie Award-winning *The Taking of Miss Janie* (pr. 1975) and in the plays from his Twentieth Century Cycle (most notably *In New England Winter*, pb. 1969, and *In the Wine Time*, pr. 1968), Bullins demonstrated a thematic power and technical versatility matched in American drama only by O'Neill.

Perhaps the best of the plays by Bullins is *The Taking of Miss Janie*, a play about racial tensions in the 1960's. The audience learns about the characters from the dramatization of the action (for example, at the party of lead character Monty) and from the characters themselves, who speak directly to the audience, sharing their thoughts. Monty, a black college student who writes poetry, wants to have sex with—and actually control—the beautiful white woman named Janie. He calls her Miss Janie, a joke that she seems unable to comprehend. To Monty, Janie, because she is a very attractive young white woman, represents the privileged and the fortunate. He realizes that she wants to be friends with him, yet he resents her, believing that she considers herself superior because of her skin color. He therefore calls her Miss Janie, seemingly calling attention to a perceived master-slave relationship. Janie enjoys his poetry, even though it is quite pessimistic and dark, and she wants desperately to be friends with him, but he doubts her sincerity, thinking that she is using him and merely wants the novelty of having a black friend. Monty doubts Janie's sincerity because she refuses to have sex with him; he considers her refusal proof that she is using him, yet Janie believes that sex hinders the opportunity for a man and woman to be friends. It is difficult to discern how truthful the characters are with the audience, with each other, and with themselves. Monty maintains a friendship with Janie, waiting patiently for his opportunity to have sex with her, which represents his ultimate goal. In the end, because she proves unwilling to have sex with him, he rapes her. The rape is not an act of sex, but rather one that exhibits power and dominance. The black man thus controls and dominates the white woman, a female whom he believes symbolizes superiority and perhaps even slave owners.

The racial tensions are complicated further in *The Taking of Miss Janie* by the presence of several other characters. Rick and Peggy are African American characters who clearly manifest hatred for whites, referring to them as devils. Their hatred for white people is returned by the prejudice toward blacks by white characters Mort Silberstein and Lonnie, Janie's jazz-playing boyfriend, both of whom make racist remarks. Rick becomes upset when meeting Lonnie because he believes that Lonnie is a usurper—a white man playing black music. Bullins clearly disapproves of Silberstein and Lonnie for their anti-African American attitudes, but his black characters such as Peggy, Monty, Rick, and Flossy do not appear to be benevolent or wholesome people either. Rather they are characters who hate white people and who are just as racist as the white characters. However, they are portrayed as more honest about their feelings than the white characters. Rick makes it clear to all the white people whom he meets that he believes that they are devils. Peggy also hates white people and blames them for the failure of her marriage to Monty. She then marries a white man. After that marriage does not work out, she decides to try a lesbian lifestyle. The characters seem to be searching for themselves, confused about their lives, and preoccupied with race.

Although the community theater movement underwent substantial changes as racial issues assumed a less prominent position in public debate during the late 1970's and 1980's, its impact is evident in the works of dramatists who have chosen to work closer to the American mainstream. Although African

American dramatists continue to confront pressure to orient their work toward a white audience, most of the simplistic stereotypes have been called into question to the extent that new playwrights, building on the achievements of Bullins and Baraka even while working from sharply differing political premises, are able to employ the power and beauty of the African American performance traditions without needing to compromise their vision of the complexity of African American life.

Dramatizing Assimilation

In the mid-1980's, African American drama began de-emphasizing the revolutionary and recolonization aspects of the political platform, searching instead for a strong dramatic voice to tell the story of African American assimilation into mainstream American ideals. That voice was found in the work of August Wilson, whose series of plays, each based on a decade in the history of African American family life, was developed in cooperation with the Yale Repertory Theatre and the O'Neill Center, officially known as the National Playwrights' Conference. The plays moved successfully from the League of Resident Theatres (LORT) circuit onto Broadway, with a new play appearing about every two years. The link between the two not-for-profit institutions was Lloyd Richards, until 1992 the artistic director of the Yale Repertory and the institutional director of the O'Neill Center. He guided Wilson's plays through the play development process, at the O'Neill Center in staged reading format, and at the Yale Repertory in their first professional productions, many of which moved to other LORT theaters before attempting a Broadway run.

Wilson's preeminence as an African American playwright was evident in his output of notable plays, which focus on separation, migration, and reunion to depict the physical and psychological journeys of African Americans in the twentieth century. These thematic explorations were heightened with his use of African American musical traditions and the depiction of the conflict between a Christian tradition and African folklore and heritage. All the works in Wilson's ten-play cycle—*Radio Golf* (pr. 2005), *Gem of the Ocean* (pr. 2003), *King Hedley II* (pr. 2001), *Jitney* (pr. 2000), *Seven Guitars* (pr. 1995), *Two Trains Running* (pr. 1990), *The Piano Lesson* (pr. 1987), *Joe Turner's Come and Gone* (pr. 1986), *Fences* (pr. 1985), and *Ma Rainey's Black Bottom* (pr. 1984), the last of which won the third Pulitzer Prize received by an African American—were produced to wide acclaim.

Fences, set in the 1950's, tells the story of Troy Maxson, his son, Cory, and his wife, Rose. Bitter because he was too old to play major league baseball when Jackie Robinson broke the color barrier, Troy resorts to hauling garbage in order to make a living. Cory shares Troy's athletic abilities, yet the father refuses to allow his son to play sports. Troy asserts that he refuses to allow Cory to waste his life playing sports when white people, who control sports and academic scholarships, will not permit African Americans to get ahead. Cory, stung by his father's refusal, becomes bitter and correctly asserts that Troy is actually jealous because Cory enjoys opportunities that were denied his father. Wilson indicates that although racism still exists, times have changed and that it is actually the father's jealousy and bitterness, not prejudice, that inhibits Cory from attending college on a football scholarship. The play focuses on the patriarchal African American family, particularly the relationships between Troy and Cory, and between Troy and Rose. When Troy impregnates Alberta, Rose becomes furious, causing permanent scars in their marriage. Troy's adultery renders him subjugated to his wife, making Cory feel that his father no longer rules the Maxson family; he subsequently challenges his father's authority, which results in Cory being forced to leave the house, never to return in his father's lifetime (he comes back for Troy's funeral). Cory had attempted to supplant his father, yet he finds that he, himself, is supplanted, being replaced by Troy's new daughter, a product of his affair with Alberta. When Cory is thrown out of the home by his father, which is part of a rite of passage and, unfortunately, a family tradition (Troy's father had thrown him out a generation before), Troy throws his belongings over the fence. Troy believes that fences are meant to keep intruders out, yet Rose believes, according to Troy's friend

Bono, that fences are designed to keep families in, to maintain the family unit.

Ma Rainey's Black Bottom, set in the 1920's, dramatizes a story about the legendary blues singer Ma Rainey and her band. The play demonstrates the racism that Rainey and other African Americans encountered. For example, Rainey purchases a new car, yet a police officer questions her about the automobile, doubting that an African American could buy such a nice car and believing that she must have stolen it. Furthermore, her musicians must insist on being paid in cash because no business is willing to cash checks presented by African Americans. Ma Rainey has an attitude problem, causing her to be habitually late and disrespectful to the record company producers, yet Wilson implies that there is a reason for her behavior. She realizes that the record producer has no respect for her and is using her to make a substantial profit. She compares herself to a prostitute: After the producer has captured her voice on tape, he has no use for her, just as a male customer has no use for a prostitute after he has satisfied his lust. Thus, she prolongs the recording session as much as possible to earn a semblance of respect.

The Piano Lesson, set in the 1930's, concerns a man, Boy Willie, who wants to sell his sister's piano, a family heirloom because it has images of their family members engraved on it. Although Berniece refuses to play the piano, she does not want to part with it because her uncles Doaker and Wining Boy, along with her father, Boy Charles, took it from the house of Sutter, the slave owner, believing that it belonged to them because of the family history engraved on it. During the removal of the piano, Boy Charles was killed; thus, Berniece cannot part with it. Boy Willie wants to sell the piano so that he can use the money to purchase land from Sutter's brother. Wilson thus creates a fascinating dilemma: Selling the piano is tantamount to betraying the family history, yet selling the piano can allow the family to thrive and to own the land on which the family was previously enslaved, thus reclaiming family history. Berniece looks back to the past, while Boy Willie focuses on the future.

Wilson's *Seven Guitars* debuted in 1995. Set in the 1940's, it tells the tragic story of blues guitarist Floyd Barton, whose funeral opens the play. The action flashes back to re-create the events of Floyd's last week of life. Floyd had arrived in Pittsburgh to try to get his guitar out of the pawn shop and to convince his former lover, Vera, to return with him to Chicago. A record he made years earlier has suddenly gained popularity, and he has been offered the opportunity to record more songs at a studio in Chicago. The play's central conflicts are Floyd's struggle to move forward in his musical career and his personal strife with Vera and his band mates. A subplot centers on Floyd's friend Hedley and his deteriorating physical and mental health as his friends attempt to place him in a tuberculosis sanatorium. The play contains some of Wilson's familiar character types, including the mentally aberrant Hedley; the troubled-by-the-law young black male protagonist, Floyd; the capable and independent woman, Louise; and the more needy, younger woman, Ruby. It also contains elements of music, dance, storytelling, violence, and food.

The 2000 play *Jitney* is about a 1970's gypsy cab service operated by Becker, a good man whose son, Booster, has just been released from prison after serving a long sentence for murdering a white woman, his girlfriend. The woman falsely accused Booster of rape after her father caught her having sex with him. While out on bail and awaiting the trial, Booster gets revenge by shooting her. Becker cannot forgive his son because Booster's imprisonment has caused his wife to be so unhappy that she dies; Becker thus blames his son for his wife's demise, permanently straining the father-son relationship. Wilson manifests again his skill in dramatizing poignant familial relationships. Another character, Youngblood, is falsely accused of adultery, when actually he is saving money and surprising his wife Rena by looking for—and purchasing—a house. When the cab company goes out of business because of Becker's accidental death, the audience realizes that Youngblood is the only one there who has a bright future. As his name implies, he is a new kind of person, an ambitious family man who thus distinguishes himself from the other characters, such as Fielding and Turnbo, whose lives are going nowhere.

Influential Women Playwrights

The death of James Baldwin in 1987 took away one of the most effective African American talents from the stage. Political activists such as Amiri Baraka became less active in the theater in the 1990's but vocal in other cultural affairs. The void left by Baldwin and the relative absence of prominent male African American playwrights in the late 1980's and 1990's opened the door for a new direction in African American theater: plays by women dramatists. Female African American playwrights, in the last decades of the twentieth century, gained attention for plays that expanded theatrical boundaries and created theater that offered unforgettable images in culturally resonant, historically significant, and deeply personal plays.

A novelist, poet, and playwright, Ntozake Shange has aptly labeled her creations "choreopoems" for their blend of poetry, drama, prose, and autobiography. Her works, labeled "militant feminism" by some critics for their portrayal of violence and their contentious relationship with black men, also display a youthful spirit, a flair with language, and a lyricism that carries them to startling and radical conclusions. Her contradictory style, such as the use of both black English and the erudite vocabulary of the educated, is at the heart of her drama. She is best known for her 1976 play *for colored girls who have considered suicide/ when the rainbow is enuf*, which was honored in that year by the Outer Critics Circle and won Obie and Audelco Awards as well as Tony and Grammy award nominations in 1977. The play is a recital, individually and in chorus, of the lives and growth of seven different black women, named according to their dress colors. The term "colored girls" in the title evokes a stereotype of black women yet also contains a germ of hope for the future (the "rainbow," both of color and of eventual salvation). These figures are representative voices of black women that express fury at their oppression both as women and as blacks. The scenes are often somber, portraying rape, abuse, city dangers, and abortion, reflecting the recurrent motif of the thwarting of dreams and aspirations for a decent life by forces beyond one's control: war, poverty, and ignorance. Yet a saving grace appears toward the end of the play, when the seven women fall into a tighter circle of mutual support, much like a religious "laying on of hands" ceremony, in which they say, "i found god in myself/ & i loved her/ i loved her fiercely." Their bitter pain, shown throughout the dramatic episodes, turns into a possibility of regeneration.

Suzan-Lori Parks gained the mainstream limelight in 2002 when she became the first African American woman to win a Pulitzer Prize in drama and earned rave reviews for her play *Topdog/Underdog* (pr. 2001). Yet Parks's career also was rewarded generously during the 1980's and 1990's. *The New York Times* called her the "year's most promising playwright" in 1989, her work was supported by grants from the Rockefeller and Ford foundations and the National Endowment for the Arts, and she received a MacArthur Award in 1986.

Parks's plays are marked by a unique use of language and speech, an approach that forefronts the vernacular in an attempt to reproduce speech both as it is spoken and as her audience assumes it may be spoken. She seeks a hypnotic and musical emphasis of words, a technique that accounts for much of the repetitive patterns in her work. Although she strives to dissect the black experience as it intersects with a white society, she often leaves room for a playfulness: As one critic noted, "[W]ith humor and insight, [she] wriggles free of political straitjackets and thumbs her nose at real racisms, too." Her early short plays include *The Sinners' Place* (pr. 1984) and *Betting on the Dust Commander* (pr. 1987). Her full-length play *Imperceptible Mutabilities in the Third Kingdom* (pr. 1989) won the Obie Award for the best play of 1990. One section of *Imperceptible Mutabilities in the Third Kingdom* takes place on the day of emancipation in 1865 and is played in whiteface by African American actors. *Venus* (pr. 1996) focuses on the life of a "sideshow freak," a black woman brought to England as the Venus Hottentot and put on public display because of her ugly figure which contradicts European notions of beauty.

Topdog/Underdog combines elements of a hip-hop riff and a Greek tragedy. The protagonist brothers, named whimsically by their father Lincoln and Booth, have been forged in a matrix of deprivation that has left them with meager family ties, little education, and few opportunities. They express their frustrations in rhythmic poetry, enhanced by a self-deprecating sense of humor. They act out their misfortunes, each dependent on the other and resentful, protective, and menacing.

Pearl Cleage is another woman who rose to prominence as a playwright in the 1990's. She uses the written word as a journalist, poet, and novelist to explore blacks' experiences in the American landscape, often employing historically accurate African American experiences and cultural lessons. Self-described as a third-generation black nationalist feminist, Cleage examines the relationships and the impacts of racism and sexism. She gained fame in 1992 with her production of *Flyin' West*, which portrayed sisters Sophie and Fannie, who, after nearly twenty years of arduous labor, are now wheat farmers and rising leaders in their community. The setting is post-emancipation Kansas, a landscape that serves as a metaphor for home, where black residents can experience a newly defined freedom as landowners. Like thousands of blacks who left Tennessee, Mississippi, and Kentucky during the Kansas Exodus of 1879, the sisters are captivated by the "free land" being given out by the American government. Cleage has said of her characters that by flying west "they were no longer the creature of another's will." The themes of *Flyin' West* include the power of memory—the sisters' recollections of the brutal South—and of imagination—their hopes for the freedom to be found in the West. Other plays by Cleage include *Hospice* (pr. 1983), *Blues for an Alabama Sky* (pr. 1994), and *Bourbon at the Border* (pr. 1997).

Playwright and performance artist Anna Deveare Smith uses a unique blend of journalistic technique—interviewing subjects from all walks of life—with the art of re-creating their words in performance, ultimately presenting controversial events from multiple points of view. In doing so, she has successfully explored issues of racial tensions, community, and character in the United States, most notably in *Twilight: Los Angeles, 1992* (pr. 1993). *Twilight* examined the 1992 Los Angeles riots and became the first play in her continuing series *On the Road: A Search for the American Character. Fires in the Mirror* (pr. 1995) followed, a play that explored the 1991 Crown Heights riots in Brooklyn that erupted after a Hasidic man's car jumped a curb, killing a six-year-old black child, and the subsequent retaliatory killing of a Hasidic rabbinical student. The play is drawn verbatim from a series of more than fifty interviews with Crown Heights residents, politicians, activists, religious leaders, gang members, street dwellers, victims, and perpetrators. *House Arrest*, the 2000 installment of the series, explores the mythic role of the presidency in American society.

Adrienne Kennedy favors a surrealistic and expressionistic form, her plays capturing the irrational quality of dreams while offering insight into the nature of the self and being. Most of her works are complex character studies in which a given figure may have several selves or roles. In this multidimensional presentation lies Kennedy's forte—the unraveling of the individual consciousness. Her plays grow out of her own experiences as a sensitive and gifted black American who grew up in the Midwest. While there is often little plot in Kennedy's plays, there exists a wealth of symbolism concerning the inherent tensions of the African American experience. Some of her best known plays include *Funnyhouse of a Negro* (pr. 1962), *The Owl Answers* (pr. 1963), *A Rat's Mass* (pr. 1966), *A Movie Star Has to Star in Black and White* (pr. 1976), *June and Jean in Concert* (pr. 1995), and *Sleep Deprivation Chamber* (pr. 1996). Kennedy's daring break from a realistic style in theatrical writing and her bold exploration of her own family history, cultural experience, and identity have arguably laid a foundation for Parks, Shange, Cleage, and Deveare Smith in their own dramatic approaches and explorations of similar topics.

Bibliography

Bean, Annemarie, ed. *Sourcebook on African American Performance: Plays, People, Movements.* New York: Routledge, 1999. A series of articles explores the period between the Black Arts movement of the 1960's and the New Black Renaissance of the 1990's. Topics include the professional, revolutionary, and college stages; concert dance; community activism; step shows; and performance art.

Elam, Harry Justin, and David Krasner, eds. *African American Per-*

formance and Theater History: A Critical Reader. London: Oxford University Press, 2000. An anthology of critical writings that explores the intersections of race, theater, and performance in the United States. Chronicles every nonmusical African American play produced from 1969 to 2000, providing an overview comment, a summary, an actor comment, and a statement about critical reception for each play.

Gavin, Christy, ed. *African American Women Playwrights: A Research Guide.* New York: Garland, 1999. A comprehensive guide to African American drama by female playwrights, helpful to scholars and students studying gender and feminist issues in African American drama.

Hill, Errol. *The Theater of Black Americans.* New York: Applause Theater Book Publishers, 1990. Traces the origins of African American theater, beginning with the Negro spiritual and the birth of the Harlem Renaissance to the emergence of a national black theater movement in the 1960's.

Krasner, David. *Resistance, Parody, and Double Consciousness in African American Theater, 1895-1910.* New York: St. Martin's Press, 1998. Using the fields of history, black literary theory, cultural studies, performance studies, and postcolonial theory, Krasner examines several major productions near the turn of the twentieth century, arguing that the period was replete with moments of resistance to racism, parodies of the minstrel tradition, and double consciousness on the part of performers.

Okur, Nilgun Anadolu. *Contemporary African American Theater: Afrocentricity in the Works of Larry Neal, Amiri Baraka, and Charles Fuller.* New York: Garland, 1997. Explores the dramatic imagination of African American playwrights during the turbulent years of the Civil Rights and Black Power movements, focusing on three playwrights in particular to reveal the roots of an Afrocentric approach to the theater.

— *Craig Werner; Thomas J. Taylor; Eric Sterling*

African American Long Fiction

Slave Narratives

Nineteenth century American fiction influenced the form and content of many of the slave narratives, while nineteenth and twentieth century African American fiction owes a great debt, in form and content, to the slave narrative. Thus the development of African American fiction can be traced to nineteenth century American fiction only by way of the slave narrative.

Just as Africans arriving in the Americas staked their claims to humanity on the basis of the cultural models available to them—European Enlightenment and Christian values—so too did the first "authors" of the slave narrative model their testimonies on the Christian confessionals of Jonathan Edwards and the sentimental fiction of Harriet Beecher Stowe. Yet despite these debts to Puritanism and sentimentality, the best and most influential narratives transcended their origins to create an entirely new prose genre. Thus an achievement such as *Narrative of the Life of Frederick Douglass, an American Slave, Written by Himself* (1845) is instructive, if rare. Because the slave narrative was, by definition, a collaborative effort between white and free black abolitionists, political or social supporters and the slave, a great number of reputed slave narratives were outright frauds concocted by abolitionists to fan the flames of the antislavery movement or, occasionally, by proslavery forces determined to demonstrate the slaves' satisfaction with their lives. Yet even in those slave narratives that have been generally authenticated by meticulous historical research, the voice of the slave is often muffled under letters of support, prefaces, introductions, reproductions of bills of sale, and appendixes, all deployed to assure the reader of the truthfulness of the tale about to be, or already, told. Indeed, insofar as many of the slave narratives are careful to depict the slave's freedom as having been the result of the aid of sympathetic white people, the narrative moral reinforces its collage format: The story of a slave's flight to freedom is inconceivable without the support and aid of northern and, occasionally, southern whites.

Narrative of the Life of Frederick Douglass, an American Slave, Written by Himself is distinguished, however, by both its literary élan and political independence. This well-known narrative boldly rises above its encumbering supplementary materials to depict one man, one slave, fighting his way to freedom. Of course luck, as well as friendly white hands, play a role in Douglass's flight to freedom, just as they do in every other slave narrative. However, the thrust of Douglass's narrative is that he, and he alone, took his life into his hands and forged for himself a new destiny. This theme was also evident in Olaudah Equiano's *The Interesting Narrative of the Life of Olaudah Equiano: Or, Gustavus Vassa, the African* (1789).

Such independence and bravado was not always available for enslaved African American women, as demonstrated in Harriet Jacobs's narrative, written under the pseudonym Linda Brent. *Incidents in the Life of a Slave Girl* (1861) has many parallels with Harriet E. Wilson's novel, *Our Nig: Or, Sketches from the Life of a Free Black, in a Two-Story White House, North. Showing That Slavery's Shadow Falls Even There* (1859). Wilson's protagonist, Alfrado, submits to a marriage with a fugitive slave who abandons her while she is pregnant, forcing her to work for an abusive white female employer. For Jacobs, affirming her gender means that she will be forced to submit to her sexual identity as an African American woman in order to escape sexual exploitation by her white master. The central psychological crisis for Jacobs occurs when she decides to take a white man as a lover in order to block the predatory sexual advances of her master. For Jacobs, the submission to sexuality as a form of power over her circumstances is humiliating, but it is a humiliation redeemed, if only in part, by her choice to decide with whom she will have illicit sexual relations. Having learned that literacy is not enough to affirm and defend her humanity (her freedom), she must affirm her racial and sexual difference—her status as a black woman—by a decision that ironically ensures her identity as both a woman and a human.

The narratives escape the limitations of their origins and

their utility as propaganda for the antislavery cause precisely because they emphasize specific individuality rather than a vague "humanity." That they differ in terms of gender stereotypes—physical prowess for the men, sexual wiliness for the woman—only underscores the narrow band of options available for those attempting to escape slavery. More important, Douglass and Equiano can demonstrate their humanity with a number of virile activities, while Jacobs has only one way to demonstrate her humanity: sexuality. This imbalance in the range of choices, along with the stereotypical, sentimental, and fiction-derived narrative of flight, disguise, concealment, near discovery, and final freedom orients the trajectory of the African American novel along lines that consistently wed identity to gender, which then orient the positions authors take on issues such as class, caste, and skin-color distinctions; individualism and integration; and cultural nationalism.

Before these themes are considered, however, it is necessary to examine a subgenre of the slave narrative known as the narrative of revolt. *The Confessions of Nat Turner* (1832) is a peculiar document of some twenty pages, a reputed record of Nat Turner's descriptions of the revolt he launched against white Virginian men, women, and children in 1831. Augmented with the usual preface attesting the truthfulness of what follows, *The Confessions of Nat Turner* resembles in form the stereotypical slave narrative. However, the witnesses in question are proslavery white men, and the content of the narrative is indeed a "confession" of the conception, planning, and execution of the revolt. This slave narrative is thus not an attempt to affirm the humanity of the "author." Instead there is only the justification of righteous violence, the inspired zealot wreaking judgment upon the sinners—that is, the slave owners. Thus, just as white abolitionists created the format of the slave narrative to depict the horrors of slavery, so too was *The Confessions of Nat Turner* created to justify not only the continuation of slavery but also the ruthless suppression of the few privileges permitted selected slaves.

The Confessions of Nat Turner may well have benefited the proslavery cause, but it also inspired other slave revolts, as well as the first "protest" novel in the African American literary tradition, *Blake: Or, The Huts of America* (1859), by William Delany, himself an African American. *Blake* did not appear as a book until 1970, but it ran serially in a black abolitionist newspaper between 1861 and 1862. *Blake* is a call to arms, an explicit justification for open slave revolt and the establishment of a black sovereignty. It is, in some respects, the novelistic version of David Walker's *Appeal in Four Articles* (1830), judged to be so inflammatory that a large number of people called for its suppression; it also allegedly cost the author his life a short time after its publication. Like *Appeal in Four Articles*, *Blake* rejects the possibility of slaves integrating into American society. Instead, Delany imagines a black-ruled Cuba as the only viable option for the enslaved Africans. Both *The Confessions of Nat Turner* and *Blake* imagine violence as the only solution to slavery and link this violence to masculinity.

Post-Reconstruction

Frances Ellen Watkins Harper's *Iola Leroy: Or, Shadows Uplifted* (1892), Charles Waddell Chesnutt's *The Marrow of Tradition* (1901), and Paul Laurence Dunbar's *The Sport of the Gods* (1902) represent three different reactions in the African American novel to the post-Reconstruction United States, although Harper's idealized treatment of injustice, suffering, and redemption stands in marked contrast to the bitterness evident in the works by Chesnutt and Dunbar.

Iola Leroy is the story of a woman who is, unbeknownst to herself and others, a mulatto. Iola Leroy believes she is white until the unexpected death of her father spurs her uncle, who has long resented his brother's interracial marriage, to sell Iola and her mother separately into slavery. Aside from the search for her mother and abolitionist arguments that function as subplots, the novel focuses on Iola's courtship by two men, one a white abolitionist doctor, the other a mulatto like Iola herself. Though tempted by the doctor's offer to "pass" into white society, Iola steadfastly rejects the opportunity. Instead, she weds herself to the cause of abolition by agreeing to marry the mulatto. The novel's happy ending suggests that Harper preferred to invoke the nineteenth century sentimental novel of manners rather than the "tragic mulatta," a figure that had already appeared in William Wells Brown's *Clotel: Or, The President's Daughter* (1853; revised as *Miralda: Or, The Beautiful Quadroon*, 1860-1861; *Clotelle: A Tale of the Southern States*, 1864; and *Clotelle: Or, The Colored Heroine*, 1867).

On the other hand, Chesnutt's *The Marrow of Tradition* and Dunbar's *The Sport of the Gods* are much darker assessments of African American life during the so-called decades of disappointment. Based loosely on the Wilmington, North Carolina, riot of 1898, Chesnutt's novel follows the lives of several white and black characters whose unacknowledged but intertwined lives culminate in a literal "revelation" amid a murderous riot. Ostensibly a depiction of the end of Reconstruction—the riot is fomented by white people who want to "take back" their town— *The Marrow of Tradition* is also a morality tale concerning the futility of hate and violence, themes that Chesnutt links to the obsession with racial purity. For Chesnutt, miscegenation is the only viable solution to the race problem.

If Chesnutt offers some hope to his audience, Dunbar's vision of the destiny of the newly freed slaves is relentlessly desolate. *The Sport of the Gods* concerns the dissolution of a post-slavery African American family forced to flee to New York City after the father is jailed on trumped-up burglary charges. Every family member ends up losing his or her moral integrity in the urban landscape; even when the parents are reunited near the end of the novel, it is clear that their lives will be cheap imitations of their shattered dreams. Dunbar's dismal vision of the urban landscape, already anticipated by *Our Nig*, looks forward to those novelists of the Harlem Renaissance whose portraits of city life effectively undermine any romantic notions of what it might mean to have come "up from slavery."

The Harlem Renaissance

The concern with skin color, particularly with miscegenation, became particularly urgent during the Harlem Renaissance (1919-1929) as the possibility of an "authentic" African American culture began, however tentatively, to take shape. Insofar as the fledgling culture had to partake of the culture of its former oppressors, the tensions and arguments over who and what was, in fact, "Negro" took on a certain urgency. Yet not every African American writer treated this issue with morbid seriousness. Wallace Thurman's *Infants of the Spring* (1932) is an excoriating roman à clef about the central figures of the Harlem Renaissance. Its vicious attacks on the petty prejudices of the leading personages of the day echo themes developed in his first and most popular novel, *The Blacker the Berry* (1929), which concerns skin-color prejudice within African American culture.

Less well known but in many respects a better work, George S. Schuyler's *Black No More: Being an Account of the Strange and Wonderful Workings of Science in the Land of the Free*, A.D. *1933-1940* (1931) is a hilarious send-up of the obsession with "race advancement" by newly formed organizations such as the National Association for the Advancement of Colored People (NAACP) and the obsession with "racial purity" by the Ku Klux Klan. Thurman's and Schuyler's satires on race, class, and gender, published during the Great Depression shortly after the Harlem Renaissance, mock the absurdities often paraded out by politicians and artists identified with the Harlem Renaissance.

For example, James Weldon Johnson's *The Autobiography of an Ex-Coloured Man* (1912) represents a logical extension of the reconciliation themes evident in the novels of Frances Harper and Charles Chesnutt. If, in their works, the mulatto/mulatta appears to embody the race's best chance for advancement, then "passing"—mulattos and mulattas "disappearing" into white society—would obviously be the next logical step. Johnson's novel idealizes the passing motif even as it rehearses its tragedy: the mulatto as a wanderer between separate cultures, never at home in either.

At the opposite end of the spectrum is Nella Larsen. Her two novels, *Quicksand* (1928) and *Passing* (1929), contain depictions of the tragic mulatta. In *Quicksand*, Helga Crane, a mulatta never at ease among African Americans or Caucasians, winds up marrying and having children. In *Passing*, Clare Kendry is a mulatta passing for Caucasian while her friend, Irene Redfield, is both disgusted and envious of her freedom. Kendry's sudden death offers her escape from the humiliation of being unveiled as a "nigger" by her white, racist husband.

Larsen's analyses of middle-class mulattas represents an extension of Jean Toomer's *Cane* (1923), a collage of poetry and fiction centered on multiple themes in early twentieth century African American life: the juxtaposition of urban and rural lifestyles, tensions between the North and the South, and "purebred"/mixed blood characteristics. As with Harper, Chesnutt and others, Toomer links the resolution of these oppositions to the mulatto. Like Larsen, however, Toomer is not optimistic about this figure, who is shunned and scorned by both African American and white cultures.

Between Johnson's idealism and Larsen's cynicism lie authors such as Claude McKay and Zora Neale Hurston on one hand and Jessie Redmon Fauset on the other hand. McKay's novel *Home to Harlem* (1928) was a commercial success, which some critics, including W. E. B. Du Bois, attributed to its exotic treatment of Harlem nightlife. Richard Wright made similar criticisms of Hurston's novel *Their Eyes Were Watching God* (1937), charging Hurston with creating laughable caricatures of African Americans.

Like the novels of Larsen, Jessie Redmon Fauset's three best novels, *There Is Confusion* (1924), *Plum Bun: A Novel Without a Moral* (1929), and *The Chinaberry Tree: A Novel of American Life* (1931), concern the plight of middle- and upper-class African American women struggling with racial passing, material possessions, marital prospects, and self-worth. Unlike Larsen, and in some respects more like Johnson, Fauset delineates the pitfalls of racial confusion without the melodrama of tragedy. At the same time, Fauset's protagonists are clearly more sensitive to, and more psychologically damaged by, the perplexing anxieties of the color caste system in African American culture.

Post-Renaissance Realism

If the problem of the color caste system dominated African American fiction as a concern before and during the Great Depression, perhaps it was because of the effects of post-Reconstruction migrations of African Americans from the South to the North. Although writers such as Dunbar attempted to unmask the urban dreamscape, the struggle by so many writers to confront color prejudice within the race is linked to the social problems associated with mass migrations: poverty, joblessness, overcrowding, and, in the case of African Americans, accelerated class distinctions tied to the presence or absence of "white" blood. Underlying the tendency to privilege or castigate on the basis of miscegenation was a belief that becoming "white" was either a way to escape the stigma attached to African blood or a way to delude oneself that white America would accept African Americans if they acted less "African."

Richard Wright's groundbreaking first novel, *Native Son* (1940), changed the terms of the debate, dramatizing the conflict between race and class. Wright's portraits of the communists—the naïve Mary, the careless Jan, and the roughhousing Max—were augmented by his negative portraits of both "liberal" Caucasians, such as the Daltons, and African American women, such as Bigger's mother, sister, and girlfriend. Wright's realist novel was widely criticized, and in this respect Dunbar's equally desolate, if less brutal, *The Sport of the Gods* can be seen as its most immediate ancestor. A similar combination of gritty realism and broad criticism can be seen in two relatively minor writers of the period, Chester Himes and Ann Petry.

Of the two, Himes is the most significant as his postwar work is an effective combination of the hard-boiled detective fiction of Raymond Chandler and the protest fiction of Wright. His best novel, *If He Hollers Let Him Go* (1945), is a masterful hybrid of these two genres. On one hand, like *Native Son*, Himes compresses his story into a short time frame (four days) that allows him to explore the effects of unrelenting racism on the consciousness of his narrator-protagonist, Bob Jones. At the same time, Himes pays tribute to the detective story as Jones struggles to figure out why a Caucasian coworker has fabricated a rape charge against him. Later novels, such as *Retour en Afrique* (1964; *Cotton Comes to Harlem*, 1965), owe more to the detective genre than the protest novel, perhaps because Himes wrote them after his expatriation to France.

Ann Petry's fame rests primarily on the basis of *The Street* (1946), the first novel by an African American woman to sell over one million copies. While some critics have compared the novel to Wright's *Native Son* because of its intense focus on urban decay and squalor, a case could also be made for linking it to Dunbar's *The Sport of the Gods* and Hurston's pioneering *Their Eyes Were Watching God.* Just as Hurston's novel concerns Janie's triumph over the patriarchal traditions of white male racism and black male chauvinism, so too does Petry's novel focus on Lutie Johnson's attempts to eke out a meager living away from the brutality of her father. Like those of the mother in Dunbar's novel, Lutie's dreams to provide for herself and her son are driven by a naïveté that drags her even further down the social ladder. If Hurston's Janie seems to be an idealized role model for all women to emulate, Petry's Lutie is a grim reminder of what so many black women actually go through in their daily lives.

Compared to the grim urban realism of Wright, Himes, and Petry, the fiction of Ralph Ellison offers a way out of the morass of frustration, rebellion, defeat, and despair. Ellison's only novel published during his lifetime, *Invisible Man* (1952), has been heralded as one of the great, if not the greatest, American novels ever written, and it is precisely the role of "Americanism" in the work that has made it a lightning rod for political debates since its appearance.

Told in a flashback by an unnamed narrator, *Invisible Man* chronicles the misadventures of a naïve high school graduate in the grand tradition of the episodic, picaresque novel. Boiled down to its essential themes, the novel traces the gradual awakening of a potential leader who believes that the key to the salvation of his community is organized group action, the most notorious of which turns out to be the Brotherhood, a political organization loosely based on the Communist Party of America. In the epilogue, however, the narrator realizes that individualism is the answer to his, and his community's, problems, that all groups are, to one degree or another, straitjackets of intolerance.

Ellison's novel was thus read as a direct rebuke to *Native Son,* though Wright himself saw more affinities than differences between the two works. Nevertheless, Ellison was heralded as the successor to Wright, whose commitment to the communist cause, if not the Communist Party, isolated him and his later work in the context of, and fallout from, McCarthyism. Moreover, a chorus of new voices began to declaim their relevancy and militancy, a phenomenon that had the effect of elevating Wright while demoting Ellison.

The writer who not only functions as a transitional figure between the 1950's and 1960's but also inherited all the contradictions and conflicts between the two decades, represented by the trajectories of Wright's and Ellison's careers, is James Baldwin. Baldwin authored six novels, but his fame rests almost entirely on his provocative essays, especially "Everybody's Protest Novel," which signaled his aesthetic break from his mentor, Richard Wright. Just as Baldwin slays his literary father in the essay, so too does his first novel, *Go Tell It on the Mountain* (1953), a depiction of the Oedipal struggle between a religious father and unconventional son, seem to be directed at his real-life stepfather, David Baldwin. Baldwin's next two novels, *Giovanni's Room* (1956) and *Another Country* (1962), explore homosexuality and black pride as avenues toward individualism. More ominous, the tone of these novels is a little more high-strung than that of the first novel, and in his subsequent novels—*Tell Me How Long the Train's Been Gone* (1968), *If Beale Street Could Talk* (1974), and *Just Above My Head* (1979)—the pitch is strident, a development reflected in the essays. In one of those ironies that permeate African American literary history, Baldwin wound up writing the same kind of protest novels, articles, and essays for which he criticized Wright and others.

How did this happen? To answer this question, it is necessary to examine the effects that the developing Civil Rights movement, the black power spin-offs, the antiwar protests, and the Black Arts movement had on Baldwin's growth as an artist. That is, it is necessary to examine the cultural, social, and political upheavals of the 1960's and 1970's through the lenses of the African American writers who would emerge as distinctive literary voices.

Sons of the 1960's, 1970's, and 1980's

The counterculture movements of the 1960's and 1970's affected all American artists, and African American novelists were no exception. Though his first two novels and various essays had gained him some notoriety, Baldwin had written himself into an aesthetic corner not unlike that inhabited by Ellison. Just as Ellison's post-*Invisible Man* essays would put distance between his nineteenth century genteel aesthetics and the politicized aesthetics of the new African American writers, so too would Baldwin's criticism of Wright's *Native Son* as mere "protest" fiction alienate Baldwin from a new generation of African American writers anxious to relate literature to social concerns. For writers attempting to forge a black aesthetic based on the values of working-class African Americans, Baldwin was aesthetically and politically irrelevant. Worse, Baldwin's avowed homosexuality only confirmed the suspicions of the largely homophobic Black Arts movement.

In 1967, one of the few novelists of the Black Arts movement, John A. Williams, penned *The Man Who Cried I Am*, a kind of roman à clef of African American literary history, featuring Langston Hughes, Richard Wright, and James Baldwin under pseudonyms. Williams's novel, about a semifamous African American male writer who struggles with illness, the envy of his peers, conniving women, and rampant racism, is composed with the crude urban realism of Himes and Wright, but its value is primarily archival.

It was during the same year, 1967, that John Edgar Wideman's first novel, *A Glance Away*, appeared, presenting Wideman as a transitional figure between Ellison and Baldwin on one hand and the Black Arts movement on the other. Perhaps influenced by Baldwin's interest in the contingencies of sexuality and race, *A Glance Away* is a concentrated study—the narrative covers a single day—in the lives of an African American drug addict and a gay Caucasian professor. *Hurry Home* (1970), Wideman's second novel, focuses on the attempt of an African American to unite his European and African cultural heritages. Both novels are less concerned with racial issues per se than philosophical ones. However, by the time of the publication of his

third novel, *The Lynchers* (1973), Wideman was under the influence of the Black Arts movement, though aesthetically the book
remains outside their camp, a stance evident in subsequent
work such as *Damballah* (1981) and *Sent for You Yesterday* (1983).

Finally, 1967 saw yet a third auspicious debut. The most important male African American novelist to follow Ellison appeared in the person of Ishmael Reed. Eschewing the simplistic
posturing of many of the Black Arts movement products, *The
Free-Lance Pallbearers* (1967) was a remarkable first novel as Reed
laid claim to being the best African American satirist since
George Schuyler. The form of his avant-garde novel was inspired as much by experimental jazz and film as James Joyce and
Ellison. *Yellow Back Radio Broke-Down* (1969), his second novel,
was an even greater triumph, a full-blown parody of the American Western as portrayed in dime-store novels and black-and-
white films. Subsequent novels during the 1970's—such as
Mumbo Jumbo (1972), *The Last Days of Louisiana Red* (1974), and
Flight to Canada (1976)—reinforced Reed's reputation as one of
the most innovative comic spirits of his generation.

Ernest J. Gaines inaugurated the 1970's as the first major African American regional novelist since Jean Toomer, though he
was soon followed by the equally talented Leon Forrest. Like
Toomer, Gaines situates his novels in the complicated racial, sexual, and class mixtures of Cajun culture in Louisiana, Gaines's
birthplace. His first novel, *The Autobiography of Miss Jane Pittman*
(1971), was a major literary and, later, television event as its 108-
year-old narrator interweaves her personal history with that of
the United States, allowing her to witness and comment on
American history from nineteenth century slavery to the Civil
Rights movement. Other significant novels would follow, including *In My Father's House* (1978), *A Gathering of Old Men* (1983),
which was also made into a television movie, and *A Lesson Before
Dying* (1993).

Leon Forrest has staked a claim as the most important regional novelist of the North as his four historical novels are all
set in Forrest's native home, "Forest County"—that is, Cook
County, Illinois. Focusing on the life and development of one
central character, Nathaniel Turner Witherspoon, *There Is a Tree*

More Ancient than Eden (1973), *The Bloodworth Orphans* (1977), *Two Wings to Veil My Face* (1984), and *Divine Days* (1992) trace the interrelated histories of two families by way of collage as Forrest draws on traditional oral storytelling, dream sequences, and mythological allusions to dramatize the intrinsic uncertainties of knowledge.

Forrest's redeployment of the serial novel—interrelated novels that follow a central theme, character, or family (for example, the Snopeses and Compsons in William Faulkner's fiction)—was mimicked by a number of other novelists, including Albert Murray. Unlike Faulkner, who used the serial novel to trace the disintegration of southern gentility, African American novelists such as Forrest and Murray used its epic possibilities to depict male heroism. Thus Murray's trilogy of novels—*Train Whistle Guitar* (1974), *The Spyglass Tree* (1991), and *The Seven League Boots* (1996)—celebrate the spirit of adventure by linking the travels of an African American musician to those of the Greek hero Odysseus. The serial novel has even been used by avant-garde writers such as the poet and novelist Nathaniel Mackey. His ongoing fiction series, *From a Broken Bottle Traces of Perfume Still Emanate*, has manifested itself in two epistolary novels, *Bedouin Hornbook* (1986) and *Djbot Baghostus's Run* (1993). Focusing on an ensemble of experimental jazz musicians, Mackey plays with polar oppositions usually taken for granted, especially those that supposedly define cultural borders, gender differences, racial and class biases, and natural and supernatural events.

Yet the traditional novel has hardly lost its viability among African American male writers. Yoking together the sophistication of northern urbanity with the penetrating eccentricity of southern folklore, David Bradley published *The Chaneysville Incident* (1981), a tour de force of historical guilt, murder, and atonement very much in the tradition of Dante's *La divina commedia* (c. 1320; *The Divine Comedy*, 1802).

Myth plays a fundamental role in the fiction of Charles Johnson. Like the early Wideman, Johnson was and remains essentially a philosophical writer. Johnson's first novel, *Faith and the Good Thing* (1974), is a good but unremarkable effort, though it already intimates the philosophical and theological concerns that would become more central to the next novel. *Oxherding Tale* (1982) could not be more different from the first book. Written under the influence of Zen Buddhism, *Oxherding Tale* revisits the slave narrative from an Asian philosophical perspective. Though not as pronounced in subsequent novels such as *The Sorcerer's Apprentice* (1986) and the award-winning *Middle Passage* (1990), Johnson's Buddhist perspective tempers all of his writings, both fiction and nonfiction. Oddly enough, Johnson's use of myth and philosophy has more in common with the experimental work of Mackey than it does with the mainstream novels of Toni Morrison, whose unique blend of myth, philosophy, folklore, and political outrage is unique, not only among African American women writers but also among all African American novelists.

African American Women Writers

No African American woman novelist has plumbed the depths of African American history with as much insight, eloquence, and passion as Toni Morrison. Along with Alice Walker, she takes seriously the feminist aphorism that "the personal is the political" and redefines the relationship between African American women and their culture.

Morrison's and Walker's most immediate predecessor, Paule Marshall, labored in relative obscurity, perhaps, in part, because of her ethnicity. Born in New York City to Caribbean parents, Marshall's work draws on myriad cultural influences. Independent girls and women dominate her fiction, and when they are not strong, Marshall's narratives lead them back to healing sources, which are invariably African (as opposed to "American") or pan-African (in other words, Caribbean) in nature. Her novels—including *Brown Girl, Brownstones* (1959), *The Chosen Place, the Timeless People* (1969), *Praisesong for the Widow* (1983), and *Daughters* (1991)—counterpoise, to varying degrees, American materialism and individualism to African American, Caribbean, and African spiritual ideals; these themes are also present in the writing of Marshall's literary descendant, Jamaica Kincaid.

Still, when all is said and done, Toni Morrison was the most important African American novelist between the 1970's and 1990's. Like the work of Alice Walker, Gloria Naylor, Gayl Jones, and Toni Cade Bambara, Morrison's fiction focuses on the relationships between African American women and Caucasian women, African American women and African American men, and African American women and white America in general from a gendered and politically engaged perspective.

Morrison's novels—including *The Bluest Eye* (1970), *Sula* (1973), *Song of Solomon* (1977), *Tar Baby* (1981), *Beloved* (1987), *Jazz* (1992), and *Paradise* (1998)—range across the landscape of African American culture. For example, while all the novels—with the lone exception of *Song of Solomon*—feature women as central protagonists, none of the novels is "feminist" in any sort of predetermined, hackneyed way. Morrison's work is primarily concerned with class and caste distinctions and divisions within African American culture; while slavery and racism, along with sexism, frame all the novels, Morrison's work cannot be reduced to protest fiction since it is not addressed primarily to either male or Caucasian readers. Nevertheless, it certainly can be said that the novels have become increasingly political insofar as slavery, sexism, and racism loom larger in each succeeding novel. Although this process has been gradual, many critics, both detractors and proponents, cite *Beloved*, Morrison's best-known work and most controversial novel, as the linchpin text.

Beloved, like *Jazz*, is based on a true story. It centers on Sethe, a former slave and mother who attempts to escape from the South but pays a tremendous personal price. Trapped by slave hunters, she tries to kill both of her baby daughters rather than see them returned to slavery, succeeding only with the youngest, unnamed one. Years later, free in Ohio but ostracized from the African American community because of the murder, Sethe and Denver, her surviving daughter, are visited by the ghost of Sethe's dead daughter, Beloved, as well as by Paul D., Sethe's lover who wants to start a new life with her. Thus the novel centers on the tug-of-war Sethe endures as she is alternately pulled back by the past (Beloved's claim of birthright) and toward the future (Paul D.'s claim on her as his wife).

The controversy over the novel centered on the question of the murder of Beloved. Was it indeed better to kill oneself or one's children than submit to the horrors of slavery? Or was it better to live, knowing that those who survived the ordeal would pass their indomitable genes and traditions on to a hoped-for, but unforeseeable, future of freedom? Morrison herself never directly addressed the issue, and readers are not helped by the ambivalence of the novel's last pages, which assert that the "story" was one "to pass on" and "not pass on."

This ambivalence, a feature of all Morrison's novels, tempers the heightened political profiles of the stories. None of Morrison's contemporaries has achieved this precarious balance between political outrage and human complexity. For example, Alice Walker, whose first novel, *The Third Life of Grange Copeland* (1970), appeared in the same year as Morrison's *The Bluest Eye*, is more an important cultural figure than a significant writer. *The Third Life of Grange Copeland* is, however, a well-written, harrowing account of women that are not only physically and psychologically abused but also driven to madness by men. To this extent, Walker is much more a feminist than Morrison. However, *The Third Life of Grange Copeland* is also about racism and class bias, as well as their relationship to violence against women. In that respect, Walker's first novel was quite promising.

Walker is best known, however, for her second novel, the controversial *The Color Purple* (1982). An epistolary novel, *The Color Purple* explores the gradual sexual and feminist awakening of a young teenager, Celie, who has been abused by both her family and her husband, whom she designates "Mister." Although she writes letters addressed to God, Celie is actually saved by Mister's mistress, Shug. The narrative of the novel implies that Shug's lesbian relationship with Celie is sparked, in part, by the oppression both undergo from Mister, a connection that understandably upset lesbians since it reduced female same-sex relationships to reactions against misogyny and sexism. At the same time, the portrait of Mister angered writers such as Ishmael Reed and Amiri Baraka, who believed that Walker and other African American feminists were unwittingly playing into the hands of a culture that had long demonized African American male sexuality. Walker's attempt to remind readers on all sides of the debate that Celie is complicit in her own abuse and oppression and that Mister is transformed by the novel's end into a humane father and friend to Celie went largely unheard. When Walker sold the screen rights of the novel to director Steven Spielberg, who produced a movie that essentially deleted the sexual politics and romanticized the South, supporters and critics of the book were dismayed. Although she continued to produce readable novels such as *The Temple of My Familiar* (1989) and *Possessing the Secret of Joy* (1992), Walker's growing interest in African American lesbianism made her a marginal figure in African American culture, a fate not unlike that suffered by Baldwin, poet Audre Lorde, and others.

Next to Morrison and Walker, other African American women novelists have shown sporadic, inconsistent promise. Toni Cade Bambara was a brilliant short story writer and a promising novelist. *The Salt Eaters* (1980) showcased complex narrative textures and jazz influences similar to those in Ishmael Reed's early novels. However, Bambara's career was shortened by her premature death in 1995.

Gloria Naylor's first novel, *The Women of Brewster Place: A Novel in Seven Stories* (1982), was a major success that was made into an even more successful television film. However, it was published in the same year as *The Color Purple*, and, worse, its similar themes of African American lesbianism and African American male cruelty echoed the inferior but more controversial book by Walker. Naylor rewrote and updated Baraka's *The System of Dante's Hell* (1965) with her second novel, *Linden Hills* (1985), revived the novel of manners in the vein of Jessie Redmon Fauset in *Mama Day* (1988), and, in *Bailey's Café* (1992), echoed the improvisational experiments of Morrison's *Jazz*.

Finally, Gayl Jones's first two novels, *Corregidora* (1975) and *Eva's Man* (1976), despite their familiar themes of misogyny, sexism, and abuse, showed promise. In many ways the most interesting of the new writers, Jones's interest in the abnormalities of psychological profiles and their link to linguistic modes suggests an intelligence only partially realized in the first two novels. Jones, however, suffered a series of personal and professional traumas, and it was more than two decades before a third novel, *The Healing* (1998), appeared. This novel, along with her fourth, *Mosquito* (1999), suggested a return to creative and psychological health for Jones, which augured well for the continued development of African American fiction.

Bibliography
Beaulieu, Elizabeth Ann. *Black Women Writers and the American Neo-Slave Narrative: Femininity Unfettered.* Westport, Conn.: Greenwood Press, 1999. Beaulieu discusses the efforts of African American women writers to redefine the slave narrative in the twentieth century. Among the novels discussed are Sherley Anne Williams's *Dessa Rose* and Toni Morrison's *Beloved.*
Braxton, Joanne M., and Andrée Nicola McLaughlin, eds. *Wild Women in the Whirlwind: Afra-American Culture and the Contemporary Literary Renaissance.* New Brunswick, N.J.: Rutgers University Press, 1990. This is the best anthology of critical writings on African American women writers, past and present. The range of writers covered is impressive, and the language is free of jargon.
Butler, Robert. *Contemporary African American Fiction: The Open Journey.* Madison, Wis.: Fairleigh Dickinson University Press, 1998. Butler's book, as the subtitle suggests, covers a wide range of subject matter, from a study of the picaresque in the fiction of Zora Neale Hurston and Richard Wright to a discussion of Octavia E. Butler's vision of the twenty-first century.
Callahan, John F. *In the African-American Grain: Call-and-Response in Twentieth-Century Black Fiction.* Middletown, Conn.: Wesleyan University Press, 1988. Callahan examines the way novelists and short story writers from Charles Chesnutt to Alice Walker have insisted on the importance of call-and-response in the creation of a personal identity that remains bound to larger ideals of African American culture.
Christian, Barbara. *Black Feminist Criticism: Perspectives on Black Women Writers.* New York: Pergamon Press, 1985. Although these brief essays read like journalistic reviews, Christian's book is valuable for the range of African American women

writers she covers, as well as the influential ideas she uses to assess sexuality and empowerment in African American women's fiction.

Davis, Charles, and Henry Louis Gates, Jr., eds. *The Slave's Narrative*. Oxford, England: Oxford University Press, 1985. This valuable addition to the growing commentary on slave narrative provides an introduction to three modes of interpreting the slave narrative: journalistic, historical, and literary.

Gates, Henry Louis, Jr. *The Signifying Monkey: A Theory of African-American Literary Criticism*. New York: Oxford University Press, 1988. This ambitious but concise text argues for the importance of the trickster figure in African American literature and its link to the problem of literacy and identity.

Greene, J. Lee. *Blacks in Eden: The African American Novel's First Century*. Charlottesville: University Press of Virginia, 1996. Greene traces the development of the African American novel through the twentieth century.

Joyce, Joyce Ann. *Warriors, Conjurers, and Priests: Defining African-Centered Literary Criticism*. Chicago: Third World Press, 1994. Joyce examines the work of neglected African American writers such as Ann Petry and Sonia Sanchez while taking on antifeminist critics such as Ishmael Reed. Joyce also provides assessments of newer writers such as Terry McMillan and E. Ethelbert Miller.

Kostelanetz, Richard. *Politics in the African-American Novel: James Weldon Johnson, W. E. B. Du Bois, Richard Wright, and Ralph Ellison*. New York: Greenwood Press, 1991. This investigation of the development of the African American novel charts the movement from the protest fiction of Johnson and Du Bois to the more complex and thus "better" work of Wright and Ellison.

Schwarz, A. B. Christa. *Gay Voices of the Harlem Renaissance*. Bloomington: Indiana University Press, 2003. Schwarz examines the work of four leading writers from the Harlem Renaissance—Countée Cullen, Langston Hughes, Claude McKay, and Richard Bruce Nugent—and their sexually nonconformist or gay literary voices.

— *Tyrone Williams*

African American Poetry

Double Consciousness

The struggle for freedom—social, psychological, and aes-thetic—is the distinguishing attribute of African American po-etry from its origins during slavery through its pluralistic flower-ing in the twentieth century. Although the impact of the struggle has only intermittently been simple or direct, it has re-mained a constant presence both for writers concentrating di-rectly on the continuing oppression of the black community and for those forging highly individualistic poetic voices not pri-marily concerned with racial issues.

Generally, two basic "voices" characterize the African Ameri-can poetic sensibility. First, black poets attempting to survive in a literary market dominated by white publishers and audiences have felt the need to demonstrate their ability to match the ac-complishments of white poets in traditional forms. From the couplets of Phillis Wheatley through the sonnets of Claude McKay to the modernist montages of Robert Hayden to the rap and hip-hop stylings of Queen Latifah, Public Enemy, Ice-T, Mos Def, Tupac, and KRS1, African American poets have mas-tered the full range of voices associated with the evolving poetic mainstream. Second, black poets have been equally concerned with forging distinctive voices reflecting both their individual sensibilities and the specifically African American cultural tra-dition.

This dual focus within the African American sensibility re-flects the presence of what W. E. B. Du Bois identified as a "double-consciousness" that forces the black writer to perceive himself or herself as both an "American" and a "Negro." The greatest African American poets—Langston Hughes, Sterling Brown, Gwendolyn Brooks, Hayden, Amiri Baraka, Maya Ange-lou, Rita Dove, Yusef Komunyakaa, and Kevin Powell—draw on this tension as a source of both formal and thematic power, helping them to construct a poetry that is at once unmistakably black and universally resonant.

1188

Caged Eagles: Early Poets

From the beginning, African American poets have continually adjusted to and rebelled against the fact of double consciousness. To be sure, this rebellion and adjustment have varied in form with changing social circumstances. Nevertheless, Baraka's statement in his poetic drama *Bloodrites* (pr. 1970) that the aware black artist has always been concerned with helping his or her community attain "Identity, Purpose, Direction" seems accurate. Over a period of time, the precise emphasis has shifted between the terms, but the specific direction and purpose inevitably reflect the individual's or the era's conception of identity. To some extent, this raises the issue of whether the emphasis in "African American" belongs on "African" or on "American." Some poets, such as Baraka during his nationalist period, emphasize the African heritage and tend toward assertive and frequently separatist visions of purpose and direction. Others, such as Jean Toomer in his late period, emphasize some version of the "American" ideal and embrace a variety of strategies for the purpose of reaching a truly integrated society.

Wheatley, the first important African American poet, was forced to confront this tension between African and American identities. As an "American" poet of the eighteenth century— before the political entity known as the United States was formed—her writing imitated the styles and themes of British masters such as John Milton, John Dryden, and Alexander Pope. Brought to America at age six, she experienced only a mild form of slavery in Philadelphia, because her owners Thomas and Susannah Wheatley felt deep affection for her and respected her gifts as a writer. Unlike other Wheatley servants, Phillis, treated more as a stepdaughter than as a servant, was exempted from routine duties and had a private room, books, and writing materials. At the same time, her career was hobbled by the blatant discrimination heaped on all "African" people. For example, in 1772, Susannah Wheatley sought patrons to help publish the then eighteen-year-old Phillis's first collection of twenty-eight poems. Colonial whites rejected the proposal because she was a slave. Phillis was forced to seek a publisher in London.

Although her poem "On Being Brought from Africa to America" views slavery as a "mercy," because it led her from "pagan" darkness to Christian light, she was never accepted as a poet on her own merits. However, in England, whose antislavery movement was stronger than that of the colonies, people of wealth and stature such as the countess of Huntingdon and the earl of Dartmouth embraced the poet. Lady Huntingdon, to whom Wheatley's first volume, *Poems on Various Subjects, Religious and Moral* (1773), was dedicated, financed the publication and put Phillis's picture on the frontispiece. Wheatley's work was advertised as the product of a "sable muse" and she was presented as a curiosity; the blind racism of the times made it impossible for her to be accepted as a poet who was as accomplished as her white contemporaries. That sentiment was made clear by Thomas Jefferson in his *Notes on the State of Virginia* (1777): "Religion indeed has produced a Phyllis Whately [sic] but it could not produce a poet. The compositions published under her name are below the dignity of criticism." Those sentiments are counterbalanced by a contemporary, Jupiter Hammon, also a slave poet, who in "An Address to Miss Phillis Whealy [sic]" praised her talent and influence as part of God's providence: "While thousands tossed by the sea,/ And others settled down,/ God's tender mercy set thee free,/ From dangers that come down."

Other early writers, such as George Moses Horton and Frances Watkins Harper, shared a common purpose in their antislavery poetry but rarely escaped the confines of religious and political themes acceptable to the abolitionist journals that published their work. The pressures on the African American poet became even more oppressive during the post-Reconstruction era as the South "reconquered" black people, in part by establishing control over the literary image of slavery. "Plantation Tradition" portrayed contented slaves and benevolent masters living in pastoral harmony. Paul Laurence Dunbar attained wide popularity in the late nineteenth and early twentieth centuries, but only by acquiescing partially in the white audience's stereotypical preconceptions concerning the proper style (slave dialect) and tones (humor or pathos) for poetry dealing with black characters.

A Voice of Their Own

Spearheading the first open poetic rebellion against imposed stereotypes, James Weldon Johnson, a close friend of Dunbar, mildly rejected Dunbar's dialect poetry in his preface to *The Book of American Negro Poetry* (1922), which issued a call for "a form that will express the racial spirit by symbols from within rather than by symbols from without." He explained:

The newer Negro poets discard dialect; much of the subject matter which went into the making of traditional dialect poetry, 'possums, watermelons, etc., they have discarded altogether, at least, as poetical material. This tendency will, no doubt, be regretted by the majority of white readers; and indeed, it would be a distinct loss if the American Negro poets threw away this quaint and musical folk-speech as a medium of expression. And yet, after all, these poets are working through a problem not realized by the reader, and perhaps, by many of these poets themselves not realized consciously. They are trying to break away, not from the Negro dialect itself, but the limitations on the Negro dialect imposed by the fixing effects of long convention.

The Negro in the United States has achieved or been placed in a certain artistic niche. When he is thought of artistically, it is as a happy-go-lucky, singing, shuffling, banjo-picking being or as a more or less pathetic figure. The African American poet realizes that there are phases of Negro life in the United States which cannot be treated in the dialect either adequately or artistically. Take, for example, the phases rising out of life in Harlem, that most wonderful Negro city in the world. I do not deny that a Negro in a log cabin is more picturesque than a Negro in a Harlem flat, but the Negro is here, and he is part of a group growing everywhere in the country, a group whose ideals are becoming increasingly more vital than those of the traditionally artistic group, even if its members are less picturesque.

The Harlem Renaissance

This call was heeded by the poets of the Harlem Renaissance, who took advantage of the development of large black population centers in the North during the Great Northern Migration of blacks from the rural South to the urban North during the 1910's and 1920's. Where earlier poets lived either among largely illiterate slave populations or in white communities, the "New Negroes"—as Alain Locke, one of the first major black critics, labeled the writers of the movement—seized the opportunity to establish a sense of identity for a sizable black audience. Locke viewed the work of poets such as McKay, Countée Cullen, and Toomer as a clear indication that blacks were preparing for a full entry into the American cultural mainstream.

The support given Harlem Renaissance writers by such white artists and patrons as Carl Van Vechten and Nancy Cunard, however, considerably complicated the era's achievement. On one hand, it appeared to herald the merging predicted by Locke. On the other, it pressured individual black writers to validate the exoticism frequently associated with black life by the white onlookers. Cullen's "Heritage," with its well-known refrain "What is Africa to me?" reflects the sometimes arbitrarily enforced consciousness of Africa that pervades the decade. African American artists confronted with white statements such as Eugene O'Neill's play *All God's Chillun Got Wings* (pr., pb. 1924) could not help remaining acutely aware that they, like Wheatley 150 years earlier, were cast more as primitive curiosities than as sophisticated artists. However, an expansion in the U.S. literary canon and evolution in African American literature could not be denied. It was celebrated in the March, 1925, issue of Van Vechten's literary journal *Survey Graphic*, guest-edited by Locke, who was then a Howard University philosophy professor.

The first flowering of Harlem as an artistic center came to an end with the Great Depression of the 1930's, which redirected African American creative energies toward political concerns. The end of prosperity brought a return of hard times to the African American community and put an end to the relatively easy access to print for aspiring black writers.

The 1930's: New Directions

If the Harlem Renaissance was largely concerned with questions of identity, the writing in Langston Hughes's *A New Song* (1938) and Sterling Brown's *Southern Road* (1932) reflects a new concern with the purpose and direction of both black artists and black masses. Hughes had earlier addressed the caution in an essay, "The Negro Artist and the Racial Mountain," published in the June 23, 1926, issue of *The Nation*:

> The Negro artist works against an undertow of sharp criticism from his own group and unintentional bribes from the whites. But in spite of the Nordicized Negro intelligentsia and the desires of some white editors we have an honest American Negro literature already with us. . . . I am ashamed for the black poet who says, "I want to be a poet, not a Negro poet," as though his own racial world were not as interesting as any other world. An artist must be free to choose what he does, certainly, but he must also never be afraid to do what he might choose.

Where many of the Harlem Renaissance writers had accepted Du Bois's vision of a "talented tenth" who would lead the community out of cultural bondage, the 1930's writers revitalized the African American tradition that perceived the source of power—poetic and political—in traditions of the "folk" community. Margaret Walker's "For My People" expresses the ideal community "pulsing in our spirits and our blood." This emphasis sometimes coincided or overlapped with the proletarian and leftist orientation that dominated African American fiction of the period. Again external events, this time World War II and the "sell-out" of blacks by the American Communist Party, brought an end to an artistic era.

The Postwar Era: Universalism

The post-World War II period of African American poetry is more difficult to define in clear-cut terms. Many new poets became active, especially during the 1960's and 1970's, while poets such as Hughes and Brown, who had begun their careers earlier, continued as active forces. Nevertheless, it is generally accurate to refer to the period from the late 1940's through the early 1960's as one of universalism and integration, and that of the mid-1960's through the mid-1970's as one of self-assertion and separatism.

The return of prosperity, landmark court decisions, and the decline of legal segregation in the face of nonviolent protest movements created the feeling during the early postwar period that African American culture might finally be admitted into the American mainstream on an equal footing. Poets such as Gwendolyn Brooks, who became the first black to win the Pulitzer Prize in poetry—for *Annie Allen* (1949)—and Robert Hayden, who later became the first black Library of Congress poet, wrote poetry that was designed to communicate to all readers, regardless of their racial backgrounds and experiences. Neither poet abandoned black materials or traditions, but neither presented a surface texture that would present difficulties for an attentive white reader. Brooks's poem "Mentors" typifies the dominant style of the "universalist" period. It can be read with equal validity as a meditation on death, a comment on the influence of artistic predecessors, a commitment to remember the suffering of the slave community, and a character study of a soldier returning home from war.

The universalist period also marked the first major assertion of modernism in black poetry. Although both Hughes and Toomer had earlier used modernist devices, neither was perceived as part of the mainstream of experimental writing, another manifestation of the critical ignorance that has haunted black poets since Wheatley. Hayden and Melvin B. Tolson adopted the radical prosody of T. S. Eliot and Ezra Pound, while Baraka, Bob Kaufman, and Ted Joans joined white poets in New York and San Francisco in forging a multiplicity of postmodernist styles, many of them rooted in African American culture, especially jazz.

The Black Arts Movement

As in the 1920's, however, the association of black poets with their white counterparts during the 1950's and 1960's generated mixed results. Again, numerous black writers believed that they were accepted primarily as exotics and that the reception of their work was racially biased. With the development of a strong Black Nationalist political movement, exemplified by Malcolm X (who was to become the subject of more poems by African American writers than any other individual), many of the universalist poets turned their attention to a poetry that would directly address the African American community's concerns in a specifically black voice. LeRoi Jones changed his name to Imamu Amiri Baraka and placed the term Black Arts in the forefront as an indicator of a new cultural aesthetic in the poem, "Black Dada Nihilismus." Brooks announced her conversion to a pan-Africanist philosophy, and community arts movements sprang up in cities throughout the United States.

A major movement of young black poets, variously referred to as the New Black Renaissance or the Black Arts movement, rejected involvement with Euro-American culture and sought to create a new "black aesthetic" that would provide a specifically black identity, purpose, and direction. Poets such as Haki R. Madhubuti (Don L. Lee), Sonia Sanchez, Nikki Giovanni, and Etheridge Knight perceived their work primarily in relation to a black audience, publishing with black houses such as Broadside Press of Detroit and Third World Press of Chicago. Most poets of the Black Arts movement remained active after the relative decline of the Black Nationalist impulse in the late 1970's and 1980's, but, with such notable exceptions as Madhubuti, their tone generally became more subdued. They have been joined in prominence by a group of poets, many of whom also began writing in the 1960's, who have strong affinities with the modernist wing of the universalist period. If Madhubuti, Knight, and Giovanni are largely populist and political in sensibility, poets such as Michael S. Harper, Ai, and Jay Wright are more academic and aesthetic in orientation. Although their sensibilities differ markedly, all the poets asserted the strength of both the African American tradition and the individual voice.

A new pluralism began to emerge, testifying to the persistence of several basic values in the African American sensibility: survival, literacy, and freedom. The publication of the anthology *Black Fire* (1968), coedited by Baraka and Larry Neal, signaled the emergence of the new age. The shift in goals, simply put, was from the uplift of the black community to the transformation of U.S. society. The collection made it clear that African American artists had moved beyond cultural navel gazing. The poets now defined themselves as a Third World people engaged in a global struggle. Neal's essay "The Black Arts Movement" became the period's manifesto:

> National and international affairs demand that we appraise the world in terms of our own interests. It is clear that the question of human survival is at the core of contemporary experience. The black artist must address himself to this reality in the strongest terms possible. Consequently, the Black Arts Movement is an ethical movement. Ethical, that is, from the viewpoint of the oppressed. And much of the oppression confronting the Third World and black America is directly traceable to the Euro-American cultural sensibility. This sensibility, antihuman in nature, has, until recently, dominated the psyches of most black artists and intellectuals. It must be destroyed before the black creative artist can have a meaningful role in the transformation of society.

Even highly idiosyncratic poets, such as Toomer in "Blue Meridian" and Ishmael Reed in his "neo-hoo-doo" poems, endorsed those basic values, all of which originated in the experience of slavery. In his book *From Behind the Veil: A Study of Afro-American Narrative* (1979), Robert B. Stepto identifies the central heroic figure of the African American tradition as the "articulate survivor," who completes a symbolic ascent from slavery to a limited freedom, and the "articulate kinsman," who completes a symbolic immersion into his cultural roots. The articulate survivor must attain "literacy" as defined by the dominant white society; the articulate kinsman must attain "tribal literacy" as defined by the black community.

In the 1960's and 1970's, the U.S. Civil Rights movement and subsequent Black Power movement breathed life into human rights struggles throughout the world. Poets in other parts of the African world began to be heard in the United States during the 1970's, which gave evidence that black bids for survival, literacy, and freedom were indeed universal. Derek Walcott of St. Lucia, South African Dennis Brutus, and Nigeria's Wole Soyinka were among the most important voices.

Walcott, like the Jamaican McKay almost a half a century before him, showed a reverence for the native Caribbean cultures. Another theme in his early work was outrage at the injustices of colonial rule. Beginning with, *The Gulf, and Other Poems* (1969), the poet begins to grapple with ideological and political questions. The strength of the reflection grows in *Sea Grapes* (1976) and comes to full potency in *The Star-Apple Kingdom* (1979).

Brutus's first volume of poems, *Sirens, Knuckles, Boots* (1963) was published while he was doing an eighteen-month stretch on Robben Island, apartheid South Africa's most infamous jail. The equivalent of the Alcatraz, it was considered escape-proof because of the water that separated its inmates from the mainland. After release in 1965, he was exiled to London. The poet joined the Northwestern University English faculty in 1970. Three years later, *A Simple Lust* detailed for American audiences the horror of South African prisons and apartheid's injustices. The collection was also influenced by medieval European sensibilities and images. In the first poem of the collection, Brutus speaks in the voice of a troubadour who fights for his beloved against social injustice and betrayal. Even though outwardly European, the poem reverberates the sense of the heroic found in many American-born black writers' works.

Like these Caribbean and South African counterparts, U.S. poets of African descent made reference to, but transformed, European influences. Maya Angelou's "Still I Rise" and Mari Evans's "Vive Noir!" convey the drama of knighthood's quests against an unjust society through plain language and images drawn from black environments. The works also tossed aside traditional notions of grammar, spelling, and punctuation as a means to emphasize the rejection of conventional European sensibilities. Evans, for example, sick of the language of oppressors as much as the slums of Inner Cities, asserts she is

weary
of exhausted lands
sagging privies
saying yessuh yessah
yesSIR
in an assortment
of geographical dialects

The Black Arts movement faded in the mid-1970's, without changing the world or stabilizing the growth it gave to African American consciousness. New Orleans poet Kalamu ya Salaam, in an essay in *The Oxford Companion to African American Literature* (1997), traced the beginning of the swan song to 1974:

As the movement reeled from the combination of external and internal disruption, commercialization and capitalist co-option delivered the coup de grace. President Richard Nixon's strategy of pushing Black capitalism as a response to Black Power epitomized mainstream co-option. As major film, record, book and magazine publishers identified the most salable artists, the Black Arts Movement's already fragile independent economic base was totally undermined.

A Shift in Emphasis: The 1970's to the 1990's

As in the 1930's, after the Harlem Renaissance subsided most of the independent publications, public forums, and other outlets for African American cultural expression had evaporated. Lotus Press and Broadside Press in Detroit and Third World Press in Chicago would continue to create outlets for excellent literature. White-owned book companies and magazines shifted focus to the movements for women's equality and against the Vietnam War. That set the stage for the emergence of Audre Lorde, Lucille Clifton, and Yusef Komunyakaa.

Lorde's *The Black Unicorn* (1978) used African symbols and myths to explore the dimensions within her existence. Adrienne Rich acknowledged the volume as a kind of declaration of independence: "Refusing to be circumscribed by any single identity, Audre Lorde writes as a Black woman, a mother, a daughter, a

Lesbian, a feminist, a visionary." In an interview with editor Claudia Tate in *Black Women Writers at Work* (1983), Lorde averred the Black Arts movement's stress on representation of the global experience of blacks and the oppressed. Tossing aside previous notions that true African American art is political at its core, she sketched a vision of poetry as a reflection of the personal:

> Black men have come to believe to their detriment that you have no validity unless you're "global," as opposed to personal. Yet our *real power* comes from the personal; our real insights about living come from the deep knowledge within us that arises from our feelings. Our thoughts are shaped by our tutoring. We were tutored to function in a structure that already existed but that does not function for our good. Our feelings are our most genuine path to knowledge. Men have been taught to deal only with what they understand. This is what they respect. They know that somewhere feeling and knowledge are important, so they keep women around to do their feeling for them, like ants do aphids.

The African American poets who rose in prominence during the 1980's, employed stylistic traditions that stretched back to Hughes and other Harlem Renaissance writers. The themes of survival and freedom remained pronounced in their works. The major difference was that, instead of grappling with outside forces, they confronted their nightmares.

Komunyakaa took on Vietnam. The Bogalusa, Louisiana, native won a Bronze Star for his service during the war as a writer and editor of the military newspaper *The Southern Cross.* His poem "Facing It," which reflects on a visit to the Vietnam Veterans Memorial in Washington, D.C., exposes the war as a personal bad dream: "My clouded reflection eyes me like a bird of prey, the profile of the night slanted against the morning." The poet becomes the black granite slab and the archetype of the tens of thousands of visitors. As the poem unfolds, it becomes clear that the conflict is a ghost that will haunt every American for generations.

In September, 1994, the largest gathering of black poets since the end of the Black Arts period was held in Harrisonburg, Virginia, at James Madison University. Thirty of the top black poets since the 1960's—old voices such as Baraka, Madhubuti, Sanchez, Giovanni, and Evans, and new voices such as E. Ethelbert Miller and Toi Derricotte—came together with more than 250 scholars, reporters, and critics. According to a report in *The Washington Post* (October 1), the one subject none of the writers wanted to discuss was what qualities set African American poetry apart from the mainstream. The reporter said that the poets "hate the question, because it reminds them of days when black poetry was relegated to the 'Negro' section of anthologies." Yet each of these poets was living with the deep awareness that African American poets were still not equal members of an elitist literary establishment.

Literacy, frequently illegal under the slave codes, both increases the chance of survival and makes freedom meaningful. Tribal literacy protects the individual's racial identity against submersion in a society perceived as inhumane and corrupt. "The literature of an oppressed people is the conscience of man," wrote Lance Jeffers in an essay printed in the January, 1971, issue of the journal *Black Scholar*:

> [N]owhere is this seen with more intense clarity than the literature of Afroamerica. An essential element of Afroamerican literature is that the literature as a whole—not the work of occasional authors—is a movement against concrete wickedness. The cry for freedom and the protest against injustice are a cry for the birth of the New Man, a testament to the Unknown World (glory) to be discovered, to be created by man.

To a large extent, black poets writing in traditional forms established their literacy as part of a survival strategy in the white literary world. Those concerned with developing black forms demonstrate their respect for, and kinship with, the culturally literate African American community.

Just Plain Folks

Against this complex of values and pressures, folk traditions have assumed a central importance in the development of the African American sensibility. Embodying the "tribal" wisdom concerning survival tactics and the meaning of freedom, they provide both formal and thematic inspiration for many black poets. African American poets have become extremely adept at manipulating various masks. Originating with the trickster figures of African folklore and African American heroes such as Brer Rabbit, these masks provide survival strategies based on intellectual, rather than physical, strength.

Existing in a situation during slavery in which open rebellion could easily result in death, the slave community capitalized on the intimate knowledge of white psychology encouraged by the need to anticipate the master's wishes. The white community, conditioned not to see or take into account black needs and desires, possessed no equivalent knowledge of black psychology. Lacking knowledge, whites typically turned to comfortable stereotypes—the loyal mammy, the singing darkie, the tragic mulatto, the black beast—for their interpretation of black behavior. The observant slave found it both easy and rewarding to manipulate white perceptions of reality by appearing to correspond to a stereotypical role while quietly maneuvering for either personal or community gain. The nature of the mask, which exploits a phenomenon of double consciousness by controlling the discrepancy between black and white perspectives, is such that the true goal must always remain hidden from the white viewer, who must always feel that he is making the "real" decisions. Brer Rabbit asks not to be thrown in the briar patch; he will be allowed to escape, however, only if Brer Bear, the symbolic white man, believes that Brer Rabbit's mask is his true face.

This folk tradition of masking adds a specifically African American dimension to the standard poetic manipulation of persona. African American poets frequently adopt personas that, when viewed by white audiences, seem transparent incarnations of familiar stereotypes. Dunbar's dialect poetry and Hughes's Harlem street poems, for example, have been both accepted and dismissed by white readers as straightforward, realistic portraits of black life. An awareness of the complex ironies inherent in the African American folk traditions on which each drew, however, uncovers increasingly complex levels of awareness in their work. Dunbar's melodious dialect songs of plantation life contrast sharply with his complaint against a world that forced him to sing "a jingle in a broken tongue." Similarly, his classic poem "We Wear the Mask" expresses the anguish of a people forced to adopt evasive presentations of self in a nation theoretically committed to pluralism and self-fulfillment. Less agonized than Dunbar, Hughes manipulates the surfaces of his poems, offering and refusing stereotypical images with dazzling speed. "Dream Boogie" first connects the image of the "dream deferred" with the marching feet of an army of the dispossessed, only to resume the mask of the smiling darkie in the sardonic concluding lines:

> What did I say?
> Sure,
> I'm happy!
> Take it away!
> Hey, pop!
> Re-bop!! Mop!
> Y-e-a-h!

The critical record gives strong evidence that Hughes is frequently taken at "face" value. His mask serves to affirm the existence of a black self in control of the rhythm of experience, as well as to satirize the limitations of the white perception.

Throughout the history of African American poetry, poets choosing to address the black political experience without intricate masks have been plagued by the assumption that their relevance was limited by their concentration on racial subject matter. Starting in the twentieth century, a new stereotype—that of the "angry black" writer—developed. The conditions of black life frequently do, in fact, generate anger and protest. African American poets, from Wheatley through Alberry Whitman in the late nineteenth century to Cullen and Giovanni, frequently protest against the oppression of blacks. McKay's sonnet "If We

Must Die" embodies the basic impulse of this tradition, concluding with the exhortation: "Like men we'll face the murderous, cowardly pack,/ Pressed to the wall, dying, but fighting back!" Far from being limited by its origins in the African American experience, such poetry embraces a universal human drive for freedom. Winston Churchill quoted lines from the poem (ironically written partially in response to British exploitation of McKay's native Jamaica) during the early days of World War II. The stereotype of the angry black, while based on a limited reality, becomes oppressive at precisely the point that it is confused with or substituted for the full human complexity of the individual poet. Giovanni, at times one of the angriest poets of the Black Arts movement, pinpoints the problem in her poem "Nikki-Rosa":

> I really hope no white person ever has cause
> to write about me
> because they never understand.
> Black love is Black wealth and they'll
> probably talk about my hard childhood
> and never understand that
> all the while I was quite happy.

The drive for freedom transcends any single tone or mode. While frequently connected with the protest against specific conditions limiting social, psychological, or artistic freedom, the impulse modifies a wide range of poetic voices. At one extreme, explicitly political poems such as Baraka's "Black Art" call for "Poems that shoot/ guns." Even Baraka's less assertive poems, such as "For Hettie" or the more recent "Three Modes of History and Culture," seek to envision a world free from oppression. At another extreme, the drive for freedom lends emotional power to "apolitical" poems such as Dunbar's "Sympathy," with its refrain, "I know why the caged bird sings." Although the poem does not explicitly address racial issues, the intense feeling of entrapment certainly reflects Dunbar's position as a black poet subject to the stereotypes of white society. Similar in theme, but more direct in confronting racial pressures, Cullen's sonnet

1203

"Yet Do I Marvel," a masterpiece of irony, accepts the apparent injustices of creation, concluding: "Yet do I marvel at this curious thing/ To make a poet black, and bid him sing." Hughes's "Mother to Son" and "I, Too" with their determination to keep moving, reflect a more optimistic vision. Despite the hardships of life in a country which forces even the "beautiful" black man to "eat in the kitchen," Hughes's characters struggle successfully against despair. It is significant that many of Hughes's poems are very popular in the Third World. "I, Too," for example, has become a kind of anthem in Latin America, which honors Hughes as a major poet in the Walt Whitman tradition.

Where Hughes and Walker frequently treat freedom optimistically, Brown's "Memphis Blues" provides a stark warning of the ultimate destruction awaiting a society that fails to live up to its ideals. McKay's sonnet "America," with its echoes of Percy Bysshe Shelley's "Ozymandias," strikes a similar note, envisioning the nation's "priceless treasures sinking in the sand." Perhaps Hayden best embodies the basic impulse in his brilliant "Runagate Runagate," which employs a complex modernist voice to celebrate the mutually nourishing relationship between the anonymous fugitive slaves and the heroic figure of Harriet Tubman, who articulates and perpetuates their drive for freedom. Blending the voices of slavemasters, runaway slaves, the spirituals, and American mythology, Hayden weaves a tapestry that culminates in the insistent refrain, "Mean mean mean to be free."

Hayden's use of the anonymous voice of the runaway slave with the voice of the spirituals underscores both the drive for freedom and the nature of the individual hero who embodies the aspirations of the entire community. It exemplifies the importance of folk traditions as formal points of reference for the African American poetic sensibility.

Music and Message

Poets seeking to assert a specifically black voice within the context of the Euro-American mainstream repeatedly turn to the rhythms and imagery of folk forms such as spirituals and sermons. During the twentieth century, the blues and jazz assume equal importance. As Stephen Henderson observes in *Understanding the New Black Poetry* (1973), these folk traditions provide both thematic and formal inspiration. Hayden's "Homage to the Empress of the Blues," Brown's "Ma Rainey," Brooks's "Queen of the Blues," and poems addressed to John Coltrane by Harper ("Dear John, Dear Coltrane," "A Love Supreme,"), Madhubuti ("Don't Cry, Scream"), and Sanchez ("A Coltrane Poem") are only a few of countless African American poems invoking black musicians as cultural heroes. Bluesmen such as Robert Johnson (who wrote such haunting lyrics as "Crossroads," "Stones in My Passageway," and "If I Had Possession over Judgement Day") and singers such as Bessie Smith frequently assume the stature of folk heroes themselves. At their best they can legitimately be seen as true poets working with the vast reservoir of imagery inherent in African American folk life. Du Bois endorsed the idea by montaging passages of African American music with selections of Euro-American poetry at the start of each chapter of *The Souls of Black Folk* (1903). Similarly, James Weldon Johnson's poem "O Black and Unknown Bards" credits the anonymous composers of the spirituals with a cultural achievement equivalent to that of Ludwig van Beethoven and Richard Wagner.

These folk and musical traditions have suggested a great range of poetic forms to African American poets. Johnson echoed the rhythms of black preaching in his powerful volume *God's Trombones: Seven Negro Sermons in Verse* (1927), which includes such classic "sermons" as "The Creation" and "Go Down Death—A Funeral Sermon." Hughes and Brown used their intricate knowledge of black musical forms in structuring their poetry. Early in his career, Hughes was content simply to imitate the structure of the blues stanza in poems such as "Suicide." As he matured, however, he developed more subtle strategies for capturing the blues impact in "The Weary Blues," which establishes a dramatic frame for several blues stanzas, and "Song for Billie." The latter mimics the subtle shifts in emphasis of the blues line by altering the order of prepositions in the stanza:

> What can purge my heart
> of the song
> and the sadness?
> What can purge my heart
> But the song
> of the sadness?
> What can purge my heart
> of the sadness
> of the song?

The persona moves from a stance of distance to one of identification and acceptance of the blues feeling. In merging emotionally with the singer, he provides a paradigm for the ideal relationship between artist and audience in the African American tradition.

Brown's blues poem "Ma Rainey" incorporates this "call and response" aspect of the blues experience into its frame story. Ma Rainey attains heroic stature because her voice and vision echo those of the audience that gathers from throughout the Mississippi Delta to hear its experience authenticated. Brown's attempt to forge a voice that combines call and response points to what may be the central formal quest of African American poetry. Such an ideal voice seeks to inspire the community by providing a strong sense of identity, purpose, and direction. Simultaneously, it validates the individual experience of the poet by providing a sense of social connection in the face of what Ralph Ellison refers to as the "brutal experience" underlying the blues impulse. Both Ellison and Hughes, two of the most profound critics of the blues as a literary form, emphasize the mixture of tragic and comic world-views in the blues. Hughes's definition of the blues attitude as "laughing to keep from crying" accurately reflects the emotional complexity of much blues poetry.

Like the blues, jazz plays a significant formal role in African American poetry. Poets frequently attempt to capture jazz rhythms in their prosody. Ambiguous stress patterns and intricate internal rhyme schemes make Brooks's "We Real Cool" and "The Blackstone Rangers" two of the most successful poems in this mode. Brown's "Cabaret" and Hughes's "Jazzonia" employ jazz rhythms to describe jazz performances. On occasion, poets such as Joans ("Jazz Must Be a Woman") and Baraka ("Africa Africa Africa") create "poems" which, like jazz charts, sketch a basic rhythmic or imagistic structure that provides a basis for improvisation during oral performance. Jazz may be most important to African American poetry, however, because of its implicit cultural pluralism. In his critical volume *Shadow and Act* (1964), Ellison suggests a profound affinity between the aesthetics of African American music and Euro-American modernism: "At least as early as T. S. Eliot's creation of a new aesthetic for poetry through the artful juxtapositioning of earlier styles, Louis Armstrong, way down the river in New Orleans, was working out a similar technique for jazz." As Ellison suggests, jazz provides an indigenous source for an African American modernism incorporating voices from diverse cultural and intellectual sources. In effect, this enables the African American poet to transform the burden of double consciousness, as manifested in the traditions of masking and ironic voicing, into sources of aesthetic power.

Many of the masterworks of African American poetry, such as Hughes's "Montage for a Dream Deferred," Brooks's "In the Mecca," Hayden's "Middle Passage," and Wright's "Dimensions of History," accomplish precisely this transformation. Choosing from the techniques and perceptions of both Euro-American and African American traditions, these works incorporate the dreams and realities of the American tradition in all its diversity. Aware of the anguish resulting from external denial of self and heritage, the African American tradition recognizes the potential inherent in all fully lived experience. Hughes's vision of individuals living out a multiplicity of dreams within the American dream testifies to his profound respect and love for the dispossessed.

The blend of the spoken word, politics, and music in the 1970's laid the foundations for rap music to become a major art form for social criticism. From Gil Scott-Heron's "The Revolution Will Not Be Televised" to Public Enemy's "Fight the Power," the rhymed critiques of life in America move beyond racial icons to indict anyone who turns away from the plight of the oppressed as the enemy. There is debate outside the community as

to whether rappers are poets or song stylists. Even some successful African American writers look upon rap and hip-hop as
clever wordplay, but lacking the discipline of traditional poetry.
Yet, anthologies edited by up-and-coming African American poets such as Kevin Powell and Clarence Gilyard give works by
some artists credibility as voices of dissent outside the "American" canon.

Focusing on concrete human experience rather than on abstract universals, the African American sensibility distrusts the
grandiose rhetoric that has too frequently glossed over the materialism, racism, and solipsism that disfigure the American
democratic ideal. The African American tradition seeks to provide a sense of identity, purpose, and direction connecting the
visions of Frederick Douglass and Malcolm X with those of
Thomas Jefferson and Walt Whitman. Drawing on folk roots
and forging a complex pluralism, it reaffirms the values of universal survival, literacy, and freedom.

Bibliography

Chapman, Abraham, and Gwendolyn Brooks, eds. *Black Voices:
Anthology of African-American Literature.* New York: Signet Classics, 2001. A reissue of a classic anthology. The book, first produced in two volumes in the late 1960's and early 1970's, was
the first great collection on black writing. It pulls together
poetry, fiction, autobiography, and literary criticism, with informative, concise author biographies.

Gilbert, Derrick I. M., and Tony Medina, eds. *Catch the Fire!!! A
Cross-Generation Anthology of Contemporary African-American Poetry.* New York: Riverhead Books, 1998. Introduces a new generation of African American poets, showcased by established
writers who include June Jordan, Amiri Baraka, Abiodun
Oyewole (of the Last Poets), Ntozake Shange, and Sonia
Sanchez. It gives the reader an understanding of what is happening in coffee houses and clubs throughout the country as
gifted spoken-word artists tie into the rap and hip-hop cultures.

Liggins Hill, Patricia, et al., eds. *The Riverside Anthology of the African American Literary Tradition.* New York: Houghton Mifflin,

1998. It took more than a decade to pull together this ground-breaking anthology. The book is hefty (more than 2,000 pages and 550 selections), but for the serious student of the culture, it will prove indispensable. Traces the literary tradition from the seventeenth century with discussions of African proverbs, folktales, and chants to contemporary writers such as Rita Dove and August Wilson.

Miller, E. Ethelbert, ed. *In Search of Color Everywhere: A Collection of African American Poetry.* New York: Stewart, Tabori and Chang, 1997. This was one of the best of a new wave of anthologies published in the 1990's, and includes works by classic artists such as Phillis Wheatley, Paul Laurence Dunbar, Countée Cullen, and Langston Hughes, as well as younger poets such as Elizabeth Alexander, Jacquie Jones, and Kevin Young. Organized by themes, for example, the "Freedom" section is followed by "Celebrations of Blackness."

Powell, Kevin, ed. *Step into a World: A Global Anthology of the New Black Literature.* New York: John Wiley & Sons, 2000. The broadest collection of hip-hop generation writers available. Includes fiction writers, poets, journalists, and commentators, as well as established authors such as Junot Diaz, Edwidge Danticat, Danyel Smith, and Paul Beatty.

Powell, Kevin, and Ras Baraka, eds. *In the Tradition: An Anthology of Young Black Writers.* New York: Writers&Readers, 1993. This is a good place to sample poetry and stories from up-and-coming authors.

Schwarz, A. B. Christa. *Gay Voices of the Harlem Renaissance.* Bloomington: Indiana University Press, 2003. Schwarz examines the work of four leading writers from the Harlem Renaissance—Countée Cullen, Langston Hughes, Claude McKay, and Richard Bruce Nugent—and their sexually nonconformist or gay literary voices.

— Craig Werner; updated by Vincent F. A. Golphin

African American Short Fiction

Introduction

Although it may be viewed as a modern genre, short fiction subsides into the mists of history in the form of fairy tales, anecdotes, myths, and historical legend. The form was known to the ancient Greeks. Actually, tales of *Alf layla wa-layla* (fifteenth century; *The Arabian Nights' Entertainments*, 1706-1708) and Geoffrey Chaucer's tales are classified as short stories. Besides the obvious difference in length, short fiction differs from longer fiction by focusing upon a single event occurring in one or two scenes and by including fewer characters. In addition, the compactness and unified effect of the literary form forces an economy of words, and setting is oftentimes simple. Edgar Allan Poe, who receives much credit for the development of the short story as a literary genre, remarked that the short story's primary distinguishing factor is the sense of aesthetic unity that can be read in one sitting. While the nineteenth century saw the development of the short story as it is understood today, the original form, passed down through oral tradition, predates recorded history and includes most cultures.

Oral tradition is especially important in African American literature. Many Africans, sold as slaves and forced into such places as Brazil, the Caribbean, and the United States, originated from cultures rich in oral traditions and oral literature. In an effort to preserve their group history, much of this spoken literature was later reworked and remade as written literature. Well-known American short-story writer John Cheever wrote: "So long as we are possessed by experience that is distinguished by its intensity and its episodic nature, we will have the short story in our literature." For African Americans, storytelling especially in the form of folk culture, as critic John Edgar Wideman writes, "preserves and expresses an identity, a history, a self-evaluation apart from those destructive incarcerating images proliferated by mainline culture." African American writers

1210

drew on the universal black experience just like Sean O'Casey and Sholom Aleichem drew upon the Irish and Jewish experiences. Influential Irish short-story writer Frank O'Connor's suggestion that short fiction is a method for "submerged population groups" to address a dominant community would certainly hold true for African American short fiction. Often the African American short story has served as a vehicle for making short, to-the-point statements: social, cultural, economic, political, or otherwise. Although the short story deals primarily with racial pride and oppression, African American short fiction also celebrates survival and deliverance. From its inception, the African American short-story genre represents a range of styles, events, and experiences and draws upon the diversity of black lives within American history.

Nineteenth Century Short-Story Writers

Before their emergence as short-story writers, African Americans in the United States launched both an oral and a written tradition in the form of slave narratives which chronicled their harrowing experiences and their compelling, never-ceasing desire for freedom. During the nineteenth century African Americans were encouraged to write only autobiographies or slave narratives, such as Sojourner Truth's *Narrative of Sojourner Truth, a Northern Slave, Emancipated from Bodily Servitude by the State of New York, in 1828* (1850) and Frederick Douglass's *My Bondage and My Freedom* (1855), in an effort to propel the abolitionist movement. These narratives became the vehicle through which African Americans' gave voice to their experiences and entered American literature. The post-Civil War era saw the emergence of African American writers. Emancipation provided opportunities for education. In 1892 Anna Julia Cooper, a leading lecturer on black women's civil rights, who at one time shared a stage with the powerful black civil rights leader W. E. B. Du Bois, published *A Voice from the South: By a Black Woman of the South.* The daughter of a North Carolina slave and graduate of Oberlin College, Cooper encouraged women, both black and white, to seek education. In addition, when her work appeared the term

"Negro" was in fashion and the term "Black Woman" in the title of her book surprised many. However, despite the fact that they wrote a great deal on a wide variety of subjects, black writers essentially remained ignored except for their slave narratives. It was not until the last quarter of the nineteenth century that Charles Waddell Chesnutt, Paul Laurence Dunbar, and his wife Alice Dunbar-Nelson, who utilized black tradition and myth to write remarkable short stories, were published—with one exception. Frances Ellen Watkins Harper's 1859 short story "The Two Offers" is recognized as the first ever published by a African American writer.

Harper was the child of free African Americans, who died when she was three. A poet, novelist, and social reformer, the youngster came under the guidance of her schoolteacher uncle. A novelist as well, Harper focused on slavery, motherhood, and Christianity and the role of the mulatto in society. American blacks, she said, "are homeless in the land of our births and worse than strangers in the land of our nativity." An active abolitionist for the Underground Railroad, which channeled slaves to freedom, Harper details the plight of a woman who goes against social conventions to advocate for the abolition of slavery in her story "The Two Offers." During an era which prescribed that women be angels in the house, Harper's story brings to light both black and white women's vulnerability, while it challenged the accepted social position of all American women.

Charles Waddell Chesnutt, recognized primarily for his psychological realism, blazed a path for African American short-fiction writers. The son of free blacks, Chesnutt spent much of his early life teaching in North Carolina. Unable to cope with the South's harsh treatment of blacks, he moved to Cleveland, Ohio, where he became an attorney and established a law firm. Although writing was merely an avocation, he published more than fifty short stories and essays, two collections of short stories, a biography of Frederick Douglass, and three novels between 1885 and 1905. In 1885, he published his first notable short story, "Uncle Peter's House," for the S. S. McClure newspaper syndicate. The tale reflects the local color of its setting, a popular literary trend during the late 1800's. Historically significant and ironic, "The Goophered Grapevine" represents the first work by a black to be accepted by *The Atlantic Monthly*. Originating from an oral tale told by the family gardener, the narrative deals with the conjuration of black voodoo practices. Beyond this, however, the heroic narrator Uncle Julius displays an ability to utilize conjure stories to frighten his white employers and oftentimes to secure a financial advantage. "The Sheriff's Children," the first significant study of the mulatto in American life, was published in the fall of 1889 and deals with the repercussions of miscegenation, hatred, and violence in the postwar South. In "The Sheriff's Children," the illegitimate son of a North Carolina sheriff and a former slave is transported to his father's jail, where he has the opportunity to remind the sheriff (who fails to recognize him at first) of his parental shortcomings. While the sheriff experiences enlightenment and repents, the son ironically commits suicide in his father's jail. The tale amplified the era's social injustice.

Chesnutt is best known for his dialect short-fiction collection detailing incidents of slavery told by an old gardener, the trickster figure Uncle Julius, to his northern employers. *The Conjure Woman*, Chesnutt's first short-story collection, was published in 1899 and was critically well received. Unlike some period writers, Chesnutt does not romanticize the slavery practices of the Old South, describing instead a world of brutal masters whose sole focus is on profit. The author admirably describes the slaves' ingenious methods of retribution and their attempts at any cost to keep their families intact. Through the practice of conjuration, slaves in "Sis' Becky's Pickaninny," "Mars Jeems's Nightmare," and "Hot-Foot Hannibal" withstand and endure their dominant abusers. In addition, tales like "The Conjurer's Revenge" and "The Gray Wolf's Ha'nt," which illustrate the dark side of voodoo, demonstrate confrontations between slaves and free African Americans. Chesnutt oftentimes illustrates racial prejudice on both sides. In his second collection of nine short stories, *The Wife of His Youth, and Other Stories of the Color Line* (1899), only one story, "The Passing of Grandison," presents the slave as trickster in a strategy to gain freedom. The rest of the stories occur after the Civil War and deal with social, psychological, and ethical implications of miscegenation. The title story, "The Wife of His Youth," deals with a free black's conflicting loyalties to the wife he married in slavery and the more refined women he meets years later. "A Matter of Principle" and "Her Virginia Mammy," drawn from Chesnutt's own experience, examine with great insight the racial prejudices of light-skinned, middle-class African Americans toward those of darker complexion. In "A Matter of Principle," the mulatto protagonist Cicero Clayton spoils his daughter's chance for happiness with a lighter-skinned congressman. In "Uncle Wellington's Wives," Chesnutt argues that southern men like Wellington, who believe they can gain equality by marrying white women, are irrational. Assimilation into mainstream American culture, Chesnutt argued, could come about only through education and hard work. The author requested that his publishers not mention his ethnicity in advertising his work because he desired to be judged strictly on literary merit. Many times compared to William Faulkner, Chesnutt remained the premier black writer until the 1930's when the Works Progress Administration (WPA) Federal Writers' Project provided a new route of emergence for African American writers. Through his indictment of racism, Chesnutt was viewed as a literary champion for the interests of middle- and working-class African Americans of the South, whom he had known growing up in North Carolina.

Pauline Hopkins counted herself a novelist, playwright, editor, actress, and singer in addition to short-fiction writer. Like many other female writers, Hopkins has been historically overlooked for her literary contributions until recently. Born in Portland, Maine, Hopkins had won a literary prize for an essay, "Evils of Intemperance and Their Remedies," by the time she was fifteen. In 1880, her first play, *Slaves' Escape: Or, The Underground Railroad* (retitled *Peculiar Sam: Or, The Underground Railroad*), was produced. Strongly influenced by Du Bois, founder and leader of the new National Association for the Advancement of Colored People, Hopkins utilized the romance model in the short-story form to explore racial violence and social themes such as the distress suffered by blacks after the Civil War. Actually, Hopkins single-handedly opened the door for black women's publishing with her 1900 novel *Contending Forces: A Romance Illustrative of Negro Life North and South*, published by the Boston Colored Co-operative Publishing Company, in which she was a shareholder. That same year, the Co-operative published the literary monthly *Colored American Magazine*, whose first issue featured Hopkins's first short story, "The Mystery Within Us," which she structured as a conversation between two men. In the time span of five years, Tom Underwood has moved from a state of down-and-out destitution to one of prosperity as a physician and an author. Tom reminisces how, on the verge of suicide, a mysterious "Presence" appeared to him and encouraged him to change his way of life. The Presence interjects into Tom's mind the thoughts of Dr. Thorn, a notable physician, who unfortunately died before bringing his medical discoveries to public attention. Deeply concerned with metaphysics, Hopkins makes such mystical and spiritual phenomena the basis of many of her works. By the time the *Colored American Magazine* ceased publication in 1909, Hopkins had published six more short stories, including "Talma Gordon," "George Washington, a Christmas Story," "As the Lord Lives, He Is One of Our Mother's Children," and her powerful "A Dash for Liberty." In "A Dash for Liberty," which focuses on the theme of escape from slavery, the protagonist, Madison, although secure and sheltered in Canada, wishes to return to Virginia to free his wife Susan. Furthermore, as editor of the magazine, Hopkins focused on discovering and publishing short stories by black women. Contributors included Frances Ellen Watkins Harper. Hopkins denounced racist myths, demonstrated outrage of the role of women as victims, and stressed that black women must resist victimization whenever possible. She attempted to reify African American humanity and believed firmly that education was the key to conquering prejudice and attaining equality.

Paul Laurence Dunbar was born in Dayton, Ohio, the son of former slaves. A well-known poet and novelist, he authored four collections of short stories. With the encouragement of William Dean Howells, a well-known American novelist, Dunbar became one of the first African American writers to gain a large public following. In particular, his southern plantation stories were deeply admired by American readers. However, Dunbar, who worked as a reading-room assistant at the Library of Congress, has experienced recent attacks upon his literary reputation because of his use of southern dialect, his degrading stereotypes of black people, and his portrayal of the Old South in romantic terms. Many of the stories in Dunbar's four collections are free of these pejorative descriptions and deserve consideration on their literary merits. His stories (plantation tall tales, didactic stories warning his readers against weakness, narratives decrying southern social repression, and protest fiction) are oftentimes aimed directly against racism.

Dunbar's first collection of stories, *Folks from Dixie*, appeared in 1898 and is concerned with plantation tales depicting southern blacks who are fiercely loyal and religious. No doubt, the idea of slaves choosing loyalty to their masters over their own well-being can indeed be considered highly offensive. His story "The Colonel's Awakening," in *Folks from Dixie*, which portrays an old Virginia aristocrat, who after losing his two sons is unable to adjust to post-Civil War life, is recognized and praised as one of Dunbar's best-constructed stories. *The Strength of Gideon, and Other Stories* (1900) remains Dunbar's most successful collection. Although it does present the South in sentimental terms, it additionally warns against the evils of northern vice. For instance, "The Trustfulness of Polly" describes the destruction of Polly Jackson's husband Sam as he falls prey to brothels. Dunbar's "The Tragedy at Three Forks" protests southern racism, and "The Ingrate" represents a fictionalized account of Dunbar's own father's escape on the Underground Railroad. The most bitter story Dunbar ever wrote, "One Man's Failure," addresses a black man's relationship to President Abraham Lincoln. His *In Old Plantation Days* (1903) makes up twenty-five short stories which unfortunately remain dependent on unpalatable stereotypes. The writer's 1904 short-story collection *The Heart of Happy Hollow* contains one of Dunbar's best short stories, "The Scapegoat," an ironic story of the political revenge that an angry black party boss takes upon the political establishment. In addition, Dunbar married Alice Ruth Moore, a writer and teacher who would achieve a measure of fame in her own right.

Alice Dunbar-Nelson, Paul Laurence Dunbar's wife, was also an early short-fiction writer. Born during Reconstruction and only a generation removed from slavery, Dunbar-Nelson felt a strong responsibility toward future generations of African Americans, and in this vein she attempted to share her knowledge and experience. Alice Ruth Moore was born in New Orleans, Louisiana. She received an M.A. from Cornell University. Incredibly versatile, she was a trained nurse, stenographer, and musician. Her first collection, *Violets, and Other Tales*, which included poetry and essays in addition to short stories, was published in 1895. "Amid the Roses," "Love and the Butterfly," "At Eventide," and "Bay St. Louis" thematically center on racism, gender roles in society, and the importance of love, war, and death. The sentimental title story tells the story of a young girl in love, who dies within a year after placing a bouquet of violets, orange blossoms, and other flowers in a letter to her sweetheart. A teacher, the writer married author Paul Laurence Dunbar after accepting a teaching assignment in New York in 1898. Dunbar-Nelson was also a journalist and wrote for many black newspapers including the *Pittsburgh Courier* and the *Washington Eagle*, for which she wrote the column "As in a Looking Glass" from 1926 to 1930. In 1920 Dunbar-Nelson founded the *Wilmington Advocate*, a weekly newspaper. Her second collection of stories, *The Goodness of St. Rocque, and Other Stories* (1899), the first collection of short stories by a black woman, focuses on New Orleans Creole culture. In "La Juanita," which incorporates a blend of Catholic and black magic practices, beautiful Juanita loves the American Mercer, despite her grandfather's objections. Known as a transitional figure to the writers of the Harlem Renaissance, Dunbar-Nelson had a great influence on rising young writers of the period.

The Harlem Renaissance

After World War I, black soldiers returned to America having fought in Europe for the concepts of equality and freedom. The 369th Battalion, "The Harlem Hellfighters," was the most decorated American unit, and when they marched up Fifth Avenue to Harlem after the war's end, the black population felt part of a new beginning. This was the celebrated time for the "New Negro." The new black writers generated a powerful and refreshing voice which was heard with a great deal of respect by the white community. These writers, artists, intellectuals, and jazz musicians came to represent the Harlem Renaissance, one of the most fertile periods in America's literary history. The Harlem Renaissance not only exemplified the advancement of black arts but also staged the independence and liberty of African American writing and publishing. Two leading African American journals of the day, *Opportunity*, edited by Charles S. Johnson, which aimed to give voice to black culture hitherto neglected by mainstream American publishing, and the magazine of Du Bois's National Association for the Advancement of Colored People (NAACP), *The Crisis*, along with newspapers such as *Baltimore African American*, continued the fashion established by Pauline Hopkins of publishing and establishing black American writers and entered the short-story competition trend between 1920 and 1935. This publishing effort dispersed the Harlem Renaissance nationwide. Both periodicals and newspapers brought great attention to the black literary market, launching the careers of such writers as Zora Neale Hurston, Dorothy West, Gwendolyn Bennett, Claude McKay, Langston Hughes, and Countée Cullen, who made up the lively Harlem writers' group. Their works began to examine the stigmatizing stereotypes of African Americans that slavery and the post-Reconstruction period promoted in white American minds.

In the 1920's, the Harlem Renaissance, also called the New Negro Movement, burst into bloom, bringing a new creative energy to African American literature and changing forevermore what had earlier been viewed as folklore or imitation "white writing" into proud, complex investigations of black culture. Although the peak of this Renaissance era extended from 1921 to 1931, it remained influential throughout the 1930's. Centered on the black neighborhoods of Harlem, in New York City, and funded by philanthropic grants and scholarships, the movement cultivated and encouraged the hopeful young black writers who were central to the Harlem domain. Sadly, the Great Depression adversely affected this dynamic group of writers and many were ultimately forced to leave New York.

Jessie Redmon Fauset is said to be a focal figure of the Harlem Renaissance because of her extensive support of other black authors. Primarily a novelist, she also wrote numerous short stories as well as acting from 1919 to 1926 as the literary editor of the highly influential *Crisis* magazine. By confronting race and sex stereotyping, Fauset demonstrated a deep awareness of the unique situation of the American black woman. Born in Camden County, New Jersey, a suburb of Philadelphia, Pennsylvania, she came from a poor family who placed a premium on education. She received a scholarship to Cornell University and graduated in 1905; she was possibly the first black woman to be elected to the academic honor society Phi Beta Kappa. During her tenure at *The Crisis*, she published a large number of women writers, black and white, who voiced convictions ranging from conservative to radical. After she left in 1926, the magazine never regained its former literary stature. In addition, she played a major influential role in the recognition and promotion of black art during the period of the Harlem Renaissance.

Zora Neale Hurston, a primary, influential African American folklorist and short-story writer, temporally captured and celebrated rural, black, southern American culture. Early in life she made her way to New York City during the Harlem Renaissance, where she associated with such writers as Langston Hughes, the prominent African American poet. Although she never finished grade school, she attended Howard University, going on to become a cultural anthropologist and ethnologist. In her scholarly endeavors, Hurston traveled to Haiti, where she researched voodoo. Hurston's first story, "John Redding Goes to Sea," was published in the literary magazine *Stylus* in 1921 and republished in 1926 in *Opportunity*, the leading periodical of the Harlem Renaissance. The story deals with young John Redding's incapacity to accomplish his goal of seeing the world (a desire brought about by a witch's spell) because the women in his life attempt to tie him down and encourage him instead to settle and marry rather than follow his dream. Throughout his life, John allows himself to be tied down and views the world only after he dies from drowning. This story set the themes Hurston was to develop throughout her career: the dream and the resistance against improving one's life and the strong, pervading sense of the supernatural.

"Drenched in Light" was published in *Opportunity* in 1924. The highly imaginative, eleven-year-old protagonist Isis (nicknamed Isie) Watts feels stifled by Grandmother Potts. Similar to the dreamer John Redding, young and impressionable Isis envisions wearing golden slippers and long princess robes while riding white horses to find the edge of the world. In vain, her grandmother disciplines the lively but mischievous girl and punishes her severely for merely whistling and playing with boys. After a white stranger, Helen, takes Isie to see a Gypsy dance performance, she is overwhelmed by the girl's exuberance and recognizes the emptiness of her own life. In what could be construed as an altruistic gesture, Helen attempts to take the youngster from her home. However, it becomes increasingly clear throughout the evolution of the story that Helen wants to absorb the child's energy only for her own delight. As one critic remarked, Helen's strategy is reminiscent of the whites who flocked to popular Harlem nightspots to be entertained by "primitive" black musicians. "Drenched in Light" describes the youthful effervescence Hurston herself exhibits in her autobiographical "How It Feels to Be Colored Me."

After moving to New York in 1925, Hurston quickly became known to and a central figure of Harlem Renaissance literary circles. Indeed, Hughes found her the most amusing member of the writers' group. That year, Hurston also received a scholarship to Barnard College, where she entered as its first black student. Hurston's popular "Spunk" is a story about a giant man, Spunk Banks, who intentionally intimidates people. Using the black, central-Florida dialect and elements of the area's folklore, the tale is set in an area much like Hurston's hometown of Eatonville, Florida. The fearless Banks suffers a decline in pride which brings about his downfall when he courts Lena, another man's wife, in public. This prompts Joe Kanty, Lena's husband, to seek revenge. Kanty, however, is killed when Banks shoots him. After the murder trial, Spunk loses his courage, believing that he is haunted by Joe's ghost, and suffers a grisly death in a mysterious sawmill accident. The townspeople believe the death was caused by Joe's spirit, who assumed the form of a black panther.

"Black Death" was also published in 1925 and highlights an Eatonville voodoo man named Old Man Morgan. Mrs. Boger consults him to seek revenge on the cold-hearted Beau Diddeley for refusing to marry her daughter Docia after impregnating her. While Beau courts another young girl, the conjure man casts his deadly spell, and soon Beau is found dead with an enigmatic powder burn found over his heart. In this tale, Hurston demonstrates her skill to connect folklore and fiction. In "Muttsy" Pinkie escapes her poverty-stricken, abusive southern home and moves to Harlem. Pinkie is directed to Ma Turner's place (a Harlem brothel and speakeasy), where she meets Muttsy Owens, a gambler who is smitten by her detached manner and superior beauty. Swearing his intentions are pure, he gives her a diamond ring, but she insists he give up gambling. Predictably, shortly after they marry, he resumes gambling.

Story magazine published Hurston's most frequently anthologized story, "The Gilded Six-Bits," in 1933. Missie May and Joe Banks live happily together in wedded bliss in an edenic setting, as delighted and innocent as two candy-eating children, until the archetypal serpent, Otis D. Slemmons, a sly woman-chaser from Chicago with gold teeth, a gold stickpin, and a ten-dollar gold piece, intrudes into their perfect garden. Like Eve, Missie May is hypnotized by the newcomer's power and falls away from her loving husband Joe. Joe returns home unannounced one evening to find his wife in bed with Slemmons. Prostrate with grief, Missie May begs her crestfallen husband Joe for forgiveness. After three months, Joe relents and returns to her and after the birth of a son, the couple continue to love each other as before.

In the highly acclaimed *Mules and Men* (1935), her collection of folktales and humorous and tragic sketches, Hurston attempted to find a balance between the folk culture of her ethnic background and her development as an artist. For Hurston, it was paramount for readers "to realize that minorities do think, and think about something other than the race problem . . . that they are just like everyone else." Perhaps best known for her controversial 1937 novel *Their Eyes Were Watching God*, about an African American woman's search for love and identity, Hurston refused to see blacks as victimized. Indeed, Hurston celebrated her rural black heritage of Eatonville, Florida, a town founded by African Americans, and the first incorporated black town in the United States. In her autobiographical "How It Feels to Be Colored Me," Hurston declares "I am not tragically colored." Despite poverty, Hurston's characters, such as Missie and Joe in "The Gilded Six-Bits" and the aggrieved husband Joe Kanty, at odds with his manhood in "Spunk," live full-flowering lives. Her characters search for fulfillment not as African Americans but as women and men. Hurston's literary characteristics can later be seen in the works of Ralph Ellison and Toni Morrison. In her autobiography *Dust Tracks on a Road* (1942) Hurston comments that she "did not know how to be humble." Sadly, although Hurston published much more than any other African American woman of her time, she died in poverty: Her work was recovered by the women's movement. However, Hurston remains central to the Harlem Renaissance.

Langston Hughes is referred to by critics as the most influential black American writer of the twentieth century. Primarily a poet, Hughes recorded the black experience in the United States. A leading luminary in the Harlem Renaissance, during the early 1920's Hughes helped to open the doors of publishing houses to young black writers, prompting them to write with racial pride. His career stretched into the Black Arts movement of the late 1960's. Born in Joplin, Missouri, Hughes grew up in Lawrence, Kansas. One of America's best-known and best-loved poets, author in particular of the famous poem "The Negro Speaks of Rivers," Hughes was inspired by D. H. Lawrence to write short stories, which are not nearly as well known as his poetry. In his short fiction, Hughes sets an example of self-determination and artistic integrity. His book of short stories, *The Ways of White Folks*, was published in 1934. Hughes helped to inspire young writers, in particular James Baldwin and Alice Walker.

A Texas native, Gwendolyn Bennett, well recognized as a poet and essayist, also utilized the short-short form to project her literary voice. As the daughter of teacher-parents, Bennett grew up on a Nevada Indian reservation before her father brought her to live in Philadelphia. Educated at Columbia University, in New York City, Bennett drew on her African roots for inspiration. In her estimation, blacks in the United States were sad people "hidden by a minstrel smile." She became the editor of *Opportunity*, writing a popular literary news column and providing a historical account of the Harlem Renaissance. Her story "Wedding Day," a popularly anthologized piece, explores the question "Who am I?"—the universal conundrum every African American faces. Paul Watson, the protagonist, believes he can escape American racial prejudice by living an expatriate existence in Europe. He succeeds in Paris, becoming a well-known musician before he falls in love with a cruel white woman. His traumatic wedding day (hence the story's title) illustrates his loss of innocence when she abandons him, leaving him only a cruel note explaining that white women simply do not marry black men. "Tokens," which appeared in *Ebony* and *Topaz* in 1927, also centers on an American in Paris who remains in France after World War I. Jenks Barnett, dying from tuberculosis, recalls an earlier happier time, when he joyfully sang with other African American expatriate entertainers. Bennett strongly disputes the humiliating treatment of blacks by whites. Her best-known story, "To a Dark Girl," is often anthologized.

Dorothy West, also known as Mary Christopher, another member of the Harlem Renaissance, wrote and published the critically acclaimed novel *The Living Is Easy* (1948) along with forty short stories. The daughter of a former slave from Virginia, West studied journalism and philosophy at Columbia University. A writer from age seven, she published her first short story in the *Boston Post* when she was fifteen. West joined the Saturday Evening Quill Club, formed in 1925 by twenty burgeoning African American writers. *Opportunity* magazine published her "The Typewriter" in 1926. The story presents a spiritually bereft father who uses his daughter's typewriting lessons to gain a sense of individual worth. Imagining himself to be his daughter's successful businessman boss, when the father dictates a letter to his daughter he comes to embody the man he dreams of being, the man, ironically, that the dominant racist culture prevents him from becoming. By the story's end, this dire pretense causes the father's death. "The Typewriter" was included in Edward J. O'Brien's *The Best Short Stories of 1926.*

In Harlem, West worked initially as a social worker and traveled the Soviet Union in 1932, with Langston Hughes and other Harlem writers, as part of a writers' project. West founded and wrote for *Challenge,* a periodical that opposed fascism, published emerging black writers, and documented the black literary attitudes of the 1930's. She also took part in the Federal Writers' Project (see below). She wrote stories twice weekly for the *New York Daily News* until the late 1960's and was one of the earliest to explore the black urban lifestyle, which most short-story writers overlooked. West, strongly influenced by Fyodor Dostoevski, accentuates psychological and social confinement. The *Saturday Evening Quill* published "An Unimportant Man," which appeared in 1928 and addressed the irony of black urban existence. Zeb, another frustrated black man like the father in "The Typewriter," has a close relationship with his daughter Essie. Through her, Zeb vicariously strives to gain self-importance. He thinks of himself merely as a forty-year-old failure, a cook unable to take the bar exam for the fourth time. However, his daughter, he swears, will become a success. What remains unclear to him, however, is that his actions ironically parallel precisely how his mother treated him, pushing him against his will into difficult careers.

The end of the Harlem Renaissance represented the termination of a rich literary era and a turning point for African American writers. Simply put, black writers had to differentiate themselves from white writers because they had the twofold task of coming to terms with white American society and simultaneously opposing its inherent racism. In the process, they had to lend dignity to the African American community.

Federal Writers' Project

In 1935, the Works Progress Administration (WPA) developed the Federal Writers' Project as part of the New Deal struggle against the Great Depression. The project provided jobs for unemployed writers, editors, and research workers. Directed by Henry G. Alsberg, the program operated in all states and at one time employed sixty-six hundred men and women. In addition to producing guides for every state, the federal plan supported ethnic studies, folklore collections, and regional histories, producing ultimately more than one thousand publications and providing a means for such top African American writers as Richard Wright and Ralph Ellison to come to public attention.

Richard Wright, short-story writer and novelist, classified as an American modernist, was deeply influenced by the famous Russian short-fiction writer Anton Chekhov. Wright ingeniously explores the concept of the internalized plot that closely examines the inner emotions of characters. He endures as one of the first African American writers to protest white prejudice and violence against blacks.

In Wright's novel *Native Son* (1940) Bigger Thomas suffers at the hands of a rich white family. In Wright's autobiography *Black Boy* (1945), which details his childhood and young manhood in the South, the voice of protest that was to influence many post-World War II writers can also be heard. The grandchild of slaves and abandoned early on by his father, Wright grew up in poverty. The Federal Writers' Project provided him with the opportunity to write.

In 1937, he became Harlem editor of the communist publication *The Daily Worker.* His first short story, "Big Boy Leaves Home," appeared in the anthology *The New Caravan* (1936). "The Ethics of Living John Crow: An Autobiographical Sketch" was published in 1937's *American Stuff: An Anthology of Prose and Verse by Members of the Federal Writers' Project.* A year later, after his first book, *Uncle Tom's Children* (1938), won a prize from *Story* magazine, Wright was catapulted into the public eye. Undoubtedly, in the genre of the short story, he was the most talented black male writer since Chesnutt. Unlike his predecessors, however, he was highly visible and received the attention and praise he richly deserved. In addition, Wright is credited with eliminating the barrier between black and white writers. In fact, he changed the tone of African American writing from one of placid petition to one of absolute insistence. In 1946, the author moved to Paris and never returned to the United States to live. After his death in 1960, a new generation of black writers, including James Baldwin, John Killens, Paule Marshall, Mary Elizabeth Vroman, London Brown, Albert Murray, William Melvin Kelley, Amiri Baraka (LeRoi Jones), Martin Hamer, and Ernest J. Gaines explored, questioned, and challenged what Ellison called "the full range of American Negro humanity."

The early years of Ralph Ellison were spent in poverty in Oklahoma City, Oklahoma, and prompted him to become an activist. An avid reader, Ellison early on set out "to look at [his] own life through the lives of fictional characters" and to connect his own world with the "worlds projected in literature." As a young adult in New York City, he met Hughes and Wright, who encouraged him in his efforts to become a writer. He served in the Merchant Marine during World War II. Immediately after the war, in 1945, he began work on his novel *Invisible Man*, which chronicles a young man's awakening to racial discrimination, and spent seven years writing it before it was published in 1952. The following year he won the National Book Award. Like Wright, Ellison's tone is insistent and demanding. "Battle Royal," Ellison's first short story and an excerpt which appeared a year before the novel, is frequently anthologized. In the story, Ellison insists that the narrator, although a man of substance, flesh, and bone, is invisible because people refuse to see him. The story details a painful episode in a young man's life; expecting a scholarship, the excited and proud youngster is invited to an elegant social function. However, instead of receiving the academic honors he expected, he is pitted against other teenage boys in a boxing match for the enjoyment of white male spectators. The broader context of the story illustrates the predictable rituals used to preserve racial lines. In "King of the Bingo Game" and "Flying Home," the main characters also undergo a trial by fire, which concludes in an elevated sense of self, a deeper maturity, and an ultimate responsibility to others. In the 1965 *Book Week* poll of two hundred writers and critics, Ellison was honored by being chosen above such black writers as Wright and Baldwin and such white writers as Ernest Hemingway, William Faulkner, J. D. Salinger, and John Steinbeck, for having penned the most celebrated novel written in the previous twenty years. However, Ellison suffered under the scathing critical scrutiny of the black nationalist writers of the Black Arts movement, such as Baraka, who insisted Ellison "sold out" by being more concerned with style than with substance. Thus, racial allegiances became suspect.

World War II

Unlike many African American writers who focus on the South, Ann Petry focused upon black life in small-town New England. A pharmacist, Petry moved early on in life to New York, where she wrote for the *Peoples' Voice* of Harlem before studying creative writing at Columbia University (1944-1946). During World War II, Petry's stories began to appear in *The Crisis*. A novelist, who numbers among her best-selling highly acclaimed works *The Street* (1946), Petry first came to public notice through such short stories as "Like a Winding Street," a complex, forceful narrative of a couple's wartime struggle, and her heart-wrenching tale of domestic abuse "The Last Day of School," which deals with a young woman's attempt to leave Harlem. Her collection of short stories *Miss Muriel, and Other Stories*, which contains "Solo on the Drums" and "Has Anybody Seen Miss Dora Dean?," was published in 1971.

Although Frank Yerby authored thirty-three novels, his short story, "Health Card," which received the O. Henry Memorial Award for best first story in 1944, is his only highly acclaimed work. "Health Card," published in *Harper's* magazine, concerns the injustices inflicted by the military, which tended to view black women as prostitutes. The story brought Yerby to national attention.

Henry Dumas wrote about the clash between black and white cultures and captured in the process the psychological tone of the black southern experience. African American folklore and music and the Civil Rights movement, in which he was an active participant, remained important influences on all his writing. Born in Arkansas, Dumas migrated to Harlem at the age of ten, attended City College of New York, and served in the Air Force. His astute short stories draw on his own southern childhood experiences. "Rain God," which uses a stream-of-consciousness technique, was published in *Negro Digest* in 1968 and deals with three boys running home on the heels of a rainstorm. This tale, reminiscent of a folktale that pronounces that when sunshine and rain occur together, the Devil is beating his wife, projects the fear experienced by the narrator, young Blue, who fears the Devil. "The Crossing," in the collection *Ark of Bones, and Other Stories* (1970), also deals with the sense of danger and fear inherent in the lives of southern blacks, particularly the vulnerability of black children amid the southern white lynch-mob mentality. Here again three young children, Jimmy, Bubba, and Essie, walk home from Sunday school, experience the fear of imminent danger, and tease one another until Bubba mentions Emmett Till, a teenager who was actually lynched in 1953. The tale of atrocity is repeated to Jimmy by Bubba. Again, the landscape figures profoundly in projecting and displacing the young characters' fear. Young sharecroppers encountering a civil rights worker and whites experiencing the mystical force of black music figure in the subject matter Dumas examined in his short stories, many of which were collected in *Ark of Bones, and Other Stories* and *Rope of Wind, and Other Stories* (1979).

The Black Arts Movement

The Black Arts movement, also called the Black Aesthetic movement, represented a literary advancement among black Americans in the 1960's and early 1970's. Based on the idea of black nationalism, the crusade sought to cultivate art forms that champion black separatism. Thus, the African American writer became activist. Using the black English vernacular, black writers discoursed on concerns of interracial tension and politics. Highly confrontational, many of these writers utilized African

American history and culture to illustrate their apprehensions and anger. Brought about by such intellectual leaders as Houston A. Baker, Jr., and Henry Louis Gates, Jr., a trailblazing literary critic instrumental in recovering African American works such as Harriet E. Wilson's *Our Nig: Or, Sketches from the Life of a Free Black, in a Two-Story White House, North. Showing That Slavery's Shadow Falls Even There* (1859), the first known novel by a black American, the Black Arts movement developed theories of black literature.

Utilizing critical methods such as semiotics and deconstruction, Baker proposed new standards, based on African American culture and values, for the interpretation and evaluation of literature and reconstructed the historical, social, political, and economic elements of African American culture. His edited collections of poetry and essays by African Americans, such as Frederick Douglass, W. E. B. Du Bois, Booker T. Washington, Richard Wright, and Ralph Ellison, brought attention to African American literary works and demonstrated the verve and vigor of black culture and its intense desire to be heard.

Tracing Caribbean and American culture back through slave narratives and folktales, Gates utilized fashionable critical theory to argue the term "signifyin'" as representative of black culture. Black writers, he claimed, are involved in an unbroken, interconnected conversation that reflects and interprets black social and cultural history. The inclusion of African American literature in the Western canon, Gates argues, cannot be ignored.

Distinguished by intense self-scrutiny, the Black Arts movement was instrumental in producing such influential works as *The Autobiography of Malcolm X* (1965; with Alex Haley) and Eldridge Cleaver's *Soul on Ice* (1968). This movement highly influenced novelist Toni Morrison, winner of the 1994 Nobel Prize in Literature. Baraka founded the Black Arts Repertory Theatre in Harlem and emerged as a powerful playwright. When it comes to recognizing the black arts as a revolutionary concept, no African American writer has better articulated the alliance of art and politics. Although the bulk of his art encompassed drama, Baraka also produced a collection of short stories, *Tales* (1967), which documents the traumatic experiences, suppressed anger, and hostility of American blacks toward the dominant white culture.

James Alan McPherson's short stories examine love, universal pain, and racial tension. Often, his realistic characters face periods of isolation and the deep, longing pangs of love. Although it could be argued that McPherson's stories represent the Black Arts movement, there is little doubt his timeless tales move far beyond politics by appealing to all classes and both genders. McPherson, strongly influenced by Ellison, addresses age, race, and class in his first short story, "Gold Coast," for which he won a short-fiction contest in *The Atlantic Monthly* in 1968. In it, the author explores the relationship between Robert, a burgeoning black writer and Harvard University student, and James Sullivan, the older white janitor who searches merely for human fellowship. A highly skilled and intricate writer, McPherson sensitively perceives human nature in all its myriad light and dark manifestations. Regarding his popular short-story collection *Hue and Cry* (1969), McPherson, born in Savannah, Georgia, remarked "it is my hope that this collection of stories can be read as a book about people, all kinds of people: old, young, lonely, homosexual, confused, used, discarded, wronged."

Despite criticism during the revolutionary 1970's, McPherson received praise for his ability to see past the color line. In his "A Matter of Vocabulary" the writer draws upon his personal experience as a grocery store clerk. Similarly, in other stories he utilizes his own life experiences as a dining-car waiter, a law student, and a janitor for fictional fodder. His first collection of melancholy short stories, *Hue and Cry*, includes the title story about interracial relationships and "Solo Song: For Doc," which examines the life of an elderly dining-car waiter, Doc Craft, whose blood runs with the "the rhythm of the wheels." Never at "home on the ground," when Doc is forced into retirement he does not know how to cope. Ultimately, he freezes to death in the Chicago train yards. The author puts the American justice system under the microscope in "An Act of Prostitution." "On Trains" documents the life of a Pullman porter, a black servant serving out his days on trains during the time of transition from train travel to airline travel in American life. After forty-three years, the elderly porter still serves in the capacity of making passengers comfortable. Throughout the night he sits and waits until one evening a sleepless racist southern woman finally engages his awareness. The title story's protagonist Margot Payne, however, belongs to the younger generation of African Americans who refused to suffer quietly. McPherson's literary talent was recognized in 1978 with a Pulitzer Prize for *Elbow Room* (1977), which illustrates the author's symmetrical division between dejection and hope. In twelve stories, McPherson explores the perplexity of individuality and diversity of American culture. In "A Loaf of Bread," Nelson Reed and his neighbors picket Harold Green for his unfair practice of charging higher food prices to the black community. While both men see themselves as good people, neither understands the other and thus look upon each other as evil enemies. In "Widows and Orphans," McPherson attains a similar level of understanding between communities.

The short stories of Alice Walker are noted for their thoughtful and insightful treatment of African American culture. As in her highly popular *The Color Purple* (1982), which won a Pulitzer Prize in 1983, Walker's work expresses with intense clarity the roles women play in the survival of the African American people. In this effort, she utilizes the history of black people in the United States, particularly in the South, where they were heartlessly enslaved. Walker grew up in Georgia and graduated from Sarah Lawrence College, in Bronxville, New York, in 1965, at which point she moved to Mississippi where she became an active participant in the Civil Rights movement. She also began teaching and publishing short fiction. Her short stories examine the relationships between black women and men and, while strongly engaging the deep spiritual tradition, center particularly on women. While African American men, Walker contends, have had to struggle with racism, black American women have to fight both racism and sexism. In 1973, the author published *In Love and Trouble: Stories of Black Women*, her first collection of short stories. This collection introduces Roselily, an impoverished mother of illegitimate children, who views her marriage to a black Muslim as a deliverance from poverty. Most of the female protagonists in this collection represent southern black women who challenge gender, race, and age. Because of its focus on the violence involved in sexism, some critics came to view it as dissident.

Walker's second collection of short stories, *You Can't Keep a Good Woman Down* (1981), her most outspoken feminist work, was also disliked by critics, who dismissed it as too controversial. In it, Walker addresses issues raised by feminists in the 1970's: abortion, sadomasochism, pornography, and rape, arguing that personal relationships reflect political issues. "Porn" examines the sexual relationship between a proud black man and an independent black woman who makes her own money. Walker explores how the male's pornographic fantasies and his need to prove himself through his sexuality inhibit him from truly loving and accepting the woman. When the woman realizes his dependence on pornography and the shallowness of their connection, their relationship is destroyed. Walker presents the stories in this collection as an ongoing process; they are not finished pieces. For example, "Advancing Luna" is a tale concerning a young southern woman's involvement in and her deepening understanding of interracial rape. The author maintains that, because of the historical alliance between lynching and rape, the story cannot be ended and thus Walker stylistically provides the tale with two conclusions. Although very different from her earlier short-story collection *In Love and Trouble*, her second, more complex collection, *You Can't Keep a Good Woman Down*, supports the Black Arts movement's impulse and establishes with certainty the freedom with which women pursue their individual selves. While the primary female characters in *In Love and Trouble* carry on and strive, the women in *You Can't Keep a Good Woman Down* are more heroic by intensely and openly confronting societal conventions.

Twentieth Century Women Writers

Women have from the beginning played a primary role in the growth of African American short fiction. In fact, more works of fiction by black women were published between 1890 and 1910 than black men had published in the previous fifty years. With the exception of Frances Ellen Watkins Harper's tale "The Two Offers," no short story by an African American woman appeared in print before 1895, when, at last, voices so long stifled were heard. In the outpouring of proud stories that followed, African American women shared their experiences, smashed stereotypes, and recorded the untold story of African American life. African American literature has further blossomed with black American women at the forefront as writers. Besides such immensely popular, award-winning novelists as Alice Walker and Toni Morrison, female short-story writers continue to proliferate. For African American women, storytelling between mothers and daughters, daughters and sisters, sisters and friends is what Paule Marshall metaphorically calls the "kitchen" of everyday experience in a world oblivious to black women's lives. As Walker observed, the woman one shares one's story with as it is happening is someone who is implicitly trusted. African American female short-fiction writers demonstrate how they survived by listening and telling.

Alice Childress, a high school dropout, developed her distinct writing style by breaking rules. Born in Charleston, South Carolina, Childress was taken to New York at the age of five. An actor and director, the burgeoning author was a director of the American Negro Theatre (1941-1952). In fact, she was nominated for a Tony for her Broadway role in *Anna Lucasta* (1944), and in 1956 she became the first woman to win an Obie Award for best Off-Broadway play for *Trouble in Mind*. Childress creates accurate depictions of black life and rejects black stereotypes, especially that black women are responsible for the problems of black men: "The Black writer explains pain to those who inflict it," she maintains. Best known for her novel directed at teenagers, *A Hero Ain't Nothin' but a Sandwich* (1973), she also gained much positive acclaim for her short-story collection *Like One of the Family: Conversations from a Domestic's Life* (1956), a series of vignettes told from the domestic's point of view. The protagonist Mildred, a dayworker based on Childress's own Aunt Lorraine, refuses "to exchange dignity for pay," as she quietly battles for human dignity and civil rights. Although others consider her job menial, she heroically declines to be debased.

As a civil rights activist and teacher, Toni Cade Bambara wrote about the concerns of the African American community while attempting to raise black American consciousness. Born Miltona Mirkin Cade in New York City, she adopted the name Bambara in 1970 when she discovered it as a signature on a family sketchbook. Bambara published her first short story, "Sweet Town," in *Vendome* magazine in 1959, as Toni Cade. The author worked as a social worker for the Harlem Welfare Center between 1959 and 1960. In the 1960's, she was directly involved in the sociopolitical activities in American urban communities. She published her second story, "Mississippi Ham Rider," in 1960 in the distinguished *Massachusetts Review.* After receiving her master's degree, Bambara taught at the City College of New York from 1965 to 1969. Active during the 1970's in the black liberation and the women's rights movements, the writer submerged herself in civil rights issues by lecturing and helping to organize rallies within the black community, all the while utilizing her personal experiences in her writing. In 1970 she edited and published *The Black Woman*, an anthology designed to demonstrate the thoughts and actions of black women in the women's and Civil Rights movements. In 1971 Bambara edited her second anthology, titled *Tales and Stories for Black Folks*, in which is included her own acclaimed "Raymond's Run." The author, who interjects black street dialect in her short fiction to create strong characters, sets her stories outside the home, where people are apt to mingle. Also, she sets her tales in both the American South and the North. Most of the stories Bambara wrote as Toni Cade between 1959 and 1970 were published in 1972 in her highly acclaimed collection *Gorilla, My Love.* The stories focus on the relationships among African Americans in both the urban North and the rural South. The title story, narrated by young Hazel, completely dissatisfied with grown-ups, describes the impact that careless adult words, particularly promises that cannot be kept, have on innocent children. In "Talkin' 'Bout Sonny," the author focuses on the coping mechanisms males utilize to maintain emotional equilibrium. Betty Butler, a social worker, dates Delauney, the father of two girls. At a local bar, Betty and Delauney discuss how their friend Sonny, while in a state of emotional collapse, stabbed his wife. Betty, appalled at first by Delauney's casual attitude, comes to realize how both men must work hard to repress and contain their sensation of free-floating rage. Delauney fully realizes that although he can understand Sonny, his own anger keeps him powerless. Bambara also published the novels *The Salt Eaters* (1980) and *If Blessing Comes* (1987).

Jamaica Kincaid was born in Antigua, in the West Indies. Finding her college experience to be a "dismal failure," the independent-minded Kincaid set about educating herself. Her early stories were published in *Rolling Stone, Paris Review,* and *The New Yorker.* Her first short-story collection, *At the Bottom of the River* (1983), which won the Morton Dauwen Zabel Award of the American Academy of Arts and Letters, features the much-anthologized, exceptional story "Girl." Although on the surface, the story reads principally like a list of rules any good mother would provide a daughter: "Don't walk barehead in the hot sun," the story also depicts maternal caution and counsel, particularly in the sexual arena. Much in keeping with the modernist movement, in which writers such as James Joyce redefined the borders and possibilities of the short-story form, this rhythmic, emotionally intense story details a young woman's life in a free-floating narrative without a conventional plot, characters, or dialogue. Kincaid's next "sister text" collection, *Annie John* (1985), contains eight stories that span Annie's childhood in Antigua to age seventeen. The poignant "The Circling Hand," portrays the author's theme of mother-child relationships. As a child, Annie trails her mother shopping, doing laundry, and cooking and experiences great anxiety when she wanders outside her mother's sphere. Ultimately, in the final chapter, Annie leaves her mother and home to take up nursing in England.

As compared to the novel, the short-story form receives

much less critical notice and much of the criticism it garners deals with techniques of writing, rather than serious criticism of the literary work. However, for many readers, the short story, which often can be read in under an hour, represents a powerful, life-changing literary method that initiates and completes catharsis. The short story as a form is open-ended, ever-changing, and continuously vigorous.

Bibliography

Andrews, William, ed. *Classic Fiction of the Harlem Renaissance.* New York: Oxford University Press, 1994. Includes a comprehensive collection of short stores by Langston Hughes, Zora Neale Hurston, Jessie Redmon Fauset, Gwendolyn Bennett, and many others.

Clarke, John Henrik, ed. *Black American Short Stories: One Hundred Years of the Best.* New York: Hill & Wang, 1993. A new introduction supplements this classic collection of stories by African Americans that features pieces by Charles Waddell Chesnutt, Zora Neale Hurston, Langston Hughes, Richard Wright, Frank Yerby, James Baldwin, Amiri Baraka, Alice Walker, and others.

Gates, Henry Louis, Jr. *The Signifying Monkey: A Theory of Afro-American Literary Criticism.* New York: Oxford University Press, 1988. Scholarly work that uses critical theory to interconnect such African American short-story writers as Ralph Ellison, Zora Neale Hurston, and Alice Walker.

Gayle, Addison, Jr., ed. *The Black Aesthetic.* Garden City, N.Y.: Doubleday, 1971. Provides excellent scholarly commentary and biographical notes for a number of African American authors.

Hughes, Langston, ed. *The Best Short Stories by Negro Writers: The Classic Anthology from 1899 to 1967.* Boston: Little, Brown, 1967. Features stories by outstanding African American writers that originally sold more than twenty-five thousand copies. An expanded edition with a new introduction offers a description of African American fiction from the nineteenth century to the present with new contributions by Alice Walker and James Alan McPherson.

Kanwar, Asha, ed. *The Unforgetting Heart: An Anthology of Short Stories by African American Women, 1859-1993.* San Francisco: Aunt Lute Books, 1993. Difficult to find but worth the effort. Contains very varied stories by well known and little know African American women writers.

Mullin, Bill, ed. *Revolutionary Tales: African American Women's Short Stories, from the First Story to the Present.* New York: Laurel, 1995. Containing forty-four stories by thirty-six authors, this collection covers 150 years of the African American short story with stories by Alice Childress, Frances Ellen Watkins Harper, Zora Neale Hurston, Alice Walker, Dorothy West, and many others.

Naylor, Gloria, ed. *Children of the Night: The Best Short Stories by Black Writers, 1967 to the Present.* Boston: Little, Brown, 1995. Includes the works of leading African American short-story writers.

Pryse, Marjorie, and Hortense J. Spillers, eds. *Conjuring: Black Women, Fiction, and Literary Tradition.* Bloomington: Indiana University Press, 1985. Provides the historical and biographical background material for such short-story writers as Pauline Hopkins.

Schwarz, A. B. Christa. *Gay Voices of the Harlem Renaissance.* Bloomington: Indiana University Press, 2003. Schwarz examines the work of four leading writers from the Harlem Renaissance—Countée Cullen, Langston Hughes, Claude McKay, and Richard Bruce Nugent—and their sexually nonconformist or gay literary voices.

— M. Casey Diana

APPENDIXES

More African American Writers

The authors listed below appear in alphabetical order by surname and are identified by the genre or discipline (essayist, novelist, dramatist, journalist, poet, anthropologist, etc.) that constitutes their main area of literary production. These books represent good places to begin in becoming familiar with the author's work.

Abdul-Jabbar, Kareem (nonfiction writer and basketball player, b. 1947)
Giant Steps: An Autobiography of Kareem Abdul-Jabbar
Kareem
Black Profiles in Courage: A Legacy of African American Achievement

Ai (poet, b. 1947)
Cruelty
Dread
Greed

Als, Hilton (journalist, b. 1961)
Fine and Mellow
Looking for Langston
Women

Andrews, Raymond (novelist, 1934-1991)
Baby Sweet's
"Jessie and Jesus" and "Cousin Claire"
Rosiebelle Lee Wildcat Tennessee

Anthony, Michael (novelist, b. 1932)
All That Glitters
High Tide of Intrigue
In the Heat of the Day

Asante, Molefi K. (nonfiction writer, b. 1942)
Encyclopedia of Black Studies
Erasing Racism: The Survival of the American Nation
One Hundred Greatest African Americans: A Biographical
  Encyclopedia

Ashe, Arthur (nonfiction writer and tennis player, 1943-1993)
Arthur Ashe: Portrait in Motion
Days of Grace
Hard Road to Glory: A History of the African-American Athlete

Attaway, William (novelist, 1911-1986)
Calypso Song Book
Hear America Singing
Let Me Breathe Thunder

Baker, Houston A. (literary critic, b. 1943)
Blues Journeys Home
No Matter Where You Travel, You Still Be Black
Renewal: A Volume of Black Poems

Beatty, Paul (novelist, b. 1962)
Joker, Joker, Deuce
Tuff
The White Boy Shuffle

Beckham, Barry (novelist and nonfiction writer, b. 1944)
The Black Student's Guide to Colleges
Double Dunk
Runner Mack

Boyd, Candy Dawson (children's author, b. 1946)
Breadsticks and Blessing Places
Circle of Gold
Forever Friends

Bradley, David (novelist, b. 1950)
The Chaneysville Incident
South Street

Brawley, Benjamin Griffith (nonfiction writer and clergyman, 1882-1939)
Negro Builders and Heroes
Women of Achievement
Your Negro Neighbor

Briscoe, Connie (novelist, b. 1952)
Big Girls Don't Cry
A Long Way from Home
Sister and Lovers

Brown, Claude (short-story writer, 1937-2002)
The Children of Ham
Manchild in the Promised Land

Brown, William Wells (novelist and nonfiction writer, 1814-1884)
Miralda: Or, The Beautiful Quadroon
My Southern Home
Narrative of William W. Brown, a Fugitive Slave, Written by Himself

Broyard, Anatole (short-story writer, 1920-1990)
Intoxicated by My Illness: And Other Writings on Life and Death
Kafka Was the Rage
Men, Women, and Other Anticlimaxes

Bryan, Ashley (children's author and artist, b. 1923)
The Ox of the Wonderful Horns, and Other African Folktales
Walk Together Children: Black American Spirituals

Carson, Benjamin (surgeon and nonfiction writer, b. 1951)
Ben Carson
Gifted Hands
Think Big: Unleashing Your Potential for Excellence

Carter, Stephen L. (nonfiction writer and lawyer, b. 1954)
The Emperor of Ocean Park
The Culture of Disbelief: How American Law and Politics Trivialize Religious Devotion
Reflections of an Affirmative Action Baby

Cary, Lorene (novelist, b. 1956)
Black Ice
The Price of a Child
Pride

Césaire, Aimé (poet and philosopher, b. 1913)
Discourse on Colonialism
Notebook of a Return to the Native Land
A Tempest

Chambers, Veronica (journalist, b. 1970)
Amistad Rising: A Story of Freedom
Mama's Girl
Marisol and Magdalena: The Sound of Our Sisterhood

Chamoiseau, Patrick (novelist, b. 1953)
School Days
Solibo Magnificent
Texaco

Chocolate, Debbi (children's author, b. 1954)
The Piano Man
Spider and the Sky God: An Akan Legend
Talk, Talk: An Ashanti Legend

Clair, Maxine (novelist and short-story writer, b. 1939)
Coping with Gravity
October Brown
Rattlebone

Clarke, John Henrik (nonfiction writer and historian, 1915-1998)
African People in World History
Harlem, U.S.A.: The Story of a City Within a City
Marcus Garvey and the Vision of Africa

Cliff, Michelle (novelist, b. 1946)
Abeng
Free Enterprise
No Telephone to Heaven

Coleman, Wanda (poet, b. 1946)
Heavy Daughter Blues: Poems and Stories, 1968-1986
Native in a Strange Land: Trials and Tremors
The Riot Inside Me: More Trials and Tremors

Collins, Patricia Hill (nonfiction writer and professor, b. 1948)
Fighting Words: Black Women and the Search for Justice
Race, Class, and Gender: An Anthology
Representations of Motherhood

Colter, Cyrus (novelist, 1910-2002)
A Chocolate Soldier
City of Light
The Rivers of Eros

Condé, Maryse (short-story writer, b. 1937)
Crossing the Mangrove
Who Slashed Celanire's Throat? A Fantastical Tale
Windward Heights

Cooper, J. California (short-story writer, b. 1931)
The Future Has a Past: Stories
Some Love, Some Pain, Sometime
Some People, Some Other Place

Cortez, Jayne (poet, b. 1936)
Jazz Fan Looks Back
Scarifications
Somewhere in Advance of Nowhere

Cose, Ellis (novelist and nonfiction writer, b. 1951)
Color-Blind: Seeing Beyond Race in a Race-Obsessed World
A Nation of Strangers: Prejudice, Politics, and the Populating of America
The Rage of a Privileged Class

Crews, Donald (children's author and artist, b. 1938)
Light
Ten Black Dots
Truck

Crouch, Stanley (nonfiction writer and literary critic, b. 1945)
All-American Skin Game: Or, The Decoy of Race
Always in Pursuit: Fresh American Perspectives
Notes of a Hanging Judge: Essays and Reviews, 1979-1989

Cruse, Harold (nonfiction writer and literary critic, 1916-2005)
The Crisis of the Negro Intellectual: A Historical Analysis of the Failure of Black Leadership
Plural But Equal: A Critical Study of Black and Minorities and America's Plural Society
Rebellion or Revolution?

Danticat, Edwidge (novelist and playwright, b. 1969)
Breath, Eyes, Memory
The Dew Breaker
Krik? Krak!

Davis, Angela (nonfiction writer and literary critic, b. 1944)
Angela Davis: An Autobiography
Are Prisons Obsolete?
Blues Legacies and Black Feminism: Gertrude "Ma" Rainey, Bessie Smith, and Billie Holiday

Davis, Ossie (playwright, 1917-2005)
Escape to Freedom: A Play About Young Frederick Douglass
Langston
Purlie

Davis, Thulani (novelist and playwright, b. 1949)
Armistad
Playing the Changes
X: The Life and Times of Malcom X

Delany, Clarissa Scott (nonfiction writer and poet, 1901-1927)
"Joy," "Solace," "Interim," and "The Mask" (in *Caroling Dusk: An Anthology of Verse by Black Poets of the Twenties*, edited and with a foreword by Countée Cullen)

Delany, Martin Robison (nonfiction writer and physician, 1812-1885)
The Condition, Elevation, Emigration, and Destiny of the Colored People of the United States, Politically Considered
The North Star

Demby, William (novelist and poet, b. 1922)
Beetlecreek
The Catacombs
Love Story Black

De Veaux, Alexis (children's author, b. 1948)
Don't Explain: A Song of Billie Holiday
An Enchanted Hair Tale
Woolu Hat

Dixon, Melvin (novelist and poet, 1950-1992)
Climbing Montmartre
Love's Instruments
Vanishing Rooms

Draper, Sharon M. (children's author, b. 1950)
Romiette and Julio
Tears of a Tiger
Ziggy and the Black Dinosaurs

Driskell, David C. (nonfiction writer and literary critic, b. 1931)
Harlem Renaissance: Art of Black America
Hidden Heritage: Afro-American Art, 1800-1950
Two Centuries of Black American Art

Du Bois, Shirley Graham (nonfiction writer and dramatist, 1907-1977)
His Day Is Marching On: A Memoir of W. E. B. Du Bois
Pictorial History of W. E. B. Du Bois
Zulu Heart

Dumas, Henry (short-story writer, 1934-1968)
Ark of Bones, and Other Stories
Goodbye, Sweetwater
Rope of Wind, and Other Stories

Dunbar-Nelson, Alice (nonfiction writer and playwright, 1875-1935)
The Author's Evening at Home
Give Us Each Day: The Diary of Alice Dunbar-Nelson
Mine Eyes Have Seen

Early, Gerald Lyn (nonfiction writer and poet, b. 1952)
One Nation Under a Groove: Motown and American Culture
*Lure and Loathing: Essays on Race, Identity, and the Ambivalence
  of Assimilation*
Tuxedo Junction: Essays on American Culture

Edwards, Louis (novelist and short-story writer, b. 1962)
N: A Romantic Mystery
Oscar Wilde Discovers America
Ten Seconds

Ellis, Trey (novelist, b. 1962)
Home Repairs
Right Here, Right Now
Tuskegee Airmen

Equiano, Olaudah (nonfiction writer and slave, 1745-1797)
The Interesting Narrative of the Life of Olaudah Equiano: Or,
  Gustavus Vassa, the African

Evans, Mari (nonfiction writer and children's author, b. 1923)
A Dark and Splendid Mass
Dear Corinne, Tell Somebody! Love, Annie
Nightstar, 1973-1978

Everett, Percival L. (novelist, b. 1956)
American Desert
Erasure
Glyph

Fanon, Frantz (philosopher, 1925-1961)
Black Skin, White Masks
A Dying Colonialism
The Wretched of the Earth

Feelings, Muriel (children's author, b. 1938)
Jambo Means Hello: Swahili Alphabet Book
Moja Means One: Swahili Counting Book
Zamani Goes to Market

Files, Lolita (novelist, b. 1964)
Blind Ambitions
Getting to the Good Part
Scenes from a Sistah

Fisher, Rudolph (short-story writer, 1897-1934)
"Guardian of the Law"
"John Archer's Nose"
"Miss Cynthie"

Forrest, Leon (novelist, 1937-1997)
Divine Days
Meteor in the Madhouse
Two Wings to Veil My Face

Franklin, John Hope (nonfiction writer and historian, b. 1915)
From Slavery to Freedom: A History of African Americans
An Illustrated History of Black Americans

George, Nelson (novelist and screenwriter, b. 1957)
Buppies, B-Boys, Baps, and Bohos: Notes on Post-soul Black Culture
The Death of Rhythm and Blues
Elevating the Game: Black Men and Basketball
Life and Def: Sex, Drugs, Money, and God

Gilliam, Dorothy Butler (journalist, b. 1936)
Paul Robeson, All-American

Gordon, Edmund W. (psychologist, b. 1921)
Day Care: Scientific and Social Policy Issues
Education and Justice: A View from the Back of the Bus
Educational Resilience in Inner-City America: Challenges and
    Prospects

Grimes, Nikki (children's author, b. 1950)
Come Sunday
Is It Far to Zanzibar?
Something on My Mind

Grimké, Charlotte L. Forten (nonfiction writer and poet, 1837-1914)
"Glimpses of New England"
"A Parting Hymn"

Guy, Rosa (children's author, b. 1928)
Billy the Great
The Music of Summer
The Ups and Downs of Carl Davis III

Hammon, Briton (nonfiction writer and slave, before 1747-after 1760)
A Narrative of the Uncommon Sufferings, and Surprizing Deliverance of Briton Hammon, A Negro Man

Hammond, Harmony (nonfiction writer and literary critic, b. 1944)
New Feminist Criticism
Wrappings: Essays on Feminism, Art, and the Martial Arts

Hansen, Joyce (children's author, b. 1942)
Between Two Fires: Black Soldiers in the Civil War
The Heart Calls Home
Yellow Bird and Me

Hardy, James Earl (novelist, b. 1966)
The Day Eazy-E Died
Love the One You're With
Spike Lee

Harper, Frances Ellen Watkins (novelist and poet, 1825-1911)
Complete Poems of Frances E. W. Harper
Iola Leroy: Or, Shadows Uplifted
Moses: A Story of the Nile

Harris, E. Lynn (novelist, b. 1955)
Abide With Me
Invisible Life
Just As I Am

Harris, Eddy L. (memoirist, b. 1956)
Mississippi Solo: A River Quest
Native Stranger: A Black American's Journey into the Heart of Africa
Still Life in Harlem

Harris, Wilson (novelist, b. 1921)
The Guyana Quartet
Jonestown
Palace of the Peacock

Haskins, James (children's author, 1941-2005)
Black Eagles: African Americans in Aviation
Count Your Way Through the Arab World
The Story of Stevie Wonder

Haynes, David (children's author and novelist, b. 1955)
Business As Usual
Live At Five
Right By My Side

Haywood, Gar Anthony (novelist, b. 1954)
All the Lucky Ones Are Dead
Going Nowhere Fast
You Can Die Trying

Heath, Roy A. K. (novelist, b. 1926)
The Ministry of Hope
The Murderer
The Shadow Bride

Hoagland, Everett (poet, b. 1942)
Black Velvet
Ten Poems: A Collection
This City and Other Poems

Holiday, Billie (singer and nonfiction writer, 1915-1959)
Lady Sings the Blues

Hooks, Bell (nonfiction writer and literary critic, b. 1952)
Ain't I a Woman: Black Women and Feminism
Bone Black: Memories of Girlhood
Killing Rage: Ending Racism

Hopkins, Pauline (novelist, 1859-1930)
Hagar's Daughter: A Story of Southern Caste Prejudice
Of One Blood: Or, The Hidden Self
Winona: A Tale of Negro Life in the South and Southwest

Horton, George Moses (poet, 1797-1883)
The Hope of Liberty
Naked Genius
The Poetical Works of George M. Horton

Howard, Elizabeth Fitzgerald (children's author, b. 1927)
Aunt Flossie's Hats (and Crab Cakes Later)
Mac and Marie and the Train Toss Surprise
The Train to Lulu's

Hudson, Wade (novelist, b. 1946)
How Sweet the Sound: African-American Songs for Children
Jamal's Busy Day
Pass It On: African-American Poetry for Children

Hunter, Kristin (novelist, b. 1931)
Breaking Away
God Bless the Child
The Landlord

Jackson, George (nonfiction writer and memoirist, 1941-1971)
Blood in My Eye
Soledad Brother: The Prison Letters of George Jackson

Jacobs, Harriet (nonfiction writer and slave, 1813-1897)
Incidents in the Life of a Slave Girl

James, C. L. R. (nonfiction writer and philosopher, 1901-1989)
Beyond a Boundary
The Black Jacobins
Minty Alley

Johnson, Dolores (children's author and artist, b. 1949)
Grandma's Hands
Papa's Stories
What Kind of Babysitter Is This?

Johnson, James Weldon (poet and nonfiction writer, 1871-1938)
Along This Way: The Autobiography of James Weldon Johnson
The Autobiography of an Ex-Coloured Man
God's Trombones: Seven Negro Sermons in Verse

Jones, Gayl (novelist and short-story writer, b. 1949)
Corregidora
Mosquito
White Rat

Kenan, Randall (novelist and nonfiction writer, b. 1963)
Let the Dead Bury Their Dead, and Other Stories
A Visitation of Spirits
Walking on Water: Black American Lives at the Turn of the Twenty-first Century

Kennedy, Randall (nonfiction writer and literary critic, b. 1954)
Nigger: The Strange Career of a Troublesome Word
Race, Crime, and the Law

Killens, John Oliver (novelist and short-story writer, 1916-1987)
And Then We Heard the Thunder
Black Man's Burden
A Man Ain't Nothin' But a Man: The Adventures of John Henry

King, Coretta Scott (nonfiction writer and memoirist, 1927-2006)
My Life with Martin Luther King, Jr.

Lamming, George (novelist, b. 1927)
In the Castle of My Skin
The Emigrants
The Pleasures of Exile

Lee, Andrea (novelist and short-story writer, b. 1953)
Interesting Women: Stories
Russian Journal
Sarah Phillips

Lee, Spike (motion picture director, b. 1957)
Best Seat in the House: A Basketball Memoir
By Any Means Necessary: The Trials and Tribulations of the Making of "Malcolm X"

Lester, Julius (children's author, b. 1939)
Basketball Game
Black Cowboy, Wild Horses
Further Tales of Uncle Remus

Lewis, David Levering (nonfiction writer and historian, b. 1936)
King: A Critical Biography
W. E. B. Du Bois, Volume I: Biography of a Race, 1868-1919
W. E. B. Du Bois, Volume II: The Fight for Equality and the American Century, 1919-1963

Locke, Alain (nonfiction writer and philosopher, 1886-1954)
The Negro in America
Plays of Negro Life: A Source-Book of Native American Drama
When Peoples Meet: A Study in Race and Culture Contacts

Loury, Glenn C. (nonfiction writer and economist, b. 1948)
One By One From the Inside Out: Essays and Reviews on Race and Responsibility in America

Lovelace, Earl (novelist, b. 1935)
The Dragon Can't Dance
Salt
The Wine of Astonishment

McCall, Nathan (journalist, b. 1955)
Makes Me Wanna Holler: A Young Black Man in America
What's Going On: Personal Essays

McKissack, Fredrick (children's author, b. 1939)
Christmas in the Big House, Christmas in the Quarters
Louis Armstrong: Jazz Musician
Sojourner Truth: Ain't I a Woman?

McKissack, Patricia C. (children's author, b. 1944)
The Dark-Thirty: Southern Tales of the Supernatural
Flossie and the Fox
Jesse Jackson: A Biography

McWhorter, John H. (linguist, b. 1965)
Authentically Black: Essays for the Black Silent Majority
*Doing Our Own Thing: The Degradation of Language and Music
   and Why We Should, Like, Care*
Losing the Race: Self-Sabotage in Black America

Malcolm X (civil rights activist, 1925-1965)
The Autobiography of Malcolm X
By Any Means Necessary
Malcolm X Speaks

Marable, Manning (journalist, b. 1950)
*Blackwater: Historical Studies in Race, Class Consciousness, and
   Revolution*
*How Capitalism Underdeveloped Black America: Problems in Race,
   Political Economy, and Society*
*Race, Reform and Rebellion: The Second Reconstruction in Black
   America, 1945-1990*

Maran, René (novelist, 1887-1960)
Batouala

Marrant, John (nonfiction writer and clergyman, 1755-1791)
A Journal of the Rev. John Marrant, from August the 18th, 1785, to the 16th of March, 1790
A Narrative of the Lord's Wonderful Dealings with John Marrant, a Black

Mathis, Sharon Bell (children's author, b. 1937)
Brooklyn Story
Running Girl: The Diary of Ebonee Rose
Teacup Full of Roses

Medearis, Angela Shelf (children's author, b. 1956)
The Adventures of Sugar and Junior
Dare to Dream: Coretta Scott King and the Civil Rights Movement
Poppa's New Pants

Meriwether, Louise (short-story writer, b. 1923)
Daddy Was a Number Runner
Fragments of the Ark
Shadow Dancing

Milner, Ron (playwright, 1938-2004)
Checkmates
Roads of the Mountain Top
Warning: A Theme for Linda

Mosley, Walter (novelist, b. 1952)
Fear Itself
Little Scarlet
The Man in My Basement

Moss, Thylias (poet, b. 1954)
Last Chance for the Tarzan Holler: Poems
Slave Moth: A Narrative in Verse
Small Congregations: New and Selected Poems

Motley, Willard (novelist, 1909-1965)
Knock on Any Door
Let Noon Be Fair
We Fished All Night

Murray, Albert (novelist, b. 1916)
The Blue Devils of Nada: A Contemporary American Approach to Aesthetic Statement
Good Morning Blues: The Autobiography of Count Basie
The Seven League Boots

Nunez, Elizabeth (novelist, b. 1944)
Beyond the Limbo Silence
Discretion
When Rocks Dance

Oliver, Diane (short-story writer, 1943-1966)
"The Closet on the Top Floor"
"Mint Juleps Not Served Here"
"Traffic Jam"

Page, Clarence (journalist, b. 1947)
Showing My Color: Impolite Essays on Race and Identity

Patterson, Orlando (nonfiction writer and sociologist, b. 1940)
Die the Long Day
The Ordeal of Integration: Progress and Resentment in America's "Racial" Crisis
Rituals of Blood: Consequences of Slavery in Two American Centuries

Phillips, Caryl (novelist, b. 1958)
Cambridge
Dancing in the Dark
A Distant Shore

Pinckney, Darryl (nonfiction writer and literary critic, b. 1953)
High Cotton
Out There: Mavericks of Black Literature

Pinkney, Brian (children's author and artist, b. 1961)
JoJo's Flying Side Kick
Max Found Two Sticks

Pinkney, Gloria Jean (children's author, b. 1941)
Back Home
The Sunday Outing

Polite, Carlene Hatcher (civil rights activist and novelist, b. 1932)
The Flagellants
Sister X and the Victims of Foul Play

Porter, Connie Rose (children's author, b. 1959)
Addy Studies Freedom
Addy's Summer Place
Addy's Wedding Quilt

Rampersad, Arnold (nonfiction writer and memoirist, b. 1941)
I Dream a World
I, Too, Sing America
Jackie Robinson: A Biography

Redding, J. Saunders (novelist and nonfiction writer, 1906-1988)
On Being Negro in America
They Came in Chains: Americans from Africa
To Make a Poet Black

Reed, Adolph L. (journalist, b. 1947)
The Jesse Jackson Phenomenon: The Crisis of Purpose in Afro-American Politics
Race, Politics, and Culture: Critical Essays on the Radicalism of the 1960's
W. E. B. Du Bois and American Political Thought: Fabianism and the Color Line

Rodgers, Carolyn M. (short-story writer, b. 1945)
Eden and Other Poems
The Heart as Ever Green
Translation

Rowan, Carl Thomas (nonfiction writer and memoirist, 1925-2000)
Breaking Barriers: A Memoir
South of Freedom
Wait till Next Year: The Life Story of Jackie Robinson

St. Omer, Garth (novelist, b. 1931)
Another Place, Another Time
The Lights on the Hill
Nor Any Country

Salkey, Andrew (novelist, poet, and children's author, 1925-1995)
Havana Journal
Hurricane
Riot

Sapphire (novelist and poet, b. 1950)
American Dreams
Push

Schuyler, George S. (journalist, 1895-1977)
Black and Conservative: The Autobiography of George S. Schuyler
Black No More: Being an Account of the Strange and Wonderful Workings of Science in the Land of the Free, a.d. 1933-1940
Slaves Today: A Story of Liberia

Scott, Nathan A. (nonfiction writer and literary critic, b. 1925)
Adversity and Grace: Studies in Recent American Literature
Albert Camus
Craters of the Spirit: Studies in the Modern Novel

Serequeberhan, Tsenay (nonfiction writer and philosopher, b. 1952)
The Eritrean People's Liberation Front: A Case Study in the Rhetoric and Practice of African Liberation
The Hermeneutics of African Philosophy: Horizon and Discourse

Shockley, Ann Allen (novelist and short-story writer, b. 1927)
The Black and White of It
Loving Her
Say Jesus and Come to Me

Staples, Brent (journalist, b. 1951)
Parallel Time: Growing Up in Black and White

Steele, Shelby (nonfiction writer and philosopher, b. 1946)
The Content of Our Character: A New Vision of Race in America
A Dream Deferred: The Second Betrayal of Black Freedom in America

Stepto, Robert B. (nonfiction writer and literary critic, b. 1945)
Blue as the Lake: A Personal Geography

Steptoe, John (children's author and artist, 1950-1989)
Marcia
My Special Best Words
Stevie

Tatum, Beverly Daniel (psychologist, b. 1954)
Assimilation Blues: Black Families in a White Community
"Why Are All the Black Kids Sitting Together in the Cafeteria?" and Other Conversations About Race

Taylor, Mildred D. (children's author, b. 1943)
The Land
Let the Circle Be Unbroken
Roll of Thunder, Hear My Cry

Taylor, Susan L. (journalist, b. 1946)
Confirmation: The Spiritual Wisdom That Has Shaped Our Lives
In the Spirit: The Inspirational Writings of Susan L. Taylor
Lessons in Living

Thomas, Joyce Carol (novelist, playwright, and poet, b. 1938)
House of Light
Joy!
Marked by Fire

Thurman, Wallace (novelist, 1902-1934)
The Blacker the Berry
Harlem
Infants of the Spring

Tolson, Melvin B. (poet, 1898-1966)
A Gallery of Harlem Portraits
Libretto for the Republic of Liberia
Rendezvous with America

Van Peebles, Melvin (novelist and screenwriter, b. 1932)
The Making of "Sweet Sweetback's Baadasssss Song"
Posse
Sweet Sweetback's Baadasssss Song

Walcott, Derek (poet, b. 1930)
The Odyssey: A Stage Version
Omeros
The Prodigal: A Poem

Walker, Margaret (poet, 1915-1998)
October Journey
On Being Female, Black, and Free: Essays by Margaret Walker, 1932-1992
This Is My Century: New and Collected Poems

Wallace, Michele (nonfiction writer and literary critic, b. 1952)
Black Macho and the Myth of the Superwoman
Invisibility Blues: From Pop to Theory

Walter, Mildred Pitts (children's author and novelist, b. 1922)
Lillie of Watts Takes a Giant Step
My Mama Needs Me
Ty's One-Man Band

Ward, Douglas Turner (actor and playwright, b. 1930)
Brotherhood
Happy Ending and Day of Absence
The Reckoning: A Surreal Southern Fable

Washington, Mary Helen (nonfiction writer and literary critic, b. 1941)
Black-Eyed Susans: Classic Stories by and About Black Women
Memory of Kin: Stories of Family by Black Writers
Midnight Birds: Stories by Contemporary Black Women Writers

Wesley, Valerie Wilson (novelist, b. 1947)
Ain't Nobody's Business if I Do
The Devil Riding
Willimena and the Cookie Money

West, Dorothy (novelist and short-story writer, 1907-1998)
The Living Is Easy
The Richer, the Poorer: Stories, Sketches, and Reminiscences
The Wedding

Whitehead, Colson (novelist, b. 1969)
The Intuitionist
John Henry Days

Wiley, Ralph (nonfiction writer and screenwriter, b. 1952)
Dark Witness: When Black People Should be Sacrificed (Again)
Why Black People Tend to Shout: Cold Facts and Wry Views from a Black Man's World

Wilkinson, Brenda Scott (children's author, b. 1946)
Ludell
Ludell and Willie
Ludell's New York Time

Williams, George Washington (civil rights activist and nonfiction writer, 1849-1891)
History of the Negro Race in America: From 1619 to 1880
A History of the Negro Troops in the War of the Rebellion

Williams, Sherley Anne (poet, 1944-1999)
Dessa Rose
Girls Together
The Peacock Poems

Williams-Garcia, Rita (novelist, b. 1957)
Stories for Strong Girls
Trapped
Twelve Shots

Wilson, Harriet E. (novelist, 1808 or c. 1827-c. 1870)
Our Nig: Or, Sketches from the Life of a Free Black, in a Two-Story White House, North. Showing That Slavery's Shadow Falls Even There

Wolfe, George C. (playwright, b. 1954)
The Colored Museum
Jelly's Last Jam
Spunk: Three Tales

Woodson, Jacqueline (children's author, b. 1964)
Between Madison and Palmetto
I Hadn't Meant to Tell You This
Miracle's Boys

Wright, Charles Stevenson (novelist, b. 1932)
Absolutely Nothing to Get Alarmed About
The Messenger
The Wig: A Mirror Image

Wright, Sarah E. (novelist, b. 1928)
Give Me a Child
A. Philip Randolph: Integration in the Workplace
This Child's Gonna Live

Bibliography

Contents

General Studies and Reference Works

Aberjhani, and Sandra L. West. *Encyclopedia of the Harlem Renaissance.* New York: Facts On File, 2003.

Andrews, William L., Frances Smith Foster, and Trudier Harris, eds. *The Concise Oxford Companion to African American Literature.* New York: Oxford University Press, 2002.

Bassett, John Earl. *Harlem in Review: Critical Reactions to Black American Writers, 1917-1939.* Selinsgrove, Pa.: Susquehanna University Press, 1992.

Bloom, Harold, ed. *Black American Poets and Dramatists: Before the Harlem Renaissance.* New York: Chelsea House, 1994.

_____. *Black American Poets and Dramatists of the Harlem Renaissance.* New York: Chelsea House, 1995.

_____. *Black American Women Poets and Dramatists.* New York: Chelsea House, 1996.

_____. *Contemporary Black American Poets and Dramatists.* New York: Chelsea House, 1995.

_____. *Major Black American Writers Through the Harlem Renaissance.* New York: Chelsea House, 1995.

_____. *Major Modern Black American Writers.* New York: Chelsea House, 1995.

_____. *Modern Black American Poets and Dramatists.* New York: Chelsea House, 1995.

Ervin, Hazel Arnett. *The Handbook of African American Literature.* Gainesville: University Press of Florida, 2004.

Fabré, Michel, comp. *The French Critical Reception of African-American Literature from the Beginnings to 1970: An Annotated Bibliography.* Westport, Conn.: Greenwood Press, 1995.

Foster, Mamie Marie Booth, comp. *Southern Black Creative Writers, 1829-1953: Bio-bibliographies.* New York: Greenwood Press, 1988.

Glikin, Ronda. *Black American Women in Literature: A Bibliography, 1976 Through 1987.* Jefferson, N.C.: McFarland, 1989.

Harris, Trudier, and Thadious M. Davis, eds. *Afro-American Writers Before the Harlem Renaissance.* Detroit: Gale Research, 1986.

_____. *Afro-American Writers from the Harlem Renaissance to 1940.* Detroit: Gale Research, 1987.

_____. *Afro-American Writers, 1940-1955.* Detroit: Gale Research, 1988.

_____. *Afro-American Writers After 1955: Dramatists and Prose Writers.* Detroit: Gale Research, 1985.

Hatch, Shari Dorantes, and Michael R. Strickland, eds. *African-American Writers: A Dictionary.* Santa Barbara, Calif.: ABC-CLIO, 2000.

Magill, Frank N., ed. *Masterpieces of African-American Literature.* New York: HarperCollins, 1992.

_____. *Masterplots II: African American Literature.* Pasadena, Calif.: Salem Press, 1994.

Metzger, Linda, Hal May, Deborah A. Straub, and Susan M. Trosky, eds. *Black Writers: A Selection of Sketches from Contemporary Authors.* Detroit: Gale Research, 1989.

Nelson, Emmanuel S., ed. *African American Authors, 1745-1945: Bio-bibliographical Critical Sourcebook.* Westport, Conn.: Greenwood Press, 2000.

Roses, Lorraine Elena. *The Harlem Renaissance and Beyond: Literary Biographies of One Hundred Black Women Writers, 1900-1945.* Boston: G. K. Hall, 1990.

Russell, Sandi. *Render Me My Song: African-American Women Writers from Slavery to the Present.* New York: Pandora, 2002.

Shockley, Ann, ed. *Afro-American Women Writers, 1746-1933: An Anthology and Critical Guide.* Boston: G. K. Hall, 1988.

Smith, Valerie, ed. *African American Writers.* New York: Charles Scribner's Sons, 2001.

Smith, Valerie, Lea Baechler, and A. Walton Litz, eds. *African American Writers*. New York: Charles Scribner's Sons, 1991.

Stanford, Barbara Dodds. *Black Literature for High School Students*. Urbana, Ill.: National Council of Teachers of English, 1978.

Yellin, Jean Fagan, and Cynthia D. Bond, comps. *The Pen Is Ours: A Listing of Writings by and About African-American Women Before 1910 with Secondary Bibliography to the Present*. New York: Oxford University Press, 1991.

Fiction

Alexander, Simone A. James. *Mother Imagery in the Novels of Afro-Caribbean Women*. Columbia: University of Missouri Press, 2001.

Ashe, Bertram D. *From Within the Frame: Storytelling in African-American Fiction*. New York: Routledge, 2002.

Auger, Philip. *Native Sons in No Man's Land: Rewriting Afro-American Manhood in the Novels of Baldwin, Walker, Wideman, and Gaines*. New York: Garland, 2000.

Beaulieu, Elizabeth Ann. *Black Women Writers and the American Neo-slave Narrative: Femininity Unfettered*. Westport, Conn.: Greenwood Press, 1999.

Bell, Bernard W. *The Contemporary African American Novel: Its Folk Roots and Modern Literary Branches*. Amherst: University of Massachusetts Press, 2004.

Billingslea-Brown, Alma Jean. *Crossing Borders Through Folklore: African American Women's Fiction and Art*. Columbia: University of Missouri Press, 1999.

Bland, Sterling Lecater. *Voices of the Fugitives: Runaway Slave Stories and Their Fictions of Self-Creation*. Westport, Conn.: Praeger, 2000.

Boesenberg, Eva. *Gender, Voice, Vernacular: The Formation of Female Subjectivity in Zora Neale Hurston, Toni Morrison, and Alice Walker*. Heidelberg, Germany: Universitatsverlag C. Winter, 1999.

Bracks, Lean'tin L. *Writings on Black Women of the Diaspora: History, Language, and Identity*. New York: Garland, 1998.

Bryant, Jacqueline K. *The Foremother Figure in Early Black Women's Literature: Clothed in My Right Mind*. New York: Garland, 1999.

Bryant, Jerry H. *Born in a Mighty Bad Land: The Violent Man in African American Folklore and Fiction.* Bloomington: Indiana University Press, 2003.

_____. *Victims and Heroes: Racial Violence in the African American Novel.* Amherst: University of Massachusetts Press, 1997.

Budick, E. Miller. *Blacks and Jews in Literary Conversation.* New York: Cambridge University Press, 1998.

Butler, Robert. *Contemporary African American Fiction: The Open Journey.* Madison, N.J.: Associated University Presses, 1998.

Calloway, Licia Morrow. *Black Family (Dys)function in Novels by Jessie Fauset, Nella Larsen, and Fannie Hurst.* New York: P. Lang, 2003.

Coleman, James W. *Black Male Fiction and the Legacy of Caliban.* Lexington: University Press of Kentucky, 2001.

Dandridge, Rita B. *Black Women's Activism: Reading African American Women's Historical Romances.* New York: P. Lang, 2004.

Dickson-Carr, Darryl. *African American Satire: The Sacredly Profane Novel.* Columbia: University of Missouri Press, 2001.

Dudley, John. *A Man's Game: Masculinity and the Anti-aesthetics of American Literary Naturalism.* Tuscaloosa: University of Alabama Press, 2004.

Elia, Nada. *Trances, Dances, and Vociferations: Agency and Resistance in Africana Women's Narratives.* New York: Garland, 2001.

Fabi, M. Giulia. *Passing and the Rise of the African American Novel.* Urbana: University of Illinois Press, 2001.

Ferguson, Roderick A. *Aberrations in Black: Toward a Queer of Color Critique.* Minneapolis: University of Minnesota Press, 2004.

Fishburn, Katherine. *The Problem of Embodiment in Early African American Narrative.* Westport, Conn.: Greenwood Press, 1997.

Folks, Jeffrey J. *From Richard Wright to Toni Morrison: Ethics in Modern and Postmodern American Narrative.* New York: P. Lang, 2001.

Gayles, Gloria Jean Wade. *No Crystal Stair: Visions of Race and Gender in Black Women's Fiction.* Cleveland: Pilgrim Press, 1997.

Gilyard, Keith. *Let's Flip the Script: An African American Discourse on Language, Literature, and Learning.* Detroit: Wayne State University Press, 1996.

Graham, Maryemma, ed. *Cambridge Companion to the African American Novel.* New York: Cambridge University Press, 2004.

Grant, Nathan. *Masculinist Impulses: Toomer, Hurston, Black Writing, and Modernity.* Columbia: University of Missouri Press, 2004.

Grasso, Linda M. *The Artistry of Anger: Black and White Women's Literature in America, 1820-1860.* Chapel Hill: University of North Carolina Press, 2002.

Grayson, Sandra M. *Visions of the Third Millennium: Black Science Fiction Novelists Write the Future.* Trenton, N.J.: Africa World Press, 2003.

Greene, J. Lee. *Blacks in Eden: The African American Novel's First Century.* Charlottesville: University Press of Virginia, 1996.

Harris, Trudier. *The Power of the Porch: The Storyteller's Craft in Zora Neale Hurston, Gloria Naylor, and Randall Kenan.* Athens: University of Georgia Press, 1996.

Hebbar, Reshmi J. *Modeling Minority Women: Heroines in African and Asian American Fiction.* New York: Routledge, 2005.

Henson, Kristin K. *Beyond the Sound Barrier: The Jazz Controversy in Twentieth-Century American Fiction.* New York: Routledge, 2003.

Jablon, Madelyn. *Black Metafiction: Self-consciousness in African American Literature.* Iowa City: University of Iowa Press, 1997.

Japtok, Martin. *Growing Up Ethnic: Nationalism and the Bildungsroman in African American and Jewish American Fiction.* Iowa City: University of Iowa Press, 2005.

Jimoh, A. Yemisi. *Spiritual, Blues, and Jazz People in African American Fiction: Living in Paradox.* Knoxville: University of Tennessee Press, 2002.

Jones, Sharon L. *Rereading the Harlem Renaissance: Race, Class, and Gender in the Fiction of Jessie Fauset, Zora Neale Hurston, and Dorothy West.* Westport, Conn.: Greenwood Press, 2002.

Kemayo, Kamau. *Emerging Afrikan Survivals: An Afrocentric Critical Theory.* New York: Routledge, 2003.

Kester, Gunilla Theander. *Writing the Subject: Bildung and the African American Text.* New York: P. Lang, 1997.

Kulkarni, Harihar. *Black Feminist Fiction: A March Towards Liberation.* New Delhi, India: Creative Books, 1999.

Leak, Jeffrey B. *Racial Myths and Masculinity in African American Literature.* Knoxville: University of Tennessee Press, 2005.

Levin, Amy K. *Africanism and Authenticity in African-American Women's Novels.* Gainesville: University Press of Florida, 2003.

Lupack, Barbara Tepa. *Literary Adaptations in Black American Cinema: From Micheaux to Toni Morrison.* Rochester, N.Y.: University of Rochester Press, 2002.

Marshall, Carmen Rose. *Black Professional Women in Recent American Fiction.* Jefferson, N.C.: McFarland, 2004.

Mitchell, Angelyn. *The Freedom to Remember: Narrative, Slavery, and Gender in Contemporary Black Women's Fiction.* New Brunswick, N.J.: Rutgers University Press, 2002.

Montgomery, Maxine Lavon. *The Apocalypse in African-American Fiction.* Gainesville: University Press of Florida, 1996.

Murdy, Anne-Elizabeth. *Teach the Nation: Public School, Racial Uplift, and Women's Writing in the 1890's.* New York: Routledge, 2003.

Newton, Adam Zachary. *Facing Black and Jew: Literature as Public Space in Twentieth-Century America.* New York: Cambridge University Press, 1999.

Page, Philip. *Reclaiming Community in Contemporary African American Fiction.* Jackson: University Press of Mississippi, 1999.

Patton, Venetria K. *Women in Chains: The Legacy of Slavery in Black Women's Fiction.* Albany: State University of New York Press, 2000.

Prince, Valerie Sweeney. *Burnin' Down the House: Home in African American Literature.* New York: Columbia University Press, 2005.

Rodgers, Lawrence R. *Canaan Bound: The African-American Great Migration Novel.* Urbana: University of Illinois Press, 1997.

Rody, Caroline. *The Daughter's Return: African-American and Caribbean Women's Fictions of History.* New York: Oxford University Press, 2001.

Rushdy, Ashraf H. A. *Neo-slave Narratives: Studies in the Social Logic of a Literary Form.* New York: Oxford University Press, 1999.

_____. *Remembering Generations: Race and Family in Contemporary African American Fiction.* Chapel Hill: University of North Carolina Press, 2001.

Simawe, Saadi, ed. *Black Orpheus: Music in African American Fiction from the Harlem Renaissance to Toni Morrison.* New York: Garland, 2000.

Smethurst, James Edward. *The Black Arts Movement: Literary Nationalism in the 1960s and 1970s.* Chapel Hill: University of North Carolina Press, 2005.

Soitos, Stephen F. *The Blues Detective: A Study of African American Detective Fiction.* Amherst: University of Massachusetts Press, 1996.

Tate, Claudia. *Psychoanalysis and Black Novels: Desire and the Protocols of Race.* New York: Oxford University Press, 1998.

Taylor, Carole Anne. *The Tragedy and Comedy of Resistance: Reading Modernity Through Black Women's Fiction.* Philadelphia: University of Pennsylvania Press, 2000.

Thompson, Carlyle Van. *The Tragic Black Buck: Racial Masquerading in the American Literary Imagination.* New York: P. Lang, 2004.

Wall, Cheryl A. *Worrying the Line: Black Women Writers, Lineage, and Literary Tradition.* Chapel Hill: University of North Carolina Press, 2005.

Washington, Teresa N. *Our Mothers, Our Powers, Our Texts: Manifestations of "Àjé" in Africana Literature.* Bloomington: Indiana University Press, 2005.

Welch, Sharon D. *A Feminist Ethic of Risk.* Minneapolis, Minn.: Fortress Press, 2000.

Wyatt, Jean. *Risking Difference: Identification, Race, and Community in Contemporary Fiction and Feminism.* Albany: State University of New York Press, 2004.

Zackodnik, Teresa C. *The Mulatta and the Politics of Race.* Jackson: University Press of Mississippi, 2004.

Harlem Renaissance

Aberjhani, and Sandra L. West. *Encyclopedia of the Harlem Renaissance.* New York: Facts On File, 2003.

Balshaw, Maria. *Looking for Harlem: Urban Aesthetics in African American Literature.* Sterling, Va.: Pluto Press, 2000.

Bascom, Lionel C., ed. *A Renaissance in Harlem: Lost Voices of an American Community.* New York: Bard, 1999.

Bassett, John Earl. *Harlem in Review: Critical Reactions to Black American Writers, 1917-1939.* Selinsgrove, Pa.: Susquehanna University Press, 1992.

Berry, Faith. *Langston Hughes, Before and Beyond Harlem.* New York: Wings Books, 1995.

Bloom, Harold, ed. *Black American Poets and Dramatists of the Harlem Renaissance.* New York: Chelsea House, 1995.

_____. *Black American Prose Writers of the Harlem Renaissance.* New York: Chelsea House, 1994.

_____. *The Harlem Renaissance.* Philadelphia: Chelsea House, 2004.

_____. *Major Black American Writers Through the Harlem Renaissance.* New York: Chelsea House, 1995.

Carroll, Anne Elizabeth. *Word, Image, and the New Negro: Representation and Identity in the Harlem Renaissance.* Bloomington: Indiana University Press, 2005.

Chambers, Veronica. *The Harlem Renaissance.* Philadelphia: Chelsea House, 1998.

Coleman, Leon. *Carl Van Vechten and the Harlem Renaissance: A Critical Assessment.* New York: Garland, 1998.

Davis, Thadious M. *Nella Larsen, Novelist of the Harlem Renaissance: A Woman's Life Unveiled.* Baton Rouge: Louisiana State University Press, 1994.

De Jongh, James. *Vicious Modernism: Black Harlem and the Literary Imagination.* New York: Cambridge University Press, 1990.

Dorsey, Brian. *Who Stole the Soul? Blaxploitation Echoed in the Harlem Renaissance.* Salzburg: Institut fur Anglistik und Amerikanistik, Universitat Salzburg, 1997.

Egar, Emmanuel Edame. *Black Women Poets of the Harlem Renaissance.* Lanham, Md.: University Press of America, 2003.

English, Daylanne K. *Unnatural Selections: Eugenics in American Modernism and the Harlem Renaissance.* Chapel Hill: University of North Carolina Press, 2004.

Fabré, Geneviève, and Michel Feith, eds. *Jean Toomer and the Harlem Renaissance.* New Brunswick, N.J.: Rutgers University Press, 2001.

_____. *Temples for Tomorrow: Looking Back at the Harlem Renaissance.* Bloomington: Indiana University Press, 2001.

Fabré, Michel. *From Harlem to Paris: Black American Writers in France, 1840-1980.* Urbana: University of Illinois Press, 1991.

Favor, J. Martin. *Authentic Blackness: The Folk in the New Negro Renaissance.* Durham, N.C.: Duke University Press, 1999.

Gallego, Mar. *Passing Novels in the Harlem Renaissance: Identity Politics and Textual Strategies.* Munster, Germany: LitVerlag, 2003.

Giovanni, Nikki, ed. *Shimmy Shimmy Shimmy Like My Sister Kate: Looking at the Harlem Renaissance Through Poems.* New York: H. Holt, 1996.

Helbling, Mark Irving. *The Harlem Renaissance: The One and the Many.* Westport, Conn.: Greenwood Press, 1999.

Hill, Laban Carrick. *Harlem Stomp! A Cultural History of the Harlem Renaissance.* New York: Megan Tingley Books, 2004.

Howes, Kelly King. *Harlem Renaissance.* Detroit: U X L, 2001.

Huggins, Nathan Irvin, ed. *Voices from the Harlem Renaissance.* New York: Oxford University Press, 1995.

Hull, Gloria T. *Color, Sex, and Poetry: Three Women Writers of the Harlem Renaissance.* Bloomington: Indiana University Press, 1987.

Hutchinson, George. *The Harlem Renaissance in Black and White.* Cambridge, Mass.: Belknap Press, 1995.

Jones, Sharon L. *Rereading the Harlem Renaissance: Race, Class, and Gender in the Fiction of Jessie Fauset, Zora Neale Hurston, and Dorothy West.* Westport, Conn.: Greenwood Press, 2002.

Kallen, Stuart A. *The Twentieth Century and the Harlem Renaissance: A History of Black People in America, 1880-1930.* Edina, Minn.: Abdo & Daughters, 1990.

Kramer, Victor A., and Robert A. Russ, eds. *Harlem Renaissance Reexamined.* Troy, N.Y.: Whitson, 1997.

Krasner, David. *A Beautiful Pageant: African American Theatre, Drama, and Performance in the Harlem Renaissance, 1910-1927.* New York: Palgrave Macmillan, 2002.

Lewis, David Levering, ed. *The Portable Harlem Renaissance Reader.* New York: Penguin Books, 1994.

Long, Richard A. *Grown Deep: Essays on the Harlem Renaissance.* Winter Park, Fla.: Four-G, 1998.

Lyons, Mary E. *Sorrow's Kitchen: The Life and Folklore of Zora Neale Hurston.* New York: Charles Scribner's Sons, 1990.

McLeod, A. L., ed. *Claude McKay: Centennial Studies.* New Delhi, India: Sterling, 1992.

Martin, Tony, ed. *African Fundamentalism: A Literary and Cultural Anthology of Garvey's Harlem Renaissance.* Dover, Mass.: Majority Press, 1991.

Mishkin, Tracy. *The Harlem and Irish Renaissances: Language, Identity, and Representation.* Gainesville: University Press of Florida, 1998.

_____, ed. *Literary Influence and African-American Writers: Collected Essays.* New York: Garland, 1996.

Nadell, Martha Jane. *Enter the New Negroes: Images of Race in American Culture.* Cambridge, Mass.: Harvard University Press, 2004.

Patton, Venetria K., and Maureen Honey, eds. *Double-take: A Revisionist Harlem Renaissance Anthology.* New Brunswick, N.J.: Rutgers University Press, 2001.

Price, Kenneth M., and Lawrence J. Oliver, eds. *Critical Essays on James Weldon Johnson.* New York: G. K. Hall, 1997.

Reid, Margaret Ann. *Black Protest Poetry: Polemics from the Harlem Renaissance and the Sixties.* New York: P. Lang, 2001.

Roses, Lorraine Elena, and Ruth Elizabeth Randolph. *The Harlem Renaissance and Beyond: Literary Biographies of One Hundred Black Women Writers, 1900-1945.* Boston: G. K. Hall, 1990.

Roses, Lorraine Elena, and Ruth Elizabeth Randolph, eds. *Harlem's Glory: Black Women Writing, 1900-1950.* Cambridge, Mass.: Harvard University Press, 1996.

Schwarz, A. B. Christa. *Gay Voices of the Harlem Renaissance.* Bloomington: Indiana University Press, 2003.

Smith, Katharine Capshaw. *Children's Literature of the Harlem Renaissance.* Bloomington: Indiana University Press, 2004.

Tolson, Melvin Beaunorus. *The Harlem Group of Negro Writers.* Westport, Conn.: Greenwood Press, 2001.

Tracy, Steven C. *Langston Hughes and the Blues.* Urbana: University of Illinois Press, 2001.

Trotman, C. James, ed. *Langston Hughes: The Man, His Art, and His Continuing Influence.* New York: Garland, 1995.

Wall, Cheryl A. *Women of the Harlem Renaissance.* Bloomington: Indiana University Press, 1995.

Washington, Robert E. *The Ideologies of African American Literature: From the Harlem Renaissance to the Black Nationalist Revolt: A Sociology of Literature Perspective.* Lanham, Md.: Rowman & Littlefield, 2001.

Wilson, Sondra Kathryn, ed. *"The Messenger" Reader: Stories, Poetry, and Essays from "The Messenger" Magazine.* New York: Modern Library, 2000.

Wintz, Cary D. *Black Culture and the Harlem Renaissance.* College Station: Texas A&M University Press, 1996.

————, ed. *The Harlem Renaissance, 1920-1940.* 7 vols. New York: Garland, 1996.

Witalec, Janet, ed. *The Harlem Renaissance: A Gale Critical Companion.* Detroit: Gale Research, 2003.

Woodson, Jon. *To Make a New Race: Gurdjieff, Toomer, and the Harlem Renaissance.* Jackson: University Press of Mississippi, 1999.

Identity

Bennett, Juda. *The Passing Figure: Racial Confusion in Modern American Literature.* New York: P. Lang, 1996.

Bland, Sterling Lecater. *Voices of the Fugitives: Runaway Slave Stories and Their Fictions of Self-Creation.* Westport, Conn.: Praeger, 2000.

Boeckmann, Cathy. *A Question of Character: Scientific Racism and the Genres of American Fiction, 1892-1912.* Tuscaloosa: University of Alabama Press, 2000.

Booker, Margaret. *Lillian Hellman and August Wilson: Dramatizing a New American Identity.* New York: P. Lang, 2003.

Bower, Martha Gilman. *"Color Struck" Under the Gaze: Ethnicity and the Pathology of Being in the Plays of Johnson, Hurston, Childress, Hansberry, and Kennedy.* Westport, Conn.: Praeger, 2003.

Bracks, Lean'tin L. *Writings on Black Women of the Diaspora: History, Language, and Identity.* New York: Garland, 1998.

Carroll, Anne Elizabeth. *Word, Image, and the New Negro: Representation and Identity in the Harlem Renaissance.* Bloomington: Indiana University Press, 2005.

Davies, Carole Boyce. *Black Women, Writing, and Identity: Migrations of the Subject.* New York: Routledge, 1994.

Fabi, M. Giulia. *Passing and the Rise of the African American Novel.* Urbana: University of Illinois Press, 2001.

Favor, J. Martin. *Authentic Blackness: The Folk in the New Negro Renaissance.* Durham, N.C.: Duke University Press, 1999.

Gallego, Mar. *Passing Novels in the Harlem Renaissance: Identity Politics and Textual Strategies.* Munster, Germany: LitVerlag, 2003.

Ginsberg, Elaine K., ed. *Passing and the Fictions of Identity.* Durham, N.C.: Duke University Press, 1996.

Gosselin, Adrienne Johnson, ed. *Multicultural Detective Fiction: Murder from the "Other" Side.* New York: Garland, 1999.

Holloway, Karla F. C. *Codes of Conduct: Race, Ethics, and the Color of Our Character.* New Brunswick, N.J.: Rutgers University Press, 1995.

Hord, Fred L. *Reconstructing Memory: Black Literary Criticism.* Chicago: Third World Press, 1991.

Kawash, Samira. *Dislocating the Color Line: Identity, Hybridity, and Singularity in African-American Narrative.* Stanford, Calif.: Stanford University Press, 1997.

Keizer, Arlene R. *Black Subjects: Identity Formation in the Contemporary Narrative of Slavery.* Ithaca, N.Y.: Cornell University Press, 2004.

Levine, Robert S. *Martin Delany, Frederick Douglass, and the Politics of Representative Identity.* Chapel Hill: University of North Carolina Press, 1997.

Lock, Helen. *A Case of Mis-taken Identity: Detective Undercurrents in Recent African American Fiction.* New York: P. Lang, 1994.

McKee, Patricia. *Producing American Races: Henry James, William Faulkner, Toni Morrison.* Durham, N.C.: Duke University Press, 1999.

Martin, Tony, ed. *African Fundamentalism: A Literary and Cultural Anthology of Garvey's Harlem Renaissance.* Dover, Mass.: Majority Press, 1991.

Mishkin, Tracy. *The Harlem and Irish Renaissances: Language, Identity, and Representation.* Gainesville: University Press of Florida, 1998.

Moses, Wilson Jeremiah. *The Wings of Ethiopia: Studies in African-American Life and Letters.* Ames: Iowa State University Press, 1990.

Nwankwo, Ifeoma Kiddoe. *Black Cosmopolitanism: Racial Consciousness and Transnational Identity in the Nineteenth-Century Americas.* Philadelphia: University of Pennsylvania Press, 2005.

Pfeiffer, Kathleen. *Race Passing and American Individualism.* Amherst: University of Massachusetts Press, 2003.

Quashie, Kevin Everod. *Black Women, Identity, and Cultural Theory: (Un)becoming the Subject.* New Brunswick, N.J.: Rutgers University Press, 2004.

Reid-Pharr, Robert. *Conjugal Union: The Body, the House, and the Black American.* New York: Oxford University Press, 1999.

Ross, Marlon Bryan. *Manning the Race: Reforming Black Men in the Jim Crow Era.* New York: New York University Press, 2004.

Sartwell, Crispin. *Act Like You Know: African-American Autobiography and White Identity.* Chicago: University of Chicago Press, 1998.

Saunders, James Robert. *Tightrope Walk: Identity, Survival, and the Corporate World in African American Literature.* Jefferson, N.C.: McFarland, 1997.

Sharadha, Y. S. *Black Women's Writing: Quest for Identity in the Plays of Lorraine Hansberry and Ntozake Shange.* New Delhi, India: Prestige Books, 1998.

Thompson, Carlyle Van. *The Tragic Black Buck: Racial Masquerading in the American Literary Imagination.* New York: P. Lang, 2004.

Tillery, Tyrone. *Claude McKay: A Black Poet's Struggle for Identity.* Amherst: University of Massachusetts Press, 1992.

Trotman, C. James, ed. *Multiculturalism: Roots and Realities.* Bloomington: Indiana University Press, 2002.

Wald, Gayle Freda. *Crossing the Line: Racial Passing in Twentieth-Century U.S. Literature and Culture.* Durham, N.C.: Duke University Press, 2000.

Wallace, Maurice O. *Constructing the Black Masculine: Identity and Ideality in African American Men's Literature and Culture, 1775-1995.* Durham, N.C.: Duke University Press, 2002.

Wallace-Sanders, Kimberly. *Skin Deep, Spirit Strong: The Black Female Body in American Culture.* Ann Arbor: University of Michigan Press, 2002.

Weiss, M. Lynn. *Gertrude Stein and Richard Wright: The Poetics and Politics of Modernism.* Jackson: University Press of Mississippi, 1998.

Wright, Lee Alfred. *Identity, Family, and Folklore in African American Literature.* New York: Garland, 1995.

Wyatt, Jean. *Risking Difference: Identification, Race, and Community in Contemporary Fiction and Feminism.* Albany: State University of New York Press, 2004.

Masculinity

Auger, Philip. *Native Sons in No Man's Land: Rewriting Afro-American Manhood in the Novels of Baldwin, Walker, Wideman, and Gaines.* New York: Garland, 2000.

Baker, Houston A. *Critical Memory: Public Spheres, African American Writing, and Black Fathers and Sons in America.* Athens: University of Georgia Press, 2001.

Bloom, Harold, ed. *Bigger Thomas.* New York: Chelsea House, 1990.

————. *"Invisible Man."* Philadelphia: Chelsea House, 1999.

————. *Richard Wright's "Native Son."* New York: Chelsea House, 1988.

Brown, Cecil. *Stagolee Shot Billy.* Cambridge, Mass.: Harvard University Press, 2003.

Bryant, Jerry H. *Born in a Mighty Bad Land: The Violent Man in African American Folklore and Fiction.* Bloomington: Indiana University Press, 2003.

Callahan, John F., ed. *Ralph Ellison's "Invisible Man": A Casebook.* New York: Oxford University Press, 2004.

Carroll, Rebecca, comp. *Swing Low: Black Men Writing.* New York: Carol Southern Books, 1995.

Clark, Keith. *Black Manhood in James Baldwin, Ernest J. Gaines, and August Wilson.* Urbana: University of Illinois Press, 2002.

————, ed. *Contemporary Black Men's Fiction and Drama.* Urbana: University of Illinois Press, 2001.

Coleman, James W. *Black Male Fiction and the Legacy of Caliban.* Lexington: University Press of Kentucky, 2001.

Dudley, David L. *My Father's Shadow: Intergenerational Conflict in*

African American Men's Autobiography. Philadelphia: University of Pennsylvania Press, 1991.

Dudley, John. *A Man's Game: Masculinity and the Anti-aesthetics of American Literary Naturalism.* Tuscaloosa: University of Alabama Press, 2004.

Grant, Nathan. *Masculinist Impulses: Toomer, Hurston, Black Writing, and Modernity.* Columbia: University of Missouri Press, 2004.

Harper, Donna Sullivan. *Not So Simple: The "Simple" Stories by Langston Hughes.* Columbia: University of Missouri Press, 1995.

Harris, Trudier. *Exorcising Blackness: Historical and Literary Lynching and Burning Rituals.* Bloomington: Indiana University Press, 1984.

_____, ed. *New Essays on "Go Tell It on the Mountain."* New York: Cambridge University Press, 1996.

Hogue, W. Lawrence. *The African American Male, Writing and Difference: A Polycentric Approach to African American Literature, Criticism, and History.* Albany: State University of New York Press, 2003.

Jackson, Edward Mercia. *Images of Black Men in Black Women Writers, 1950-1990.* Bristol, Ind.: Wyndham Hall Press, 1992.

Johnson, Michael K. *Black Masculinity and the Frontier Myth in American Literature.* Norman: University of Oklahoma Press, 2002.

Kinnamon, Keneth, ed. *Critical Essays on Richard Wright's "Native Son."* New York: Twayne, 1997.

Leak, Jeffrey B. *Racial Myths and Masculinity in African American Literature.* Knoxville: University of Tennessee Press, 2005.

Morel, Lucas E., ed. *Ralph Ellison and the Raft of Hope: A Political Companion to "Invisible Man."* Lexington: University Press of Kentucky, 2004.

Riley, Dorothy Winbush, ed. *Black Men, in the Image of God.* Cleveland: Pilgrim Press, 1999.

Rosen, Steven. *Gita on the Green: The Mystical Tradition Behind Bagger Vance.* New York: Continuum, 2000.

Ross, Marlon Bryan. *Manning the Race: Reforming Black Men in the Jim Crow Era.* New York: New York University Press, 2004.

Schwarz, A. B. Christa. *Gay Voices of the Harlem Renaissance.* Bloomington: Indiana University Press, 2003.

Thompson, Carlyle Van. *The Tragic Black Buck: Racial Masquerading in the American Literary Imagination.* New York: P. Lang, 2004.

Wallace, Maurice O. *Constructing the Black Masculine: Identity and Ideality in African American Men's Literature and Culture, 1775-1995.* Durham, N.C.: Duke University Press, 2002.

Warren, Kenneth W. *So Black and Blue: Ralph Ellison and the Occasion of Criticism.* Chicago: University of Chicago Press, 2003.

Wilson, Charles E. *Walter Mosley: A Critical Companion.* Westport, Conn.: Greenwood Press, 2003.

Poetry

Anderson, T. J. *Notes to Make the Sound Come Right: Four Innovators of Jazz Poetry.* Fayetteville: University of Arkansas Press, 2004.

Bloom, Harold, ed. *African-American Poets: Phillis Wheatley Through Melvin B. Tolson.* Philadelphia: Chelsea House, 2003.

_____. *African-American Poets: Robert Hayden Through Rita Dove.* Philadelphia: Chelsea House, 2003.

Bolden, Tony. *Afro-blue: Improvisations in African American Poetry and Culture.* Urbana: University of Illinois Press, 2004.

Brown, Fahamisha Patricia. *Performing the Word: African American Poetry as Vernacular Culture.* New Brunswick, N.J.: Rutgers University Press, 1999.

Clarke, Cheryl. *"After Mecca": Women Poets and the Black Arts Movement.* New Brunswick, N.J.: Rutgers University Press, 2005.

Coyle, Michael, ed. *Ezra Pound and African American Modernism.* Orono, Maine: National Poetry Foundation, 2001.

Dorsey, Brian. *Spirituality, Sensuality, Literality: Blues, Jazz, and Rap as Music and Poetry.* Vienna: Braumuller, 2000.

Egar, Emmanuel Edame. *Black Women Poets of the Harlem Renaissance.* Lanham, Md.: University Press of America, 2003.

Feinstein, Sascha. *Jazz Poetry: From the 1920s to the Present.* Westport, Conn.: Greenwood Press, 1997.

Gabbin, Joanne V., ed. *The Furious Flowering of African American Poetry.* Charlottesville: University Press of Virginia, 1999.

Georgoudaki, Ekaterini. *Race, Gender, and Class Perspectives in the*

Works of Maya Angelou, Gwendolyn Brooks, Rita Dove, Nikki Giovanni, and Audre Lorde. Thessaloniki, Greece: Aristotle University of Thessaloniki, 1991.

Giovanni, Nikki, ed. *Shimmy Shimmy Shimmy Like My Sister Kate: Looking at the Harlem Renaissance Through Poems.* New York: H. Holt, 1996.

Hull, Gloria T. *Color, Sex, and Poetry: Three Women Writers of the Harlem Renaissance.* Bloomington: Indiana University Press, 1987.

Melhem, D. H. *Heroism in the New Black Poetry: Introductions and Interviews.* Lexington: University Press of Kentucky, 1990.

Neff-Mayson, Heather. *Redemption Songs: The Voice of Protest in the Poetry of Afro-Americans.* Bern: Francke Verlag, 1989.

Nielsen, Aldon Lynn. *Black Chant: Languages of African-American Postmodernism.* New York: Cambridge University Press, 1997.

———, ed. *Reading Race in American Poetry: An Area of Act.* Urbana: University of Illinois Press, 2000.

Redding, J. Saunders. *To Make a Poet Black.* Ithaca, N.Y.: Cornell University Press, 1988.

Reid, Margaret Ann. *Black Protest Poetry: Polemics from the Harlem Renaissance and the Sixties.* New York: P. Lang, 2001.

Sherman, Joan R. *Invisible Poets: Afro-Americans of the Nineteenth Century.* Urbana: University of Illinois Press, 1989.

Smethurst, James Edward. *The Black Arts Movement: Literary Nationalism in the 1960s and 1970s.* Chapel Hill: University of North Carolina Press, 2005.

———. *The New Red Negro: The Literary Left and African American Poetry, 1930-1946.* New York: Oxford University Press, 1999.

Thomas, Lorenzo. *Extraordinary Measures: Afrocentric Modernism and Twentieth-Century American Poetry.* Tuscaloosa: University of Alabama Press, 2000.

Tracy, Steven C. *Langston Hughes and the Blues.* Urbana: University of Illinois Press, 2001.

Race

Arac, Jonathan. *Huckleberry Finn as Idol and Target: The Functions of Criticism in Our Time.* Madison: University of Wisconsin Press, 1997.

Baker, Houston A. *Critical Memory: Public Spheres, African Ameri-*

can Writing, and Black Fathers and Sons in America. Athens: University of Georgia Press, 2001.

Balfour, Katharine Lawrence. *The Evidence of Things Not Said: James Baldwin and the Promise of American Democracy.* Ithaca, N.Y.: Cornell University Press, 2001.

Bergner, Gwen S. *Taboo Subjects: Race, Sex, and Psychoanalysis.* Minneapolis: University of Minnesota Press, 2005.

Boeckmann, Cathy. *A Question of Character: Scientific Racism and the Genres of American Fiction, 1892-1912.* Tuscaloosa: University of Alabama Press, 2000.

Bryant, Jerry H. *Victims and Heroes: Racial Violence in the African American Novel.* Amherst: University of Massachusetts Press, 1997.

Champion, Ernest A. *Mr. Baldwin, I Presume: James Baldwin and Chinua Achebe: A Meeting of the Minds.* Lanham, Md.: University Press of America, 1995.

Crane, Gregg David. *Race, Citizenship, and Law in American Literature.* New York: Cambridge University Press, 2002.

Crowe, Chris. *Presenting Mildred D. Taylor.* New York: Twayne, 1999.

Dempsey, Terrell. *Searching for Jim: Slavery in Sam Clemens's World.* Columbia: University of Missouri Press, 2003.

Dussere, Erik. *Balancing the Books: Faulkner, Morrison, and the Economies of Slavery.* New York: Routledge, 2003.

Erkkila, Betsy. *Mixed Bloods and Other Crosses: Rethinking American Literature from the Revolution to the Culture Wars.* Philadelphia: University of Pennsylvania Press, 2005.

Goldner, Ellen J., and Safiya Henderson-Holmes, eds. *Racing and (E)racing Language: Living with the Color of Our Words.* Syracuse, N.Y.: Syracuse University Press, 2001.

Graham, Arthur J. *The Manichean Leitmotif: The Ideology and Psychology of Racism in American Fiction.* Los Angeles: Image Analysts, 2000.

Hakutani, Yoshinobu. *Richard Wright and Racial Discourse.* Columbia: University of Missouri Press, 1996.

Heneghan, Bridget T. *Whitewashing America: Material Culture and Race in the Antebellum Imagination.* Jackson: University Press of Mississippi, 2003.

Ladd, Barbara. *Nationalism and the Color Line in George W. Cable, Mark Twain, and William Faulkner.* Baton Rouge: Louisiana State University Press, 1996.

Lemire, Elise Virginia. *"Miscegenation": Making Race in America.* Philadelphia: University of Pennsylvania Press, 2002.

Lindqvist, Sven. *Exterminate All the Brutes.* New York: New Press, 1996.

MacCann, Donnarae. *White Supremacy in Children's Literature: Characterizations of African Americans, 1830-1900.* New York: Routledge, 2001.

Maddy, Yulisa Amadu. *African Images in Juvenile Literature: Commentaries on Neocolonialist Fiction.* Jefferson, N.C.: McFarland, 1996.

Miller, Ericka M. *The Other Reconstruction: Where Violence and Womanhood Meet in the Writings of Wells-Barnett, Grimké, and Larsen.* New York: Garland, 2000.

Mullen, Bill. *Afro-Orientalism.* Minneapolis: University of Minnesota Press, 2004.

Muller-Hartmann, Andreas. *The Discourse of Race and Southern Literature, 1890-1940: From Consensus and Accommodation to Subversion and Resistance.* New York: P. Lang, 2000.

Myers, Jeffrey. *Converging Stories: Race, Ecology, and Environmental Justice in American Literature.* Athens: University of Georgia Press, 2005.

Reddy, Maureen T. *Traces, Codes, and Clues: Reading Race in Crime Fiction.* New Brunswick, N.J.: Rutgers University Press, 2003.

Robinson, Charles F. *Dangerous Liasons: Sex and Love in the Segregated South.* Fayetteville: University of Arkansas Press, 2003.

Ryan, Susan M. *The Grammar of Good Intentions: Race and the Antebellum Culture of Benevolence.* Ithaca, N.Y.: Cornell University Press, 2003.

Samuels, Robert. *Writing Prejudices: The Psychoanalysis and Pedagogy of Discrimination from Shakespeare to Toni Morrison.* Albany: State University of New York Press, 2001.

Spillers, Hortense J. *Black, White, and in Color: Essays on American Literature and Culture.* Chicago: University of Chicago Press, 2003.

Stinchcomb, Dawn F. *The Development of Literary Blackness in the*

Dominican Republic. Gainesville: University Press of Florida, 2004.

Stokes, Mason Boyd. *The Color of Sex: Whiteness, Heterosexuality, and the Fictions of White Supremacy*. Durham, N.C.: Duke University Press, 2001.

Taylor, Gary. *Buying Whiteness: Race, Culture, and Identity from Columbus to Hip Hop*. New York: Palgrave Macmillan, 2005.

Thompson, Carlyle Van. *The Tragic Black Buck: Racial Masquerading in the American Literary Imagination*. New York: P. Lang, 2004.

Weierman, Karen Woods. *One Nation, One Blood: Interracial Marriage in American Fiction, Scandal, and Law, 1820-1870*. Amherst: University of Massachusetts Press, 2005.

Wonham, Henry B., ed. *Criticism and the Color Line: Desegregating American Literary Studies*. New Brunswick, N.J.: Rutgers University Press, 1996.

Wylie, Dan. *Savage Delight: White Myths of Shaka*. Pietermaritzburg: University of Natal Press, 2000.

Zackodnik, Teresa C. *The Mulatta and the Politics of Race*. Jackson: University Press of Mississippi, 2004

Sexuality

Awkward, Michael. *Negotiating Difference: Race, Gender, and the Politics of Positionality*. Chicago: University of Chicago Press, 1995.

Barnett, Pamela E. *Dangerous Desire: Sexual Freedom and Sexual Violence Since the Sixties*. New York: Routledge, 2004.

Bergner, Gwen S. *Taboo Subjects: Race, Sex, and Psychoanalysis*. Minneapolis: University of Minnesota Press, 2005.

Coser, Stelamaris. *Bridging the Americas: The Literature of Paule Marshall, Toni Morrison, and Gayl Jones*. Philadelphia: Temple University Press, 1995.

Davies, Carole Boyce. *Black Women, Writing, and Identity: Migrations of the Subject*. New York: Routledge, 1994.

Davis, Thadious M. *Games of Property: Law, Race, Gender, and Faulkner's "Go Down, Moses."* Durham, N.C.: Duke University Press, 2003.

DuCille, Ann. *The Coupling Convention: Sex, Text, and Tradition in*

Black Women's Fiction. New York: Oxford University Press, 1993.

DuPlessis, Rachel Blau. *Genders, Races, and Religious Cultures in Modern American Poetries, 1908-1934.* New York: Cambridge University Press, 2001.

Ellis, Trey. *Platitudes and "The New Black Aesthetic."* Boston: Northeastern University Press, 2003.

Ferguson, Roderick A. *Aberrations in Black: Toward a Queer of Color Critique.* Minneapolis: University of Minnesota Press, 2004.

Gayles, Gloria Jean Wade. *No Crystal Stair: Visions of Race and Gender in Black Women's Fiction.* Cleveland: Pilgrim Press, 1997.

Golden, Maria, ed. *Wild Women Don't Wear No Blues: Black Women Writers on Love, Men, and Sex.* New York: Doubleday, 1993.

Gourdine, Angeletta K. M. *The Difference Place Makes: Gender, Sexuality, and Diaspora Identity.* Columbus: Ohio State University Press, 2002.

Hernton, Calvin C. *The Sexual Mountain and Black Women Writers: Adventures in Sex, Literature, and Real Life.* New York: Anchor Books, 1990.

Holloway, Karla F. C. *Moorings and Metaphors: Figures of Culture and Gender in Black Women's Literature.* New Brunswick, N.J.: Rutgers University Press, 1992.

Hudson-Weems, Clenora. *Africana Womanist Literary Theory.* Trenton, N.J.: Africa World Press, 2004.

Jenkins, McKay. *The South in Black and White: Race, Sex, and Literature in the 1940s.* Chapel Hill: University of North Carolina Press, 1999.

Jones, Sharon L. *Rereading the Harlem Renaissance: Race, Class, and Gender in the Fiction of Jessie Fauset, Zora Neale Hurston, and Dorothy West.* Westport, Conn.: Greenwood Press, 2002.

Kolmerten, Carol A., Stephen M. Ross, and Judith Bryant Wittenberg, eds. *Unflinching Gaze: Morrison and Faulkner Reenvisioned.* Jackson: University Press of Mississippi, 1997.

Meisenhelder, Susan Edwards. *Hitting a Straight Lick with a Crooked Stick: Race and Gender in the Work of Zora Neale Hurston.* Tuscaloosa: University of Alabama Press, 1999.

Mitchell, Angelyn. *The Freedom to Remember: Narrative, Slavery, and Gender in Contemporary Black Women's Fiction.* New Brunswick, N.J.: Rutgers University Press, 2002.

Myrsiades, Kostas, and Linda Myrsiades, eds. *Race-ing Representation: Voice, History, and Sexuality.* Lanham, Md.: Rowman & Littlefield, 1998.

Robinson, Charles F. *Dangerous Liasons: Sex and Love in the Segregated South.* Fayetteville: University of Arkansas Press, 2003.

Ross, Marlon Bryan. *Manning the Race: Reforming Black Men in the Jim Crow Era.* New York: New York University Press, 2004.

Samuels, Shirley, ed. *The Culture of Sentiment: Race, Gender, and Sentimentality in Nineteenth-Century America.* New York: Oxford University Press, 1992.

Schreiber, Evelyn Jaffe. *Subversive Voices: Eroticizing the Other in William Faulkner and Toni Morrison.* Knoxville: University of Tennessee Press, 2001.

Schwarz, A. B. Christa. *Gay Voices of the Harlem Renaissance.* Bloomington: Indiana University Press, 2003.

Smith, Felipe. *American Body Politics: Race, Gender, and Black Literary Renaissance.* Athens: University of Georgia Press, 1998.

Stokes, Mason Boyd. *The Color of Sex: Whiteness, Heterosexuality, and the Fictions of White Supremacy.* Durham, N.C.: Duke University Press, 2001.

Twagilimana, Aimable. *Race and Gender in the Making of an African American Literary Tradition.* New York: Garland, 1997.

Weinstein, Philip M. *What Else but Love? The Ordeal of Race in Faulkner and Morrison.* New York: Columbia University Press, 1996.

Winter, Kari J. *Subjects of Slavery, Agents of Change: Women and Power in Gothic Novels and Slave Narratives, 1790-1865.* Athens: University of Georgia Press, 1992.

Slavery

Brock-Sallah, Sabine. *White Amnesia—Black Memory? American Women's Writing and History.* New York: P. Lang, 1999.

Carey, Brycchan, Markman Ellis, and Sara Salih, eds. *Discourses of Slavery and Abolition: Britain and Its Colonies, 1760-1838.* New York: Palgrave Macmillan, 2004.

Creed, Barbara, and Jeanette Hoorn, eds. *Body Trade: Captivity,*

Cannibalism and Colonialism in the Pacific. New York: Routledge, 2001.

Diedrich, Maria, Henry Louis Gates, Jr., and Carl Pedersen, eds. *Black Imagination and the Middle Passage.* New York: Oxford University Press, 1999.

Gould, Philip. *Barbaric Traffic: Commerce and Antislavery in the Eighteenth-Century Atlantic World.* Cambridge, Mass.: Harvard University Press, 2003.

Keizer, Arlene R. *Black Subjects: Identity Formation in the Contemporary Narrative of Slavery.* Ithaca, N.Y.: Cornell University Press, 2004.

Mackenthun, Gesa. *Fictions of the Black Atlantic in American Foundational Literature.* New York: Routledge, 2004.

Sandiford, Keith Albert. *Measuring the Moment: Strategies of Protest in Eighteenth-Century Afro-English Writing.* Selinsgrove, Pa.: Susquehanna University Press, 1988.

Thomas, Helen. *Romanticism and Slave Narratives: Transatlantic Testimonies.* New York: Cambridge University Press, 2000.

Theater

Allen, Carol. *Peculiar Passages: Black Women Playwrights, 1875 to 2000.* New York: P. Lang, 2005.

Anadolu-Okur, Nilgun. *Contemporary African American Theater: Afrocentricity in the Works of Larry Neal, Amiri Baraka, and Charles Fuller.* Studies in African American History and Culture. New York: Garland, 1997.

Bean, Annemarie, ed. *A Sourcebook of African-American Performance: Plays, People, Movements.* Worlds of Performance. New York: Routledge, 1999.

Bloom, Harold, ed. *Contemporary Black American Poets and Dramatists.* New York: Chelsea House, 1995.

_____. *Modern Black American Poets and Dramatists.* New York: Chelsea House, 1995.

Bosch, Susanna A. *"Sturdy Black Bridges" on the American Stage: The Portrayal of Black Motherhood in Selected Plays by Contemporary African American Women Playwrights.* Vol. 8 in *Aachen British and American Studies.* New York: P. Lang, 1996.

Bower, Martha Gilman. *"Color Struck" Under the Gaze: Ethnicity and the Pathology of Being in the Plays of Johnson, Hurston, Childress, Hansberry, and Kennedy.* Contributions in Afro-American and African Studies 208. Westport, Conn.: Praeger, 2003.

Brown-Guillory, Elizabeth. *Their Place on the Stage: Black Women Playwrights in America.* Contributions in Afro-American and African Studies 117. New York: Greenwood Press, 1988.

Effiong, Philip U. *In Search of a Model for African-American Drama: A Study of Selected Plays by Lorraine Hansberry, Amiri Baraka, and Ntozake Shange.* Lanham, Md.: University Press of America, 2000.

Elam, Harry J., Jr., and David Krasner. *African American Performance and Theater History: A Critical Reader.* New York: Oxford University Press, 2001.

Euba, Femi. *Archetypes, Imprecators, and Victims of Fate: Origins and Developments of Satire in Black Drama.* Contributions in Afro-American and African Studies 126. New York: Greenwood Press, 1989.

Hay, Samuel A. *African American Theatre: A Historical and Critical Analysis.* Cambridge Studies in American Theatre and Drama. New York: Cambridge University Press, 1994.

Hill, Errol. *A History of African American Theatre.* Cambridge Studies in American Theatre and Drama. New York: Cambridge University Press, 2003.

_____, ed. *The Theater of Black Americans: A Collection of Critical Essays.* New York: Applause, 1987.

King, Woodie. *The Impact of Race: Theatre and Culture.* New York: Applause Theatre & Cinema Books, 2003.

Krasner, David. *A Beautiful Pageant: African American Theatre, Drama, and Performance in the Harlem Renaissance, 1910-1927.* New York: Palgrave Macmillan, 2002.

_____. *Resistance, Parody, and Double Consciousness in African American Theatre, 1895-1910.* New York: St. Martin's Press, 1997.

Marsh-Lockett, Carol P., ed. *Black Women Playwrights: Visions on the American Stage.* Vol. 11 in *Studies in Modern Drama.* New York: Garland, 1999.

Olaniyan, Tejumola. *Scars of Conquest/Masks of Resistance: The In-*

vention of Cultural Identities in African, African-American, and Caribbean Drama. New York: Oxford University Press, 1995.

Sanders, Leslie Catherine. *The Development of Black Theater in America: From Shadows to Selves.* Baton Rouge: Louisiana State University Press, 1988.

Sharadha, Y. S. *Black Women's Writing: Quest for Identity in the Plays of Lorraine Hansberry and Ntozake Shange.* New Delhi, India: Prestige Books, 1998.

Smethurst, James Edward. *The Black Arts Movement: Literary Nationalism in the 1960s and 1970s.* Chapel Hill: University of North Carolina Press, 2005.

Wetmore, Kevin J. *Black Dionysus: Greek Tragedy and African American Theatre.* Jefferson, N.C.: McFarland, 2003.

Williams, Mance R. *Black Theatre in the 1960s and 1970s: A Historical-Critical Analysis of the Movement.* Contributions in Afro-American and African Studies 87. Westport, Conn.: Greenwood Press, 1985.

Wilson, August. *The Ground on Which I Stand.* Dramatic Contexts. New York: Theatre Communications Group, 2001.

Women's Studies

Allen, Carol. *Black Women Intellectuals: Strategies of Nation, Family, and Neighborhood in the Works of Pauline Hopkins, Jessie Fauset, and Marita Bonner.* New York: Garland, 1998.

———. *Peculiar Passages: Black Women Playwrights, 1875 to 2000.* New York: P. Lang, 2005.

Awkward, Michael. *Inspiriting Influences: Tradition, Revision, and Afro-American Women's Novels.* New York: Columbia University Press, 1989.

Bacon, Jacqueline. *The Humblest May Stand Forth: Rhetoric, Empowerment, and Abolition.* Columbia: University of South Carolina Press, 2002.

Baker, Houston A. *Workings of the Spirit: The Poetics of Afro-American Women's Writing.* Chicago: University of Chicago Press, 1991.

Birch, Eva Lennox. *Black American Women's Writing: A Quilt of Many Colours.* New York: Harvester Wheatsheaf, 1994.

Bloom, Harold, ed. *Black American Women Poets and Dramatists.* New York: Chelsea House, 1996.

Braxton, Joanne M., and Andrée Nicola McLaughlin, eds. *Wild Women in the Whirlwind: Afra-American Culture and the Contemporary Literary Renaissance.* New Brunswick, N.J.: Rutgers University Press, 1990.

Calloway, Licia Morrow. *Black Family (Dys)function in Novels by Jessie Fauset, Nella Larsen, and Fannie Hurst.* New York: P. Lang, 2003.

Clarke, Cheryl. *"After Mecca": Women Poets and the Black Arts Movement.* New Brunswick, N.J.: Rutgers University Press, 2005.

Dandridge, Rita B. *Black Women's Activism: Reading African American Women's Historical Romances.* New York: P. Lang, 2004.

Egar, Emmanuel Edame. *Black Women Poets of the Harlem Renaissance.* Lanham, Md.: University Press of America, 2003.

Foster, Frances Smith. *Written by Herself: Literary Production by African American Women, 1746-1892.* Bloomington: Indiana University Press, 1993.

Glikin, Ronda. *Black American Women in Literature: A Bibliography, 1976 Through 1987.* Jefferson, N.C.: McFarland, 1989.

Golden, Maria, ed. *Wild Women Don't Wear No Blues: Black Women Writers on Love, Men, and Sex.* New York: Doubleday, 1993.

Hebbar, Reshmi J. *Modeling Minority Women: Heroines in African and Asian American Fiction.* New York: Routledge, 2005.

Hooks, Bell. *Remembered Rapture: The Writer at Work.* New York: Henry Holt, 1999.

Hudson-Weems, Clenora. *Africana Womanist Literary Theory.* Trenton, N.J.: Africa World Press, 2004.

Hull, Gloria T. *Color, Sex, and Poetry: Three Women Writers of the Harlem Renaissance.* Bloomington: Indiana University Press, 1987.

Jackson, Edward Mercia. *Images of Black Men in Black Women Writers, 1950-1990.* Bristol, Ind.: Wyndham Hall Press, 1992.

Jordan, Shirley M., ed. *Broken Silences: Interviews with Black and White Women Writers.* New Brunswick, N.J.: Rutgers University Press, 1993.

Kraft, Marion. *The African Continuum and Contemporary African American Women Writers: Their Literary Presence and Ancestral Past.* New York: P. Lang, 1995.

Kubitschek, Missy Dehn. *Claiming the Heritage: African-American*

Women's Novels and History. Jackson: University Press of Mississippi, 1991.

Levin, Amy K. *Africanism and Authenticity in African-American Women's Novels.* Gainesville: University Press of Florida, 2003.

Logan, Shirley Wilson. *We Are Coming: The Persuasive Discourse of Nineteenth-Century Black Women.* Carbondale: Southern Illinois University Press, 1999.

————, ed. *With Pen and Voice: A Critical Anthology of Nineteenth-Century African-American Women.* Carbondale: Southern Illinois University Press, 1995.

McDowell, Deborah E. *"The Changing Same": Black Women's Literature, Criticism, and Theory.* Bloomington: Indiana University Press, 1995.

Marshall, Carmen Rose. *Black Professional Women in Recent American Fiction.* Jefferson, N.C.: McFarland, 2004.

Melhem, D. H. *Gwendolyn Brooks, Poetry and the Heroic Voice.* Lexington: University Press of Kentucky, 1987.

Murdy, Anne-Elizabeth. *Teach the Nation: Public School, Racial Uplift, and Women's Writing in the 1890's.* New York: Routledge, 2003.

Perkins, Margo V. *Autobiography as Activism: Three Black Women of the Sixties.* Jackson: University Press of Mississippi, 2000.

Puri, Usha. *Towards a New Womanhood: A Study of Black Women Writers.* Jaipur, India: Printwell, 1989.

Quashie, Kevin Everod. *Black Women, Identity, and Cultural Theory: (Un)becoming the Subject.* New Brunswick, N.J.: Rutgers University Press, 2004.

Roses, Lorraine Elena, and Ruth Elizabeth Randolph. *The Harlem Renaissance and Beyond: Literary Biographies of One Hundred Black Women Writers, 1900-1945.* Boston: G. K. Hall, 1990.

Russell, Sandi. *Render Me My Song: African-American Women Writers from Slavery to the Present.* New York: Pandora, 2002.

Shockley, Ann, ed. *Afro-American Women Writers, 1746-1933: An Anthology and Critical Guide.* Boston: G. K. Hall, 1988.

Stover, Johnnie M. *Rhetoric and Resistance in Black Women's Autobiography.* Gainesville: University Press of Florida, 2003.

Tate, Claudia. *Domestic Allegories of Political Desire: The Black Hero-*

ine's Text at the Turn of the Century. New York: Oxford University Press, 1992.

Wall, Cheryl A. *Worrying the Line: Black Women Writers, Lineage, and Literary Tradition.* Chapel Hill: University of North Carolina Press, 2005.

Washington, Teresa N. *Our Mothers, Our Powers, Our Texts: Manifestations of "Àjé" in Africana Literature.* Bloomington: Indiana University Press, 2005.

Wyatt, Jean. *Risking Difference: Identification, Race, and Community in Contemporary Fiction and Feminism.* Albany: State University of New York Press, 2004.

Yellin, Jean Fagan, and Cynthia D. Bond, comps. *The Pen Is Ours: A Listing of Writings by and About African-American Women Before 1910 with Secondary Bibliography to the Present.* New York: Oxford University Press, 1991.

Zackodnik, Teresa C. *The Mulatta and the Politics of Race.* Jackson: University Press of Mississippi, 2004.

— Anna A. Moore

Electronic Resources

Electronic Databases

Electronic databases are integrated electronic sources to which public, college, and university libraries subscribe, installing links on their Web sites that are available only to library card holders or specified patrons. Readers can check library Web sites to see if these databases are installed or can ask reference librarians if these databases are available.

General

Academic Search Premier

The world's largest scholarly full-text database, *Academic Search Premier* has indexed and created abstracts for more than eight thousand journals. Searches are presented in an easy-to-use format and can be narrowed by date published, format (academic journal, magazine, or newspaper), number of pages, and presence of images.

African American Newspapers: The Nineteenth Century

For those looking for articles published between 1827 and 1902, this will prove an extremely useful tool. It presents complete articles from significant African American publications like *The Christian Recorder, The Colored American, Frederick Douglass Paper, Freedom's Journal, The National Era, The North Star,* and *Provincial Freeman.*

Black Studies on Disc

One of the most comprehensive bibliographic resources available to those studying the history and culture of people of African ancestry, this database lists sources from the eighth century A.D. to the present. It provides citations for many types of resources, culled from the catalog of the Schomburg Center for Research in Black Culture and the Index to Black Periodicals.

First Search
Commonly found in academic libraries, this system covers dozens of databases, some of which have links to full-text articles. Students of African American literature will find helpful information in the *Contemporary Women's Issues, Dissertation Abstracts, MLA Bibliography, Wilson Select,* and *WorldCat* databases.

Gale Virtual Reference Library
The database contains more than eighty-five reference books, including encyclopedias and almanacs, allowing users to find information about a broad range of subjects quickly.

J-STOR
J-STOR has organized hundreds of journals in both single- and multidisciplinary formats in order to streamline the search process. Their collection includes several journals on African American history, as well as the literary journals *African American Review, Callaloo, Journal of Black Studies,* and *Phylon.* Several journals that specifically deal with African history and literature are also available.

Oxford Reference Online
A virtual reference library of more than one hundred dictionaries and reference books published by Oxford University Press. *Oxford Reference Online* contains information about a broad range of subjects, including art, architecture, military history, science, religion, philosophy, political and social science, and literature. The site also features English-language and bilingual dictionaries, as well as collections of quotations and proverbs.

African American Studies and Other Subject-Specific Databases

African American Biographical Database
This collection bills itself as "a resource of first resort" for images and information about more than thirty thousand African Americans. Gathering material from periodicals, encyclopedias, biographical texts, and other sources, it allows researchers to

search by city, state, country, religion, and occupation, among other fields. Though updated every two months, results are limited to the years between 1790 and 1950.

America: History and Life

This database, produced by ABC-Clio, provides access to a number of important literary journals and some books. *America: History and Life* contains almost a half million entries from more than fifteen hundred journals devoted to American and Canadian history.

Arts and Humanities Citation Index

This database allows users to search across disciplines to find bibliographic and reference material in more than a thousand scholarly journals.

Biography Resource Center

This database, produced by Thomson Gale, includes biographies of more than 320,000 prominent people from throughout the world and from a wide range of disciplines. Searches for African American writers returned more than two thousand hits.

The Columbia Granger's World of Poetry

Columbia University Press compiles thousands of works by hundreds of poets (more than 150 of Gwendolyn Brooks's poems are indexed, for example) in this database, which also includes a comprehensive glossary of poetry-related terms. Biographies and critical essays are available for some writers, and users can search for anthologies by title, category, and editor.

Contemporary Authors

Thomson Gale's database organizes biographical information on approximately 112,000 novelists whose work has been published since 1960.

Contemporary Literary Criticism Select
Published by Thomson Gale, this system catalogs critical essays on approximately six hundred major authors. Students can search by author, title, and subject.

Ethnic News Watch
This database combs through a half a million articles that have appeared in ethnic and minority publications since 1990. Archived material from the mid-1980's is also available. An especially useful resource for hard-to-find newspaper and magazine articles from important African American newspapers such as New York's *Amsterdam News,* Los Angeles' *The Sentinel,* Florida's *The Miami Times,* Boston's *Bay State Banner,* and Chicago's *The Chicago Defender.*

GLBT Life
This database is devoted to discussing issues related to gay, lesbian, bisexual, and transgender issues. The system searches dozens of periodicals specializing in GLBT issues; students will find a number of reviews, interviews, and other articles on such authors as James Baldwin, Alice Dunbar-Nelson, and Audre Lorde.

Historical Census Browser
This is an invaluable resource for students of African American history. It provides U.S. Census information on the U.S. political and economic climate between 1790 and 1960, but it also allows users to create maps of population density based on number of slaves, literacy rates, ethnicity, place of birth, and various agricultural and economic factors.

History Reference Center
A product of EBSCO Information Services, the *History Reference Center* is a comprehensive world history database. It contains the contents of more than 650 encyclopedias and other books, the full text of articles published in about sixty history periodicals, and thousands of historical documents, biographies, photographs, and maps.

Literature Resource Center

Literature Resource Center, produced by Thomson Gale, includes biographies, bibliographies, and critical analyses of authors from a wide range of literary genres, movements, countries, and eras. The database also features plot summaries, the full text of articles from literary journals, critical essays, and links to Web sites. Users can search by author nationality, theme, literary movement, and genre; for example, a search for writers of African American descent returned nearly three hundred results.

MagillOnLiteraturePlus

Salem Press has placed many of its literature reference sources on this database, including *Masterplots, Cyclopedia of World Authors, Cyclopedia of Literary Characters,* and *World Philosophers and Their Works.* The database covers the works of more than 8,500 writers, poets, dramatists, essayists, and philosophers, featuring plot summaries, critical analyses, biographical essays, character profiles, and up-to-date lists of each author's works. Searches can be narrowed according to author's national and cultural identity and literary characters and locales, among other fields; for example, a search for African American authors returned more than fourteen hundred results.

MLA International Bibliography

Thousands of journals and book citations can be found in the Modern Language Association's electronic bibliography, which is a particularly valuable source of literary theory and critical articles.

Virtual Reference Library

Infotrac's *Virtual Reference Library* combines access to six helpful resources: the four-volume *Africa: An Encyclopedia for Students* (2002), the ten-volume *Dictionary of American History* (2003), *African American Almanac* (2003), *African-American Years: Chronologies of American History and Experience* (2003), the three-volume *Encyclopedia of Lesbian, Gay, Bisexual, and Transgender History in*

America (2004), and the three-volume *Gale Encyclopedia of Multicultural America* (2000).

Wilson Biographies Illustrated
Produced by H. W. Wilson Co., this database offers more than ninety-five thousand biographies and obituaries, and more than twenty-six thousand photographs, of prominent people throughout history.

World History FullText
A joint product of EBSCO Information Services and ABC-Clio, this database provides a global view of history with information on a wide range of topics, including anthropology, art, culture, economics, government, heritage, military history, politics, regional issues, and sociology.

World History Online
Facts On File, Inc., has created this reference database of world history, featuring biographies, time lines, maps, charts, and other information.

Web Sites

The sites listed below were visited by the editors of Salem Press in September, 2005. Because URLs frequently change or are moved, the accuracy of these sites cannot be guaranteed; however, long-standing sites—such as those of university departments, national organizations, and government agencies—generally maintain links when sites move or upgrade their offerings.

African American Literature Book Club
http://aalbc.com
A popular site that offers book reviews and recommendations, author biographies, and tips for aspiring writers. Those interested can post their thoughts and read others' opinions on several discussion boards. Also includes a useful source of information about upcoming literary events.

African American Literature Online
http://www.geocities.com/afam_literature
A good source for brief summaries of the state of African American literature during the twentieth century. Pages are divided by the decades they discuss, and each includes a summary of that period's more notable works.

The African American Mosaic: A Library of Congress Research Guide for the Study of Black History and Culture
http://www.loc.gov/exhibits/african/intro.html
This site accompanies an exhibit that took place between February and August, 1994. Rather than focusing on slavery, its first section summarizes the efforts of the American Colonization Society, which offered nineteenth century African Americans the chance to return to Africa rather than be emancipated in the United States. Later sections discuss the roles of abolitionists and the Works Progress Administration and African Americans' migration to Kansas, Chicago, and other Western and midwestern cities.

African American Writers: Online E-texts
http://falcon.jmu.edu/~ramseyil/afroonline.htm
Forty-six African American authors are listed here, and each author's entry has several links to sites with further biographical information and samples of text (sometimes available in their entirety) in electronic format.

Africans in America
http://www.pbs.org/wgbh/aia/home.html
This site was built as a companion to the Public Broadcasting Service (PBS) television series of the same name. It is divided into four sections: The Terrible Transformation (1450-1750), Revolution (1750-1805), Brotherly Love (1791-1831), and Judgment Day (1831-1865). Each page's concise, logical format presents information unavailable anywhere else. Each section contains a Resource Bank with extraordinary images and stories and comprehensive teacher's guides.

American Slave Narratives: An Online Anthology
http://xroads.virginia.edu/~HYPER/wpa/wpahome.html

An amazing collection of audio files and texts excerpted from the Works Progress Administration's interviews with former slaves in the 1930's. Some of the interviews are difficult to understand, but all are worth the effort. Other sites of interest are also listed.

The Black Renaissance in Washington
http://www.dclibrary.org/blkren/index2.html

This project, sponsored by the District of Columbia's public library, includes biographies of dozens of important Renaissance writers, a list of the Harlem Renaissance's major works, a time line, and links to additional resources.

The Martin Luther King, Jr. Papers Project
http://www.stanford.edu/group/King

Stanford University's Martin Luther King, Jr. Papers Project contains summaries of King's published works, his most popular speeches, sermons, and audio clips, biographies and chronologies, and lesson plans for teachers.

Our Shared History: African American Heritage
http://www.cr.nps.gov/aahistory

The National Parks Service sponsors this site, which contains a wealth of information about notable places in African American history (such as Baltimore, Detroit, and St. Louis), and major figures (such as Frederick Douglass, Mary McLeod Bethune, and Booker T. Washington). This is a particularly helpful place for those interested in the Underground Railroad.

Resources in Black Studies
http://www.library.ucsb.edu/subjects/blackstudies/black.html

The University of California, Santa Barbara, maintains a fairly comprehensive list of direct links to institutions, publications, and projects throughout the field of African American studies. Section titles include "Slavery and the Slave Trade," "Radio, TV, and Film," and "Historical Texts and Documents."

San Antonio College LitWeb: African American Literature Index

http://www.accd.edu/sac/english/bailey/aframlit.htm

Presents a detailed time line of major contributions to African American literature. Many entries include links to biographies, images, lists of works created, and bibliographies, though the site is limited to works produced between 1746 and 1999.

Schomburg Center for Black Culture

http://www.nypl.org/research/sc/sc.html

The New York Public Library's Schomburg Center regularly sponsors exhibits on important African American issues, and their Web site holds a considerable amount of information about exhibitions past and present, as well as summaries of their important collections (which include rare manuscripts, recordings, and photographs).

Voice of the Shuttle: Minority Literatures

http://vos.ucsb.edu/browse.asp?id=2746

Produced by the University of California, Santa Barbara, the African American section of this page presents samples of work, biographies, home pages, and teacher's guides for dozens of African American writers. Other sections of this page have interesting (though more general) links.

Voices from the Gaps: Women Writers and Artists of Color

http://voices.cla.umn.edu/vg

An especially useful source for teachers, this site (maintained by the University of Minnesota's English department) contains teaching and planning tips and profiles authors and their works, provides discussion boards for viewers, and lists links to related material.

— *Anna A. Moore*

Chronological List of Authors

Below, the authors covered in these volumes are arranged chronologically by year of birth.

To 1800
1753   Phillis Wheatley

1801-1900
1817   Frederick Douglass
1856   Booker T. Washington
1858   Charles Waddell
           Chesnutt
1868   W. E. B. Du Bois
1872   Paul Laurence Dunbar
1882   Jessie Redmon Fauset
1889   Claude McKay
1891   Zora Neale Hurston
1891   Nella Larsen
1894   Jean Toomer

1901-1910
1901   Sterling A. Brown
1902   Arna Wendell Bontemps
1902   Langston Hughes
1903   Countée Cullen
1908   Ann Petry
1908   Richard Wright
1909   Chester Himes

1911-1920
1912   Gordon Parks, Sr.
1913   Robert Hayden
1914   Owen Dodson
1914   Ralph Ellison
1914   Dudley Randall
1916   Alice Childress
1916   Frank Yerby
1917   Gwendolyn Brooks

1921-1930
1921   Alex Haley
1924   James Baldwin
1925   John A. Williams
1928   Maya Angelou
1929   Martin Luther King, Jr.
1929   Paule Marshall
1930   Edward Kamau
           Brathwaite
1930   Lorraine Hansbury

1931-1940
1931   Lonne Elder III
1931   Adrienne Kennedy
1931   Etheridge Knight
1931   Toni Morrison
1933   Ernest J. Gaines
1934   Amiri Baraka
1934   Audre Lorde
1934   Sonia Sanchez
1935   Ed Bullins
1935   Joseph A. Walker
1935   Jay Wright
1936   Lucille Clifton
1936   Virginia Hamilton
1936   June Jordan
1936   Clarence Major
1937   William Melvin Kelley
1937   Walter Dean Myers
1938   Michael S. Harper
1938   Ishmael Reed
1939   Toni Cade Bambara
1939   Barbara Chase-Riboud
1939   Charles Fuller
1939   Al Young

1941-1950

1941	Toi Derricotte
1941	John Edgar Wideman
1942	Samuel R. Delany
1942	Haki R. Madhubuti
1943	Nikki Giovanni
1943	James Alan McPherson
1944	Alice Walker
1945	August Wilson
1947	Octavia E. Butler
1947	Yusef Komunyakaa
1948	Charles Johnson
1948	Ntozake Shange
1949	Victor Hernández Cruz

1949	Jamaica Kincaid
1950	Bebe Moore Campbell
1950	Henry Louis Gates, Jr.
1950	Gloria Naylor

1951-1960

1951	Terry McMillan
1952	Rita Dove
1953	Cornel West
1954	Cornelius Eady
1956	Reginald McKnight

1961-

1963	Suzan-Lori Parks

INDEXES

Genre Index

Personages Index

Title Index

Subject Index